NUTRITION AND POVERTY

WIDER

Studies in Development Economics embody the output of the research programmes of the World Institute for Development Economics Research (WIDER), which was established by the United Nations University as its first research and training centre in 1984 and started work in Helsinki in 1985. The principal purpose of the Institute is to help identify and meet the need for policy-oriented socio-economic research on pressing global and development problems, as well as common domestic problems and their inter-relationships.

Nutrition and Poverty

Edited by

S. R. OSMANI

A study prepared for the World Institute for Development
Economics Research (WIDER) of the United Nations University

CLARENDON PRESS · OXFORD
1992

Oxford University Press, Walton Street, Oxford OX2 6DP
Oxford New York Toronto
Delhi Calcutta Madras Karachi
Kuala Lumpur Singapore Hong Kong Tokyo
Nairobi Dar es Salaam Cape Town
Melbourne Auckland Madrid
and associated companies in
Berlin Ibadan

Oxford is a trade mark of Oxford University Press

Published in the United States
by Oxford University Press Inc., New York

WIDER: World Institute for Development Economics Research (WIDER)—The United
Nations University, Annankatu 42c, 00100 Helsinki, Finland

British Library Cataloguing in Publication Data
Data available

Library of Congress Cataloging in Publication Data
Nutrition and poverty / edited by S.R. Osmani.
p. cm.—(Studies in development economics)
"A study prepared for the World Institute for Development Economics Research
(WIDER) of the United Nations University."
Includes bibliographical references and index.
1. Malnutrition—Social aspects. 2. Nutrition—Evaluation.
3. Nutrition surveys. 4. Poor—Nutrition. I. Osmani, Siddiqur
Rahman. II. World Institute for Development Economics Research.
III. Series.
RA645.N87N85 1991 363.8—dc20 91–41487
ISBN 0–19–828396–2

Typeset by Pure Tech Corporation, Pondicherry, India
Printed in Great Britain on acid-free paper by
Bookcraft (Bath) Ltd

World Institute for Development Economics Research (WIDER). The United Nations University, Annankatu 42C, 00100 Helsinki, Finland.

LIST OF CONTRIBUTORS

DR SUDHIR ANAND, St Catherine's College, Oxford.

PROFESSOR JERE R. BEHRMAN, Department of Economics, University of Pennsylvania.

PROFESSOR RODERICK FLOUD, City of London Polytechnic.

PROFESSOR ROBERT W. FOGEL, Director, Graduate School of Business, University of Chicago.

DR C. GOPALAN, Director, Nutrition Foundation of India, New Delhi.

DR CHRISTOPHER J. HARRIS, Nuffield College, Oxford.

PROFESSOR NANAK C. KAKWANI, Department of Economics, University of New South Wales.

DR S. R. OSMANI, Research Fellow, World Institute for Development Economics Research, Helsinki.

PROFESSOR PHILIP R. PAYNE, London School of Hygiene and Tropical Medicine.

PROFESSOR T. N. SRINIVASAN, Department of Economics, Yale University.

PREFACE

HUNGER and poverty constitute an important area of WIDER research. Four volumes incorporating policy-oriented conclusions from studies under this theme have already been published. While earlier research was focused mainly on questions relating to the food problem in terms of *Hunger and Public Action* and *The Political Economy of Hunger*, the papers in this volume address issues arising from the definition and measurement of poverty in terms of nutritional status. A high degree of nutritional deprivation is considered to be an indicator of poverty. Hence the definition of an appropriate nutritional yardstick and its measurement are of crucial significance for determining the level and magnitude of poverty.

This volume is essentially a critical appraisal of the 'state of the art', and focuses on differing views and perceptions on the related questions of assessing poverty and nutritional status. The chapters cover a range of issues and have been contributed by a representative cross-section of distinguished nutritionists and economists. Early versions of these papers were presented at a conference held at WIDER in the summer of 1987.

Is it possible to define a reference standard of nutritional status for comparative assessment purposes? This question has elicited conflicting responses. One school of thought argues that a reference standard can be defined as a state of nutrition in which there is no deficiency in any of the nutrition-related functions. Another view considers this definition as too much of an ideal, since a state of perfect all-round nutritional adequacy seldom exists. This approach suggests that a meaningful and realistic reference standard has to be in terms of a state of serious deficiency, posing a threat to life. In this context, the capacity of the human body to 'adapt' itself to minimize the effects of inadequate nutrition is another factor to be taken into account.

A further question that is taken up in these papers refers to energy-related nutritional deprivation. The issue under debate is whether to compare calorie intake against an average reference standard or to compare anthropometric measurements of the body with some reference standard. Both viewpoints have been rigorously advanced in the chapters that follow. In this context, the presence of interpersonal and intrapersonal variation in energy requirements further complicates the assessments of nutritional deprivation.

Among other issues considered below is that of gender bias in the incidence of nutritional deprivation. The evidence suggests the existence of bias against females, but the study cautions that further research is necessary to arrive at firm conclusions.

It is hoped that this set of papers will certainly contribute to the ongoing debate and to advancing the level of knowledge on questions relating to the definition and measurement of nutritional status, though not necessarily reaching a consensus on all the issues raised.

L. J.

CONTENTS

LIST OF FIGURES

LIST OF TABLES

ABBREVIATIONS

ACN   average calorie norm
BMI   body mass index
BMR   basal metabolism rate
BSI   body size index
CDR   crude death rate
LBM   lean body mass
MCM muscle cell mass
MMM mild to moderate malnutrition
PAI   physical activity index
PEM   protein–energy malnutrition
PWC   physical work capacity
RDA   recommended daily allowance

1

Introduction

S. R. Osmani

Nutrition and poverty are two very closely related themes. Many elementary aspects of being poor, such as hunger, inadequate health–care, unhygienic living conditions, and the stress and strain of precarious living, tend to impair a person's nutritional status. In consequence, being poor almost always means being deprived of full nutritional capabilities, i.e. the capabilities to avoid premature mortality, to live a life free of avoidable morbidity, and to have the energy for work and leisure. The study of poverty is, therefore, very much a study of people's state of nutrition.

There are two related ways in which the study of nutrition can illuminate the study of poverty. The first has to do with the processes of poverty, and the second with the assessment of the extent of its prevalence.

An understanding of the processes through which chronic malnutrition comes to afflict a household or a community—e.g. the processes leading to inadequate entitlement to food and health care and those perpetuating unhygienic environment—can reveal a good deal about the processes leading to endemic poverty. Such analyses may also yield useful guides for policy. For example, by delineating the relative roles of food, health care, and environment in the genesis of malnutrition, such analyses may help policy-makers to rationalize priorities among different components of anti-poverty programmes.

The assessment aspect is no less important, although there is at times a tendency to play it down. It is not unusual to encounter the argument that assessing the magnitude of poverty is superfluous because we all know that massive poverty exists, say, in Asia or Africa—it is there for all to see! Eminently commonsensical though it may seem, this argument really misses the point. The objective of measuring poverty is usually not to show the existence of poverty, or even to prove its massiveness, but

I wish to express my gratitude to Amartya Sen, Carlo Fonseca, and especially the contributors to this volume for making many helpful comments. I also want to emphasize that, while an attempt has been made in this Introduction to tie together the various themes running through the volume and to compare and contrast the views of different contributors, the interpretations offered are entirely my own. I have tried to check with the contributors that my interpretations do not do gross injustice to their views, but there is always scope for difference in nuances and matters of emphasis; this is especially true in a subject matter as controversial as the one addressed in this volume.

to compare the magnitude of poverty across time and space. In this comparative context, what is there 'for all to see' may depend a great deal on the eyes of the beholder. There may not exist any basis for agreement among different observers without an agreed framework of measurement. Economists, therefore, have been rightly concerned with the framework of measuring poverty; and in pursuit of this concern they have long been drawing upon the science of nutrition. Since absolute poverty and the loss of nutritional capabilities tend to go hand in hand, it has seemed natural to measure poverty by the extent of a population's failure to achieve desirable nutritional status.

However, as economists delved into the question of nutrition, they soon discovered that there were no ready-made answers waiting for them. Whether the problem was one of understanding the processes of poverty or assessing its magnitude, the relevant nutritional issues were found to be matters of ongoing, and sometimes very contentious, debate among the nutritionists themselves. Economists soon joined this debate, and nutritionists in turn brought their own perspectives to bear on the questions being asked by the economists. The resulting interchange, both within and across the disciplines, has spawned a large and interesting, if at times somewhat confusing, literature. The present book grew out of the felt need to consolidate the outcome of this interchange and to carry it forward. Accordingly, the papers, all written especially for this volume by a group of nutritionists, economists, and economic historians, collectively offer both stock-taking of existing knowledge and attempts to break fresh ground.

Without trying to be exhaustive, I shall proceed to highlight some of the major issues the authors have grappled with.

One recurring theme concerns the reference standard of nutritional status. Whether we are interested in the processes or the magnitude of nutritional deprivation, we need to define a reference standard of nutritional status against which the actual status can be compared. Ideally, the reference standard should refer to that coveted nutritional status in which a person suffers from no disability in any of his nutrition-related functions (such as immunological competence, physical work capacity, cognitive function, reproductive capacity, etc.). But does such an ideal state exist?

Gopalan and Payne take conflicting positions on this matter. Gopalan's paper (Chapter 2), which in fact reflects much of the mainstream views on the range of issues covered in this volume, clearly suggests that such a state does exist. This is evident from his criticism of some of the criteria of nutritional adequacy that have been suggested by Payne and others. His method of criticism is to show, through empirical evidence, that the achievement of adequacy as judged by these criteria would still leave people deficient in at least some of the nutrition-related functions.

His own preferred criteria are designed not to allow for these functional deficiencies. This implies that he believes in the existence of a state of nutrition in which there is no deficiency in any of the nutrition-related functions.[1]

Payne, on the other hand, argues in Chapter 3 that there can be no state of nutrition in which all the functions are simultaneously maximized. He takes the view that the evolutionary process through which the human body has come to acquire its potential for functional abilities is 'sufficing' rather than 'optimizing' in nature. This is taken to mean that the human body has not acquired the ability simultaneously to attain maximal capabilities in respect of all the functions: there is always a trade-off between the functions so that improvement in one function typically entails the loss of another.

These differences on the question of whether or not an ideal nutritional state exists lead directly to controversies regarding the practical methods for assessing the magnitude of undernutrition. The proposed methods of assessment differ because the standards of comparison differ. Since, from Gopalan's perspective, the standard of comparison is the ideal state, his method of assessment is meant to capture all those who are suffering from any degree of deficiency in any kind of nutritional functioning. Not so for Payne, from whose perspective there will always be deficiencies of one kind or the other. For him, the only practical thing to do is to assess the magnitude of very serious deficiencies—so serious as to pose a threat to life.

A crucial concept that Payne invokes in this context is that of 'adaptation', a concept that appears frequently in the other papers as well. When faced with a nutritional constraint, the human body adapts itself in a number of ways to minimize the adverse consequences of that constraint. Essentially, this is an exercise in damage limitation. As Payne notes, it may not be possible to avoid damage to nutritional functions completely, but adaptation does help to limit the damage. Of course, at some point, when the nutritional constraint is too severe, it may no longer be possible to contain the damage. It is at this point—the threshold of the breakdown of adaptation—that the threat to life begins to emerge. Payne is in effect suggesting that this threshold exists and is identifiable, while the threshold of an ideal nutritional status does not exist. This is the basis of his claim that the only practical way of assessing nutritional deprivation is to do so relative to the threshold of life-threatening risk rather than to that of an imaginary ideal. He then goes

---

[1] It ought to be emphasized that all those who use the traditional reference standards (that is, the ones that are advocated by Gopalan) do not necessarily hold the view that these standards reflect an ideal nutritional status. For many of them, the standards are no more than a reference point for measuring relative changes over time: the question of idealness of the standard remains an open issue. This is indeed the approach taken in the historical papers by Fogel and Floud included in this volume.

on to suggest various criteria for assessing the prevalence of such life-threatening risk.

But for Gopalan, all this amounts to an unacceptable 'policy of brinkmanship'. What he objects to is not so much the call for assessing the prevalence of life-threatening risk as the idea that the assessment of deprivation should be confined to this task. He argues that functional impairments, even when not so serious as to pose a threat to life, are serious enough to merit attention. Besides, what is not so serious today may become so in due course; for after all, severe malnutrition does not develop overnight—it is the culmination of a protracted process in which a person passes successively through the stages of mild, moderate, and severe malnutrition. Thus, from a dynamic point of view, Gopalan rejects the notion that life-threatening risk confronts only those among the deprived who have already sunk below Payne's threshold of adaptation. Accordingly, he makes a strong defence of the usual practice of assessing deprivations of all degrees, not just the most serious ones, and of counting all such deprivations as cases of undernutrition.

This particular debate concerns the choice of the level of functional competence that should be used as the standard of comparison for assessing the degree of nutritional deprivation. But there are also other, no less contentious, issues in the context of assessment. Whatever level of functional competence is chosen as the standard, there is the subsequent problem of how to judge whether or not the chosen levels have been attained. Very intense controversies surround this issue. The problem stems from the fact that it is virtually impossible to make direct measurements of functional competence in large populations. Such measurements are of course routinely made by researchers, but almost always on small samples and usually for one function at a time. In fact, even a single function usually consists of several dimensions—for example, immunological competence refers to immunity against a whole range of diseases, and mental ability to a number of different kinds of cognitive functions—and actual tests often have to be confined to a subset of these dimensions. Given such diversity of nutritional functions and the complexity of their measurement, direct tests of nutritional achievement in a large population would be prohibitive in terms of time and cost. The only practical course is to make indirect assessments with the help of proxies. And that is where the problem begins.

In the context of energy-related nutritional deprivation, which is the principal focus of this book, two types of proxies are used in practice. One is to compare caloric intake with some standard of requirement, and the other is to compare anthropometric measurements of the body (height, weight, etc.) with some reference standard. The standards of both caloric intake and anthropometric achievements are obtained in practice from the actual intake and achievements of a sample of individuals who are believed to be healthy. The presumption is that the failure to achieve these reference standards will indicate suboptimal achievement in at least some of the nutrition-related functions. But doubts are now being expressed from many quarters on whether deviations from these standards truly reflect loss of functional competence. In particular, it has been suggested that these standards may be too high—a suggestion that has been hotly contested by others. Note that the issue here is not the rationale behind the choice of the reference nutritional status; that is, this debate is not about the level of functional capabilities we should aim at while defining a standard of comparison—that problem we have already discussed. The issue now is whether it is really necessary to attain the chosen reference levels of caloric intake or anthropometric achievement in order to achieve the chosen level of functional capabilities. In other words, this particular debate is not about the content of the reference standard of nutritional status, but about the validity of the proxies employed to reflect that status. Most of the papers of this volume have grappled with this issue, by taking up positions on opposing sides of the debate, clarifying the nature of the arguments involved, and in some cases also proposing solutions.

In the course of this debate, both caloric and anthropometric standards have been called into question. In the case of calories, the source of dispute lies in the usual practice of measuring undernutrition by comparing actual intake of calories with a fixed standard set by the average intake of healthy people.[2] Comparison with a fixed standard carries the implication that energy requirement of a given type of individual is a fixed quantity, and that any shortfall from this fixed level must entail impairment of at least some nutritional functions. But the critics have argued that, just because a person's calorie intake falls short of the standard specified for his type, one cannot say that his functions are impaired. The level of intake at which functions begin to be impaired—in other words, the energy required by a person to maintain his functions—is believed to be variable rather than fixed.

There are said to be two types of variation in energy requirement: interpersonal and intrapersonal. Interpersonal variation arises from genetic differences between individuals, while intrapersonal variation occurs through temporal variation, within the same body, of the determinants of energy requirement. These are also known as genotypic and phenotypic variations, respectively. These variations have important implications for the assessment of nutritional deprivation. This makes it necessary to address the questions of whether requirements do in fact vary and, if so, what amendments are required to the method of assessment. These questions figure prominently throughout this volume.

[2] Actually, the standard is fixed for people of the same type but varies between types—the type being defined in terms of age, sex, body weight, and levels of physical activity.

Srinivasan's paper (Chapter 4) deals with the problems posed by the presence of intrapersonal variation in requirement. Taking his cue from the writings of P. V. Sukhatme, who has brought this issue to the forefront of discussion in recent years, Srinivasan argues strongly for the abandonment of the 'fixed requirement' model and for the adoption of what is called the 'process view of nutrition'. There are two aspects of this view of nutrition: one operates in the long run and the other in the short run. In the long run, a person tries to come to terms with nutritional constraints by taking recourse to a process of adaptation, which occurs through changes in metabolic efficiency, physical dimension, and behavioural pattern. This process may or may not enable him to maintain a desirable nutritional status in response to a particular constraint. This can only be judged, argues Srinivasan, by looking into the *process* of adaptation: the mere comparison of intake with a fixed requirement cannot tell us much.

In the short run, too, there is believed to be a process of adjustment which occurs through changes in metabolic efficiency (i.e. the efficiency with which food is converted into energy). This process enables a person to vary his intake from day to day and from week to week while maintaining the same nutritional status when seen over a longer period. This is the much debated theory of homeostasis. From the perspective of this theory, the intake of a healthy person, as recorded during a short period of observation, may well be seen to fall short of average requirement, which is essentially a long-term concept. That is why a major inference of the homeostatic theory is that the usual practice of comparing short-period intake with the average requirement norm overestimates the magnitude of nutritional deprivation. While elaborating this theory, Srinivasan offers a generalization of the original 'process view' of nutrition as developed by Sukhatme, and also suggests what would be the ideal method of assessing nutritional deprivation consistent with this theory. As it happens, however, the data requirement for this type of assessment is quite demanding—one typically needs a long time-series of intake rather than the information for a day or a week as is commonly available. For the common case, where longitudinal data are not available, Srinivasan suggests that it may be sensible under certain assumptions to follow Sukhatme's advice, that undernutrition should be assessed by comparing calorie intake with a reference point that is well below the usual standard of average requirement. He also cites evidence in support of the process view of nutrition, and goes on to review the appropriateness of standard policies for combating undernutrition as seen from this altered viewpoint.

The process view of nutrition, as expounded by Srinivasan, seeks to replace the notion of fixity in calorie requirement by that of intrapersonal variability. Opinions are however sharply divided on the possibilities of such variation, either through homeostasis in the short run or through adaptation in the long run. These divisions are also reflected in the papers of this volume. Gopalan, for example, strongly argues against both the short-run and the long-run versions of the concept of variable requirement. Payne, on the other hand, lends vigorous support to the possibility of altering requirement through adaptation in the long run but holds a rather cautious view on the short-run process of homeostasis. While not doubting the theoretical possibility of homeostasis, he none the less believes that the scope of altering requirements through this process is quantitatively small, that the process cannot be assumed to apply to the physical activity component of energy expenditure, and that the process should not be presumed to leave all functional capabilities intact.[3] In expressing these divergent views, the authors have reopened an argument that has been much debated by nutritionists over the last two decades.

This argument, over a patently technical matter, has aroused deep passions in the past because each group believes that the opposing group's viewpoint is not only wrong theoretically but also harmful socially. As noted above, the theory of intrapersonal variation provides a justification for assessing undernutrition by comparing calorie intake with a standard that is lower—in fact much lower—than the one postulated by the conventional view. This means that, if this theory is found wanting on scientific grounds, we would be understating the magnitude of nutritional deprivation by following its logic. This would have unfortunate consequences for a society trying to rid itself of the scourge of malnutrition. On the other hand, if this theory is right, then the conventional practice would overestimate the extent of deprivation and thus run the risk of wasting scarce resources by trying to help the well nourished (as well as the undernourished) in the name of fighting undernutrition. Much, therefore, hangs on the scientific validity of the theory. But before commenting on the weight of scientific evidence, I should mention a couple of points that have been raised regarding the implications of accepting the theory of intrapersonal variation.

First, even if one accepts the hypothesis of homeostatic variation in requirement, does it necessarily mean that nothing useful can be said by comparing calorie intake with average requirement? In the case of a single individual, such comparisons will indeed be useless, since the theory of homeostasis tells us that even a healthy person may have an intake that falls short of average requirement during a short period of observation. But the same argument is difficult to apply when the average intake of a large group of people, rather than that of an individual,

---

[3] Taken together, these reservations bring Payne's views on homeostasis much closer to those of Gopalan than to Sukhatme's, although sharp differences remain on the role of adaptation in the long run.

is seen to fall below average requirement. This is because it is highly unlikely that all members of the group will simultaneously be on the wrong side of the norm in the course of homeostatic variation. One could, therefore, infer that at least some members of the group are likely to have shortfalls that are not homeostatic in nature; such people would be genuinely undernourished. In fact, the bigger the shortfall, the greater the likelihood that at least some members of the group are genuinely undernourished.[4]

Another implication of accepting the theory of intrapersonal variation arises from an interesting observation made by Gopalan in his paper. It has been accepted by nutritionists for quite some time that, if a person subsisting on a cereal-based diet gets enough calories according to the conventional standard of requirement, his protein needs will also be met. This has in fact been the standard justification in much of the nutrition literature for focusing, as we also do in this book, on calorie deficiency alone while discussing the general problem of protein–calorie malnutrition. However, if the theory of intrapersonal variation now leads to a lowering of the standard of calorie requirement, there is no assurance that a calorie-adequate diet will also be protein-adequate. In that case, a calorie-adequate diet will no longer indicate that the nutrition-related functions are all intact, for the functions that are causally linked with calories are in most cases joint functions of protein and calories. This means that, by following the recommendation of those who wish to bring down the requirement norm in view of intrapersonal variation, one would in general underestimate the prevalence of nutritional deprivation.

It should be noted, however, that this is not an argument against the hypothesis of intrapersonal variation as such, but rather a cautionary reminder that, if this hypothesis is accepted and the cut-off point is accordingly lowered, the impairment of functions (related to protein–calorie nutrition) can no longer be inferred from calorie intake alone. Whether or not the hypothesis should be accepted is of course a separate matter—it depends on the weight of scientific evidence on the existence of intrapersonal variation in requirement. The relevant evidence has been reviewed in several of the following papers.

Both Payne and Srinivasan cite evidence in support of the existence of significant intrapersonal variation in requirement. But Gopalan remains unimpressed. Much of the evidence is indirect in nature; and such

---

[4] This point was made by Amartya Sen in a meeting organized at WIDER to discuss the papers assembled in this volume. He also noted that probabilistic assessment of this kind could be further strengthened by going beyond the information on calories and looking at various other socioeconomic indicators of the people concerned. How to make good use of such extraneous information is in fact a chief concern of the paper by Anand and Harris (Ch. 7), but in the context of inter- (as opposed to intra-) personal variation in requirement.

direct evidence as there is does not, in his view, lend support to the theory. Osmani in Chapter 5 concurs with this assessment. Critically evaluating the arguments of Sukhatme, the original and most forceful proponent of the theory, he finds that there are in fact two separate hypotheses implicit in Sukhatme's arguments. Both are based on the notion that intrapersonal variation in requirement arises from variation in the efficiency of energy utilization, but in one hypothesis efficiency varies in a spontaneous manner (the stochastic model), while in the other it is induced by variation in calorie intake (the adaptive model).

On reviewing the internal logic of these two hypotheses and the scientific evidence bearing on them, Osmani is led to the following conclusions. The existing scientific evidence, scanty as it is, does not lend support to the idea that efficiency, and thus the nutritional requirement, of an individual varies over time in a spontaneous manner. Besides, even if spontaneous variation were to occur, Sukhatme's proposed methodology of assessing undernutrition would not be justified, on purely logical grounds. In contrast, the adaptive model, if valid, would logically justify lowering the standard of requirement as Sukhatme proposes to do. But the existing scientific evidence does not attest to its validity. On the other hand, the evidence does not disprove the model, either, so the final resolution of this issue must await further experiments.

On the other type of variation, namely interpersonal variation in requirement, there is a much greater measure of agreement among nutritionists. It is widely recognized that genetic differences in metabolic efficiency can indeed lead to different levels of energy requirement for individuals of the same type. Sukhatme and a few others have recently suggested that interpersonal variation is of relatively minor order of magnitude, and that the observed variation between individuals is really a reflection of intrapersonal variation. However, this claim is contingent on the validity of the thesis of intrapersonal variation itself, for which the present scientific evidence is far from convincing, as argued by Gopalan and Osmani. Besides, as Kakwani (Chapter 6) and Anand and Harris (Chapter 7) point out, even if intrapersonal variation is accorded a pre-eminent role, the problem of interpersonal variation does not vanish. One must recognize the possibility that different persons may have different ranges of intrapersonal variation, which reintroduces the problem of variation between persons.

There is also a practical reason why the assessment of undernutrition in large populations cannot avoid the problem of interpersonal variation, even if theory tells us that there is no interpersonal variation in requirement for a given 'type' of individual. It may be recalled that the level of physical activity is one of the defining characteristics of an individual 'type', since energy requirement depends, *inter alia*, on the level of activity. This means that different individual 'types' should be defined for different levels of activity. But this is difficult to do in practice because activity levels will vary more or less continuously in large populations. A practical short-cut procedure is to classify the individuals into broad bands of activity levels such as heavy, moderate, and light. Such broad-banding, however, makes it inevitable that there will remain significant variation in activity levels, and hence in requirements, within the same 'type'.

The presence of interpersonal variation in requirement creates a rather serious problem in the assessment of nutritional deprivation. When requirements vary between individuals, the standard practice of comparing calorie intake with a fixed standard of requirement will lead to two types of errors: some individuals will be wrongly classified as undernourished, and some will be wrongly classified as well nourished. The fact that these two errors pull in opposite directions is of little comfort. In the first place, there is no assurance that the errors will even roughly cancel each other out. As shown by Kakwani, much depends on the correlation between intakes and requirements. Besides, even if the errors happen to cancel out, we shall at best get a good estimate of the proportion of people undernourished; but the set of people identified as undernourished will not be the true set—it will contain some well nourished people who should not be there and will exclude an equal number of people who should be. In the terminology used by Anand and Harris, the problem of 'comprehensiveness' will be solved but that of 'purity' will remain. This is clearly unsatisfactory if our interest extends beyond merely obtaining the percentage of undernourished people to knowing, for example, something about the socioeconomic characteristics of the undernourished, or doing something about their plight.

In theory, the problems of estimation arising from the presence of interpersonal variation in requirement could be neatly resolved if one knew the joint distribution of intake and requirement. In that case a precise estimation would be possible without resorting to the crude method of comparing average intake with average requirement. But the practical problem is that the requirements distribution is never fully known—all that may be known are a couple of parameters such as mean and variance. So one has to look for ways of making the best use of this limited information. This challenge is taken up by Kakwani and by Anand and Harris. Kakwani shows how one can squeeze the most out of any given level of information about the requirements distribution. He also develops a new class of measures of undernutrition, which takes note of the severity of individual deprivations as well as the proportion of undernourished people. Anand and Harris take a somewhat different route. They are concerned, among other things, with the twin problems of 'comprehensiveness' (i.e. the accuracy of estimating the number of undernourished people) and 'purity' (i.e. capturing only the truly undernourished people) that confront the estimation of undernutrition when only limited information exists on the requirement distribution, and they suggest various ways of dealing with them. They show how the 'comprehensiveness' of estimation can be improved by using extraneous information—specifically, information on welfare distribution. They also explore ways of improving the 'purity' of assessment by using supplementary information, especially information on food expenditure in addition to data on calorie intake. The search for purity generally involves a trade-off with comprehensiveness, and the objective of the Anand–Harris methodology is to minimize this trade-off.

It is evident from the preceding discussion that the route of measuring nutritional status with the help of calorie intake presents many challenges. The alternative (and to some extent complementary) route, through anthropometric measurement, presents equally tough challenges, and several of the papers take up some of these challenges as well.

To begin with, there are problems concerning the choice of the reference standard. As mentioned before, nutritional deprivation is measured in the anthropometric approach by comparing actual physical dimensions (height, weight, etc.) with the standard set by the achievements of a chosen sample of healthy people. As in the case of calorie requirement, the questions of interpersonal and intrapersonal variation also arise in this context. Do we have a fixed standard for everyone, or do we allow for variability within the standard? There is a presumption in the prevailing orthodoxy in favour of a fixed standard. The theory underlying this presumption is known as the 'genetic potential' theory. This contends that, if free from all nutritional constraints, most population groups in the world are capable of achieving the same physical dimensions; that is, they all have the same genetic potential.[5] The reference standard is supposed to reflect this common genetic potential,[6] so that if a particular population fails to achieve this standard, its members may be presumed to suffer from nutritional deprivation.[7] Recent research has indeed shown that most population groups in the world do have remarkably similar genetic potential. Whatever differences remain can be taken

[5] An allowance is however made for random variation of genetic potential among the individuals of each group.

[6] However, the point made in n. 1 also applies here. For some purposes, as can be seen in Floud's paper (Ch. 8), it is not necessary to assume that the reference standard reflects genetic potential. For Floud, the use of the standard is simply as a marker for measuring relative changes over time.

[7] It should be noted though that, unlike in the case of caloric measurement, which indicates whether or not nutritional deprivation exists at present, anthropometric measurements may indicate either present or past deprivation, depending on which measure is used. Measures such as weight-for-height indicate current (strictly speaking, recent past) situation, while there are measures such as height-for-age which indicate (long-term) past experience and still others such as weight-for-age which reflect the *combined* effect of past and present experience.

care of by choosing the reference sample from the nutritionally unconstrained subset of the same population. So, for practical purposes, most
nutritionists no longer regard genetic variation as a serious problem for
anthropometry.

However, the question of intrapersonal variation remains a highly
contentious one. There is an unorthodox view which contends that the
anthropometric achievement of a person may vary within a certain (fairly
wide) limit without causing any damage to his functional competence.
This point has been made most forcefully in the context of height, and
especially in the case of children. The argument, simply, is this. When
faced with a nutritional constraint, the child's body initiates a process
of adaptation by reducing its growth. With lower growth, and thus
smaller body size, the child can live better with the constraint since a
smaller body needs a smaller amount of nutrients to maintain itself—this
is the essence of adaptation. It is then argued that, although the child
may fail to achieve its genetic potential of height as a result of this
'stunted' growth, it need not suffer from any functional impairment so
long as the stunting is not too severe and weight remains normal in
relation to height. This has come to be known as the 'small but healthy'
hypothesis.

For the proponents of this hypothesis, the usual anthropometric measurements made against the standard of genetic potential overstate the extent
of nutritional deprivation. They recommend comparison with a lower
standard—a threshold of adaptation up to which functions do not suffer
despite smallness of size. But this, according to the proponents of traditional practice, would give an underestimate of deprivation, because any
smallness relative to genetic potential must, in their view, impair functions.
These disputations are similar to those involving the standard of calorie
requirement, and, as in the case of calories, a high degree of passion has
marked the controversy over the 'small but healthy' hypothesis.

Payne is sympathetic to this hypothesis and cites supportive evidence
for the process of adaptation. But Gopalan is sharply critical and pro-
duces an array of evidence to show that the adaptive process does entail
functional impairment. Osmani contends that the controversy has been
much bedevilled by a misunderstanding of each other's position. He
restates the contending positions in a manner that clearly shows what
kinds of empirical evidence are needed to settle the matter, reviews the
existing evidence in that light, and finds that such scanty evidence as
there is does not seem to refute the 'small but healthy' hypothesis.
However, he also points to the need for collecting more evidence before
drawing any firm conclusions, and also for applying caution in interpreting the hypothesis.

One problem of interpretation is as follows. Suppose we find, upon
collecting more evidence, that the biochemical processes of growth re-

tardation do not impair any functions when retardation remains within certain bounds. Then it would be right to say that growth retardation, within bounds, does not degrade one's nutritional status, and in that sense the 'small but healthy' hypothesis would be valid. But it still may not be right to say that lower height, within bounds, does not imply lower nutritional status. This is because the nutritional constraints that bring about growth retardation may have other consequences, for example reduction of physical activity, which may impair the cognitive functions of a child. In that case, a child with retarded height could be said to be nutritionally impaired even though the process of retardation did not in itself cause the impairment of functions.

Another problem of interpretation may arise from the failure to appreciate that the measurement of height can serve two distinct purposes. As Floud explains in Chapter 8, height can be used as a predictor of future capabilities and also as an indicator of past nutritional experience of a population. The question of whether the retardation of height necessarily entails functional impairment belongs to the problem of predicting future capabilities; and this is where the arguments surrounding the 'small but healthy' hypothesis become relevant. But how well the present height of a population indicates its past nutritional experience is a separate matter. Here, regardless of the validity of the 'small but healthy' hypothesis, one can independently postulate the hypothesis that greater height indicates better nutritional experience (which, it may be recalled, includes disease environment as well as the consumption of nutrients). In this 'indicative' role, the measurement of height can be a very useful tool in socioeconomic analysis. Gopalan emphasizes this point by drawing on the current experience of developing countries. The papers by Floud and Fogel (Chapter 9) make the same point by looking at the historical experience of the present-day developed world.

Floud first clarifies the statistical picture of changes in height in the industrialized world over the last two and a half centuries. Several interesting features emerge from this analysis. First, there has been a secular increase in height over the period as a whole but the progress was halted, probably even reversed, during the nineteenth century. Second, there are significant differences between countries in their time profiles of height change. Third, even today there are notable differences in the average heights of different socioeconomic groups within the same country. Floud demonstrates that all these features of the history of height can be largely explained by the nutritional experience of the populations concerned. His study thus vindicates the use of height in its 'indicative' role.

Fogel makes powerful use of this indicative role of height in throwing light on an aspect of the economic history of Europe. His concern is to explain the decline in mortality that has occurred in Europe in the modern era. Not long ago, most economic historians believed that the high mortality levels of the earlier centuries arose from periodic famines, which were in turn caused by periodic failures of crops. This hypothesis thus attributed the recent decline in mortality to the conquest of famines. Fogel disputes this hypothesis on several grounds, drawing mostly from the experience of England. First, he demonstrates that most of the famines occurred not through severe failures of harvest but through sharp falls in the entitlement of certain social classes following rather mild shortfall of crops. Second, he cites recently collected evidence to argue that periodic excess mortality, whether caused by famines or otherwise, can explain only a small part of the overall high mortality in the earlier centuries. Finally, he suggests the hypothesis that it is the *secular* improvement in the nutritional experience of the population that explains the secular decline in mortality. It is at this stage of the argument that Fogel makes use of the indicative role of height: he invokes the history of European heights to support the thesis of secular improvement in nutritional experience.

Apart from its 'predictive' and 'indicative' roles, anthropometry can have other uses too. Payne points to a possibility which we may call the 'discriminating' role of anthropometry. The task here is to identify the binding constraint among many possible factors that contribute to the genesis of undernutrition. The nutritional status of a person is almost always the outcome of a complex interaction between nutrient intakes and disease environment. The intake of nutrients may itself be constrained by a number of distinct factors, such as economic conditions determining the availability of intake, incidence of diseases affecting appetite and absorption, and the multitude of forces determining the distribution of available nutrients among the members of a household. The usual methods of assessing undernutrition can at best tell us about the existence and magnitude of deprivation: they cannot discriminate between the many possible constraints that may have led to that deprivation. Payne suggests a novel way of getting around this problem. He shows how, by using the information on a particular anthropometric measure, called the bodymass index, for both children and adult members of a household, it may be possible to classify different households according to the binding constraint each of them faces.

One other major issue covered in this volume is that of gender bias in the incidence of nutritional deprivation. It has been suggested on the basis of empirical observation that females are systematically more deprived than males in certain parts of the developing world. Behrman (Chapter 10) investigates this phenomenon within the framework of a household decision model. He looks at a number of issues of relevance in this context. First, how firm is the evidence for this bias? Second, what are the possible reasons for the observed bias? Third, how well do existing studies deal with the various problems of nutritional assessment, such as those discussed in other papers of this volume? To answer these questions, Behrman undertakes a critical survey of those among the existing studies whose estimating equations can be interpreted as being generated by his household decision model. He finds evidence for the existence of bias against females and tries to locate this phenomenon within the explanatory framework of his decision model, but cautions against drawing any firm conclusions at this stage. He notes the preliminary nature of the existing models of household decision and points to the need for developing them further. He also notes the many problems the existing studies get into by trying to assess nutritional deprivation from calorie intake alone, and urges the use of anthropometric indicators supplemented by more direct health indicators such as morbidity.

Taken together, the papers of this volume have dealt with most of the important problems that arise when economists engaged in the study of deprivation try to use nutrition as a tool of analysis. This has inevitably required a much deeper probe into the technicalities of nutrition than an economist would expect to encounter. But we hope this would be a price worth paying for a better understanding of the possibilities and limitations of the tools of nutrition as used in socioeconomic analysis.

2

Undernutrition: Measurement and Implications

C. Gopalan

2.1 INTRODUCTION

In this chapter it is the measurement of undernutrition in population groups rather than individuals that is under consideration. It is important to make this distinction at the very outset, because yardsticks and procedures that may be adequate for evaluation of the nutritional status of whole communities may not be suitable for the assessment of the nutritional status of a given individual. Individual genetic variations with respect to requirements of nutrients and response to their deprivations could get largely neutralized when large population groups in nearly similar socioeconomic and environmental status are considered.

Economists and planners, understandably, look for tidy methods of quantifying undernutrition in population groups. Biologists, however, would readily recognize the inherent limitations and pitfalls of exercises that seek to 'measure' undernutrition with mathematical precision. These limitations stem from the very nature of the undernutrition process—the multiplicity of interacting, often mutually reinforcing, factors involved in its causation; its evolution, often so insidious that it is hard to decide where normalcy has ended and subnormality (or abnormality) has set in; and its multiple clinical dimensions. It is not the purpose of this paper to discuss these limitations in detail, but a broad appreciation of them is essential for any meaningful discussion of the problem of measuring undernutrition.

The paper is organized as follows. Section 2.2 describes the biological processes involved in the genesis and development of undernutrition. Section 2.3 reviews the conceptual issues involved in the two major approaches to the measurement of undernutrition. These issues have been the subject of intense controversy in recent times, leading to sharply contrasting views on how undernutrition should be measured. These controversies are reviewed briefly, and my own views on the subject are presented. Section 2.4 is concerned with some of the practical problems of measuring undernutrition, bearing in mind the limitations of data on the one hand and the multi-faceted nature of undernutrition on the other. Here I argue that the measurement of undernutrition in large populations should be based on dietary surveys supplemented by weight-for-age measurements of children under the age of five.

My emphasis on the weight-for-age criterion is in sharp opposition to a recent trend which favours the alternative weight-for-height criterion. As I explain, the choice between these alternative criteria has a lot to do with the views one holds on the conceptual issues discussed in Section 2.3. It is, however, important to point out that my choice of the weight-for-age criterion for the under-fives in no way implies a negative judgement on the usefulness of height-for-age measurements: it is just that there are certain special problems in the height-for-age measurement of very young children. However, as is argued in Section 2.5, monitoring the height of older children is an exceedingly useful exercise; indeed, it is perhaps the best possible way of assessing the long-term changes in the nutritional status of a community. Finally, my major conclusions are summarized in Section 2.6.

2.2 THE BIOLOGY OF UNDERNUTRITION

The aetiology Undernutrition, widely prevalent among socially and economically deprived population groups around the world, is associated with a cluster of related, often coexistent, factors which together constitute what may be termed the 'poverty syndrome', the major attributes of which are (1) income levels that are inadequate to meet basic needs of food, clothing, and shelter; (2) diets that are quantitatively and often qualitatively deficient; (3) poor environment, poor access to safe water, and poor sanitation; (4) poor access to health care; and (5) large family size and high levels of illiteracy—especially female illiteracy. Among most undernourished population groups, these factors often tend to coexist, though their relative severity and extent may vary in different locations. In the evelation of undernutrition, and indeed in its progression and perpetuation, these factors often act synergistically.

The effects of all these factors, both socioeconomic and environmental, are, however, ultimately mediated through a final common pathway. The ultimate determinant of nutritional status is the availability at the cellular level—in adequate amounts, in proper combinations, and at appropriate times—of all the essential nutrients required for normal growth, development, maintenance, repair, and functioning of the organism. This, in turn, is determined by two broad sets of factors: (1) the diet, which must provide adequate amounts of the essential nutrients, and (2) factors that condition the requirement, absorption, assimilation, and utilization of the nutrients of the diet. These latter include the activity level and environmental factors, particularly infections and stress situations.

2.2.1 Correlation between dietary intake and nutritional status

The correlation between the levels of dietary inadequacy prevailing in households and communities on the one hand and the degree of severity of undernutrition (as assessed by anthropometric criteria and clinical signs) obtaining among them on the other is not always strict. Three major reasons for this may be mentioned.

1 The severity of effects of primary dietary inadequacy in a population can be aggravated by superadded conditioning factors, such as infections and parasitic diseases, the extent of such aggravation being determined by the nature of such infections, their duration, frequency, and severity, and the promptness and efficiency with which they are prevented and treated in the community. Infections can increase requirements of nutrients and inhibit their absorption and assimilation.

For example, in communities subject to the same order of dietary deficiency right through the year, clinical manifestation of undernutrition could be more pronounced in seasons characterized by a high prevalence of infections than at other times. Thus, in Coonoor in India, in poor communities subject to the same monotonous dietary deficiency throughout the year, the peak incidence of 'kwashiorkor' (a disease caused by severe protein–calorie deficiency) in children in successive years was noticed in May–June, following the peak incidence of diarrhoeal diseases in the 'fly season' of April–May (Gopalan 1955). In parts of Kerala in India, nearly three decades ago, when health services were less adequate than at present, the peak prevalence of 'kwashiorkor' was noticed in the weeks following the monsoon when, again, diarrhoeal diseases attained their peak.

While the level of dietary inadequacy is undoubtedly the dominant determinant of undernutrition, the level of primary health care in the community can significantly modify the severity of its clinical manifestations.

2 Where diets of entire households rather than of individuals within the family are being used as yardsticks in the assessment of community nutritional status, differences in the nature of intrafamilial distribution of food, and in particular in infant feeding and child-rearing practices, between the families and between communities can result in important differences with respect to nutritional status (especially of children) between households, and between communities with nearly similar overall levels of dietary inadequacy.

Differences with respect to nutritional status of infants and young children between households with nearly similar dietary and socioeconomic status can arise from differences with respect to duration and intensity of breast-feeding, the time of introduction of supplements, and the nature and amount of such supplements. Relatively small proportions of the overall family diet can make a significant difference to the level of adequacy or inadequacy of the diet of the preschool child. The level of female literacy in the household is often a major determinant of child-rearing practices and, therefore, of the level of child nutrition in poor households.

3 Furthermore, except in acute famine situations, the current nutritional status of a community is often a reflection of its erstwhile rather than (necessarily) its present dietary status. There is a variable time-lag between dietary deprivation and the onset of clinical undernutrition. This consideration, however, may not matter in the case of communities wherein no significant or striking changes in dietaries have taken place, and where seasonal fluctuations in dietaries are not marked. Current dietaries may then well reflect the situation responsible for the prevailing nutritional state.

The time-lag between the onset of nutrient deprivation and the appearance of clinical (or functional) manifestation can vary, depending on the nutrient and the clinical sign. Thus, for example, it could take much longer for eye lesions to appear following a vitamin A deprivation than for growth retardation to occur following calorie–protein undernutrition. In the case of growth retardation consequent on calorie–protein undernutrition itself, retardation in linear growth (stunting) is generally the outcome of a more longstanding dietary deprivation than retardation in body-weight increment (wasting).

These considerations will underscore the limitations with respect to the measurement of nutritional status of communities on the basis of the level of dietary inadequacy alone, and will highlight the need for additional yardsticks. This is not to minimize the importance of diet surveys in the assessment of nutritional status of population groups, but only to explain some of the seeming incongruities such as the lack of strict parallelism between dietary intakes and nutritional status. It will also explain the reasons why nutrition scientists rely not only on diet survey data but also on nutrition surveys (actual examination of human subjects—both adults and children) for the assessment of nutritional status of population groups.

Growth retardation In children of poor communities, habitually subsisting on inadequate diets, there is a continuous and insidious transition from the stage of normalcy usually obtaining up to about the fourth or sixth month (many infants being small-for-date may never start from normalcy) to that of fully fledged, clinically manifest undernutrition which generally supervenes before the third year. The speed of this downward slide from normalcy to fully fledged disease will depend on the extent of the dietary inadequacy, its duration, and the presence or absence of superadded aggravating factors such as infection. In poor communities we may expect to see children in different stages of this transition. Not all will go through the entire transition: the downward slide may be arrested at different stages, or it may be so slow that the child may manage to cross the critical age period of four to five years before the 'end-point' is reached. It is necessary to emphasize that, unlike many infectious diseases, in the case of undernutrition there is no point of striking or dramatic onset and no easily (visually) discernible dividing line between normalcy and the commencing of 'disease'. In children whose growth is carefully monitored, a faltering in the growth rate and the point at which the growth curve begins to flatten and deviate away from the normal standard could provide the earliest indication of undernutrition; however, few children in poor communities of the developing world enjoy the benefit of such close and careful growth-monitoring. Biochemical tests could reveal sub-clinical undernutrition, but these are hardly feasible in large-scale community surveys.

Retardation of growth and the downward deviation from normalcy becomes progressively more pronounced with the passage of time, and children pass insidiously from the so-called 'mild' to the 'severe' grades of growth retardation. A considerable proportion of children presently in the 'mild' grades of growth retardation are potential candidates for the 'moderate' and 'severe' grades; those presently in the 'severe' grades were probably in the 'mild' and 'moderate' categories a few weeks or months earlier. A fortunate small proportion may even reverse their direction.

In order to arrive at a given level of growth retardation, not all children need follow the same route in the growth chart. The shape of the growth curve could vary. The speed and intensity of growth retardation and the consequent duration over which a given order of growth retardation results will differ depending on the nature and extent of dietary inadequacy and of superadded infections. Under these circumstances, as important as the child's current position in the growth chart will be the route which that child took in order to arrive at the point—whether the child is the victim of an acute fairly severe deficiency over a short duration, or of a chronic less severe deficiency spread out over a longer period. For the same low weight-for-age, the child in the latter category could be more 'stunted' (less height for age) than the one in the first, and might require a much longer duration of more intensive nutritional rehabilitation for recovery. Quantification of undernutrition purely on the basis of degree of deficit of weight-for-age thus has its complexities and limitations. These have been discussed in detail in an earlier communication (Gopalan 1984).

Multiple nutrient deficiencies Children in poor communities suffer not merely from calorie deficiency but from other nutrient deficiencies as well. Thus, Indian children in poor rural communities often suffer from moderate and severe iron deficiency, anaemia (63 per cent of children below three years belonging to poor rural communities were found to suffer from such anaemia, according to one study of the National Institute of Nutrition), vitamin A deficiency, and less frequently from deficiencies of vitamins of the B group. Iodine deficiency resulting in endemic goitre is a massive problem of a special kind, and may be treated as a separate category; it lends itself to a simple technological solution capable of successful implementation even within the prevailing context of poverty.

The severity of deficiency of the different nutrients does not necessarily run parallel, possibly because of differences in the composition of diets and in the efficiency of absorption of different nutrients. The severity of iron deficiency or vitamin A deficiency may show a much lower positive correlation with the degree of weight deficit than the severity of calorie deficiency. Under the circumstances, different combinations of multiple nutrient deficiencies of varying orders of severity are seen in poor children. To quantify undernutrition under these circumstances, we need to be able to give a 'value' to different specific nutritional deficiencies in the total composite of undernutrition.

A recognition of these complexities inherent in the biology of the process of undernutrition will help us understand the problems and difficulties involved in the measurement of undernutrition in a community.

2.2.2 Practical approaches to measurement

Despite these difficulties and limitations, a fairly reliable estimate of the quantum of undernutrition in a community may be made through two approaches which are practicable under the real-life conditions obtaining in the field, and which will largely serve the needs of the public health scientist and developmental economist:

1   a survey of the diets of representative households (supported by a survey of diets of individual members of the family in a sub-sample of households) in a community, in order to derive information on nutrient intake—especially the calorie intake;
2   anthropometric and clinical examination of children—especially the under-fives (who constitute the 'most sensitive' segment of the population from the point of view of nutritional vulnerability).

In the conventional procedure employed by nutrition scientists for the assessment of nutritional status of communities, these two approaches are combined with a broad survey of the socioeconomic and environmental status of the community, which not only could facilitate the interpretation of data but also could provide valuable practical leads for combating undernutrition in the community.

The approaches described above have been widely used, and, subject to their inherent limitations, they are valid. The major controversies with respect to measurement of undernutrition pertain not so much to the choice of the above two approaches, as to the interpretation and evaluation of the data derived from them.

2.3 SOME BASIC ISSUES

In any discussion about the measurement of undernutrition, there are some basic issues which need to be considered and some crucial questions which need to be answered.

If we are going to use the two practical approaches described above, the following questions arise: What are the normal standards against which the prevailing level of calorie intake and the observed growth performance should be compared in order to determine adequacy or otherwise? Are the widely used standards that are recommended by international agencies and adopted with slight variations by most countries valid for both the rich and the poor? More specifically, with respect to calorie intake, is it necessary to use the recommended mean requirement level (M), or will it be more appropriate, especially in the case of poor populations, to use a level equivalent to the mean minus two standard deviations $(M - 2\ SD)$ as the standard yardstick? With respect to growth, how appropriate are the 'international standards' for developing countries? Even if we accept the position that the genetic potential for growth between populations is nearly similar, can we not accept some levels of growth retardation (as revealed by comparisons with international or the 'best indigenous' standard) as acceptable for poor children consistent with their 'economy and ecology'? Should small body size cause any concern, and is it of any functional significance? Does 'stunting', so widely seen in developing countries, really matter?

We may consider some recent hypotheses which touch on these questions.

Sukhatme's hypothesis   With respect to calorie intake, a sharp debate as to whether, for the purpose of assessing the adequacy of a given level of calorie intake, the recommended mean energy requirement level (M) need be used as the standard for comparison, or whether a level corresponding to the mean minus two standard deviations $(M - 2\ SD)$ would suffice has been ongoing for some time. This debate was touched off largely by the postulate of Sukhatme (1978, 1981a) that a human subject can permanently 'adapt' himself to a low calorie intake level representing the lowest limit of his 'intra-individual variation' and that, therefore, $M - 2\,SD$ rather than M would be the appropriate yardstick for comparison. Sukhatme's postulate has been dealt with in earlier publications (Gopalan 1983a), and it is therefore proposed to touch on it only briefly here.

Sukhatme's contention that the energy requirement of normal individuals is not static and that there is intra-individual variation in calorie intake may not be disputed. In fact, it is to be expected that calorie intake of individuals not subject to socioeconomic constraint will show daily variation depending on the level of activity and the presence or absence of stress.

What is unacceptable, however, is the second postulate of Sukhatme, that subjects permanently obliged to subsist on calorie intakes representing the lowest levels of what he terms 'intra-individual variation' (equivalent to recommended mean level minus the standard deviations) can permanently adapt their requirement to this low intake without any functional impairment. In short, Sukhatme suggests that the pendulum of daily calorie intake in an individual, which normally oscillates between two points on either side of the mean, can be safely and permanently arrested at the lowest end of its oscillation. If intra-individual variation in energy intake is a physiological mechanism providing for daily variation in energy requirements, Sukhatme's postulate would imply that the human organism could do without this physiological adjustment and that that requirement will somehow get adjusted to a lower level in keeping with the lowered intake. A healthy subject responds to alterations in energy intake by burning body fat when dietary energy is deficient or by storing body fat when dietary energy is in excess, resulting in a continuous process of breakdown and synthesis of body energy reserves. Individuals subsisting permanently on low-energy intakes have no scope for this and lose the advantage of an important regulatory mechanism. We have no evidence that fluctuations in efficiency of energy utilization in the absence of variations in levels of activity or stress contribute significantly to prevailing intra-individual variation even over a short period. We have no evidence to believe that populations engaged in their expected levels of occupational activity and obliged permanently to subsist at nearly 70 per cent of the recommended mean energy intake can 'adapt' themselves to such a low level of calorie intake without suffering loss of body weight and consequent impairment of function.

Seckler's and Payne's hypotheses   Seckler (1982) had gone so far as to suggest that 'smallness' is an appropriate and welcome attribute of poor people, consistent with their good health. He advised Indian nutrition scientists not only not to use 'international standards' of growth (as these would yield an 'overestimation' of undernutrition) but also not to use even the 'best indigenous standard' of the Indian high socioeconomic groups, because even these will be 'abnormally large' for the majority of Indians who are poor. This subject has been dealt with by the author in an earlier publication (Gopalan 1983*b*).

More recently, Payne has argued that, even if children of developing countries have the same genetic potential for growth as those of the more fortunate countries of Europe and the USA, they will settle for a lower level of growth in keeping with their 'economy and ecology' (Pacey and Payne 1985). It is not surprising that this plea for acquiescence in growth retardation has been sharply rejected as an exercise in 'perpetuation of undernutrition' (Jaya Rao 1986).

The three hypotheses referred to above have one thing in common: they have all relied on the body's ability to permanently 'adapt' itself to environmental and dietary stress without any detriment whatsoever to functional competence. Unfortunately, 'adaptation' has apparently been loosely interpreted in the debate to signify an acceptable state of normalcy instead of being viewed as no more than a 'strategic retreat from normalcy' on the part of the organism ('a contraction of its metabolic frontiers') in order to face the stress and escape with minimal permanent damage to its vital tissues. 'Adaptation' thus represents a state of siege. A population that is permanently reduced to this state cannot be normal. I shall discuss this central issue at some length in the next section and shall try to highlight the 'cost' and functional implications involved in the so-called 'adaptation' process.

2.3.1 'Adaptation': meaning and implications

When an organism is subject to the stress of dietary inadequacy, it responds to the stress in a number of ways in order to minimize permanent tissue damage. A reduction of physical activity to conserve energy and a retardation of growth to minimize nutrient requirement are well-known responses. However, these responses are not without their inevitable functional consequences and costs. Individuals responding to stress in this way should not be considered normal and indeed are not normal, as several functional studies have shown. They generally function at a substandard level.

Thus, an adult can (within limits) successfully 'adapt' himself to low calorie intake through a corresponding reduction in work output to reduce energy expenditure. Such adaptation will, however, result in limiting his productivity and earning capacity and thus could only serve to perpetuate his poverty. Payne would perhaps argue that the individual is 'adapted' to function as well as he needs to in his 'economy and ecology', meaning his poverty situation, in which he is often either unemployed or underemployed. This would imply that we accept a situation in which the economic status of a poor country decides the level of development of its human resources, and that efforts at improvement of the quality of human resources of a country could wait until economic improvement has been registered. This would be contrary to the present strategies, whereby vigorous efforts at promoting the quality of human resources go hand in hand with efforts at economic improvement.

To take another example, children can adapt to energy deficiency by reducing play and other physical activities, but such restriction could impair their mental and physical development. The fascinating work of Torun *et al.* (1975) has in fact shown the importance of physical activity in children in promoting linear growth and ensuring an efficient pattern of energy utilization. A restriction of physical activity in children can, by reducing opportunities for stimulation and learning experiences, retard mental development as well. Adjustment to low energy inputs through restriction of necessary physical activity cannot, therefore, be considered an acceptable form of adaptation.

Rutishauser and Whitehead (1972) observed that the level of physical activity of Ugandan children was less than that of European counterparts of comparable age and that their caloric intake was also correspondingly low (80 kcal per kilogram of body weight as against 100 kcal for European children). We should avoid drawing the conclusion that the low physical activity of the African children is perhaps a 'cultural attribute' and that the low energy intake is the result rather than the cause of the decreased activity. We may safely predict that, if the European children were to subsist on the habitual diets of Ugandan children, their activity pattern would be no different. Several 'natural' and controlled studies have clearly demonstrated that the response of human beings to calorie undernutrition is identical, irrespective of their race and nationality. The picture of semi-starvation was the same in Belsen and Bengal, in Madras and Minnesota. There is no scientific evidence to show that people of different cultures will show different physiological responses when faced with the same order of restriction in calorie intake.

Implications with respect to protein nutrition An important point that seems to have been totally lost sight of in discussions of Sukhatme's hypothesis of 'adaptation' to low calorie intake is its serious implications with respect to protein nutrition. Policy-makers, planners, and some economists apparently labour under the mistaken impression that, with the acceptance of that hypothesis, the current estimates of undernutrition among populations in developing countries will be reduced to 'manageable proportions'. Far from this being the case, the acceptance of this hypothesis would actually imply that the nutrition situation in many developing countries is far worse than what the present estimates indicate—indeed, that the solution of the problem will be possible only through a drastic qualitative upgrading of the current dietaries, which would be clearly well beyond the economic resources of these countries. Let me explain why this is so.

At the height of the great protein debate, which finally led to the 'protein fiasco' and the winding up of the PAG (Protein Advisory Group of the UN), we in India had argued that the problem of protein–calorie malnutrition was essentially a problem of calorie deficiency, and that such protein deficiency as existed was an incidental secondary by-product of primary calorie deficiency. Sukhatme himself was very much in the forefront in this endeavour. We had shown that, if the habitual cereal–legume dietaries of poor Asian population groups were consumed at levels adequate to meet the full caloric needs (and here we were talking of caloric needs as conforming to present international recommended mean levels of intake, and not of $M - 2SD$ levels), then protein needs would be automatically met. A study carried out at the National Institute of Nutrition (Gopalan *et al.* 1973), which had then attracted international attention, actually helped to demonstrate how, in an under-nourished community of children, an additional provision of 310 calories (even when such calories were derived from food sources practically devoid of proteins—'empty calories') could bring about a significant improvement in their nutritional status and a reduction in protein-calorie malnutrition. We therefore took the position that, under the circumstances, the right and feasible strategy was to bridge the calorie gap with existing habitual dietaries and not to go in for expensive protein concentrates or for drastic dietary changes which in any case were well beyond the economic resources of these countries. Our policy was based on the principle that children needed to be fed the cereal–legume diets, which alone they could afford, at levels that would at least provide their full calorie needs as per internationally accepted recommendations—levels at which they would not need to restrict play and physical activity in order to conserve energy. We sought to overcome the problem of low calorie density ('bulk factor') of cooked cereal diets through invoking traditional practices like malting, so that children could be fed such predominantly cereal-based diets in quantities that would provide them their full caloric needs as per current recommendations (and therefore also, incidentally, their protein needs).

If, in consonance with Sukhatme's hypothesis, we now take the position that what children (and adults) need is no more than 70 per cent of the recommended mean levels of calorie intake, then on such restricted levels, clearly, they cannot meet their protein requirements with their present habitual cereal–legume diets. As the intake of energy is restricted, protein requirement increases—by as much as 20–30 per cent. Individuals will need to include in their dietaries other, relatively expensive, items of protein-rich foods. Several studies carried out at the National Institute of

Nutrition in Hyderabad provide experimental support for this in both children and adults, as shown in Tables 2.1 and 2.2. Not only is the protein concentration in the habitual poor Asian dietaries too low to provide the protein requirement at the $M - 2SD$ levels of calorie intake, but the utilization of protein at this lower level is also relatively poor.

Table 2.1. Recommended dietary intakes of protein and energy for Indians, 1981

	Net calories (kcal)	Proteins (g)	Protein–calorie %	Net calories at 70% level	Protein–calorie % at low level of energy requirement
Men					
Sedentary work	2400	55	9.2	1680	13.1
Moderate work	2800	55	7.9	1960	11.2
Heavy work	3900	55	5.6	2730	8.1
Women					
Sedentary work	1900	45	9.5	1330	13.5
Moderate work	2200	45	8.2	1540	11.7
Heavy work	3000	45	6.0	2100	8.6
During pregnancy	2500	59	9.4	1750	13.5
Lactation	2750	70	10.2	1925	14.5
Children					
1–3 years	1220	22.0	7.2	854	10.3
4–6 years	1720	29.4	6.8	1204	9.8
7–9 years	2050	35.6	6.9	1435	9.9
Boys 10–12 years	2420	42.5	7.0	1694	10.0
Girls 10–12 years	2260	42.1	7.5	1582	10.6
Boys 13–15 years	2660	51.7	7.8	1862	11.1
Girls 13–15 years	2360	43.3	7.3	1652	10.5
Boys 16–18 years	2820	53.1	7.5	1974	10.8
Girls 16–18 years	2200	44.00	8.0	1540	11.4

Note: This table presents the RDA of calories and proteins for adults (at different physiological levels) and children. Also, it provides the protein–calorie percentage at requirement level and at the low level of energy intake. This shows that at low level of energy ($M - 2SD$) intake the protein–calorie percentage of the dietaries should be at higher levels to meet the recommended allowance of protein. The protein–calories percentage of the habitual rice/legume–based Indian dietaries is around 8–9 per cent. Also, since the protein requirement is known to increase when calories are restricted because of poorer utilization, the actual protein–calorie percentage required at the low energy will be higher by another 20–50 per cent.

Source: Recommended Dietary Intakes for Indians 1981 (Indian Council of Medical Research)

Table 2.2.   Effect of energy restriction on protein requirements in India

Preschool children

Energy intake (kcal/kg/day)	Protein requirement [a] (g/kg)
100	1.33
80	1.64

Adults 1

Protein intake (g/day)	Energy required for nitrogen(N) balance (cal)
60	2066
40	2249

Adults 2: Heavy casual labourers

Energy intake (kcal/kg/day)	Protein intake (g/kg/day)	Mean N balance (g/day)
55.5	1.0	+ 1.0
44.4	1.0	− 0.3

[a]A retention of 40 mg of nitrogen per kilogram was taken on meeting the requirement of preschool children.

Source: Provided at the author's request by Dr B. S. Narasinga Rao, Director, National Institute of Nutrition, Hyderabad, India.

Thus, a child of 3 years subsisting on a 1200 calorie diet could obtain 22 g protein daily with a diet that provides no more than just 7.2 per cent of its overall calorific value through protein. (Low-cost cereal–legume diets provide more than 8 per cent of protein calories.) Against this, if calorie intake using the same diet is reduced to 70 per cent of mean recommended levels ($M - 2SD$ level), the protein–calorie percentage in the diet that will be needed to provide the same 22 g of protein daily would be 10.3 per cent (clearly, more than what is possible with existing poor Indian dietaries). Moreover, we have also to take into account the fact that with low levels of calorie intake the utilization of protein is poor. Thus, in a study of under-fives it was found that, while with a calorie intake of 100 kcal/kg per day the children need 1.35 g protein per kilogram to achieve a retention of 40 mg of nitrogen per day, they would need 1.64 g per kilogram from the same protein source to achieve the same level of nitrogen retention when calorie intake is reduced to 80 kcal/kg per day. Thus, a decrease in calorie intake to 70 per cent will call for an increase of protein intake by an additional 20 per cent. In a study of adults it was found that, with a calorie intake of 2066 kcal daily, as much as 60 g protein was necessary to achieve nitrogen balance, while with a calorie intake of 2250 calories, the protein intake needed for achieving nitrogen balance was just 40 g daily.

In effect, then, it would appear that, in recommending lower levels of calorie intake for poor populations in the expectation that they will 'adapt' to such low levels, we are also implying that they substitute 'cake' for their usual 'bread'.

2.3.2   Growth retardation: the minimal role of genetic factor

It has now been conclusively shown, on the basis of data from countries throughout the world, that differences currently observed with respect to growth patterns of children in the rich countries of Europe and North America on the one hand and in the poor countries of Asia, Africa, and Latin America on the other (and between the rich and poor within the developing countries themselves) are mostly attributable to differences in their socioeconomic status, and not to genetic differences (Habicht *et al*. 1974; Stephenson *et al*. 1983). The remarkable secular trend in heights of children and adults witnessed in post-war Japan underscores this fact. While a great majority of Indian children show varying degrees of growth retardation, Indian children who are not subject to dietary constraints have been shown to have growth levels that correspond closely to the international (Harvard) standards (Gopalan 1989). The genetic potential for growth and development is nearly similar among most peoples of the world.

The Lancet (1984), discussing the use in developing countries of international growth standards (particularly the WHO/NCHS standards), on the basis of data from different parts of the world, concluded in its editorial that 'recent evidence suggests that the growth of privileged groups of children in developing countries does *not* differ importantly from these standards' and that 'the poorer growth so commonly observed in the underprivileged is due to social factors—among which malnutrition–infection complex is of primary importance—rather than to ethnic or geographic differences'.

Also, there are no known ethnic differences in human physiology with respect to metabolism of nutrients. Africans and Asians do not burn their dietary calories or use their dietary protein any differently from Europeans and Americans. It follows, then, that dietary requirements for normal growth, development, and function cannot vary widely between different races, unless we accept different standards between them with respect to normal growth and function.

It is not so much the retardation of physical growth *per se* and the relatively small body size of the poor that need bother us: it is the fact that there is now mounting evidence, thanks to sophisticated functional tests which measure physical stamina and work capacity on the one hand and mental development and learning ability on the other, that impairment in physical growth (as assessed by the failure to achieve the full genetic potential for the attainment of physical stature) is accompanied by varying degrees of functional incompetence. The fascinating work of Spurr *et al.* (1982, 1983, 1984) in Colombia, Chavez and Martinez (1982) in Mexico, Viteri (1971) in Guatemala, and Satyanarayana *et al.* (1977) in India has provided ample evidence of the functional implications of growth retardation. Indeed, there is often a linear relationship between the degree of growth retardation and the degree of physical and mental functional impairment. Measurement of the degree of growth retardation thus could serve as a proxy for the assessment of functional competence.

It will be difficult for any biologist to agree with Payne's strange suggestion that the term 'undernutrition' should be reserved only for children whose state of nutrition has deteriorated to the point where they are .close to death, and that other children with less severe degrees of nutritional deprivation, who do not actually face the risk of imminent death, even if they happen to show clear evidence of functional impairment of various kinds, should not be included in the 'undernourished' category. This is almost like saying that a person should be considered 'unhealthy' only when he has reached the point of death.

Weight-for-height A view that is now being widely propagated is that, irrespective of deficits in height-for-age or weight-for-age, children with weights 'appropriate' to their heights ('normal' weight–height ratio) could be considered to have successfully adapted themselves to their dietary deprivation, and to be practically 'normal' and free from undernutrition! According to this postulate, it is not so much height-for-age or weight-for-age that matters but the weight–height ratio that is the crucial indicator of normalcy. This convenient hypothesis could lend legitimacy to the 'small but healthy' hypothesis. However, there is not an iota of hard scientific evidence to justify this sweeping postulate. Indeed, such evidence as is available points to a near-linear relationship between deficits in height-for-age or weight-for-age and functional impairment, irrespective of weight-for-height.

The above postulate is an unwarranted distortion of Waterlow's morphological classification of growth retardation into stunting, wasting, and stunting + wasting . Waterlow clearly did not invest this classification with functional significance. All that he implied was that, in the case of such stunted children with a normal weight–height ratio, it could be argued that their *current* level of calorie intake is probably adequate to sustain them in the context of their stunted stature. He did not claim that stunted children with appropriate weights for their heights were functionally normal or that stunting, even if associated with appropriate body weight-for-height, was an acceptable state.

Satyanarayana has shown a direct correlation between productivity and body weight in industrial workers drawn from the poor socioeconomic groups, even with respect to operations in which body weight may not be expected to make a difference. In a longitudinal study on undernourished boys in India, Satyanarayana and colleagues (1979) showed that the wages earned by adolescent boys employed by farmers in rural areas were significantly related to body weight and height. Men and women with better nutritional anthropometry earned 30–50 per cent additional incentive money (over and above the uniform basic pay) in factories where an individual incentive system based on work output was in operation.

Agarwal *et al.* (1987) have provided convincing evidence, on the basis of an intensive study of over 1300 children in rural areas of Uttar Pradesh in India, that stunted children with a 'normal' weight–height ratio show the same order of functional (physical and mental) impairment as equally stunted children with poorer weight–height ratios. The view that a stunted child may be considered 'adapted' if it happens to have a weight appropriate to its stunted height is apparently untenable.

A considerable proportion of girls in developing countries who are stunted and of low body size because of undernutrition during the crucial years of their growth and development end up with heights of below 145 cm when they enter motherhood. It is now known that there is a direct relationship between stunting of mothers and the occurrence of low birth weights in their offspring. According to the recommendations of international agencies, maternal heights below 145 cm may be considered indicative of risk of obstetric complications and low birth weight. It will be seen from the data presented in Table 2.3 that a distinctly higher proportion of offspring of mothers with heights of less than 145 cm were of low birth weight. In India, as in many other developing countries, more than one-third of all infants born alive have birth weights below 2500 g. It is now known that, with respect to both height and weight, infants who start with the initial handicap of a low birth weight apparently never fully recover from it. Thus, low birth weights in full-term infants make a lasting contribution to stunting.

Stunting is the outstanding feature of so-called 'adaptation'. It is the feature that ensures that not only this generation, but also the next, does not escape from the poverty trap. Stunted children with impaired learning abilities and schooling end up as stunted adults with low levels of productivity, educational attainment, and resourcefulness, earning low incomes and thus continuing to be enmeshed in the poverty trap, and so proving unable to feed their children adequately. Stunted women beget offspring with low birth weights who start their lives with an initial handicap from which they never fully recover. Thus, stunting and the poverty with which it is invariably associated continue from one generation to another. To view this scenario as 'acceptable adaptation' is cruel irony!

Table 2.3. Maternal height and incidence of low birth weight (LBW) in offspring, India

Maternal height (cm)	Income group (Rs/head/month)	Incidence of LBW (%)
< 145	< 50	35.5
> 145	< 50	24.2
> 145	> 200	15.0

Source: Shanti Ghosh *et al.* (unpublished research)

A country or community in which large segments of the population suffer from growth retardation is one in which the quality and calibre of human resources is eroded and of substandard quality. A level of dietary intake and nutrition which can permit only substandard growth must inevitably lead to an erosion of the quality of human resources in developing countries or a perpetuation of such erosion where it already exists.

A sensible developmental policy of any country must obviously aim at providing for a level of calorie intake that will permit the full productivity and work output from its labour force, and a level of growth and development for its children that represents the fullest expression of their genetic potential. It is possible that many poor countries may be in no position to achieve these targets in the near future, and may have to settle for a policy that will enable them to reach these goals in a phased manner. It will, however, be an act of self-deception and political expediency to tailor standards of growth, physical and mental function, and dietary requirements in order to minimize the problem of undernutrition and win the war against poverty *on paper*. Standards are meant to determine the magnitude of a problem: it will be perverse to let this magnitude frighten us or tempt us to tailor the standard so that the 'problem' is reduced to 'manageable proportions'.

There is no scientific justification for double standards between rich and poor countries in the matter of dietary requirements of their populations or growth levels of their children. We may, of course, argue as to whether current levels of body weight (not height) observed in European and American infants and preschool children are not somewhat high and are representative of *over*nutrition and obesity. This is a different matter; it could call for a revision of standards for American and European children as well. Establishment by each country of a standard yardstick of its own in conformity with the pattern observed among affluent children of that country, who are not subject to dietary and environmental constraints, will be in order. On the basis of all available evidence, we may expect that the standards thus established by different countries (including developing countries) will not be widely different. What we should guard against, however, is an acceptance of the concept that levels of growth and of dietary intake known and accepted to be subnormal and substandard for the affluent are appropriate and good enough for the poor and consistent with their poverty status. In the measurement of undernutrition, we should be guided by these considerations.

2.4   SOME PROBLEMS IN MEASUREMENT

I shall now briefly consider the two practical approaches referred to earlier. There are inherent practical limitations involved in the use of these approaches as measures of undernutrition. For our present purpose, we will not consider the limitations that pertain to the actual collection of data and the possibilities of measurement errors, but merely the broader issues.

2.4.1   The calorie intake yardstick

Estimations of levels of dietary intake of calories have been widely used in the evaluation of nutritional status of population groups. The limitations of the calorie intake yardstick have been discussed in an earlier communication (Gopalan 1983*a*); these need only be recapitulated briefly here.

First, as pointed out earlier, poor diets are deficient not in calories alone but in several nutrients as well, though in dietaries based mostly on a single major staple there is a close correlation between calorie intake and intake of essential nutrients. Where the major dietary item is lacking in an important nutrient (as is the case with cassava and tapioca with respect to protein), the diet could be quite adequate with respect to calories while being highly deficient with respect to protein. This is not unusual in Africa. Under the circumstances, calorie intake levels may provide a flattering picture of the nutritional status. Therefore calorie intake measurements generally provide a quantitative and not necessarily a qualitative measure of the adequacy of diets.

Second, measurements of calorie intake, especially under field conditions, lack precision; daily and seasonal fluctuations in dietary intake could add to this problem, which even seven-day weighment methods cannot entirely solve. Repeated diet surveys in different seasons may be necessary to obtain a reliable picture.

Third, where diets of entire households (and not of individual members therein) are estimated, as is generally the case, the actual calorie intake of the most vulnerable segment of the population, namely the children, is often indirectly derived through the application of certain arbitrary coefficients based on the assumption that the intrafamilial distribution of food conforms to relative physiological needs—an assumption not often valid. Actual estimations of individual dietary intakes within families in a representative sub-sample of households surveyed, and the application of necessary correction based on these data to the figures for individual intakes, may obviate the error to some extent.

For the purpose of assessment of dietary/nutritional status, the actual observed calorie intake for a given age/sex/occupational group is compared with the mean energy requirement level for that group as recommended by international (and national) expert bodies on the basis of well conducted, fairly reliable intensive studies in several laboratories of the world. The Indian Council of Medical Research, for example, has recommended energy intake levels appropriate for different categories (age, sex, and occupation) based on Indian studies as well as on published observations from elsewhere and the recommendation of international agencies. Through such comparison, it will be possible to determine proportions of population groups—manual labourers (male and female), sedentary workers (male and female), children between 5 and 12 years of age, and children below 5 years of age—in the community surveyed, obtaining, say, 90, 80–90, 70–80, 60–70, and less than 60 per cent of the respective recommended intake energy level.

2.4.2 Growth retardation as a measure of undernutrition

Children under 5 years of age represent the most vulnerable segment of the population from the nutritional standpoint. For all practical purposes, the growth performance of children of this age group is a convenient measure of the nutritional status of the community. This procedure is now being widely employed in many developing countries. The pitfalls and limitations of this approach have been discussed in an earlier publication (Gopalan 1984).

Among the different anthropometric measurements—namely, weight-for-age, height-for-age, weight-for-height, and arm circumference—taking practical considerations into account, the balance of advantage rests heavily with weight-for-age measurements as far as infants and under-fives are concerned. Heights (or lengths) for age in children are more difficult to measure accurately, and height measurements are also less sensitive to dietary deprivation. The significance of weight-for-height measurements, and of the classification of growth retardation into 'wasting' and 'stunting', are debatable. Arm circumference measurements are simple to carry out but there are doubts on the one hand about their being age-independent (a merit often claimed in their favour), and on the other hand about their reliability in comparison to weight measurements. For all practical purposes, therefore, as far as under-fives are concerned, it may be best to rely on weight-for-age surveys.

The procedure that is now being widely adopted is to compare the weight-for-age of the child with the weight-for-age in the international (Harvard or NCHS) standard. According to the Gomez scale, which is generally used (Gomez *et al.* 1956), children with weights within 90 per cent of the standard are considered 'normal', those between 90 and 75 per cent of the standard as being in 'mild' malnutrition, those between 75 and 60 per cent of the standard as being 'moderately' malnourished, and those below 60 per cent of the standard as being 'severely' malnourished.

The cut-off points of 90, 75, and 60 per cent, are admittedly arbitrary and have no real scientific basis. The use of the international standard rather than the 'best indigenous' standard as the yardstick for comparison has also been questioned. Even so, Gomez's classification has proved useful in enabling health/nutrition scientists to quantify undernutrition in the children of a community and to assess the impact of nutrition intervention programmes. However, in order that weight-for-age measurements in under-fives could be thus used for comparisons of nutritional status between population groups and between two time-points in the same population group, some precautions are absolutely necessary. These precautions are not being currently observed, with the result that the data from different locations and at different time-points are not truly comparable.

In all comparisons that use cut-off points that are percentages of the standard median, it is extremely important to ensure that the age and sex composition of the under-five groups are very similar. A given order of weight deficit in a child under 2 years of age carries a far greater significance than the same order of weight deficit in a child of 5 years. Also, where there are wide seasonal fluctuations with regard to food availability, comparisons of measurements between two populations in two such different seasons may prove fallacious. Mistakes in age assessment, especially in children under 3 years, can modify results significantly.

According to available data, generally less than 10 per cent of under-fives in South-East Asian countries suffer from 'severe malnutrition' (weight-for-age less than 60 per cent of the standard), less than 15 per cent are normal (weight-for-age more than 90 per cent of standard), while the remaining belong to the 'mild' and 'moderate' grades of under-nutrition.

If used with due precautions, weight-for-age surveys among under-fives and the quantification of the order of weight deficit observed among them provides the health/nutrition scientist with a convenient and prac-ticable tool for the quantification of weight deficits in children and therefore, indirectly, for the quantification of undernutrition. This pro-cedure will be specially useful in comparisons of different population groups within a country in order to identify the most depressed groups requiring special attention, and also to monitor changes in the profile of undernutrition (the quantum and pattern) following from nutrition in-tervention programmes.

The Gomez scale and other similar methods attempt to classify under-nutrition in terms of various cut-off points defined as a stipulated per-centage of the median of the reference population. The limitation of this approach is that it does not take into account the variability of the relative width of the distribution of weight-for-age across different age periods. For example, 60 per cent of median weight-for-age indicates a much more severe state of malnutrition for infants and young children than for older children. In order to overcome this problem, a new method has been developed which measures the deviation of the antho-ropometric measurement from the reference median in terms of standard deviation units or 'Z' scores (Waterlow et al. 1977). This is coming into increasing use.

Unfortunately, weight-for-age measurements are now being put to the improper use of subserving a nutrition policy of brinkmanship in some developing countries, not for the promotion of child health/nutrition and prevention of undernutrition, but mainly to identify cases of so-called 'severe' malnutrition (that is, children with weight-for-age of less than 60 per cent of the standard) who could be chosen as beneficiaries for supplementary feeding programmes. In a longitudinal study in children of Bangladesh, Chen et al. (1980) observed that the risk of increased mortality was observed only in under-fives who suffered from 'severe' malnutrition. This has been unfortunately misinterpreted to imply that children suffering from 'mild' and 'moderate' malnutrition can somehow muddle through and that only the 'severely' malnourished need attention in nutrition intervention programmes. Though Chen tried to rebut this inference in a later publication (Chen et al. 1982), the impression con-veyed by his original paper has continued to misguide health workers in developing countries.

Such exclusive attention to the severely malnourished to the point of neglect of the 'moderately' and 'mildly' malnourished (nutrition policy of brinkmanship) can only result in reducing the size of the tip of the iceberg and in further increasing the pool of moderate and mild malnutrition cases in the community. But children who are currently in the so-called 'moderate' stage could move into the 'severe' stage within a few weeks or months. To withhold action until they are actually at that end-stage would be poor strategy. The inputs needed to prevent children who are in the mild and moderate stages of malnutrition from passing into the severe stage are far less than those that would be needed to rehabilitate the severely undernourished ones. It may even be possible for mothers of poor households to provide the inputs of the former category in their own homes with their own resources, if they are properly assisted and educated by health workers in the course of domiciliary visits. The inputs needed for rehabilitation of the severely undernourished, on the other hand, will be clearly beyond the means of poor households and will need expensive institutional support. Apart from this practical consideration, there is now evidence that even the so-called moderately undernourished children show functional (physical and mental) impairment.

2.5   HEIGHT AS AN INDICATOR OF NUTRITIONAL STATUS

It was earlier pointed out that, as far as infants and very young children are concerned, height measurements may not be feasible in large-scale field studies; moreover, height (length) is less sensitive to dietary fluctuations in the short run. For these reasons, it was recommended that weight-for-age measurements would suffice for all practical purposes as far as under-fives are concerned.

However, the merit of height measurements as an indication of socioeconomic status of a community deserves special emphasis. Serial height measurements of children of 6–7 years of age have an important place in national nutrition surveys. Cross-sectional measurement of heights in adult populations of different classes can provide valuable indicators of disparities with respect to nutritional status arising from socioeconomic inequalities. Tanner (1982), in his remarkable paper on 'The Potential of Auxological Data for Measuring Economic and Social Well-being', has provided a fascinating historical account which highlights the great value of height measurements as an instrument for monitoring progress with respect to the state of health, nutrition, and well-being of communities. Steckel (1983) found a close correlation between height and per capita income in a study based on the result of 56 height studies and per capita income estimates for 20 countries. When it is recognized that 'socioeconomic' factors and per capita income could affect height only by mediating changes in nutritional inputs, the importance of height as a measure of nutritional status of a community becomes obvious.

The most convenient age group that could be captured for large-scale height surveys would be schoolchildren of the 6–7-year age group—i.e. those belonging to the first or second standard (the stage at which drop-outs are few). In fact, such surveys must constitute an important item of any national nutrition survey.

Height measurements and quantification of height deficit (in comparison with an international or national standard) will help to identify differences in nutritional status between different regions, population groups, and social classes in a country and to monitor changes over a period of time. Indeed, height deficits in a population group could be considered to provide an even more reliable indication of nutritional status than weight deficits. It may be argued that the standards against which weight measurements are being compared have been derived from relatively obese affluent American subjects and may not necessarily reflect optimal nutrition. Also, temporary diminution in weights occurring in communities of children or even adults can be caused by short-lived epidemics. These criticisms will not apply to height measurements. Overnutrition and resultant obesity can result in more than optimal weights, but not in more than optimal heights.

Height-for-age deficits can be quantified in the same way as weight-for-age deficits using international standards and applying the procedures of 'Z' scores. Where facilities exist, each country could develop its own weight-for-age and height-for-age standards based on measurements carried out on truly affluent sections of its own populations which are free from dietary and environmental constraints. Many developing countries do not at present have such standards of their own. Under the circumstances, in view of the mounting evidence that genetic differences with respect to growth potential between population groups are relatively minor, it will be quite in order for international standards (WHO/NCHS/Harvard) to be used for all practical purposes for the assessment of weight and height deficits. It is possible that even standards developed by each developing country based on observations on its affluent sections could fall short of the widely used international standards to some extent. This is because of the strong likelihood that the secular trend with respect to growth has not as yet reached its maximum limit in many developing countries. It may probably need two or three generations of affluence for populations in many such countries to attain their fullest growth potential, which can be expected to be almost similar to the prevailing pattern in Europe and America, as has been revealed by experience in Japan during the last two to three decades.

Biological significance of height measurement   Tanner (1982) quotes Villerme, who wrote as long ago as 1928 that 'Human height becomes greater and growth takes place more rapidly, other things being equal, in proportion as the country is richer, comfort more general, houses, clothes and nourishment better, and labour, fatigue and privations during infancy and youth less; in other words, circumstances which accompany poverty delay the age at which complete stature is reached and stunt adult height.'

In Japan, between 1957 and 1977 average mature height increased by 4.3 cm in males and 2.7 cm in females; age at maximum increment dropped by 0.97 years in males and 0.53 years in females. Practically all the height increase was due to increase in leg length, not in sitting height, with the result that within 20 years of economic advancement the entire body proportions of the Japanese had changed. This is perhaps the most striking and spectacular evidence of the importance of height measurements as an index of the nutritional status of a population which parallels economic advancement, and it reveals that height measurement is clearly an indicator of as much importance to the developmental economist and planner as it is to the health/nutrition scientist.

There is a large body of evidence pointing to a relationship between height and mental function. Indeed, as early as 1893, William Porter (quoted by Tanner 1982) had shown in the schools of St Louis that pupils who were academically advanced for their age were also taller. There have been quite a few similar observations in recent years pointing to a correlation between height and IQ.

Tanner also quotes findings from a massive study in Norway, in which height measurements were recorded in 1.8 million subjects over 15 years of age: there it was found that mortality in those 185–9 cm tall was half the rate of that in those 150–5 cm tall. A similar lower mortality among taller children less than 5 years old in Ghana has also been reported by Billewicz and McGresor (1982).

Reviewing all the available evidence on height measurements and attempting an answer to the question, 'Is being taller better?', Tanner (1982) concludes: 'It does look, therefore, as though height indeed can be a proxy for health and for the attainment of biological potential. This is true, of course, only when comparing groups, not in comparing isolated individuals, the variation between whom is due overwhelmingly to genetic causes. But between social classes, urban and rural dwellers, educated and uneducated, height is a useful proxy for 'aisance de vie'.

Height measurements will not only be helpful in monitoring *secular* trends in nutrition and economic status: they will also be useful in making interregional and interclass comparisons of nutritional status. Height measurements could help to bring out glaring socioeconomic inequalities and the consequent disparities in nutritional status among classes within countries. Tanner refers to a report on Trinidad slaves in 1815 which showed that Trinidad foremen were on average an inch taller than the fieldhands. Bielicki *et al.* (1981) showed that the sons of Polish peasants raised in villages in families containing four children had an average height of about 172 cm, while sons of professional men with small families working in large cities averaged 176 cm. Goldstein (1971) reported a similar phenomenon in the UK on the basis of a national sample survey of heights of 7-year-olds in 1971.

The difference between the average heights of non-manual classes (class III) and labouring classes (classes IV and V) was also reported as being roughly 1 in. by Clements and Picket in 1957 (quoted by Tanner 1982); strangely enough, the data of the office of Population Censuses and Surveys of 1980 show that this difference still persists.

It is only with respect to Scandinavian countries—Sweden and Norway—that there is, today, convincing evidence of an absence of significant differences with respect to height between occupational classes. The attainment of such a situation of equity and distributive justice wherein there are no striking differences with respect to nutritional status between different occupational and income groups must be considered the hallmark of truly successful socioeconomic development; in such a situation, even the groups with the lowest income levels are apparently able to achieve an optimal level of nutrition. Unfortunately, most developing countries still appear to be far away from this goal. Not only is the general level of health and nutrition in their populations low, but there is also apparently far greater evidence of disparities among populations. Evidence of differences in height between different occupation groups in India are unfortunately quite striking, as the observations that follow will show.

Indian studies   Three Indian studies covering fairly large numbers of subjects indicate the value of height as a measure of nutritional status. In these studies, height measurements (along with weight measurements) have been carried out in subjects of different socioeconomic groups. It was presumed that the dietary intake would largely parallel the socioeconomic status; and in any case, as was pointed out earlier, there is no way in which socioeconomic or occupational status can exert a direct metabolic effect on the body in order to influence height except through its effect on nutritional inputs. So it will be justifiable to view the observed relationship in these studies between height and economic status as in fact a relationship between height and nutritional status.

1   Shanti Ghosh and her colleagues have carried out an extensive longitudinal study on growth and development of children of different socioeconomic groups, from birth to nearly 15 years of age. Nearly 8,200 children were covered in the study. The communities investigated

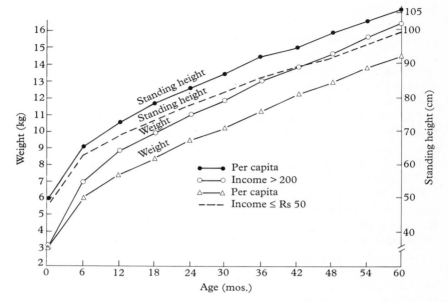

Fig. 2.1. Weight and standing heights of Indian girls, by per capita income and age

Source: Shanti Ghosh *et al.*, unpublished research

ranged from the poorest (less than Rs 50 per head per month—1969 level) to the fairly well-to-do upper middle class (more than Rs 200 per head per month—1969 level). The longitudinal data from children belonging to these two income groups (Figure 2.1) show a clear relationship between socioeconomic status and heights and weights of children.

2 Satyanarayana and colleagues (1980) have assembled data from longitudinal observations on the heights and weights of children of different socioeconomic groups in rural Hyderabad observed over a 15-year period from 5 to 20 years of age. The children belonging to their Group I, with heights between M and $M - 2SD$ of Boston standard, mostly came from families of affluent landlords owning more than 5 acres of fertile land; those of their Group III were from the poorest rural households owning no land of their own, with adults being illiterate and eking out their living from seasonal agricultural wage-labour. In Table 2.4 some of their observations have been set out. The table also shows data on heights and weights of children of the most affluent Indian communities as observed and reported by Hanumantha Rao and Sastry (1977) on the basis of their cross-sectional studies. The striking differences between the different socioeconomic groups will again be obvious.

Table 2.4. Longitudinal studies of growth of Indian children of different socioeconomic groups

Group	Initial (aged 5)		Final (aged 20)	
	Ht (cm)	Wt (kg)	Ht (cm)	Wt (kg)
Mostly from families of well-to-do landlords [a] (owning about 5 acres of fertile land)	104.7	15.3	167.8	51.5
Mostly from families of agricultural labourers on seasonal/daily wages[a]	89.2	11.5	157.8	44.0
Highly affluent[b]	108.0	18.3	171.8	59.6

[a] Based on Satyanarayna (1986)
[b] Based on Hanumantha Rao and Sastry (1977)

3   The National Nutrition Monitoring Bureau (1980) has recently completed a study of the dietary, nutritional, and anthropometric status of 32,332 subjects (12,925 adults and the rest children) drawn from 15 major cities of India. The sample households were classified into five major socioeconomic categories. The high income group (HIG) and the slum labour (SL) represented the two extreme ends of the economic spectrum, with the other three groups lying in between. SL was the group subject to the greatest socioeconomic deprivation—poor, largely illiterate or semi-literate, living in highly overcrowded and unhygienic conditions, and having to depend mostly on unskilled manual labour to eke out a precarious livelihood. Their diets were decidedly lower in energy content, and their children showed a higher prevalence of signs of vitamin deficiencies. The heights and weights of children and adults faithfully reflected the socioeconomic gradient, with HIG at one end, SL at the other, and the remaining groups falling in between. For the sake of convenience, only part of the data from the two groups at the extreme ends (HIG and SL) have been set out in Tables 2.5 and 2.6.

The poverty trap   The outstanding finding in all the three Indian studies cited above is the striking relationship between income and occupational status on the one hand and physical stature on the other. It would appear that the more *lowly* (using the expression for the sake of convenience) the job that a community is engaged in, the greater the degree of stunting in its children and adults. The cart-pullers, scavengers, manual labourers (including those engaged in strenuous work), stone-cutters, porters having to carry heavy loads, and agricultural labourers are apparently the ones who are most stunted and have the lowest body weights; unfortunately, these are precisely the occupation groups (rather than the business executives and academicians) who are in greatest need of a strong and sturdy body for optimal productivity and output and for earning a reasonable wage from their occupation.

Table 2.5. Heights and weights of children in urban India, 1975–1979

	Height (cm)		Weight (kg)	
	HIG[a]	SL[b]	HIG[a]	SL[b]
At 5 years				
Boys	110.4	99.8	18.2	13.9
Girls	107.6	98.7	16.2	13.6
At 12 years				
Boys	144.2	132.6	30.8	25.1
Girls	140.4	133.7	29.9	26.8
At 16 years				
Boys	164.5	154.7	46.2	38.6
Girls	156.2	148.6	43.1	39.1

[a] High-income group   [b] Slum labour

Source: National Nutrition Monitoring Bureau (1980)

Table 2.6. Heights and weights of adults in India, 1975–1979

	Height (cm)		Weight (kg)	
	HIG[a] (1)	SL[b] (2)[c]	HIG[a] (3)	SL[b] (4)[c]
At 20–25 years				
Males	166.4	161.4 (161.0–164)	50.4	46.6 (47.2–49.8)
Females	154.6	150.1 (149.4–151.9)	46.8	41.7 (41.0–44.2)
At 40–45 years				
Males	166.8	161.2	66.3	48.1
Females	153.1	149.6	56.0	41.6

[a] High–income group   [b] Slum labour
[c] Figures in parentheses in columns (2) and (4) are measurements of corresponding rural groups

Source: National Nutrition Monitoring Bureau (1980)

As was pointed out earlier, my concern is not over small body size *per se*. Earlier in this chapter I pointed out the functional implications of stunting. Stunting in a community is but a proxy for current substandard function and for past malnutrition which must have involved a considerable cost to society.

A community in which a considerable part of the population is stunted is usually a community with high infant and child mortality, high levels of morbidity in children, a high rate of drop-outs from schools. This is also a community in which children have lost valuable time for learning skills, mothers have lost considerable part of their daily wages, and health services are so overburdened with curative work that preventive and promotive health programmes are relegated to the background.

2.6 SUMMARY AND CONCLUSIONS

The major propositions of this chapter can be briefly recapitulated.

1 There are two practical approaches to the measurement of undernutrition: (*a*) through a survey of diets of representative households (supported by surveys of diets of individual members of the family in a sub-sample of households), in order to derive information about the nutrient intake, especially calorie intake; and (*b*) through an anthropometric and clinical examination of children, especially the under-fives. These two procedures, combined with a broad survey of socioeconomic and environmental status of the community, will yield data which, when properly interpreted and evaluated, could provide valuable practical leads for combating undernutrition in the community.

2 The basic issue that arises in the interpretations of the data gathered through these above approaches is, what are the normal standards against which prevailing levels of calorie intake or observed growth performance should be compared in order to determine adequacy or otherwise? The three hypotheses—of Sukhatme, Seckler, and Payne—that have been advanced in this connection have been critically examined. Sukhatme has argued that human subjects can permanently adapt themselves to a low calorie intake level representing the lowest limit of their intra-individual variations and that, therefore, $M - 2SD$ (recommended mean energy requirement level M minus two standard deviations) rather than M would be the appropriate yardstick for an assessment of calorie intake. Sukhatme's hypothesis is unacceptable because there is no convincing evidence that populations engaged in their expected levels of occupational activity and obliged to subsist on only about 70 per cent of their recommended mean energy intake can permanently adapt themselves to such a low calorie intake through metabolic adjustment and increased efficiency of energy utilization with-

out suffering a loss of body weight or consequent impairment of function. With a calorie intake that is around 70 per cent of the currently recommended levels, it will be difficult for children to meet their protein requirements with cereal-based diets: a drastic qualitative upgrading of current cereal-based diets would be necessary. This implies a reversal to the discredited view that the answer to the problem of protein–calorie malnutrition in developing countries lies in increasing use of expensive protein concentrates, a view that has been convincingly rejected on the basis of extensive studies.

3   Seckler's hypothesis that moderate degrees of growth retardation are a welcome attribute of poor people consistent with their good health and an acceptable form of adaptation is untenable because of the evidence that even moderate degrees of growth retardation have been shown to be associated with an impairment of physical and mental function.

4   Payne's hypothesis that, even if children of developing countries have been shown to have the same genetic potential for growth as those of the more fortunate countries of Europe and the USA, their lower levels of growth should not be viewed as evidence of undernutrition but as an adjustment to their 'economy and ecology' is also untenable. Payne does not deny that such growth-retarded children suffer from impaired function; but he considers that, despite such impairment, the subjects can function as well as they need to in their economy and ecology, and therefore, he would not consider them undernourished. The acceptance of this postulate can lead to the perpetuation of the present substandard state of growth and development in populations of the poor countries and is therefore wholly unacceptable.

5   In all the above three hypotheses the word 'adaptation' has been loosely employed to signify an acceptable state of normalcy instead of being viewed as a strategic retreat from normalcy which involves compromise with respect to both physical and mental function.

6   The view propounded by Payne that only those children whose state of nutrition has deteriorated to the point where they face the risk of imminent death should be considered undernourished obviously cannot be accepted. This is almost like saying that a person is 'unhealthy' only when he is on the point of death. The so-called moderately malnourished children of today could gravitate into severe malnutrition in a few weeks or months. It is far easier and far less expensive to prevent them from sliding to such a severe stage of undernutrition than to rehabilitate them after they have reached that stage. Moreover, the so-called moderate degree of growth retardation is also associated with impaired function. Populations subjected to such retardation represent a substandard human resource.

7   The view sometimes propagated that, irrespective of deficit in height-for-age or weight-for-age, children with weights appropriate to

their heights (normal weight-for-height ratio) could be considered adapted is also untenable. Stunting, irrespective of body weight, has been shown to be associated with impaired function. Stunted children with normal weight-for-height ratio also show evidence of impaired physical and mental function.

8 A level of dietary intake and nutrition which can permit only substandard growth must inevitably lead to an erosion of the quality of human resources of developing countries or a perpetuation of such erosion where it already exists. It must, therefore, be the policy of developing countries to achieve for their children a level of growth and development which represents the fullest expression of their genetic potential.

3

Assessing Undernutrition: The Need for a Reconceptualization

P. Payne

3.1 INTRODUCTION

Some social scientists seem recently to have discovered to their dismay that nutrition is still an area of active research and enquiry, characterized as much by disagreements about the interpretation of measurements and the validity of theories as by consensus. I can well appreciate the frustration. The answers to such apparently simple questions as how to assess the nutritional adequacy of a person's diet, or how to measure a person's state of nutritional health, seem to command a reasonable measure of agreement from nutritionists only when couched in terms that are either so general as to be of doubtful value, or refer to such closely controlled circumstances as to have little relevance to real-life situations. It must be all the more puzzling because the subject of nutrition is so manifestly successful in some respects. For example, we know how to keep astronauts in good nutritional health for almost indefinite periods of time, and the formulation of least-cost diets for animal production has reached an almost embarrassing degree of efficiency.

However, the history of the subject shows that throughout the past century, progress has been marked by a sequence of controversies and more or less abrupt changes of viewpoint. It is significant that some of the fiercer disputes between nutritionists centre around issues that have very direct implications for human welfare and come to involve members of other professions.

For example, in the 1920s and 1930s there were major controversies between the followers of Chittenden (1905) and Lusk (1906) about how to determine protein requirements. These remained unresolved, but resurfaced in the 1960s as the 'Great Protein Fiasco'. Quite suddenly, or so it must have seemed to those outside the subject, it emerged that there was no consensus among the 'experts' about the scientific validity of the amounts of protein currently recommended as necessary for health. When the implications of drastically reducing these became clear to economists, food planners, relief agencies, and the like, it seemed that policies based on the idea that low protein intakes were the cause of malnutrition of the poor had suddenly to be abandoned in favour of the supposition that low energy intakes were the critical factor. This ought really to be understood as a change of consensus rather than as a sudden new discovery of research scientists. Research had been continuing all the time, and opposition to the established consensus had built up over the years to a point where disagreement between the 'experts' could not be contained. The lesson is that social scientists should not expect natural scientists to display any narrower diversity of views than they do themselves: the best they can hope for is an invitation to join the argument. Consensus, on the other hand, should be viewed as much with caution as with satisfaction.

There is another aspect of the exchange of ideas between disciplines which is important in relation to the current disputes about measuring undernutrition. This is the confusion between survival thresholds and acceptable minimum standards. Osmani (1987) comments on the long held interest of economists in nutritionally based poverty indices. He cites Rowntree (1901) as basing his dietary standards for the poor of the working class in terms of satisfying a minimum standard of nutrition. In fact, these diets were described in terms of specific food items and the weekly expenditures needed to secure them. Although Rowntree was advised by nutritionists, notably Attwater, his objective was not to define a minimum standard, but to describe the extent of poverty in the city of York in such a way as to shock and disturb the conscience of the public about how many people were living at a level where, regardless of nutritional adequacy, they certainly could not meet any reasonable standard of social decency.

Apart from the problem that nutritionally adequate diets may be either uneatable or socially unacceptable, survival thresholds sometimes get misused by subsequently being redefined as minimum acceptable standards. In 1933 the British Medical Association (BMA) was asked by the government to advise on a minimum family food expenditure for the purpose of defining levels of unemployment benefit. The BMA appointed a committee of experts, who proceeded by calculating the energy and nutrient contents of Rowntree's poverty-line diets and then estimating the minimum cost at which these nutrients could be purchased. The results were types and combinations of foods that were not only socially unacceptable, but literally unusable with the recipes and cooking facilities available to poor people at that time. In effect, using the 'scientific' principles of nutrition helped the government of the day to peg welfare benefits at on arbitrary level without taking any regard for what was a minimally 'decent' standard, or even what foods it was possible for the poor to use (Woolf 1946).

Besides the problem of standards versus minima, this example also illustrates a more general problem. Social scientists, concerned with measuring and characterizing poverty, face problems that are at the same time conceptually complex, greatly varied according to context, and, above all, subject to problems of valuation. It must be tempting to think that a nutritional approach would not only overcome some of the technical difficulties of measurement but also bypass those of social valuation. Undernutrition could then be presented as an objective 'scientific' measure of poverty—one which, moreover, pointed to some fairly well focused types of intervention.

I believe that this is almost always likely to lead to frustration. Thus, the discovery that man *could* live on bread alone and satisfy his biological needs for protein was for many people embarrassing. The current arguments about adaptation have not only revealed the gaps in our knowledge about nutritional requirements, but have given rise to the suggestion that the poor could be smaller, could be less physically active both at work and at leisure, and could even have lower rates of metabolism, without showing any clear signs of loss of biological function. This is regarded as outrageous and unacceptable by many of those who hoped that nutrition would provide a scientific basis for measuring poverty. Up to now there seem to have been three kinds of responses: (1) to argue that the scientific measurements must be wrong—that experiments have been misconceived, that the statistical interpretation of data has been in error, or simply that biological function is an inadequate basis for assessing the acceptable limits of adaptation; (2) to insist that nutrient requirements must only be based on levels that are sufficiently high to ensure something called 'optimum' health and performance; (3) to maintain that in any case minimum survival levels must never be specifically identified because of the risk, referred to above, that they may subsequently be misused.

It would be more than optimistic to imagine that these differences can easily be resolved. Probably the best that can be hoped for is the clarification of some of the issues. In order to try to contribute to this, it may help to begin by describing the controversy as one between sharply polarized groups. Each group has in practice a somewhat heterogeneous membership, but the primary division is between those on the one hand whose concern it is to distinguish classes of people for whom levels of food availability and environmental health are so poor that either constraints are imposed on their opportunities for self-sustaining improvement or they are exposed to a life-threatening risk, and those on the other hand whose interest is in defining levels of food consumption that would constitute a minimum standard of welfare. That second group is, however, also divided. There are some who think that the standard should be based on the best estimates we have of what nutrients are needed to support an optimal state of health: this standard is presumed to be universally applicable across all population groups. There are others—the adaptationists—who believe that dietary requirements should take account of people's ability to change either their behaviour or their metabolism in response to changes in food supply—always provided there is no evidence of detriment to them in so doing.

Not surprisingly, these approaches result in very different estimates of the numbers of people experiencing undernutrition. Thus, the Food and Agriculture Organization in its Fourth (1977) and Fifth (1985) *World Food Surveys* puts the proportion of Third World populations living below a *minimum survival level* of energy consumption at about 15 per cent, whereas the World Bank (1986) assesses the numbers living on diets with less than *optimum energy* content at between 14 and 51 per cent. Sukhatme (1977a) (the most committed adaptationist) estimates that in India the numbers of people whose energy intakes are below the *lower limit of adaptation* comprise 20 per cent of the population, whereas Dandekar and Rath (1971) estimated about twice that proportion to be unable to purchase a *minimum adequate diet*.

Notwithstanding the different conceptual bases of these calculations, the producers of the low estimates accuse the advocates of optimum levels of inflating the magnitude of the food problem, and in so doing of failing to identify a critical sub-section of the population: those below the minimum, whose condition is not only bad but is different in character from the rest of the poor. It is argued that such people are at high risk of becoming ill, having exhausted all of their capabilities for adaptive adjustment, and may therefore need different kinds of policies or interventions. For their part, the advocates of the higher estimates accuse the others of 'talking down' the size of the nutrition problem by, in effect, setting low standards of diet and health for poor people.

If one strips these arguments of their emotional content, there seems no obvious reason why they should be mutually exclusive. Indeed, in terms of policy guidance they ought to be complementary, providing elements of diagnosis as well as prescription. In regard to advocacy, also, one can sympathize with both, although obviously for different reasons. However, the special needs of advocacy in particular circumstances are rarely discussed except in highly emotional terms.

By far the greatest heat has been generated by the question of 'adaptability', i.e. of whether, and by how much, people can change their state of nutrition so as to adjust to low food intakes without threat to life or livelihood. As we shall see, some aspects of adaptation are gradually beginning to be accepted, and the implications of this can be discerned in the more recent pronouncements of expert committees. One particular issue remains a source of inflammatory exchanges. It centres primarily on the ideas of Sukhatme and Margen that there can be changes in metabolic efficiency of energy use which reduce requirements without any measureable loss of function or body weight. This is by no means as simple an issue to resolve as it might seem. From the biologist's point of view, the hypothesis poses quite difficult problems in the design and interpretation of research. Fascinating though this is from a scientific point of view, it is probably a pity that it has become so distractingly contentious, because other aspects of adaptation—changes in body weight or composition and of physical activity, for example—are almost certainly of far greater magnitude and importance to the question of dietary standards and the measurement and characterization of undernutrition.

In fact, the inclusion of these aspects of adaptation has extended the arguments beyond the area of the efficiency of nutrient and energy conversion in the body. We are now faced with the need to reassess the significance of differences in adult body size between populations and of the relative rates of growth of children in poor as compared with affluent populations. Thus, there is a school of thought, exemplified by Seckler (1982), which is unconvinced by evidence that smallness is associated with any important loss of functional capacity. Down to a certain point at least, Seckler says, people might be said to be 'small but healthy'. Perhaps not surprisingly, this arouses even more passionate responses from some paediatricians than the possibility that the poor might adapt to reduced energy consumption.

One positive aspect of these disputes is that they have given new impetus to questions about the nature of the consequences to health of different modes of living and production. This is interesting, partly because it forces us to ask more precise questions about the definition of undernutrition, but also because many of the ideas are remarkably convergent with those that are taking place concerning diet and health in richer societies.

It is more than just ironic that, in countries where access to food is virtually unrestricted, upwards of 25 per cent of the population at any one time is desperately trying to lose weight; that health professions are urging the virtues of regular experience of hunger as opposed to indulgence, of bodily thinness, and of high-fibre diets, and are beginning to qualify, or even reverse, the advice given to the last generation of parents about the overriding needs of their children for meat and dairy products. By far the most significant feature of these changing ideas regarding the nutrition problems of both the poor and the affluent is that the concept of good nutrition as the maintenance of optimum health, defined in terms of an ideal body weight, or of desirable levels of energy expenditure, is gradually having to be abandoned. Part of the general uncertainty within the subject arises from the fact that this means that we have also to abandon the definition of undernutrition simply as any state that is below that optimum. I shall argue the case for this abandonment in Section 3.2 by showing the limitations of the current approaches to measuring undernutrition. In Section 3.3 the alternative view will be offered that measurement should be concerned more with identifying those people who have failed to avoid life-threatening risk even after making all possible adjustments to nutritional stress. This will be done, first, by reviewing the existing knowledge on the scope for adjustment and adaptation, and then by suggesting the criteria for identifying life-threatening risk ensuing from the failure of adjustments (Section 3.4). A brief summary and conclusions are offered in Section 3.5.

3.2 CURRENT APPROACHES TO MEASURING UNDERNUTRITION

For the remainder of this chapter the word 'undernutrition' will be used to describe the effects of low intakes of dietary energy as distinct from the broader term 'malnutrition', which is intended to cover the effects of deficiencies of any or all nutrients besides energy.[1]

In principle, there are two alternatives. Either we can try to measure *nutritional status*, i.e. the outcome of previous nutrition, directly in terms of the presence or absence of deficiency signs, the failure of growth, or some important aspect of functional capacity; or we can try to assess whether or not a person's intake of food is sufficient to ensure that those deficiency symptoms are unlikely to arise. Of course, the two methods are interdependent. If we choose to look at intakes, we need to compare them with some estimate of requirements, and these will have to be derived from past experience—research on the relationship between level of intake and the symptoms that we have agreed to accept as evidence of deficiency. It is useful to bear this in mind, together with the further implication that, if we choose to rely only on intake assessment, then we can only draw certain kinds of conclusions. If we believe that our meas-

---

[1] The critically minded might justifiably ask, 'If there is so much uncertainty about the required levels of energy, and if this is also true of the various other nutrients, how can we ever establish with certainty that low energy intakes are the most likely dietary factor which is limiting health in any given situation?' Quite so, and the honest answer is that we should be cautious about the kind of generalization that a few years ago had so many people convinced that more protein in the diet was the universal answer to child malnutrition. Vitamin A and iodine deficiencies are still considerable public health problems in many developing countries. In the Asian countries, the high prevalence of such problems and large size of the populations at risk combine to produce an estimated half million cases per year of children with active corneal lesions and 5 million non-corneal xeropthalmias. About 800 million people are at risk of iodine deficiency diseases which include endemic cretinism as well as goitre. Although it is possible to show approximate geographical distributions of populations 'at risk', there is a shortage both of national representative studies and of within-country distributions. Methodologies for measurement of status are technically demanding and expensive. However, the magnitude and persistence of these problems might justify a fairly intensive effort, at least in some carefully selected countries. Such an exercise would impose almost impossible demands for data, and it is quite unrealistic to suppose that an analysis of food consumption data is ever likely to reveal causally explicit relationships.

urement represents the long-term habitual intake of a person, then we may be able to make a statement such as 'There is a probability of X that this person will show symptoms of deficiency.' In practice, we cannot as a rule be sure that the measurement reflects the long-term past experience of the person (because the period of measurement is always finite; indeed, in practice it usually has to be quite short). We may, however, have reason to believe that it represents the likely future level of consumption, in which case we could make a conditional predictive statement. Thus, in practice, the bold assertion, 'Tell me what a man eats and I will tell you what he is', becomes a rather cautions, 'Tell me what he ate last week, and I might hazard a guess about what he will be like in a month's time.'

I shall now explain how difficult it is to measure undernutrition through either the 'intake approach' or the 'nutritional status' approach, if undernutrition is to be understood as the deviation from an optimum level of health. This will lead to the contention that the only practical thing to do is identify those individuals whose state of nutrition is so bad as to expose them to a life-threatening risk.

3.2.1 Assessing the adequacy of dietary energy supply

Measuring intakes It often comes as a surprise to non-nutritionists to discover that direct measurement of food intakes is in fact the most difficult, the most expensive, and probably the least satisfactory way of identifying malnourished people. Besides the methodological problems mentioned above, there is the question of observer interference. Given sufficient resources, intakes can be measured with precision, but only at the expense of invasiveness as well as money and time. Thus, it is possible to know accurately how much food a person or a family has eaten over a period, but only with so much observer interference as to cast doubt on the result as an estimate of normal habitual intake. This kind of observer error could produce either over or underestimations, and is likely to be systematic within any particular cultural context. Individual intakes are rarely measured, and are prone to greater technical problems and errors at younger ages of subjects. Because of all these problems, it is perhaps not too surprising that very few countries have comprehensive regular surveys of food consumption, even at the household level. Measurements of the intakes of individuals are very rare indeed.

Because of this, most of the head-counting exercises that purport to estimate the numbers of undernourished people at country or global region level (FAO 1977, 1985; Reutlinger and Alderman 1980) do so on the basis of distributions of 'consumption' that are synthesized from a combination of food balance sheets and household food expenditure data. Food balance sheets, which are used as a substitute for direct information about the average energy intake, are in fact estimates of total food moving into supply over a year, and they have systematic errors which lead to underestimation of consumption for low-income countries and overestimation for higher-income populations (Poleman 1981a; Dowler and Seo 1985). Household food expenditure is used to derive information about the distribution between households. However, as Casley and Lury (1981) have pointed out, there seems to be something fundamentally unsatisfactory about household expenditure as a measure of energy intake: most of the data sources, when stratified by income, generate class means which span a range from intakes that are, from a physiological point of view, impossibly low to those that are impossibly high. Finally, the level of aggregation of these data sources necessitates expression in terms of consumption units, thus making the implicit assumption that intakes are allocated between age/sex groups in proportion to requirements.

When to all of this is added the need to choose an algebraic function that is supposed to represent the shape of the lower tail of the distribution of intakes (obviously the most important part for estimation of undernutrition), the whole exercise is perhaps most kindly described as 'heroic'. Although sensitivity analyses are applied, e.g. by Reutlinger and Alderman, to the values assumed for *requirements*, there is no independent assessment of the probable range of error associated with the lower end of the *intake* distribution. One suspects that if this were done the uncertainties about requirements would pale into insignificance!

Defining energy requirements The difficulties of measurement, which are common to all dietary assessment, are further complicated by the particular problems of defining energy requirements.

1 Unlike many of the other essential nutrients, there are no very clear and unequivocal signs or symptoms which can be used to establish the threshold between adequacy and inadequacy of energy intake. *Any* change of intake results in compensatory adjustments in activity, body size/growth, body composition, or metabolism, either singly or all together. Moreover, the range of these adjustments is very wide. In addition, the two examples given above suggest that chronicity is always likely to be a crucial factor: not only do requirements change continuously as a result of infectious episodes and seasonal demands for physical work, but the pattern of adjustments will also shift in response to those factors.

2 In the absence of clear and specific deficiency symptoms, energy requirements have until very recently been based on the average observed intakes of groups of people living in relatively affluent circumstances and presumed to be healthy.

3   In practice, therefore, the intakes of groups of poorer people, or of the populations of poorer countries, have in effect been assessed by comparing them with those of richer people or richer countries. In this way, the 'standards' of size and growth upon which these requirements are implicitly based have also been those of affluent populations. This has always posed problems for committees advising on requirements— first, because people in developing countries are generally smaller at all ages than those of rich ones; second, because the body weights of adults in affluent circumstances are in many cases considered too high to be consistent with optimum health. Since the first FAO (1950) committee report on calorie requirements, successive reports have suggested increasingly elaborate procedures for scaling the recommended levels to take account of age, sex, and body size differences between countries, although the basic figures for requirements per unit of body weight have remained substantially unchanged.

4   At least until 1985, all these committees have seen their function primarily as making recommendations about the amounts of food energy supply at the national level that would be consistent with a nutritionally healthy population. This has led to a general tendency to err on the side of safety, and to avoid any accusations of planning for suboptimal standards. (The one exception to this has been body size, because it has been considered difficult and in any case possibly undesirable to advocate that the body weights of poorer populations should be rapidly increased to match those of affluent countries.)

5   Until 1985 all the UN reports have been emphatic that these recommended levels should not be applied to individuals, but only to groups. Furthermore, they were not intended to be used as a yardstick for the detection of undernutrition, but only as a basis for planning adequate supplies.[2]

In effect, many of the disputes about measuring the extent of undernutrition have been about how to apply standards which were never intended for that purpose! Although we should not expect the debate to be ended by some once-and-for-all pronouncement about whether autocorrelation analysis shows what Sukhatme says it does, or that metabolic adaptation to low energy intakes does or does not exist, it might help to remove some of the heat from the exchanges if we can agree that there

---

[2] 'The energy requirement of persons is the energy intake that is considered adequate to meet the energy needs of the average healthy person in a specified category.'
'Their use is in the planning of food supplies for groups, institutions or countries, and for this purpose, the mean values for the age/sex groups may be aggregated to provide a weighted mean applicable to a whole population'; 'The recommendations cannot be used for examining the nutritional status of a population. Comparisons [of intakes with requirements] cannot in themselves justify statements that undernutrition, malnutrition or overnutrition is present in a community or group, as such conclusions must always be supported by clinical or bio-chemical evidence' (FAO/WHO 1973).

could be more than one legitimate way in which requirements can be used. One of the more interesting features of the latest FAO/WHO/UNU (1985) report on energy and protein requirements is its open-mindedness about exactly that. For the first time, a clear distinction is made between *prescriptive* purposes, i.e. making recommendations about what consumption levels ought to be in a population with reasonable levels of health and social welfare, and *diagnostic* applications, i.e. assessing existing situations.[3]

In addition, the basis of the recommendations is radically different: the new figures are estimates of expenditure rather than the observed average intakes of individuals presumed to be healthy. This involves separate estimates of three factors: maintenance, growth, and physical activity components.

Table 3.1. The factorial components of energy requirements

Age	Weight (kg)	Maintenence energy 1.5 × BMR (kcal/day)	Energy for growth (kcal/day)	Activity energy (kcal/day)	Observed intake (kcal/day)
< 3 months	4.6	370	128	57	550
9–12 months	10	800	60	150	1010
10 years	31	1750	30	640	2420
Adult	65	2600	0	400	3000

Source: FAO/WHO (1973)

Payne and Waterlow (1971) reviewed evidence from both human and animal balance studies which suggest that maintenance energy expenditure is approximately 1.5 times the basal metabolism rate (BMR), and hence can be predicted from measured or calculated rates of BMR.

The FAO/WHO (1973) committee outlined a factorial method for predicting total daily expenditure, but did not actually use this as a basis for their recommendations. The figures in Table 3.1, which are taken from that report, illustrate the nature of the calculation. Perhaps the most striking aspect of this is the very small contribution of the growth component to total requirements. Starting at 25 per cent of the daily intake, this has fallen to 6 per cent by the end of the first year, and is little more than 1 per cent of total needs by the age of 10.

---

[3] 'In prescriptive applications the estimates are used to suggest what intakes should be. . . it has frequently been pointed out in this report that for some purposes different estimates of energy requirement might be used. In diagnostic applications the estimates are used to judge the probable adequacy or inadequacy of observed intakes, e.g. assessing the existing situation given existing body sizes and activity patterns versus predicting the energy needs that would be associated with a new situation' (FAO/WHO/UNU 1985).

The problem with this method of estimating requirements is the need to specify activity expenditure rates. The figures in Table 3.1 were derived by difference, i.e. by subtracting the maintenance and growth components from the observed intakes. The FAO/WHO/UNU (1985) report admits that there is still no basis for specifying desirable activity expenditure rates for children under 10 years of age, and opts for the retention of observed intakes of 'healthy' populations as a basis for recommendations. For adults and children over 10 years of age, a method for estimating physical activity expenditures is proposed, based on the energy cost of various occupational and recreational activities, and the lengths of time spent in these activities in different occupational groups. These Physical Activity Index (PAI) figures are expressed in terms of multiples of BMR. Since BMR can be calculated from body size, the entire daily expenditure can be predicted.

The lowest possible level of physical activity, allowing for standing, dressing, washing, eating, etc., during the day and assuming a basal level overnight, gives what the report describes as a 'survival' level of $1.27 \times BMR$. The three conventional categories of 'light', 'moderate', and 'heavy' occupational work levels are then identified as 1.54, 1.78, and $2.14 \times BMR$ BMR, respectively.

This is a neat and simple procedure, but it is open to criticism for a number of reasons. In particular, the accuracy depends entirely upon the estimation of BMR, and, as will be shown later, the prediction equation proposed in the report for doing this overestimates the BMRs of smaller subjects by a significant amount.

Table 3.2 illustrates the results of these and earlier approaches. All the figures relate to a 55 kg male subject, chosen because it corresponds to the standard 'consumer unit' for India used as the basis for calculation of poverty-line consumption levels by Sukhatme and Dandekar, and for the 'ultra poverty' levels of food consumption by Lipton (1983). The first four values show the energy needs of a 'moderately active' man of this body weight as recommended by various committees over the past 30 years. The figure of 2700 proposed by FAO/WHO/UNU (1985) report is nicely in line with its predecessors, doubtless reflecting the careful choice of expenditure rates and times employed in constructing the PAI figure. However, if the BMR is calculated using a regression equation known to give good predictions of values for Indian subjects, this reduces the requirement by 12 per cent. Even this estimate includes a component to cover desirable social and recreational activities (which the report refers to as 'discretionary'). If we were to adopt Rowntree's (1901) approach to defining absolute poverty as a condition in which life is sustainable *without decency*, then this discretionary component, which amounts to between 200 and 300 kcal per day, would be omitted. This brings the figure very close to the 2100 kcal suggested by Lipton as the threshold for ultra-poverty.

Table 3.2. Energy requirements of a male adult with a nominal body weight
of 55 kg (BMI 22.4)

Basis of calculation	kcal/day
(1) FAO (1957) Moderate activity	2830
(2) FAO/WHO (1973) Moderate activity	2530
(3) FAO/WHO/UNU (1985) Moderate activity	2710
(4) ICMR (1981) Moderate activity	2700
(5) FAO/WHO/UNU (1985) Corrected for over estimation of BMR [a]	2450
(6) As above, without 'discretionary' activity [b]	2200
(7) As above, with body weight adjusted to 44 kg (BMI 18)	1960
(8) 80% of ICMR: Lipton (1983) 'ultra–poor'	2100
(9) FAO (1985) 'survival' requirement $(1.2 \times BMR)$[c]	1550
(10) As above, with BMR adjusted downwards by 15% (1.2 BMR)	1470

[a] BMR calculated using the equation of Quenouille *et al.* (1951).

[b] Discretionary activities are described in FAO/WHO/UNU (1985) as those
connected with social and recreational pursuits: they amount to about 250 kcal
per day for a man of 55 kg.

[c] Allows for minimal activities such as washing, dressing, standing, etc. No
discretionary or occupational activities.

So far it has been assumed that the body weight remains at 55 kg. The
actual body sizes of poor Indian men are lower than this. If a downward
adjustment to 44 kg is made (as will be seen later, this is about the lowest
body weight consistent with survival for a person of average Indian
height), the calorie requirement falls still further. All of these figures still
allow for occupational expenditure at the 'moderate' level, and do not
include any metabolic component of adjustment. Rows (8) and (9) in
the table pertain to unemployed persons surviving perhaps on food relief
programmes, and denied the level of social and recreational activities
consistent with a 'decent' life-style.

Finally, row (10) of the table includes a downward adjustment of 15
per cent of the basal metabolic rate component of maintenance to allow
for the possibility of metabolic adjustment. This represents the best
estimate of the magnitude of 'metabolic' adaptation that can be made
on the basis of current experimental evidence, the justification for which
will be discussed in the next section. It is interesting, however, that it
happens by chance to correspond with $1 \times$ standard BMR (i.e., uncor-
rected for any metabolic adaptation), which is the lower of the two cut-
off points adopted by the FAO for its World Food Surveys.

These figures perhaps offer a more balanced perspective from which
to view the controversy over adaptation. Lipton (1983), in a very detailed review of the various causes of overestimation of energy require-

ments, while agreeing with Sukhatme's position on intra-individual variation, concludes that the major factor has been a tendency of committees to include safety factors, i.e. always to err on the side of over rather than underestimation of the mean value—understandable perhaps in view of the largely prescriptive intention behind most of the estimates.

Analysis of individual situations Unlike its predecessors, the 1985 report (FAO/WHO/UNU 1985) suggests that the new approach to defining energy requirements can be used for diagnosis, i.e. for analysing existing situations at the individual level, as well as for groups. Perhaps the greatest problem here is how to allow for the activity component of the requirement. Table 3.3 shows the results of some measurements on elderly men and women living in rural India. Calculation of the minimum amounts of energy needed for maintenance, and subtraction of these from the observed intakes, gives estimates of the amounts of energy that were available to these subjects for physical activity.

Given sufficient resources, it would of course have been possible to measure the actual levels of expenditure during work and leisure activities, and hence to compare the total energy expenditure of these people with their energy intakes. With sufficient care in measurements of metabolic rates, activity expenditures, and changes in body composition, we would have been able to discover whether or not their intakes matched their expenditures over the period of the measurement—in effect, a tedious and very costly reconfirmation of the first law of thermodynamics!

If it turns out that balance (i.e. intake – expenditure) is negative—or positive—this in itself tells us nothing, since there is no reason to expect that short-term equilibrium is either a normal or indeed a desirable state. By themselves, such measurements cannot tell us about either the existence or the nature of constraints to output or productivity. Would the individuals' work output increase if their food intake were raised? Or would they gain weight? If so, would they be healthier or less at risk of illness?

The 1985 FAO/WHO/UNU report offers no practical advice about how to answer these questions. After commenting that recommendations for energy needs depend at least as much on value judgements about what levels of activity, growth rates, and body sizes are deemed to be socially desirable as on biological needs, almost nothing is said on the subject of how to diagnose undernutrition.

3.2.2 Measurement of nutritional status

If assessment of intake is so problematic, why not just rely on the direct measurement of nutritional status? The usual process of developing a method for diagnosis of disease conditions is one by which accumulating experiences and knowledge of mechanisms results in either a single symptom or a set of symptoms coming to be recognized as characteristic of a specific causal agent—a disease organism, the presence of a particular toxic substance in the environment, or, in the case of nutrition, the lack of energy or of a specific chemical entity in the diet. Thus, the name attached to a disease condition comes over time to be more and more confidently identified not only with a distinct syndrome but with the cause, with appropriate treatment, and with efficacious strategies for prevention. This is of course true of some kinds of malnutrition. For example, the clinical signs and distinctly different functional consequences of deficiencies of vitamin A and of iodine are well identified.

Table 3.3. Energy intakes and minimum requirements of rural Indian men and women aged 60–90 years [a]

	Men	Women
Weight (kg)	46.8	41.4
BMI	17.7	18.7
Minimum requirements (kcal/day)[b]	1560	1250
Intake (kcal/day)	1840	1390
Energy available for activity (kcal/day)	280	140

[a] Data from McNeill (1986)
[b] Calculated as BMR × 1.27; BMRs from Adbritton (1954)

Logically, then, a discussion of techniques for measuring nutritional status should begin with the identification of some symptom or symptoms that exist in all individuals suffering from lack of energy, but not in those suffering from any other deficiency or disease condition. The basic technique of measurement would then consist of assessing the extent and severity of these symptoms in affected populations. As we have seen, however, in respect of energy there is no set of symptoms that is unique to that particular cause. What is usually meant by people who speak of the extent of undernutrition in populations is the existence of individuals who are either relatively small in size for their age, or whose energy intakes imply levels of physical activity that are lower than is considered desirable.

A good many different anthropometric indicators have been devised for defining different classes or grades of severity of growth retardation. These are far too numerous and well reviewed (WHO 1978) to deal with in any detail here. Generally they are based on estimates of the total mass of body tissues, assessed as weight, arm circumference, or skinfold thickness. These are often complemented by measures of linear size—most commonly height, but sometimes head or chest circumference.

Not surprisingly, as in the case of requirements, there have been problems with the definition of standards. If undernutrition is to be assessed in terms of deficits from some 'well nourished' state, can we define this as a fixed point, and, if so, how do we grade the importance of different deviations from it? As with standards for requirements, the solution has been to use the mean or median values of body dimensions of affluent populations as a reference point and to use the inter-individual variation of these as an indication of how much deviation from the mean could be assumed to be of genetic, or at least of non-nutritional, origin. The various anthropometric classifications of individuals—'normal', 'mildly', 'moderately', or 'severely' undernourished—have all been derived in this way. The different grades of severity are in effect levels of probability that individuals are undernourished rather than genetically small.

There are two more recent developments of ideas in this area. (1) There is now an accumulation of evidence of the probability of finding, in association with low body size, an actual loss of function relating to cognitive ability, work capacity, immune function, or the risk of disease or death. This has led to a growing tendency to regard the anthropometric classes as defining different levels of risk rather than as measures of actual debility or loss of function. In this way they have come to assume much of the same probabilistic and predictive qualities as does assessment of intake. (2) It has been suggested that the linear measurements, notably height, have a different significance from those of tissue mass. This is partly because height represents more of an 'integrated' record of all past experiences (people do not lose significant amounts of height when they are ill or deprived of food: they simply fail to gain more), and also for the practical reason that correcting weight-for-height substantially reduces the genetic variation between people in well nourished populations. This has the effect of sharpening the discriminatory power of anthropometry as a means of specifically identifying malnourished individuals.

Various methods have been proposed for 'factoring out' the influence of height. The oldest, and possibly still the best, was an index suggested by the astronomer Quetelet in 1871, and is simply weight divided by height squared. Since body density varies only over a very small range, we can think of this ratio as a good approximation to volume divided by height squared, and hence as having the dimensions of a 'length'. This turns out to conform quite well to subjective assessments of 'thinness', but also is a very good predictor of risk. Quetelet's index has rather inappropriately been renamed the 'Body Mass Index' (BMI) and is rapidly becoming accepted as the best parameter to use for comparing mortality risk of people of different weights and body build.

The method that is now most widely used for children is that popularized by Waterlow (1972). Actual body weights are expressed as a percentage of the median weight of a child of the same height and age in a standard healthy population. Obviously, correcting for height differences in this way is useful only if we are either prepared to regard shortness or 'stunting' as an index in its own right, possibly of some other kind of deprivation, or if we believe it to be of relatively little importance. This is still an unresolved issue. Although it is very likely that there are degrees of 'shortness' and 'tallness' that are associated with disadvantages, in terms of either morbidity or mortality experience, or indeed in social or economic competence, we do not as yet have any basis for defining these.

The practical effect of using height-corrected indices is a fairly drastic reduction in the numbers of children falling into the various categories of undernutrition: obviously, if we do not count as undernourished children who are simply small rather than thin, then the numbers will be lower. This has been the cause of as much dismay and argument as have the consequences of lowering dietary requirement levels. Once again, these disputes have been caused as much by differences of viewpoint about the purpose of measuring the extent of child undernutrition as by differences about scientific evidence. Some see the greater discriminatory power of the height-corrected indices as focusing attention more effectively on those whose condition is life-threatening, whereas others see the much smaller numbers as detracting from advocacy, and understating the need for better standards of nutrition for all.

One of the problems of this subject is the semantic confusion resulting from common usage through which the condition 'smallness' has come to be identified with the description 'undernourished'. It is almost universal practice to refer to anthropometry as a technique for measuring 'nutritional status'. However, time and the growth of knowledge, instead of increasing confidence in the specificity of this diagnosis, have actually reduced it. But the semantic problems sometimes make it quite difficult for those outside the immediate subject to interpret the results of research. For example, work at the ICDDR in Bangladesh has made a major contribution towards teasing out the complex association between growth and the incidence and duration of diarrhoea. The title of a recent paper by Black et al. (1984) illustrates the problem: 'Malnutrition as a Determining Factor in Diarrhoeal Duration but not in Incidence among Young Children in a Longitudinal Study in Rural Bangladesh'. This describes the content well. However, 'malnutrition' was in fact measured by anthropometry, so that the title could just as well have read 'Growth Retardation as a Determining Factor . . . '. But if we accept the evidence, much of which has been provided by the authors, that extended episodes of diarrhoea themselves predispose towards growth retardation, it seems that children assessed as small are subsequently found to suffer most from diarrhoea and hence perhaps tend to remain small. It is by now well known that growth can be affected by disease, as well as by the lack of other nutrients, through mechanisms that include direct metabolic effects influencing the control of growth, but also depression of appetite and the reduction of food absorption.[4]

Faced with this, it has become fairly common to describe the 'nutrition problem' as a multi-factorial one, with the implication that achieving significant improvements may require the removal of a number of possible constraints—increased food availability, better housing and water supplies, better basic health services, better standards of personal hygiene, better knowledge of child care and nutrition, and greater motivation. Thus, Osmani (1987) uses the two terms 'food' and 'non-food' causes of undernutrition, and suggests that we should consider undernutrition as arising from deficiencies in either of two entitlements: a food entitlement and a hygiene entitlement.

I have some sympathy with this, particularly in so far as it discourages the idea that malnutrition in young children is simply a particularly visible aspect of inadequate household food availability. However, it would be dangerous to over-generalize. There are some situations in which a causal analysis is essential: it does little to help health administrators in Kenya, for example, to tell them that differences in average height of children between districts are a measure of undernutrition (even if we qualify this by saying that it might be a 'non-food factor' type of undernutrition) when there is good reason to suspect that the cause is malaria.

In addition to the problem of the multiple causes of growth-faltering in children and the technical problems of measurement, the two approaches, i.e. dietary analysis and anthropometry, suffer from the same difficulty of interpretation. Both have been seen to require the specification of an ideal reference state, a level of consumption, or a body size consistent with optimum health. Quite apart from the illogicality of the notion of such a unique state, this position is under attack, as we have seen, from two directions. First, the realization that many of the diseases of affluence may be associated with diet has made it difficult to accept any existing population as a standard for good nutrition. Second, the idea that individuals may adapt to different levels of intake, or assume different body sizes without loss of function, means that we may have to

---

[4] Grantham-McGregor (1984), writing about this, says: 'Currently there is much confusion about the diagnosis and classification of malnutrition. Terms such as kwashiorkor, marasmus, 'moderate' and 'severe' malnutrition are used indiscriminately by different researchers. Some of these terms represent quite different clinical conditions which are probably associated with different social backgrounds . . . A further problem is that the diagnosis of malnutrition does not reflect aetiology, and malnutrition is generally caused by a combination of inadequate food intake and infections. It is not clear exactly how important the role of infection is in the aetiology of malnutrition.'

consider the possibility of differing patterns of adaptation between individuals.

The way forward seems to be to set aside for the time being the problem of how, if at all, it is possible to define a perfectly adequate state of nutrition, and to concentrate instead on identifying critical limits of intake and body size below which there is clear evidence of risk of loss of functional capacity measured in some objective terms, or indeed life-threatening risk. Adoption of this minimalist position does not imply that policies and interventions would be restricted to 'worst-case' situations. It is based on the view that there is a primary need to assert priorities between people: to design interventions to meet differing circumstances, and to reduce differential deprivation progressivly over time—a strategy, in fact, of 'putting the last first' (Chambers 1983).

In order to identify the 'worst-case' situations, we would of course need some criteria for determining the critical thresholds of risk. These are discussed in Section 3.4. The critical thresholds are determined by the range beyond which the human organism fails to adjust itself in its effort to minimize the risk to its survival. So first we need to know more about the biological principles behind the various adjustment mechanisms and the limits to their efficacy.

3.3 ADJUSTMENTS, ADAPTATIONS, AND FAILURES

First of all some definitions will be needed. This subject is already overloaded with terms, many of which clearly mean different things to different people. For example, the terms 'response', 'adjustment', and 'accommodation' have all been used to signify the actual changes that take place in the body as a consequence of changes in the environment. The word 'adaptation' has had a variety of adjectives attached to it—'successful', 'acceptable', 'metabolic', 'cost-free', and even 'pure' (Osmani 1987).

I have already used the words 'adjustment' and 'adaptation', and will try to explain the meanings I attach to them. This is not because it is necessary or even desirable to fix the definitions for all time—rather the reverse, in fact. The advice 'define your terms' is bad counsel to biologists. Where the observations to be described have no sharp limits, if definition makes the argument simpler it does so at the expense of truth. It is arguable that the numerous attempts to invest the idea of nutritional adaptation with too precise a meaning have actually led to a confusion of thought and argument. For the purpose of what follows, however, the word 'adjustment' will be used to describe *co-ordinated* changes which take place within a self-organizing system as a result of that system's response to alterations in the external environment. Thus, a change in available food may result in adjustments of the size of the whole body, of the relative sizes of organs or tissues such as the liver or fat deposits, or of their metabolic rates or temperatures. In addition, there may be adjustments in the levels of interaction between the system and its environment, such as the type and extent of exploratory activity, rates of physical work, and social interactions.

The notion of co-ordination between these different components of adjustment is important because it implies the existence of patterns of information flow between the various component parts of the system—in particular, of compensatory feed-back loops which operate so as to maintain certain important aspects of the internal environment within acceptable limits. I shall try to avoid over use of the word 'adaptation', and especially to refrain from using the various qualifications such as 'successful', 'pure', etc. In biological usage, 'adaptation' refers to the whole set of characters and strategies by which organisms attain a sufficient degree of 'fit' with their environments, and through which they maintain that fit. That is to say, adjustments are *ways of handling the world* and are characteristics of adaptation.

In the same way as the length of the giraffe's neck represents a strategic balance between the advantages of long reach and the difficulties of maintaining an adequate blood supply to the brain, we expect to find limits to the capacity to make adjustments together with some prioritization of the various components—for example, giving up body fat stores before using muscle, and giving up both before depleting the brain, in response to a reduced food supply. In other words, not only the patterns but also the limits to the extent of the adjustments that individuals can make will be just as much a result of natural selection as is the length of neck.

The process of natural selection, however, intrinsically depends upon the continued existence of individual variability; it operates by favouring those individuals who are more successful at handling dynamic changes in their environment and hence continue to survive and reproduce. This means that we should expect to find differences between individuals in respect of their capacity to make adjustments. Moreover, because the process of ontogeny is a continuing one, we must regard that range of capacities as a kind of storehouse of variability which enables a species to respond to adverse changes, or to capitalize on potentially advantageous alterations in its environment. It does so because there are always some individuals with a greater capacity to adjust to any one of a whole range of possible stresses. However, since the process of natural selection is essentially a 'sufficing' one rather than an 'optimizing' one, an individual needs only to be sufficiently better adapted to an altered environment than others of the same species in order to gain a comparative advantage in terms of reproducing its own particular version of the genotype.

The suggestion that we should regard capacity to adjust to dietary or other environmental stresses by changes of size or metabolism as no more and no less than adaptive characteristics often meets with the objection that successful reproduction of an individual's genes is not a sufficient criterion for defining those adjustments that we *ought* to accept as consistent with a healthy life. Health, it is said, should be more than 'mere survival', so that requirements should not be based on adjustments down to survival level. In terms of human values, that is indisputable. The problem then is, How do we establish what kinds and degrees of adjustments should be regarded as acceptable? Remembering the earlier discussion about the history of attempts to set requirement scales, it seems that there are only two possibilities:

1 Persist in the belief that there is an optimizing process which, freed from constraints, will produce a state of health. This led to the adoption of actual intakes and body sizes of well-to-do active populations having free access to food as the norm. Faced with evidence that real populations freed from constraints eat and idle themselves to death in droves, this has to be modified by proposing idealized standards such as the FAO reference man and woman, who have a specified body size and are 'healthy'.

2 Accept the nature of the biological processes that have made us what we are, as a point of departure, but add some additional criteria of our own. In practice, this means finding out about the relationships between such things as body size, composition, and energy expenditure and specified disabilities, losses of function, or risks of these. This is clearly not a self-limiting research agenda, as the recent concerns with long-run health effects of diet illustrate. The best we will ever be able to say is what the health implications of particular adjustments are *within the limits of current knowledge*. Whether or not they, or their social implications, are acceptable depends on what value judgements we want to make: appealing to 'nature' will not help us to do that.

There are two other fairly common attempts to avoid this choice. One is to say, at least in respect of children, that the achievement of 'genetic potential' is an important criterion. This is meaningless except as a variant of the first of the above possibilities; i.e., it expresses the implicit assumption that 'potential' means optimal. The other is to say that only 'cost-free' adjustments are acceptable. Taken to its logical conclusion, this again is the same as the first possibility above, since it implies either the existence of some optimum state of individuals against which the 'costs' of having made an adjustment could be assessed, or the fact that there is some particular kind of adjustment that can be regarded as intrinsically benign. Some of the confusion and disputes that currently surround the subject of metabolic adjustments arise from the common but quite unwarranted assumption that changes of metabolic rate, or of efficiency of energy conversion if such occur, would not carry any cost.

This idea that some kinds of adjustments could be assumed to be cost-free, or 'pure', seems to rest on the additional assumption that, if they can be shown to happen in subjects without change in body weight or composition, this would be sufficient evidence of benignity. However, as we have seen, constancy of body weight is not by itself a criterion of optimum health. There is no reason to assume that a lowered rate of metabolism is any more an intrinsically safe kind of adjustment than is a change of size or of total energy expenditure.

This might seem like a rejection of the adaptationist school. However, I am simply making the point that being an adaptationist by no means implies a denial of the importance of costs. Dawkins (1982) writes: 'That every evolutionary adaptation must cost *something*, costs being measured in lost opportunities to do other things, is as true as that gem of traditional economic wisdom "There is no such thing as a free lunch".' What we have to remember is that we are looking at a biological system in which the priorities and trade-offs between different elements of adaptive strategies have been shaped by the process of natural selection. Bearing in mind the sufficing character of those strategies, the systems of adaptive organization are likely to be, as Dawkins says, 'a patchwork of makeshifts' and a 'tangle of compromises'. We may well decide that, in order to assess nutritional status, we ought to be using a set of criteria that reflect different priorities and trade-offs, i.e. those that derive from social valuations. One of my objectives in this paper is simply to make the point that we are unlikely to succeed in doing so unless we start with some understanding of the nature of that tangle of compromises. What follows is an attempt to give an outline of what we know so far.

3.3.1 Patterns and ranges of adjustment

The range of adjustments to altered energy intake is defined by responses of the following components: (a) change of body size or growth rate; (b) change in the proportion of adipose tissue; (c) change in the composition of the lean tissue mass (i.e. changes in the relative weights of one or more organs); (d) change in the specific metabolic activity (the metabolic rate per unit mass of tissue) of one or more organs; and (e) change of the level of physical activity. It is response (d) that is often termed 'metabolic adaptation'.

All of these are known to occur in people subjected to experimental or other deliberately imposed changes in intake of energy, whether these are upwards or downwards of their habitual diets. What we would like to know of course is:

1   Over what range can such responses be made without a serious threat
    to life or irreversible damage to function resulting?

2   What reversible changes in functional capacity occur within this
    range?

3   When, as is usually the case, all of these combine in various propor-
    tions to constitute the total adjustment, what priority rules prevail
    between them?

Needless to say, only a rather incomplete answer can be given to these
questions.

Growth and body size   At least three factors probably contribute to the
range of sizes found between various groups of populations.

First, the adverse effects of diet and of infectious diseases during early
life exert a lasting influence on subsequent growth. A very young child
will respond in a relatively reversible fashion to infectious episodes or
short-term restrictions of diet, and will compensate for a period of
reduced growth in height, by a fast 'catch-up'. With increasing age,
however, this potential for fully reversible responses is progressively
reduced, and height growth becomes more and more irreversibly 'programmed' on to a lower path. This degree of plasticity, i.e. the capacity
of the mechanism of growth control to reset itself in response to environmental influences, is an adaptive characteristic. It is the way the
organism responds to information about the outside world, the levels of
disease, food supply, etc., that are current and are likely to be encountered in the future.

We do not know exactly at what age improving the diet or the health
environment ceases fully to reverse the effects of early deprivation on height
growth, but it does occur very early. Beaton and Ghassemi (1982) reviewed
the literature on the impact of supplementary feeding programmes on the
growth of children under 6 years old. They concluded that the impacts were
very much less than the theoretical increments implied by the amounts of
supplement consumed (making corrections for losses, leakages, displace-
ments, etc.). Martorell *et al* (1980) showed that dietary supplements contributing an average of 258 Kcal and 18.2 g of protein per day from birth
onwards reduced the height deficits at 3 years of Guatemalan children, but
still left them below the 5th centile (− 2.0 standard deviations below the
mean) of the NCHS reference growth standard.

Second, this process of interaction and the plasticity of response can
be carried over and reinforced over time-spans longer than one generation. Shorter women tend to have smaller, slower-growing children,
who in turn do likewise.

Third, there are genetic differences in stature between ethnic groups.
These can be demonstrated quite easily. Well-off Asian boys have aver-

age heights at 7 years of age corresponding to the 25th percentile of the NCHS reference growth standard, whereas well-off Africans, Latin Americans, and North Americans of the same age average close to the 50th centile, i.e. about 3.5 cm taller (Martorell 1985). In some populations the endogenous control mechanism responsible for controlling height can be studied directly. Adult male Pygmies; whose height averages 32 cm lower than Europeans, have correspondingly lower blood levels of insulin-like growth factor throughout childhood and adolescence (Merimee *et al.* 1987).

Although they may be completely or largely irreversible during the lifetime of the individual, all three of these factors do change over longer periods, and all contribute to the secular increases in adult height, and the trend towards earlier sexual maturity, that have occured in European and American populations during the past century and are now being seen in other industrializing populations. An additional factor contributing to secular trends is likely to be hybrid vigour—increases in growth rate and final size of offspring as compared with either parent, owing to intermarriage between members of previously more genetically isolated populations (Wolanski 1970).

In addition to these complex effects, height growth is affected by other environmental factors, for example seasonal changes. These have been studied in well-to-do as well as deprived populations. During the period of the 1920s and 1930s, the effect of seasonal factors on child growth was the subject of great interest. Reviews by Nylin (1929), Orr and Clark (1930), and Palmer (1933), all agree on the following:

1 Seasonal changes in growth rates occur in children at all ages and in many different countries. Palmer says, of her own study of 2500 children living in Hagerstown, USA, that the magnitude of these is 'such as quite completely to dominate any change in growth rates which may be expected to occur in successive calendar years'.

2 Growth in weight proceeds at maximal rates during the late summer and early autumn and declines during winter to a minimum during spring and early summer, with velocities of weight gain frequently falling to zero. The same pattern has been found in Australian children, not at the same time, but at the corresponding seasons for the southern hemisphere (Fitt 1924).

3 Palmer's study of school children showed that the effect was not due to cyclic patterns of infectious diseases.

4 Growth in height is also affected, but with a difference in phase such that maximum height increase comes at the time when weight gains are at their minimum—just as Brown *et al.* (1982) found in Bangladesh.

Dugdale and Eaton-Evans (1985) studied a sample of 1000 infants born in Brisbane, and compared the 'summer' and 'winter' weight gains during the first to third month of age. They found significantly slower growth during the winter months. Griffiths (personal communication, 1985) has recorded daily weights for two-year periods of a group of preschool and early school-age children of professional parents living in London. All show signs of a marked 'staircase' effect of the season of the year on the course of weight gain. In some individuals growth virtually ceased for three-month periods, resulting in the crossing of a number of percentiles of standard NCHS growth charts, an effect as great as that observed by Billewicz and McGregor (1982) for Gambian children.

This discussion is not intended to dispose of height altogether as an index of undernutrition, but rather to underline the problems of interpretation. Stature at a given age is determined by a whole complex of environmental and genetic factors. Diet and disease are only a part of this, and their effect is probably dominant only during the very first year or so of life. After this period, during which the more important adjustments to nutritional factors are made, attained height becomes increasingly a record of the past history of environmental effects rather than an index of current conditions. It is for these reasons that anthropometric indicators of undernutrition are now based mainly on height-independent measurements. The relatively irreversible nature of these adjustments accounts for the fact that, over the years, methods for estimating the food requirements of populations have increasingly been based on existing, rather than desirable, body sizes of adults and older children.

Of course, this does not dispose of the need to ask about the costs of adjustments, or the limits to the range that are possible without risk of failure. The main problem in answering those questions arises from the strong interactions between the effects of adjustments of height and adjustments of weight.

It is fairly obvious that there will be a problem if, for example, we are interested in the effects of undernutrition on cognitive development, or on disease resistance in children. An adverse environment in early life is likely to produce concurrent changes in both weight and height. The problems of measurement of cognitive functions are such that there is no way at the moment of determining whether length or any other measure of skeletal size is specifically associated with the level of competence. In later years, height measures and weight measures will be increasingly divergent in their significance. The height of a schoolchild may be more a reflection of the environmental insults encountered in the first months of life, and hence might be expected to correlate with the early development of cognitive function, while the weight-for-height, or thinness, might be expected to reflect the impacts of current hunger and tiredness on attention and on social interactions.

Table 3.4. Physical work capacity of adult males with various occupations

Group	Age (yrs)	Weight (kg)	BMI	VO$_2$ (max) (1/min)	VO$_2$ (max) ml/kg/min
Sedentary British	24	72	23.3	2.95	41
Italian shipyard workers					
Light category	36	75	24.6	2.63	35
Moderate category	38	78	25.9	2.96	38
Heavy category	37	76	25.4	2.81	37
USA Civil Service Labour	27	76	25.4	3.04	40
Physical education students and instructors					
S. Africa, untrained	21	74	23.8	3.18	43
S. Africa, trained	20	74	23.8	3.48	47
Sweden, trained	20–33	70	21.7	4.06	58
British military personnel					
Sedentary	32	80	25.3	2.64	33
Well trained	22	67	22.7	3.81	57
Physical education instructors	25	71	23.6	3.62	51
Elite weight-trained athletes	27	96	29.2	4.70	49
New Guinea subsistence farmers					
Coastal	18–29	58	21.1	3.17	55
Highlanders	18–29	59	21.9	3.82	65
Guatemala farmers					
Unsupplemented	19	51	25.4	2.13	42
Supplemented	26	58	17.6	2.37	41
Colombia farmers					
General farm labourers	26	61	22.4	2.70	44
Agricultural workers	30	60	21.6	2.75	46
Sugarcane loaders	33	60	22.8	2.95	49
Sugarcane cutters, normal	29	58	21.1	2.60	45
Sugarcane cutters, mild malnutrition	33	52	20.9	2.18	42
Sugarcane cutters, moderate malnutrition	40	48	20.0	1.69	35
Sugarcane cutters, severe malnutrition	38	43	16.9	1.06	25
East Africa sugarcane cutters					
High producers	26	63	21.7	3.21	51
Medium producers	26	61	22.4	2.95	48
Low producers	27	59	21.9	2.78	47
Older	39	64	22.5	2.77	43
Sudanese sugarcane cutters					
Young	21	59	19.5	2.83	48
Older	32	58	19.9	2.73	47

[Table continued overleaf]

Group	Age (yrs)	Weight (kg)	BMI	VO₂ (max) (1/min)	ml/kg/min
Yoruba Africans					
Villagers	25	62	20.9	3.02	49
Sedentary	26	62	20.9	3.83	46
Factory workers	25	62	20.9	3.45	56
Middle East farmers					
Kurd Jews	26	64	22.5	2.83	44
Yemenite Jews	25	64	23.7	3.00	47
Caribbeans					
Trinidad sedentary	26	67	21.5	2.74	41
Jamaica hill farmers	28	60	20.4	3.19	53

Source: Ferro-Luzzi (1985)

For older children and for adults, there are almost certain to be some interactions between the effects of height and weight adjustments on capacity for physical work. Considered as a measure of frame size, height must place some constraints on muscle mass, if only for the same reasons that chassis size imposes a constraint on the size of engine that can be mounted in a motor car.

These constraints are not well understood. It is often assumed (e.g. FAO/WHO 1973) that, since extra food does not increase the heights of people 'above the age of 13', it would 'only lead to obesity'. Indeed it might, and as we shall see there are very good health reasons for setting an upper limit to weight for a given height. But we also know that there are such things as training programmes for army recruits and athletes, and that these increase muscle mass rather than just fat. They do so of course at the cost not only of the food needed to gain the extra muscle, but also of an increased maintenance requirement.

It has been suggested that the cumulative and irreversible effects of early deprivation impose some additional constraints to work capacity per unit of muscle mass. Many comparisons have been made across social class groups and between countries of the physical performance of children (Davies 1973a; Desai et al. 1984; Ferro-Luzzi et al. 1979; Parizkova 1977; Spurr et al. 1983; Satyanarayana et al. 1979). While these authors differ in respect of the implications they derive from their research, they agree essentially on two things: (1) smaller sized children have smaller peak work capacities than larger ones, and (2) their peak work capacities are proportional to body weight. When they become adults this still holds. Ferro-Luzzi (1985) has compiled data on 36 different occupation, country, and ethnic groups (Table 3.4) which reveal the same thing. Although there are differences in absolute terms in maximum work capacity, most of these are accounted for by differences in body size, the next source of variance being the degree of training, judged either by formal (physical education) gradings or by the intensity of occupational work. The training effect in particular is quite substantial. Out of all these groups, the only ones that show significantly low values for VO_2 per kilogram of body weight are those with BMIs below 17 (and some with values more than 24).

Finally, there is increasing evidence that the effects of environmental deprivation in early life are themselves part of the determinants of adult health. In so far as adult height is also an outcome of early experience, short stature can be expected to be a marker for poorer adult health. The recent prospective study of height and mortality in the Norwegian population clearly shows this (Waaler 1984). Thus, independently of the effects of over- or under-weight, height alone is an important predictor of life expectancy. In that particular population, however, there is little to suggest that the environmental factors responsible for stunting are nutritional.

As might be expected, there are two main views about the significance of these findings: (1) that undernutrition reduces peak work capacity, and hence must *reduce* productivity; (2) that peak work capacity is not a universally appropriate index—many kinds of work are more dependent on such things as endurance, skill, motivation, and even perhaps smallness and lightness. Still others say that the important question is the availability of employment which will bring returns over and above the extra cost of food needed. Longhurst and Payne (1981) suggest that poor Nigerian farmers are often in an 'energy trap', requiring them to make an expenditure at the margin of many more calories per 100 calories of purchasing power than the non-poor. I would add to that that, if their extra employment opportunities were of the kind that demanded sustained heavy work, they might well have to make a prior 'investment' in terms of food in order to increase their weight to a sufficient level.

The question therefore is, How far it is useful to generalize? Whether people are limited primarily by current food supply, by the effects of past undernutrition, or by some other constraint of resources or environment seems to be essentially dependent on the context. Whether, in any particular context, increasing energy intake would raise net production requires some understanding of how people currently cope with their circumstances over time as well as space. One of the conceptual limitations of the conventional nutritional assessments is that they encourage the view that we are dealing with steady states or quasi-steady states, or at least with systems that would be stable if they were not constrained in some way. Inclusion of a time dimension often leads to the realization that constant body weights or growth rates are the exception rather than the rule.

In the context of energy regulation, adjustments of body weight can be thought of as having two main aspects:

1   the deposition or utilization of stored energy: it is useful to remember
     that, with the exception of the brain and nervous system, all kinds of
     body tissues take some part in this—not only fat;
2   a change of maintenance costs: thus, an adjustment of body weight,
     or of growth rate, is a two-part strategy for countering an immediate
     shortfall or excess of food supply, and for dealing with future events
     of the same kind.

An interesting question for adaptationists is, If, as there is every reason
to believe, adjustments in metabolism without weight change are not
only theoretically possible, but very likely to exist, why do they not
feature quite largely in regulation and adjustment? We spend our time,
it seems, squabbling about the magnitude, or even the very existence, of
an effect that seems at first sight to be potentially so 'useful'. The answer
perhaps is that in survival terms the double strategy of paying off immediate energy debts and at the same time reducing future overheads is a
very powerful one, and for the most part probably suffices.

As in the case of height, it is likely that there is an early period of
plasticity, followed by one in which growth is increasingly subject to
endogenous control. The time course of height and weight deficits (as
compared with international standards) is shown for Bangladesh in Fig.
3.1, which is modified from Martorell (1985). This shows that, whereas
the prevalence of *stunting* (short stature) rises rapidly until it includes
more than 80 per cent of the population and then remains constant,
wasting (low weight in relation to height) rises to a peak between 1 and
2 years of age and then declines, so that at 5 years 90 per cent of the
population is more than two standard deviations below the mean of the
reference standard for height, and 90 per cent is less than two standard
deviations below the mean of the standard for weight-for-height.

This emphasizes the major impact of environment during the very
early months. Height deficits, once established, remain (probably
throughout most of the remaining growth period); weight deficits in
relation to height tend to decline. This picture is much in accord with
clinical experience. Mortality from diarrhoeal and nutritional causes is
highest during the first year of life, and it is during that period that the
nutrition–infection complex has its most critical effects. Waterlow
(1986), writing about nutrition issues for the 1980s and 1990s, concludes that the programmes in recent decades that focused on the
preschool child have to a large extent been misdirected and wasteful, in
that they have not taken enough account of the biology of the young
child. The catching up of weight deficits to an extent that is dictated by
attained height is also consistent with what happens when malnourished
children are re-fed in hospital: they grow very rapidly until their weight
reaches the normal value for their height, at which point the superfast

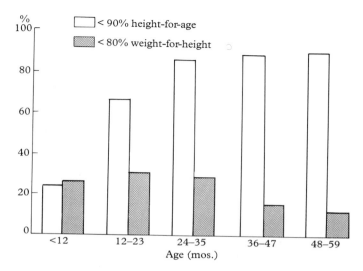

Fig. 3.1. The time course of height and weight deficits in Bangladesh, 1975–1976
Source: Martorell (1985)

catch-up growth ceases abruptly, and subsequently proceeds along a course that is normal for the height.

It seems that height itself is a part of the control mechanism for the regulation of weight growth, acting as a kind of built-in reference for the guidance system. Of course weight, unlike height, can be lost and regained, and appetite can be influenced by many things, including palatability, level of stimulation, physical activity, and illness; and of course food supply may be restricted, so that weight-for-height still varies throughout life, both within and between people.

It is important to realize that after the first few years the small size and relative thinness of the child populations of developing countries is likely to be mainly the result of altered patterns of growth, which have their origins in the adjustments made to environmental insults during very early life. Except for intermittent episodes of disease and food shortage or other dietary factors, it is not likely to be continuously determined by the current level of energy intake.

As always, the question is, What are the costs of being small, and what are the safe limits? Attention has been directed mainly towards associations between undernutrition in early life and aspects of performance, such as resistance to infectious diseases and cognitive development. One problem of interpretation that is common to all of the studies of nutrition–infection relationships has already been noted. Undernutrition is assessed by anthropometry, so that no 'first cause' inferences can be drawn.

Two recent reviews by Martorell (1985) and Tomkins and Watson (1989) reach similar conclusions. First, with respect to incidence, i.e. the frequency with which children with different levels of growth performance suffer illness, for measles, diarrhoea, and pneumonia there seems to be no relationship between incidence rates over the full range of anthropometric measurements except for the possibility that growth deficits caused in the first place by measles may be subsequently followed by increased susceptibility to diarrhoea (Tomkins 1981). There is, however, evidence of high rates of incidence of diarrhoea in children who are severely growth-affected.

With respect to severity of illness, again the evidence seems to point to none or only slight differences between normal and mildly growth-affected individuals, but to very markedly worse effects on the severely undergrown particularly for the important childhood diseases such as measles and diarrhoea. The one exception to this pattern seems to be that of duration of the infection with respect to diarrhoea: even moderate growth reduction is associated with an extension of the duration of symptoms. Martorell summarizes in this way: 'In a nutshell, nutrition seems to have little to do with *who* gets sick. On the other hand, more studies indicate an association between nutritional status (anthropometry) and the severity of infections,' (Martorell 1985: 22).

It is only fair to say, however, that Martorell does not support the 'small but healthy' hypothesis. Lack of evidence that stunting in particular does not seem to carry any adverse indications does not mean, he says, that we should regard it as benign, rather as we would 'scar tissue'. Tomkins and Watson conclude:

> The implication is that families with malnourished children are usually the underprivileged families with greatest difficulties in obtaining employment, food, potable water, decent housing or access to even the most basic medical care facilities. It is at this stage (i.e. analysis of nutrition in relation to outcome of infection) that the significance of PEM (protein-energy malnutrition measured by anthropometry) as a risk factor for infection is seen not just as a biological influence on immune response or physiological function during an infective process, but as a marker for those who are without sufficient power to survive in the environment. (Tomkins and Watson 1989)

There is general agreement about the implications of more severe degrees of undernutrition. In particular, anthropometry has been shown to be a good predictor of mortality, at least for those individuals whose growth is badly affected. Sommer and Loewenstein (1975), Kielmann and McCord (1978), Chen et al. (1980), and Heywood (1986) have all demonstrated a nonlinear relationship between anthropometric assessments and subsequent mortality. The last three of these also show evidence of a 'threshold' effect; i.e., mortality risk rises very rapidly when weight or height or arm circumference falls below a critical level. Comparison of the Heywood (Papua New Guinea) study with that of Chen *et al.* (Bangladesh) suggests that the position of the threshold on the anthropometric scale may depend on the nature of the spectrum of infectious diseases to which the children are exposed.

With respect to mental development, there is again general agreement that there is a level of deprivation in very early life at which some irreversible damage is done to brain function (Brozek 1979). With respect to milder or later episodes, problems of measurement and of correcting for confounding factors are very severe. An illustration of this comes from some of the most extensive studies involving food intervention, which have been made in Guatemala (Barrett *et al.* 1982). The results show that, on average the growth and behavioural performance, measured in terms of spontaneous exploratory levels, competitiveness, persistence, etc., of the children, were poorer for the group whose uptake of supplementary food was smaller. (In fact, these differences in behaviour were seen for the most part in boys rather than girls.) At the age of 6–8 years, these children continued to show differences in mood, levels of play activity, and dependency on adults.

There are, however, arguments about these implications, if not about the findings. Klein (1979) says: 'At age seven, the independent impact of earlier or current moderate malnutrition as measured by anthropometric indicators—though not that of quality of home or of parental contacts—on "school performance" (unlike that of psychological test performance) is not significantly different from zero.' However, Barrett *et al.* (1982) assert that nutrition is the causal agent, and that food supplementation of whole populations would greatly increase social performance and productivity.[5] As in the case of work capacity, the general impression is one of the relatively small costs of adjustments, at least up to a point, although there clearly is a degree beyond which regulation fails.

With some reservations about the possibility that different disease backgrounds might imply the need for different thresholds, the evidence suggests that the point on the weight-for-height scale at which the risk of significant functional impairment begins to rise is close to the lower end of the range of individual variation found in well-to-do populations.

Changes in body composition　　Adjustment of body fat stores is the most obvious component of the response to changes of energy intake, in either an upward or a downward direction. It is not always appreciated that these are inevitably linked to some extent with changes in lean tissue as

[5] But even if these effects can be attributed to some intrinsic damage arising from previous undernutrition, it is difficult to see the practical implications of a trial which shows that low *voluntary* acceptance of food supplements is associated with poor performance.

well. Studies of partial or total starvation show that as fat stores are
mobilized there is always some loss of lean body mass. Moreover, the
proportion of energy mobilized from fat as compared with lean varies
quite widely from one individual to another. When a transient downward
change is reversed and energy stores are replenished, this happens in the
same proportions, so that the continual swings of positive and negative
balance which are a normal part of existence do not lead to cumulative
changes in body composition. Payne and Dugdale (1977) suggest that
the range of inter-individual variation is from 97 per cent of energy stored
as fat and 3 per cent as lean to 70 per cent as fat and 30 per cent as
lean, with a median value of 85 and 15 per cent. They also suggest that
a propensity to use and replace fat as an energy store, rather than rely
on depletion of lean body mass, is a useful adaptation of population
groups to situations in which food supply and energy expenditure fluc-
tuate throughout the agricultural production season. A population that
is adapted to subsistence agriculture would be likely to comprise a high
proportion of 'fat' storers. These people would not actually become
obese, however, until such time as they began to make use of a wider
range of production possibilities, perhaps with mechanical aids, or
moved to an urban environment. This is consistent with the fact that
there is known to be a large genetic component to obesity and that the
prevalence increases very rapidly with urbanization.

   Very little is known about changes in the proportions of non-fat tissues
in response to changes in intake, although it is certain that such changes
do occur. Moreover, some organs like the liver actually function as
short-term 'buffer' stores, smoothing out the intermittent flow of nutrients. The effects of relative changes of weight of some of the more
metabolically active tissues such as liver, gut, heart, kidney, etc., on the
whole body metabolic rate could be very substantial, and might be quite
difficult to distinguish from those arising from an alteration of metabolic
efficiency.

Changes in specific metabolic rates of tissues, or 'metabolic adaptation'
There has been continuous speculation and dispute about this subject
during the past few years, despite the fact that there is very little in the
way of direct experimental data that can be referred to. I have already
made some comments about the possibility of such an effect, and of the
need to regard it as a possible, even a probable, component of the whole
strategy of adjustment. I have no intention of adding to the speculation
or of arguing about the statistical analysis of autocorrelation. I will
simply state my position on the issue.

   1   I know of no theoretical reason why such an effect should not exist.
It would not contravene any of the laws of thermodynamics, nor would
it require any revision of our present view of how energy is transformed

in biological systems. There is nothing in the way metabolism is regulated in the whole body which dictates a constant efficiency of conversion.

Apart from the BMR itself, there are other components of maintenance expenditure which might be reducible. For example, many experiments on animals have shown that body weight cannot be maintained unless energy intake is sustained at some 40 per cent above the minimum resting metabolic rate or BMR. (In fact, as we have already seen, the FAO/WHO/UNU (1985) requirements committee used this as the basis of its recommendations.) But this is a puzzling observation. The 40 per cent cannot all be accounted for in terms of muscle tone or minimum obligatory physical activity (Milligan and Summers 1986). Furthermore, Girardier and Stock (1983), writing about the control of thermogenesis, point out that even the rates of energy consumption measured as BMR under the standard fasting and resting conditions cannot be taken as a fixed and irreducible minimum, since these are up to 60 per cent higher than those measured under anaesthesia or with sensory deprivation.

2   In any case, we still need to bear in mind the possibility that costs may be incurred as a result of this kind of adjustment, just as with any other.

Integrated adjustments   At this stage it might be asked, Why cannot the question of metabolic adjustment be settled by experiment? The major reason for this is simply that, if we reduce habitual intake in experimental subjects, the result is always an integrated response in which changes of body weight, composition, and physical activity all play a part. In fact, several trials involving underfeeding of volunteers have been mounted during the past 60 years. In most of these, resting metabolic rates were substantially reduced. The problem of interpretation of these lies in the uncertainty about how to correct the results for the accompanying changes in weight and fat content. If we wish to compare the metabolic rates of subjects of different body sizes, there are regression equations involving terms for height, weight, age, sex, and environmental temperature which give quite accurate comparisons. These variables in effect account for a very large part of inter-individual variation in metabolic rates. When applied to the subjects of underfeeding trials, however, they generally do not account for the intra-individual changes. The question is, Is it fair to use them?

The discrepancies are quite large. For example, the most often quoted is a semi-starvation trial reported by Keys *et al.* (1950). Thirty-two men were given half their normal energy intake for 24 weeks and lost on average 24 per cent of their initial body weight; body mass indices fell from 24 to 17.5. The basal metabolic rates fell by an average of 39 per cent: applying the standard regression equations gives a predicted fall of only 22 per cent, leaving a possible 17 per cent to be counted as metabolic adjustment. But the validity of this calculation is questionable: there were major changes in body composition, and the subjects were not equilibrated at their reduced weights, but were almost immediately placed on a recovery regime. Physical activity fell to a very low level, and this study is generally discounted by opponents of adaptability, because of its very severe effects. However, it should be noted that the decline in BMR was progressive throughout the 24 weeks, and by 8 weeks was already greater than could be accounted for by the change in weight.

A study by Benedict et al. (1919) usually receives less attention, but is in fact much more relevant to the question of adaptation. Twelve men were subjected to a 10 per cent reduction in body weight (a change of BMI from 22.8 down to 20.0) by a careful adjustment of each individual's energy intake, which amounted on average to a 30 per cent reduction. Their weights were stabilized at the lower level, and maintained for three months. The subjects were urged to maintain their habitual patterns of physical activity as far as they possibly could, both during work and at recreation. Very detailed studies were made of changes of physiological and psychological function, including, for example, the energy cost of a 10 km walk before and after weight reduction. In these subjects there was a decline in BMR of 12 per cent greater than could be accounted for on the basis of body weight change. The energy cost of walking, however, was reduced simply in direct proportion to the weight loss.

Garby (1987) has used a different method for analysing the effects of both over- and underfeeding trials. He calculates the changes in BMR that would be expected from the gains or losses of fat and lean tissue, i.e. assuming constant values for the metabolic rates per kilogram of fat and lean tissue, which he derived from independent studies. Garby finds that in three studies on overconsumption there was an average of 5 per cent (range 3–7 per cent) of excess of metabolic rate unaccounted for by change of weight, and in eight underfeeding trials there was an average of 7.5 per cent (range 0–17 per cent) reduction of BMR below the predicted values.

Comparisons of the metabolic rates of free-living subjects in different socioeconomic circumstances are complicated by the same problems of the need to correct for differences of size, body composition, climate, and, finally, for the possibility of genetic differences between ethnic groups. Shetty (1984) found values for BMR in a group of poor Indian agricultural labourers that were significantly below those of a control group. However, part of this can be accounted for by the untypically high values of the controls (McNeill 1986); in addition, the poor labourers had endured a period of unemployment and had BMI values as low as 16.6.

3.4 PRACTICAL IMPLICATIONS

It was shown in Section 3.2 why it is a hopeless task to try and measure undernutrition as a deviation from some notion of optimum health. What, then, can our measurements hope realistically to achieve? The answer emerges from our discussion of adjustment and adaptation in Section 3.3. We have seen there that, faced with a nutritional stress, the human organism can adjust its energy expenditure in a number of ways. Such adjustments are not likely to be without cost, but over a relatively wide range of adjustment those costs will be balanced by increased chances of survival. Beyond that range, the cost might not be acceptable. Accordingly, a realistic as well as useful objective of our measurement exercise would be to try and identify those vulnerable people whose adjustments have gone far enough to expose them to life-threatening risk. In this section, I suggest the criteria for such identification through both the 'intake approach' and the 'nutritional status approach'.

3.4.1 Defining energy requirements

Any proposed level of energy needs of population groups, whether for minimum survival or for a standard of adequacy, will necessarily consist of two components: an estimate of the mean value for the group, and an estimate of the extent of variation about the mean.

As Lipton (1983) suggests, the evidence so far is that by far the most important factors affecting the definition of energy requirements are those that influence the selection of the mean values. In the past, partly because of their technical limitations and partly because of the preoccupation of committees with prescriptive uses, requirements have included large safety factors. It is the recognition of this that will have the greatest impact on the 'head counts' of the numbers of malnourished. For the future, the really difficult problems stem from the wide extent of possible adjustment of body size, and the great uncertainties about appropriate levels to cover work expenditures. The question is not so much whether metabolic adjustments happen, but whether they are large enough to materially worsen the already large uncertainties of the methods.

For the mean value, according to the FAO/WHO/UNU (1985) committee on energy and protein requirements, we need to take an estimate of the basal metabolic rate and increase this by 40 per cent. This committee, presumably in pursuit of simplicity, proposed equations for predicting the metabolic rates of adults which assume a linear relationship with body weight. (All the regression equations proposed previously had been of an exponential form.) The UN equation has a positive intercept; i.e., it predicts a positive metabolic rate for zero body weight and was derived by 'forcing' a linear regression on to a large collection of data culled from the literature. Finding that the figures for Asian subjects reduced the strength of the correlation, the committee decided to leave them out. The result is that the method recommended considerably overestimates the energy requirements, certainly of Asian people, and probably of all populations of small body weights. McNeill *et al.* (1987) describe the results of measurements on 58 rural Indian men, all of whom had low body weights and fat stores. Their BMRs were on average 12.1 per cent lower than those predicted by the UN equation— which might suggest a metabolic adjustment. However, they were only 0.2 per cent lower than an equation proposed by Quenouille *et al.* (1951) which is based on Asian men of higher average body weight, includes exponential terms for both height and weight, and takes account of climate. This group of subjects did not show evidence of metabolic adjustment, but none the less they had maintenance energy requirements some 12 per cent below those recommended by the FAO/WHO/UNU report for people of the same weight and age.

If all individuals could be shown to undergo a metabolic adjustment in response to reduced energy intake, then, if our estimate of the mean requirement of a group was based on measurements on people whose food intakes were unrestricted, we would be justified in reducing that mean by the amount of downward metabolic adjustment that members of the group could be presumed to be able to make. The question is, How much should that be? We really need an estimate of the maximum extent of intra-individual adjustment. Sukhatme's approach is to use twice the standard deviation of the intra-individual variation derived from measurements on unstressed populations. This might be regarded as a conservative estimate on the grounds that few people in such a group would have adjusted their requirement to an absolute minimum. However, I would agree to do this only for the maintenance component. I think we should be much more cautious about the possibility of comparable changes in the metabolic efficiency of physical work. In practice, therefore, we are considering the effect of taking an estimate of the mean requirement as 140 per cent of the BMR and subtracting twice the standard deviation of the inter-individual variation of BMR. This is about 15 per cent, and is similar to the range of reduction of BMR in underfed subjects which Garby says is not accounted for by changes of body weight or composition. It was on this basis that the lowest figure of all for the survival minimum for an adult male was calculated in Table 3.2.

3.4.2 *Nutritional status measurements*

The discussion in Sections 3.2 and 3.3 identified a number of concerns about anthropometric indicators of nutritional status:

1 the evidence for and against the existence of functional defects associated with smallness;
2 the problems of distinguishing the effects of current deprivation from the cumulative effects of past episodes; the different significance to be attached to height or length, as compared with weight;
3 the near impossibility of distinguishing between the effects of restriction of available food and self-restriction, combined with increased metabolic losses that accompany infections.

In respect of the first of these problem areas, there is an accumulation of evidence on which it is possible to establish the safe limits to downward adjustments of body size. Anthropometry can then give us two kinds of information:

1 It can identify individuals whose weight-for-height (or BMI in adults) lies below a critical threshold. These are suffering from a life-threatening situation, and can be regarded as currently undernourished. There will of course be a wide variety of possible causes—disease, neglect, food constraints—perhaps coupled with high demands for physical work. By itself, anthropometry can tell us nothing about these, and needs to be related to independent indicators of those factors.
2 It can identify individuals who are above the critical threshold and are not currently at great risk of a breakdown. For such people the extent of the adjustments they have already made gives a measure of their capacity to make additional responses without incurring a threat to life. Thus, low BMIs in older children and adults indicate not so much limited capacity for current work demands, as a limited capacity to cope with any further adverse changes—such as regular seasonal fluctuations, or irregular 'bad year' situations, losses of employment opportunities, illness of family members, an additional child to support.

With the present state of knowledge, it seems practical to use weight-for-height in children. Since the risk of mortality rises steeply for values below 80 per cent of the median of the NCHS reference, this could be taken as defining the point below which individuals are classed as currently undernourished.

With regard to body weight in adults, information is beginning to accumulate about the relation between weight-for-height and mortality risk, so far mainly in relatively well-off populations. By far the best source is of a prospective study of the Body Mass Index (BMI) of 1.8 million Norwegians (Waaler 1984). Figure 3.2 shows that, in this population at least, the form of the relationship between general mortality experience and 'thinness' is very similar at the lower end to that for weight-for-age in children.

Cause-specific mortality follows generally similar patterns, but for low BMI values obstructive lung diseases exert a strong effect on the shape of the curve, suggesting that the risks of being underweight may be less for non-smokers. Values less than 18 or 19 for BMI in males seem to carry about 10 per cent excess mortality risk, but the curves are markedly steeper for women, which might suggest the need for a higher threshold value of between 19 and 20 for them.

In addition to this, Keys (1980) analysed actuarial data to show that mortality in middle-aged American males from various occupations is higher for those with BMIs below 20. Cole et al. (1974) studied British and Danish men in the age range 55–65, and showed that mortality rates were three times higher for the group with BMIs below 19.7 than for those between 19.7 and 22.4. (They were twice as high as for those above 22.4.)

We also have estimates of mean values of BMI for a number of population groups. For example, Eveleth and Tanner (1976) quote 18.3 and 20.4 respectively for national samples of Indian and Javanese males. Shetty (1984) found 20.7 and 16.6 for two small groups of Indian subjects. Those with the low values were employed labourers who, while showing no signs of clinical malnutrition, had adapted to very reduced levels of daily energy intake and resting metabolic rate during a prolonged period of drought and underemployment. The data given in Table 3.4 suggest that maximum work capacity is reduced in men with BMI values below 17.[6]

More epidemiological evidence will be needed in order to extend the usefulness of adult anthropometry. In particular, we need more information about the effects of age. Nutritional assessment of adults is generally a very neglected area of research, but never more so than in respect of the elderly. McNeill (1986) studied 100 people over the age of 60 (range 60–90) in a rural *panchayat* in Tamil Nadu. Table 3.5 shows that the average BMI of these elderly people was not only lower than that of younger adults, but was also less than the critical levels of 18 for men and 19 for women.

---

[6] It is of course the steeply rising risk associated with high values that underlies the current concern about overnutrition in richer populations. The problems of being overweight, hypertension, diabetes, heart diseases, etc., are well reviewed elsewhere. There is, in addition, a substantial body of evidence from animal studies pointing to an inverse relationship between the velocity of growth in early life and maximum body size on the one hand, and the age at onset of degenerative diseases and at death on the other. A recent review by Pariza (1987) concentrates particularly on cancer risk. Pointing out that calorie restriction is one of the most effective ways to decrease cancer risk in animals, Pariza notes the growing emergence of epidemiological evidence for similar relationships in man. Those who see the value of requirements as primarily prescriptive need to bear in mind that obesity seems to be a problem which arises very rapidly in populations which acquire even quite modest levels of improved food supply and leisure.

Table 3.5. Anthropometric measurements of young and elderly adults in rural Tamil Nadu

	BMI
Men	
20–49	19.3
60–90	17.7
Women	
20–49	19.1
60–90	18.7

Source: McNeill (1986).

Of course, loss of lean body mass is a characteristic of ageing, particularly during the final decade of life, so that the significance of these findings is not clear. Nevertheless, the productive contribution of this age group is often of critical significance to the maintenance of the household. These elderly women in particular were spending on average three times as long each day on child care as were the younger women, who were hence free to engage in agricultural and other earning activities. It is therefore clearly important to understand better the implications of low BMI for the productivity of such people.

The use of adult anthropometry can indeed be extremely useful in a number of ways. One is to help us sort out the problem of multiple causality in the genesis of undernutrition: by using adult anthropometry in conjunction with child anthropometry, it may be possible to identify which households suffer from a binding constraint of food availability and which households face other limiting constraints. Table 3.6, which is taken from Dugdale (1985), shows some of the possible household patterns that might be distinguished. In addition to the probable logistic advantages, this method offers the possibility of longitudinal assessment on a sample basis, enabling a determination of the effects of, for example, seasonal availability of food in relation to work demands on women, on men, and on other productive members. (Adolescent girls, for example, are often noted as being a vulnerable but neglected group.)

Pattern A shows that the current nutrition of all family members is adequate. The parents and older children may be small in stature, reflecting undernutrition in early childhood, but their present nutritional status is satisfactory.

In pattern B the adults, infants, and older children are all adequately nourished, but the preschool children show evidence of present undernutrition. This is a very common pattern in poor communities: infants are generally protected for the first few months of life by breast-feeding, but from the later months of infancy to about four years of age they are undernourished, with resulting decreases in height-for-age, weight-for-

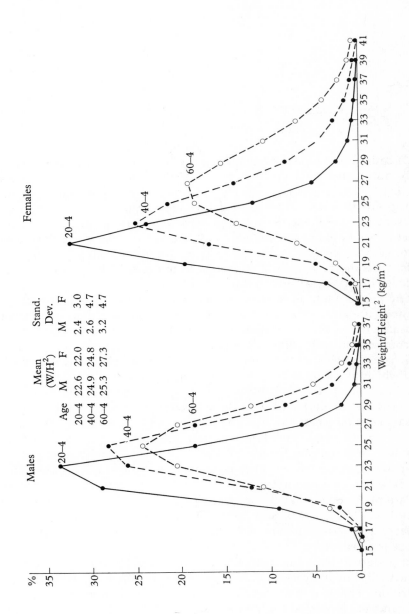

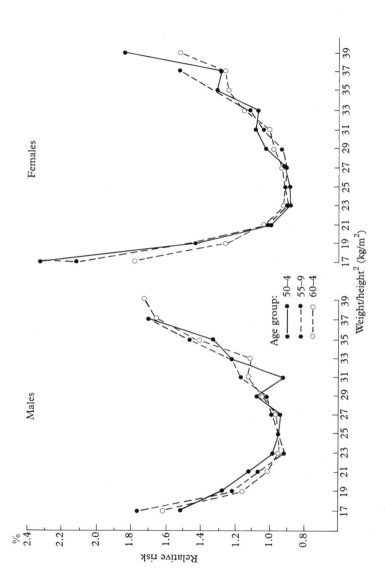

Fig. 3.2. The distribution of body mass index (BMI) in the Norwegian adult population and the relationship between BMI and prospective risk of death, 1963–1979
Source: Waaler (1984)

age, and weight-for-height. By the time these children reach school age they can cope adequately with their environment. From then on their current nutrition, as indicated by weight-for-height, approaches normal, but they are left with a deficit in height-for-age and weight-for-age. This pattern of malnutrition does not reflect an absolute deficiency of food in the family home: rather, it suggests either a lack of satisfactory foods for young children or other deficiencies in their care. These are common causes of malnutrition in developing countries, where young children are expected to eat the same foods as adults and where both parents may spend their days in the fields, leaving the care of young children to older siblings.

Table 3.6. Some patterns of undernutrition in families

Pattern	Present nutrition in families							
	Father	Mother	Infant	Preschool child		School child		
				1	2	1	2	3
A	+	+	+	+	−	+	+	−
B	+	+	+	0	0	+	+	−
C	+	+	0	0	−	+	−	−
D	+	0	0	0	−	+	+	−
E	0	0	0	0	0	0	−	−
F	+	+	+	+	−	+	0	+

+ Weight for height satisfactory.
0 Weight for height below critical level.
− No family member.

Source: Dugdale (1985)

Pattern C suggests poor practices of infant and child care, perhaps with a working mother who cannot feed and care for her infant and younger children during the day. In pattern D, poor nutrition or disease in the mother is almost certainly the primary factor leading to secondary effects in the younger children. The school-age children can fend for themselves. Pattern E indicates an absolute lack of food in the family. Pattern F, with isolated 'malnutrition' of a school-age child, is much more likely to result from disease than from food restriction.

Many other family patterns are possible, and each could be interpreted as a result of specific family problems.

Malnutrition and disease tend to cluster in problem families. When such families are identified and the pattern of their needs is determined, intervention can be targeted more accurately and efficiently. Anthropometry has its limitations and cannot detect all diseases, but it will increase the efficiency in the use of field data for action programmes.

By itself, of course, anthropometry, at a single point in time, tells us very little about the processes that may result in serious nutrition problems. Reference was made earlier to the importance of coping strategies: those by which households deal with the problems of illness, particularly of dependent members, but also the ways in which regular and irregular changes in food supply (or income) and in labour demands are met. Perhaps one of the most constraining effects of the more traditional approaches to measuring undernutrition is the way in which concentration on population prevalence rates, in particular age/sex groups, and on the adequacy of aggregate food supplies has tended to reinforce the notion that good nutrition consists of some kind of steady state. Indeed, the definition of 'requirement' is based on the idea of an equilibrium, or at least of a steady rate of growth. The real world is never like that; even in well-to-do populations body weights are not constant except over relatively short time periods. In rural societies, still largely dependent upon physical labour and intermittent food supplies, the dynamic nature of energy regulation is even more marked. For example, in their studies on the energy requirements of reproduction, Roberts et al. (1982) and Laurence et al. (1984) have shown that, in Gambian women, normal strategies for dealing with the combination of seasonal food availability and the changing requirements of pregnancy and lactation are complex, and continuously changing over time. They include adjustments of energy expenditure on work as well as of basal metabolism. These authors conclude, very reasonably, that 'FAO/WHO-recommended intakes during pregnancy and lactation are "inappropriate" for this community'. The problem of course is that the whole armamentarium of recommended intakes, and of techniques for measuring and comparison of consumption patterns with respect to these standards, is premised not only on the desirability of the levels chosen, but on the maintenance of a steady state of equilibrium. If the 'normal' state is one of a dynamic disequilibrium, with repeated cyclic adjustments over a range of values, then we shall need more than just 'appropriate' levels of recommended energy intake in order to establish whether seasonal effects contribute to malnutrition, and if so when.

This is just as true, of course, for anthropometry. Reference was made earlier to the confounding effects of seasonal changes of climate and day-length on child growth. The impact of the agricultural cycle on body weights of adults is even greater. Dugdale and Payne (1987) described and contrasted the cyclic changes of energy balance in subsistence farmers in the Gambia and in Burma in terms of the different strategies employed to deal with the problems of labour peaks and 'hungry' periods.

Up to now, this kind of analysis has been based on little more than static comparison of intakes and requirements, both of which are usually assumed to have been averaged over a sufficient length of time to remove the effects of fluctuations. We need to take a much more dynamic view of the relationship, one that recognizes the human subject as part of a system which includes the fluctuating demands of his or her annual work pattern. An important outcome is likely to be a replacement of the simple notion of an 'adequate' or 'inadequate' food supply with a capacity to identify critical situations and points in the calendar when the viability of the system may be at risk. For the Gambian type of livelihood, attaining sufficient weight (such as the muscle mass to enable intense but relatively short periods of work to be performed and the body stores needed to fuel that work) may be more important than always sustaining a level of food intake that matches expenditure. If this can be ensured by a particular pattern of food use, then advantage can be taken of reduced maintenance needs at other times.

By contrast, the Burmese situation seems to demand endurance rather than a high peak power output and to do so over lengths of time such that body energy stores are of relatively smaller significance. For these people food intakes must prevent already low body weights from falling below the point at which endurance suffers. Of course at the moment we know very little about these critical weights and muscle masses, and much more research will be necessary before we can predict the probability of the failure of farm systems because of nutritional inadequacy. But this seems to point precisely in the direction in which more research is needed.

Most importantly, there is the question of how to interpret the critical levels of body weights and compositions and the implications of these for health and function. For the present we have to accept that we are a long way from being able to identify the nutritional constraints that characterize different peasant livelihood systems. We are even further from being able to predict the effects of interventions in those systems.

3.5   SUMMARY AND CONCLUSIONS

This paper began by describing the current controversy about adaptation, as only the latest in a long history of conflicts that have characterized the growth of knowledge in nutrition. A straightforward controversy about whether or not changes in metabolic efficiency play some part in adaptation to changes in food supply is in itself quite insufficient to account for the bitterness and personal nature of the disputes of the past ten years. It is rather the implications for policy, and for advocacy of the possibility that energy requirements are lower than had previously been thought, that causes such offence. It is feared that acceptance of these ideas would result in a drastic reduction in the numbers of people considered to be undernourished, and would in effect imply a reduction in standards of adequacy. In other words, much of the emotion is due to different attitudes towards the policy implications of defining either poverty lines or minimum standards.

There is no doubting Rowntree's intentions when he defined his poverty-line diet as a means of assessing the condition of the poor in York in 1899. He wanted to shock by demonstrating the starkness of the conditions of those families who could afford bare sufficiency (in health terms) but not decency. His emphasis was upon what such a family would be *unable* to do: no omnibus fares, no newspapers, no letters to absent children, no contributions to church or chapel, trade union or sick club, no tobacco, no pretty clothes—'nothing must be bought but what is absolutely necessary for the maintenance of physical health. Should a child fall ill it must be attended by the parish; should it die it must be buried by the parish. The wage-earner must never be absent from his work for a single day.' Moreover, 'if any of these conditions are broken, the extra expenditure is met and can only be met by limiting the diet'—in contemporary terms, we would say by falling below the threshold of risk.

Rowntree had no intention that his poverty line should be used as a standard, but by the time of the 1933 BMA committee, and the 1943 Beveridge report, it had, with the help of 'scientific' calculations, been transformed into a measure of minimum sufficiency. No longer to be used as a warning about the nature of the trap into which 30 per cent of the population of York had fallen, but a prescription or minimum recommendation to be used as a basis for public policy.

This 'prescriptive' purpose has been the basis of all of the international committee reports on energy requirements since the Second World War. The international community, for most of this time, perceived undernutrition as being due primarily to lack of food production, so that public policy and the needs of international assistance were best served by making recommendations about adequate levels of food energy supply at country level.

But there is a problem about setting standards of adequacy in nutrition which is probably at its most difficult in respect of energy. This is well summed up in the final words of FAO/WHO/UNU (1985): 'No longer can we bypass the question—Requirements for what?' In the past this question has been bypassed in two ways, both of which now seem suspect. First, the intakes and body sizes of well-to-do populations have been used as a reference standard. An increasing conviction that such populations are not healthy has disposed of that, especially now that energy requirements are supposed to be regarded as recommended expenditures rather than intakes. For example, the requirements for children under 10 years of age given by the 1985 report are higher than any known consumption levels, because the committee saw themselves as prescribing 'desirable' levels of physical activity!

The second attempt to bypass the question of standards has been by appealing to the concept of a genetically defined optimum for nutritional health. This idea is essentially a residuum of the way in which the Victorians accommodated (and modified) the theories of Charles Darwin. They needed to see evolution as a directed and optimizing process, rather than a random, exploratory, and essentially sufficing one. From such a perspective, it seems natural to suppose that, if the capacity of an individual to express any characteristic such as body size or growth velocity is determined by genetic factors, then a state of health should be defined as being one in which those factors are fully expressed. Optimum health is thus the full expression of all such characteristics simultaneously.

This concept is now giving way to the view that individuals have the capacity to adjust over a range of states of 'health', which may all be different, in so far as they represent different balances and trade-offs between physiological and behavioural components of adjustment, but are sustainable in the sense of not carrying severe functional penalties or threat to life. The idea of a single optimum state of nutrition is replaced by a zone of relative safety and effective adjustment to different environments, bounded by limits beyond which the risk of severe consequences rises more steeply. The implications of this are that, in respect of older children and adults, indicators for assessment of undernutrition, whether in terms of anthropometry or food intake, should be constructed and used primarily for detecting people who are either always or frequently having to adjust beyond those limits. This reorientation of the measurement exercise calls for corresponding redefinition of the concepts of 'energy requirement' and minimum anthropometric standard.

It is not suggested, however, that the traditional concept of 'requirement' has no useful purpose whatever. There are some aspects of macrolevel planning for which it is useful to be able to predict the likely future levels of aggregate food consumption, and to assess the effects on these of demographic trends, secular changes in body size, changes of employment, mechanization, etc. It seems likely that current knowledge of energy requirements is sufficient to meet these needs, especially bearing in mind the limitations of the data available for estimating present and future food supplies. Notwithstanding the likelihood that some degree of adaptation or reduced energy intakes does exist and may come to be acknowledged as a part of the theory of requirements, it is most unlikely that the magnitude of the effect of this on aggregate consumption will be such as to influence materially the decisions of food planners.

At the level of the household or the individual, it seems more profitable to concentrate on identifying those whose intakes place them at a significant risk of malnutrition. As discussed in Sections 3.2 and 3.3 above, the theoretical approach to defining energy requirements adopted by the latest FAO/WHO/UNU committee can lead to an estimate of the minimum survival needs of an adult male equivalent consumer which is very close to that proposed by Lipton as an index of ultra-poverty—always provided (a) that the error implicit in the equation recommended by the committee for predicting BMR are avoided, and (b) that no allowance is made for so-called 'discretionary activities'. In the absence of data on intakes, household cash expenditure data could be used to identify those unable to purchase food equivalent to that amount of energy without exceeding 80 per cent of disposable income (Lipton 1983).

There is some purpose in defining, in this way, levels of intake that are on the borderline between survival and malnutrition. People living at such levels would belong to the class that Lipton has described as the ultra-poor. For such people, availability of food is a binding constraint: without more food-energy, any attempt they may make to change their livelihood situations will imply a threat to life or health. Besides deserving the highest priority for assistance, they may need different kinds of interventions and policies from those who, while also poor, are in a position to choose from a wider range of options.

There is as yet no method of dietary assessment which can reveal the existence of another kind of energy trap—people whose livelihood demands a high level of work output, but whose intake is only sufficient to balance expenditure when they have made the maximum adjustments to body size and energy stores consistent with survival. To detect such situations, we need to apply anthropometry to adult working people much more widely than we have in the past. Interpretation of adult weights and heights will also depend on our ability to identify the lower limits of the range of sizes that are consistent with sustaining life and working capacity.

For young children, the stresses of infectious diseases not only induce some of the same kinds of physiological adjustments as direct food deprivation, but actually cause undernutrition by reducing appetite. These strong interactions between food and non-food (disease) factors during the first year or so of life have led to the view that undernutrition must be regarded from a 'holistic' perspective, a result of both food and non-food factors operating to limit the household food and health entitlements. From the point of view of the dependent child, this is perhaps a reasonable perspective, and of course there are sound arguments for public policy aimed at improving both of these entitlements for poor people anyway. Problems arise however when, as all too often is the case, the only evidence there is about nutritional status in the population consists of measurements of young children. Precisely because the causes of their condition are so complex, it is likely that there will be no consistent relationship between these and household resources generally, or even between these and food availability.

From the point of view of intervention policy, the question is whether child growth is an indicator that enables us to distinguish the need to improve food availability from the need to improve control of the disease environment. With the present state of knowledge, the answer seems to be No. Of course, this is not to conclude that no action is needed: simply that anthropometry does not indicate priorities.

There is a fair amount of evidence that interventions which seek to alter single factors in the environment of the child, such as food intake alone or the health environment alone (either directly or through education of mothers), have on the whole had rather little impact. Such vertical programmes have raised doubts about the significance of the benefits to recipients, as well as about the justification of the cost. It seems that the interrelationships between nutrients, and even more the interactions between diet, disease, and behavioural factors, are such that, operating over time, they are often in effect all more or less equally limiting, so that the probability of being able to bring about a significant improvement through direct intervention affecting just one factor is small. In this respect, the continued existence of the undernutrition of children in poor communities is now perceived as part of the wider problem of how to improve child survival and development through specific public health interventions. Lincoln Chen (1986), in a review of 20 years of the Matlab disease control programme in Bangladesh, concludes that, despite the proven efficacy of single interventions for the control of cholera, neonatal tetanus, etc., the actual impact of these on infant and child survival are disappointing, notwithstanding the fact that life expectancy after the age of 5 is now very comparable to that of developed countries.

It would appear that improved chances of survival and better development of young children are likely to depend ultimately on the level of household resources: food, time, and health care.

4

Undernutrition: Concepts, Measurements, and Policy Implications

T. N. Srinivasan

4.1 INTRODUCTION

The problem of hunger and undernutrition (primarily meant to describe inadequate long-term energy intakes in some sense) in developing countries has rightly attracted the attention of scholars.[1] However, the underlying concepts, and the hazards of quantifying the extent of undernutrition with widely available data, appear to be poorly understood. An appalling consequence of this is the wide range in the estimated extent of undernutrition in developing countries. The World Bank (1986) estimates that in 1980 34 per cent of the population of developing countries, or 730 million people, did not have sufficient energy intakes through their diets to enable them to live an active working life, and that the diets of nearly half of them (340 million) were so deficient in energy that they ran the risk of stunted growth and serious health problems. The Food and Agriculture Organization (FAO) provides two alternative estimates of the proportion of undernourished population in developing market economies for the period 1979–81; one of 15 per cent (335 million) and one of 23 per cent (494 million). FAO (1985) emphasizes that these estimates do not allow for any activity other than maintenance of bodily functions, and as such these estimates may understate the prevalence of undernutrition. Even if one allows for the differences in methods of estimation and of coverage between the two studies, the difference between the two on the extent of undernutrition is substantial.

It will be argued below that the conceptual basis underlying the available estimates of undernutrition is faulty, and even if it were to be faultless, the data-base with which the concepts are used to derive the

I thank Jere Berhman, Angus Deaton, Burton Singer, John Strauss, P. V. Sukhatme, and participants of the July 1987 WIDER Conference on Poverty, Undernutrition, and Living Standards for their comments. Siddiq Osmani's detailed, probing, and constructive comments have been extremely valuable. Of course, none of the above is responsible for the errors still remaining in the paper.

[1] This paper is concerned only with the problems of defining the adequacy of energy intake and of measuring the extent of undernutrition in the sense of the proportion of population having inadequate energy intake. The broader and more inclusive concept of malnutrition will not be addressed. The differences between the two concepts are laid out in Srinivasan (1983b).

estimates most often cannot support such use without making a number of essentially untested, if not untestable, assumptions primarily of a statistical nature.

Section 4.2 introduces the *process approach* to energy balance. It is natural to view the energy intakes, expenditures, and energy balance for an individual as a vector stochastic process. First, analytical and policy interest lies in the health and well-being of each individual over a lifetime and not just at an arbitrary point in time. Second, it is unrealistic to assume that intakes or expenditures are deterministic: after all, even if we ignore everything else, avoidance of monotonicity in diets may induce an individual to vary in an unpredictable way the composition, and hence the energy content, of his diet from day to day. Since many of the components of this stochastic process are subject to the choice of the individual, the evolution of the stochastic process will depend on such choices as well as on any other exogenous shocks to the system, and not only on the metabolic processes involved. To take a mundane example of an exogenous shock, unusually cold or hot weather may affect one's intake of food. It is therefore conceivable that, depending on the exogenous shocks and choices actually made, the system may or may not be stable, and, if the stochastic process converges, the (joint) distribution to which it converges need not be unique. Indeed, as we shall see below, multiple equilibria are the rule rather than the exception.

Once again, it is natural to ask whether the metabolic processes have a tendency to maintain the system along a stable path towards convergence if the processes relating to choice and exogenous variables satisfy such a property. A system with such a tendency is said to be *homeostatic*. Suppose the system exhibits homeostasis and is in stochastic equilibrium, but the processes relating to a subset of exogenous variables is altered at some point from one stable convergent set to another. Then, if the processes relating to the choice variables can be suitably altered and the metabolic processes also adjust, if necessary, to steer the system towards another stochastic equilibrium, the system is said to exhibit *adaptation*. Thus, homeostasis relates only to the metabolic processes, while adaptation also involves choice variables in an essential way.

It was pointed out earlier that what is of interest is the health and well-being of an individual throughout her life. From such a point of view, the entire time-path of the relevant indicators of health and nutrition would be relevant. However, in conformity with common practice, and for the sake of analytical simplicity, the long-term nutritional status, or in the above context the steady-state distribution of the relevant processes, will be used to assess the nutritional status of an individual. Thus, unsatisfactory *nutritional status* will arise if the steady-state joint distribution of the relevant processes is deemed unsatisfactory in some well-defined sense. Clearly, with nutritional status identified with long-term consequences, if the system does not exhibit homeostasis, the question of evaluating the nutritional status does not arise. As such, if *nutritional stress*, as exhibited by disruption of homeostasis, is not reversed, the nutritional status of the individual is ill-defined. Thus, the presence of nutritional stress at a point in time raises the presumption of impairment of nutritional status. On the other hand, the absence of nutritional stress does not preclude the possibility that the individual is moving towards an unsatisfactory nutritional status; that is, even though the individual is presumably moving towards a stable equilibrium, the equilibrium itself may be unsatisfactory.

Section 4.3 is devoted to issues relating to measurement. Even if the relevant processes are identified conceptually at an individual level, the issue of finding empirical proxies for theoretically appropriate variables has to be addressed if empirical analysis is to be undertaken. And if, as is usually the case, interest lies not in the nutritional status of a specific individual but in that of a group of individuals, problems of aggregation arise at a conceptual as well as an empirical level. An analytical description of various types of data that have been used in the measurement of the extent of undernutrition will therefore be attempted, with particular attention being paid to the level of aggregation with respect to units of observation (individuals, households, income groups, etc.), durations of observation (day, week, month, etc.), and the object of observation (actual intake of cooked food, uncooked ingredients of food consumption, expenditure on such ingredients, etc.). Statistical procedures used, starting from concepts and data and ending up with estimates of the extent of undernutrition, will be critically examined. Section 4.4 is devoted to a brief discussion of policy issues, and Section 4.5 summarizes and concludes the paper.

4.2   THE PROCESS APPROACH TO ENERGY BALANCE[2]

It is convenient to start with an identity dictated by laws of thermodynamics. In any process (physical or biological), the sum of inflows of energy into the process from all sources must equal exactly the sum of all outflows, the flows being defined as rates of energy per unit of time, e.g. kilocalories per day, megajoules per day, etc. In applying this identity to energy balance in human beings, inflows are essentially two: energy content of food intake (I_t) and the energy withdrawn from stores within the body. Energy outflows or expenditures consist of (*a*) energy expended by metabolic processes $\{M_t\}$, including energy needs for system

---

[2] This section was inspired by the stimulating papers of Professors P. V. Sukhatme and Philip Payne. They are not of course responsible for any errors or misrepresentations!

(blood circulation, respiration, etc.), maintenance, and growth (if relevant); (b) energy expended on activities (A_t) relating to one's occupation or profession, exercises, or other physical activities aimed at maintaining good health, recreation, etc.; (c) energy added to bodily stores; and (d) energy content of bodily wastes (W_t), including dissipated heat not included in other flows. Clearly, for flow-accounting what matters is the rate of net addition (positive or negative) to bodily stores per unit of time, so that we can transfer from the inflow side of the identity the energy withdrawal from stores to the outflow side and treat the net addition S_t (positive or negative) formally as an outflow. Although one should allow for changes in body composition as well as mass, in particular changes in stores of different types of tissue, for simplicity we will ignore this aspect and proceed as if there is only one store from which energy is drawn or to which energy is added. With this convention, we can write the fundamental identity[3] as

$$I_t \equiv M_t + A_t + S_t + W_t \qquad (1)$$

The fact that the above is an identity (i.e. an equation that holds by virtue of the definition of variables involved in it) implies that it conveys nothing about the process itself, for example about whether the process is stable in some well defined sense, and, if stable, whether the process maintains the system in a state that is satisfactory in some appropriate sense. In the context of energy balance in human beings, stability may be identified with the absence of nutritional stress in some well-defined sense at any point in time, and the desired state of the system may be identified with the ability to maintain good health and pursue one's occupation as well as any desired recreational and other discretionary activities. In order to pose the issues of stability and desirability in a meaningful way, one has to describe the processes that determine $\{I_t\}$, $\{M_t\}$ etc. (all but one of them, since the identity determines the one remaining).

It is useful to begin with the hypothetical case of an individual whose energy expenditure on activities A_t remains constant at $\bar{A}$. Assume further that the net addition to bodily stores S_t is constant at zero. Clearly, if S_t remains constant and positive (negative), it would mean a continuous increase (decrease) in body mass. This is impossible if the individual has an infinite life-span and unlikely unless S_t is sufficiently small if the individual has a finite life-span.[4] The energy needs for metabolic processes are a function of age, sex, and body weight and the intake itself.

---

[3] A computer simulation model based on this identity for prediction of energy balance and body weight can be found in Payne and Dugdale (1977).

[4] In populations in which there is a large seasonal component in energy needs for work and energy availability from food, there may be an accumulation of body weight in some season/s which is depleted during the rest of the year. Payne (1985a) provides evidence from the Gambia for this phenomenon. Clearly, such seasonal factors are not ruled out in a covariance stationary $\{S_t\}$ process.

If we ignore the variation arising from ageing, then for an individual (with a constant intake $\bar{I}$) maintaining body weight, M_t could be assumed to be a constant $\bar{M}$ as well. If W_t can be assumed to be negligible relative to $\bar{A} + \bar{M}$, and if his constant energy intake $\bar{I}$ equals $\bar{A} + \bar{M}$, then the individual is in energy balance. As long as the body mass and the levels of activities that are being maintained are satisfactory, the process has a satisfactory outcome. Then $\bar{A} + \bar{M}$ could be defined as the (hypothetical) energy requirement of the individual under discussion. Of course, the issue of stability does not arise since neither the inflow nor the outflows vary over time.

In order to pose the stability problem in a simple yet meaningful way, let us proceed by stages of increasing realism and complexity. First, assume that the intake processes $\{I_t\}$ and activity process $\{A_t\}$ are exogenous and stationary and that the processes $\{S_t\}$, $\{M\}$ and $\{W_t\}$ are endogenous, so that they adjust to maintain identity (1). Clearly, adjustments that indefinitely increase or decrease body mass are not meaningful. As such, one would like to ensure that $\{S_t\}$ is stationary with mean zero. Thus, the stability of the system in enabling the individual to perform exogenously specified activities $\{A_t\}$ with exogenously given intakes $\{I_t\}$ depends on whether the endogenous metabolic processes $\{M_t\}$ and $\{W_t\}$ can adjust to maintain $\{S_t\}$ stationary at mean zero. Clearly, the variance of the exogenous processes together with the adjustment 'capability' of the endogenous processes will determine whether the system is stable in the above sense. This suggests that one can define the system to be *homeostatic*, and the variances of the exogenous processes to be within its homeostatic range, if the system is stable in the above sense, i.e. if the endogenous processes adjust to keep the individual in energy balance (in a stationary stochastic equilibrium) with no drift in his body mass while enabling him to perform the exogenously specified activities given the exogenously specified intake.

Adaptation, as contrasted with homeostasis, can be defined for the above model as follows. Suppose a system that has been in stationary stochastic equilibrium, given $\{I_t\}$ and $\{A_t\}$, is shocked at some point T so that the intake process is shifted to another stationary process $\{\tilde{I}_t\}$ $t \geq T$, with a different mean but with the same variance. Then adaptation is the process of achieving a new stationary stochastic equilibrium. Of course, by definition, the new equilibrium will involve a stationary $\{S_t\}$ with mean zero: adaptation then involves changes in $\{M_t\}$ and mean body mass. The changes in $\{M_t\}$ involve changes in energy expended in metabolic processes, a large component of which is a function of the change in body mass. Analogous to the shock to $\{I_t\}$, one can visualize a shock to $\{A_t\}$ in the form of a change in its mean. If the $\{I_t\}$ process is unchanged, once again, adaptation will involve changes in mean body mass and the associated change in $\{M_t\}$.

It is evident that, analogous to the limits on process variances within which homeostatis applies, there are likely to be limits, this time on the changes in means of the relevant process, applicable to adaptation. Put another way, stationary stochastic equilibrium may be infeasible, for instance, if mean body mass to be maintained at such an equilibrium is too high or too low. That is to say, even if one reduces all energy expenditures other than for the functions of metabolic processes to zero, one may not be able to maintain too high a body mass. Equally, too low a body mass may be inconsistent with survival.

In the above discussion, the processes $\{I_t\}$ and $\{A_t\}$ were treated as exogenous. For some purposes this is appropriate. For instance, the $\{A_t\}$ process could be normatively specified so as to ensure that it is 'economically necessary and socially desirable' and 'consistent with long-term good health' (FAO/WHO/UNU 1985). If the $\{I_t\}$ process is viewed as being derived from the allocation of income between consumption of food and non-food commodities, given their prices, and if the income generation process is determined by the normatively specified economic activities (and accumulated assets), then $\{I_t\}$ is also exogenous to the energy balance system. In this view, the above framework is essentially an apparatus for assessing whether $\{I_t\}$ and $\{A_t\}$ are compatible with stationary stochastic equilibrium. If they are, the resulting equilibrium is by definition satisfactory, since the intake and activity processes are normatively specified.

It is clear that it is not realistic to assume that $\{I_t\}$ and $\{A_t\}$ are exogenous if the analytical framework is to have any descriptive validity. The intake of an individual in any particular period may depend in part on his or her health status, which in turn may depend on past intakes, episodes of illness, etc. Also, current intakes may be influenced by past physical activities and even by the level of current physical activity if the unit of time defining a period is sufficiently long. In the energy-accounting identity (1), $\{A_t\}$ and $\{I_t\}$ are defined in energy units per unit of time. However, if instead we measure $\{I_t\}$ in physical units of different types of uncooked food, then possibly the energy content, and certainly the nutrient contents, of cooked food ingested will depend on the method of cooking! If we measure physical activity in units of time spent in performing that activity, then the energy expended on that activity will depend on how intensively that activity is performed, which may depend not only on the state of health of the individual but on incentives. For example, an unsupervised worker may shirk work: even though he may spend as much time on some activity whether he is supervised or not, his effort, and hence the energy he expends, may be considerably less when he is not supervised.

There is a further problem. The energy spent on some of the discretionary activities may depend on the energy available from intake, with any excess (shortfall) in intakes being accommodated by an increase (decrease) in such activities. A trivial example of this is an individual who decides to jog a few extra kilometers to use up the energy ingested through an exceptionally large and rich meal! More seriously, it has been suggested that severely constrained intake levels arising from poverty force the very poor to curtail not only discretionary activities, but also economic activities, which in turn restricts their income, thus keeping them in poverty. In extreme situations, adjustment to intake constraints will result in an individual not performing any physical activity other than a bare minimum associated with bodily functions, and/or in a loss of body mass.

The above discussion suggests a general model analogous to 'error correction' models of economic time series (Salmon 1982; Engle and Granger 1987) for describing energy balance regulation. The basic idea is to specify models in which comparative-static or steady-state equilibria and the process of dynamic adjustment in moving from one equilibrium to another are specified in a consistent way. Salmon argues that 'consistency in this sense requires that the short-run dynamic adjustment be directed by the perceived disequilibrium and that eventual convergence to the equilibrium position be ensured' (Salmon 1982: 615). The equilibrium path is viewed as a target according to whose behaviour the error correction mechanism is specified to ensure zero steady-state error. The mechanism could be derived from a dynamic stochastic optimization exercise, or on feedback effects based on the observed 'error' or extent of disequilibrium in the relevant variables.

The homeostasis and adaptation processes are analogous to the error correction mechanisms, the former being directed by 'optimization' by the body's internal metabolic processes, and the latter by both metabolic processes and actions initiated by the individual to correct perceived energy imbalance[5] or disequilibrium. A formal model that may be appropriate can be formulated based on the one discussed in Davidson (1986), whose presentation is reproduced below. One distinguishes a vector of variables (y_t) endogenous to the health–nutrition–energy balance process, and a vector (z_t) of truly exogenous variables connected by a system of auto-regressive distributed lag equations,

$$B(L)y_t + \Gamma(L)z_t = u_t \tag{2}$$

where $B(L)$, $\Gamma(L)$ are matrix polynomials of maximum order p so that

$$B(L) = \sum_{i=0}^{p} B_i L^i \text{ and } \Gamma(L) = \sum_{i=0}^{p} \Gamma_i L^i.$$

[5] The imbalance is the difference between exogenous inflows and outflows, prior to the endogenous balancing flow initiated by the correction mechanism. To repeat, once *all* inflows and outflows, exogenous and endogenous, are correctly measured and accounted for, identity (1) holds and there is no imbalance.

B_i is of order $n \times n$ and Γ_i is of order $n \times m$, where $n(m)$ is the dimension of the column vector $\mathbf{y}_t(\mathbf{z}_t)$.

For example, $\mathbf{y}_t$ will include energy expended on activities, possibly distinguished by the nature of activities (work-related, recreational, etc.) The corresponding equations will specify the variables (current and past, endogenous and exogenous) that determine such energy expenditures. In the general nutrition–health status model, it is clear that other variables that describe the current health status will be included in $\mathbf{y}_t$. In $\mathbf{z}_t$ any of the variables that are relevant to a person's choices and that affect his energy intake, expenditure, and health status but are exogenous to his decision-making will be included. Examples include the current (and possibly past) wage rates facing a worker, or crop shares facing a share-cropper (to the extent these are market-determined), relevant interest rates, environmental variables such as ambient temperature, parasite vectors, etc. $\mathbf{u}_t$ is a latent, zero mean, stationary *innovation* process. As argued by Davidson, it is natural to assume that $\mathbf{u}_t$ is an innovation process, that is that it cannot be predicted by lagged values of observable variables. For if it can, these variables should be explicitly in the model.

In the context of energy intakes, health, and nutrition, although there is nothing in theory to suggest linearity of the relationships involved, it is analytically convenient to start by assuming them to be linear, though linearity in logarithms may be more appropriate. Of course, whether the underlying metabolic pathways associated with homeostasis and long-term adaptation (which may involve genetic adaptation as well) are adequately described by such a model, only biologists can say! The stability of the system and the steady-state distribution of $\mathbf{y}_t$ (conditional on suitably specified $\mathbf{z}_t$) are of interest. Davidson shows that, as is well known, the necessary and sufficient condition for stability is that all roots of the determinantal equation $|B(\xi)| = 0$, $\xi \varepsilon$ complex number space, lie outside the unit circle.

The nature of the lagged relationship between the endogenous variables as reflected in B(L) affects the stability of the system. This conforms to one's intuition: if past intakes, activities, and health status together affect current values of these variables, clearly, the stability of the system depends on whether some of these effects are cumulative and reinforcing or damped and eventually die out. The steady-state distribution of $\mathbf{y}_t$ corresponds to the stochastic stationary equilibrium discussed earlier. Whether or not this equilibrium is satisfactory—that is, whether the stable adjustment process as implied in the lag structure leads to an equilibrium that is satisfactory—can be judged by looking at the steady-state joint distribution of some set of overall indicators that are functions of $\mathbf{y}_t$.

It is worth emphasizing that a rationalization of the error correction model based on stochastic optimization or control comes closest in spirit to the process view of energy balance, once we recognize that $\mathbf{y}_t$ includes the endogenous metabolic process variables as well as the non-metabolic choice variables. Thus, the parameters of the model reflect 'optimal' responses to changes in the relevant distributions. The definition of homeostatic range based on restricting the variances of the exogenous processes can be generalized and restated in the context of the error correction model as follows. If the parameters of the lag structure corresponding to 'optimal' adjustment through metabolic processes (i.e. a subset of $\mathbf{y}_t$) to changes in the distribution of exogenous variables lead to stability of the system, then the system is homeostatic, and such changes in the distribution of exogenous variables are within the homeostatic range. The generalization consists in allowing other changes in the relevant distribution besides variances. Similarly, the earlier definition of adaptation can be generalized by allowing 'optimal' adjustment through non-metabolic as well as metabolic processes included in $\mathbf{y}_t$ and examining the resulting parameters of lag structure for stability.

The above model can be used to judge the health–energy status of an individual if enough longitudinal data on $\mathbf{y}_t$, $\mathbf{z}_t$ are available so that the parameters of the system can be estimated well and the estimated system tested statistically for the presence of unit roots. It is also possible to extend the model to cover several individuals if it can be assumed that individual-specific and lag effects of the adjustment process have sufficient common structure. For example, if the lag parameters of the system are the same for all individuals and the only individual-specific effects are random shifters in each equation, with the shifters being drawn from a specified joint distribution (i.e. whose functional form though not parameters is known), then, with longitudinal data from a cross-section of individuals, the system can be estimated.

4.3   MEASUREMENT ISSUES

4.3.1   Intra-individual variation, habitual intakes, and nutritional stress

In contrast with the process approach described above, most of the literature on measurement of the extent and severity of undernutrition ignores homeostasis (and hence intra-individual variation in intakes) altogether by implicitly assuming, in essence, that energy inflows and outflows are kept unchanged at their long-term mean. For instance, the latest joint FAO/WHO/UNU expert consultation report defines the energy requirement of an individual as 'the level of energy intake from food that will balance energy expenditure when the individual has a body size and composition, and level of physical activity, consistent with long-term good health; and that will allow for the maintenance of economically necessary and socially desirable physical activity', and states that 'all requirement estimates refer to needs persisting over moderate periods of time. The corresponding intakes may be referred to as "habitual" or "usual" to distinguish them from intakes on a particular day' (FAO/WHO/UNU 1985: 12). Since most procedures of estimation of energy-related undernutrition compare an estimated intake of an individual for a day, week, or month with a requirement estimate derived from FAO/WHO/UNU (1985) or its antecedents (which, as quoted above, refer to a much longer period), such procedures have to assume that the estimated intake is a good estimate of the long-term average, even if it is based on a single day's data! Even if one were to assume that averaging over a week or a month is adequate to provide a good estimate of the long-term average, and that this equals the long-term requirement needed for maintenance of good health, etc., there is still the question of whether the variance in daily intakes is within a homeostatic range. To put the point dramatically, an alternating feasting-and-fasting regime may yield an average intake equalling requirement as defined by FAO/WHO/UNU (1985); but clearly, there is no presumption that it is healthy!

Once intra-individual variation in intakes associated with homeostasis is recognized, it is clear that observed intakes for whatever period (sufficiently short) can differ from long-term requirements without either creating stress or invoking the process of long-term adaptation, as long as the intake process is stationary with its mean equal to the long-term requirement and has a variance that is within the homeostatic range. Only when the observed intake is outside the range of homeostasis will there be a presumption of nutritional stress. And unless it can be inferred from the short-period data that the long-term mean of the intake process differs from requirement, there is no presumption that adaptation is taking place either.

4.3.2 Homeostatic range and inter-individual variation

How does one estimate the range of variation in intakes compatible with homeostasis? Clearly, if one observes the intakes of a healthy individual in stationary stochastic equilibrium, then the range of variation in his intakes provides an estimate. However, if one can assume that the homeostatic range is symmetric around the long-term mean requirement, and that the length of the range is the same for all healthy individuals in equilibrium, one can use the estimate of within-individual variance $\hat{\sigma}^2$ in observed intakes of these individuals to obtain the length of the range (say as $6\hat{\sigma}_w$).[6] The assumption of symmetry can be disputed:

[6] This procedure assumes that there is no autocorrelation in intakes. If autocorrelation is present, then it has to be allowed for in estimating the true intra-individual variance from

adjustment to a negative deviation in, say, intakes from long-term requirement may be more difficult than adjustment to a positive deviation of the same magnitude. Alternatively, one could assume the length of the homeostatic range to be proportional to the long-term mean requirements. Then different individuals, because of differences in their age, sex, body weight, and activity, will have different mean requirements, and hence different homeostatic ranges. However, with an estimate of the coefficient of variation in the intakes of healthy individuals with the same mean requirement, one can obtain the homeostatic range of individuals with different mean requirements in an obvious manner. It must be emphasized that, in the absence of properly controlled clinical trials, the various alternative hypotheses about homeostasis have to be treated with caution. For instance, there is no biological basis to assert whether $6\sigma_w$ or $4\sigma_w$ is the appropriate estimate of the homeostatic range.

Sukhatme (1982b) suggests that, once allowance is made for differences in sex, age, activity, body mass, etc., there is not significant inter-individual variation in long-term equilibrium mean intakes, i.e. in requirements. In terms of the above framework, what this means is that, if we consider the intake processes of a number of individuals in stationary stochastic equilibrium, these processes will differ in their means. This in turn implies that, by shifting the mean of the equilibrium intake processes of different individuals to account for differences in the factors mentioned above, one can make all the shifted intake processes have the same mean, namely, the mean μ of the intake process of a reference individual (e.g. a male of a given age, who is healthy and in equilibrium). As argued earlier, the range $[\mu - 3\sigma_w, \mu + 3\sigma_w]$ could be considered as the range within which homeostasis operates, where σ_w is the intra-individual standard deviation in intakes. Now with intake data for a given period (of the same length as the period on which σ_w is based) for a

within individual variance in intakes. Waterlow (1984), as quoted in Sukhatme (1987), attributes to Sukhatme the argument that autocorrelation necessarily implies homeostasis, which he finds difficult to accept because the former is a statistical concept and the latter a physiological concept. This is not a convincing argument since the underlying physiological mechanism may induce an autoregressive process on the measured variables representing the outcomes. However, it is true that Sukhatme writes as if autocorrelation in *intakes* implies homeostasis. But properly interpreted, his analysis is really about autocorrelation in *energy balance*, defined as the difference between energy intakes and presumed average energy expenditure on metabolic processes and physical activities. In fact, Sukhatme and Margen (1982) came to their mode of energy balance by analogy to their model of nitrogen balance. In our error correction model of energy regulation, autocorrelation in energy balance as defined by Sukhatme arises naturally if the adjustment to perceived imbalance through endogenous mechanisms has a lag structure implying partial response to shocks within any period. More simply put, energy balance as defined by Sukhatme is a function of several omitted adjustment variables including changes in bodily energy stress, energy content of bodily wastes, etc. Since identity (1) holds by definition if all the relevant flows are included, any autoregressive structure in the omitted variables implied by the error correction or adjustment process will be reflected in the energy balance measure, even though intakes themselves may have no autocorrelation.

number of individuals, we first subtract or add the adjustment in mean requirements for any difference in their relevant characteristics compared with the reference person. Then, as long as the adjusted intakes fall within the range $[\mu - 3\sigma_w, \mu + 3\sigma_w]$, it could be presumed that none of the individuals will be subject to nutritional stress.

It should be kept in mind that the above statement is only a presumption and not a prediction. One reason for this is that, unless one has information about the intake process rather than a single observation from that process, one cannot judge whether an individual's intake will at some point in the future put him outside the homeostatic range; to make a probabilistic statement about the future course, one has to make additional assumptions about the processes. Another reason is that, if the error correction model of energy balance regulation is appropriate, one needs information about the parameters of the model to judge its stability. Just as the parameters of an econometric model that represents private behaviour in response to public policy are policy-regime-dependent (the so-called Lucas critique), the relevant parameters in this context are also dependent on the distribution of exogenous processes to which the system is 'optimally' responding through homeostasis or adaptation. In any case, even if there are no changes in the distribution so that the parameters do not change, if the parameters are estimated, then the stability judgement will be probabilistic. Further, it should be recalled that any intake within the homeostatic range, whether at the extremes or in the middle, is consistent with the absence of nutritional stress. And by definition, there is no 'cost' to homeostatic adjustment to variation in intakes in terms of changes in body mass, activity levels, etc. This fact has not been grasped by some critics of Sukhatme (e.g. Dasgupta and Ray 1990), who confuse long-term adaptation with shorter-term homeostasis!

4.3.3 Aggregation over individuals and averaging

Knowledge of the relevant characteristics of each individual is essential along with her intake, if the above procedure is used for determining whether she can be presumed to be free of nutritional stress. Without such knowledge, the adjustment in mean requirement relative to that of the reference individual cannot be made. However, if the joint distribution of characteristics and intakes among individuals in a population (or at least a representative sample of the population) is known, one can arrive at the proportion of individuals who can be presumed to be free of stress without being able to say whether any specified individual is free of such stress or not. The minimal set of relevant characteristics will include age, sex, body mass, and activity status. Very rarely, if at all, is such information available together with intake for the same set of individuals. Certainly, none of the global estimates of the extent of undernutrition is based on actual data on such a joint distribution.

The data-base most often used for estimating the extent of undernutrition consists of a distribution of energy intakes for some specified period, such as a day, week, month, or even a whole year. The intake may refer to individuals, but more often is likely to be the average intake per person in a household, or per consumption unit where each person in a household is weighted differently according to age and sex in arriving at the total number of consumption units. The weights may have little to do with the metabolic processes involved, and some may not agree that aggregation makes sense in this context. The distribution may be based on household survey data on actual intake of cooked food at one extreme or on expenditure on various food items at the other. Alternatively, as in FAO's world food survey (FAO 1985), it may be a synthetic distribution whose parameters are either exogenously specified or indirectly estimated from aggregate data. Given the distribution function $F(x)$ of intakes x and a cut-off point R dividing adequate from inadequate intakes, the proportion of the relevant population (individuals or households) with inadequate intake is then estimated as $F(R)$. In some studies R is set as the average energy requirement of the population, the average being computed from WHO norms using the usually available information on the distribution of population according to age and sex and (largely untested) assumptions about activity. Usually no account is taken of variation in actual body mass of individuals within each age–sex activity cell in computing this average.

There are serious problems associated with aggregating or averaging intake requirements of members of a household. This is because, in addition to the processes of homeostasis and adaptation at the individual level, at the household level some adjustment in activity and food allocation to changes in aggregate food availability is likely to take place to reduce any adverse impact of such changes. Payne (1985a) reports a finding of Abdullah and Wheeler (1985) that there were seasonal changes in the physical activity of small children, as well as of adults, in a Bangladeshi village, so that food allocation within households cannot easily be interpreted in terms of either 'requirement' levels or shares relative to the total. Be that as it may, we shall see below that, under certain assumptions about the household allocation process, one can overcome the aggregation problem. For the moment let us ignore it by assuming that the intake distribution refers to individuals and that intakes are accurately measured, and explore the implications of allowing for the range of intra-individual variation associated with homeostasis.

Suppose we had information of the *joint* density $j(x, R)$ of intakes x and requirements R in the population. If $[R - H(R), R + H(R)]$ denotes the homeostatic range (we have allowed for the possibility that the range depends on the requirement R), then the proportion of individuals presumed to be free of nutritional stress is by definition

$$P = \int dR \int_{R-H(R)}^{R+H(R)} j(x, R)\,dx.$$

On the other hand, if we ignore homeostasis and classify an individual as free from undernutrition only if his intake exceeds his requirement, then the proportion of population adequately nourished will be

$$\tilde{P} = \int dR \int_R j(x, R)\,dx.$$

If we ignore the threat of nutritional stress of those with intakes exceeding the upper limit of homeostasis in analogy with treating everyone with intakes exceeding requirement as free from undernutrition, then

$$P - \tilde{P} = \int [F(R\,|\,R) - F(R - H(R)\,|\,R)]\,g(R)\,dR > 0 \quad \text{since } H(R) > 0,$$

where $F(-\,|\,R)$ is the cumulative distribution of x conditional on R and $g(R)$ is the marginal distribution of R. Thus, using requirement as a cut-off point and ignoring homeostasis will understate the proportion of the population that is free of undernutrition. If, instead of using each individual's requirement as the cut-off intake as in $\tilde{P}$ above, we used the mean requirement $\bar{R}$ for the population, the associated estimate $\bar{P}$ would be $1 - F(\bar{R})$. One could attempt to approximate the extent of the understatement of the stress-free proportion P if we use $\tilde{P}$ or $\bar{P}$ as Kakwani does in Chapter 6 below. But this is of little more than illustrative significance, since there is very little empirical basis for determining $g(R)$.

4.3.4 Estimation of extent of undernutrition from household data

Sukhatme (1982*b*) has estimated the extent of undernutrition among individuals in a population, given a distribution of households by average intake of the household per consumer unit, as the proportion of households having average intakes below $R^* - H(R^*)$, where R^* is the requirement per reference person. This procedure can indeed be justified under certain strong assumptions. Consider a household with total intake X, consisting of n individuals with requirements R_i. Let the allocation of X among the members of the households be such that individual i is allocated an intake

$$X_i = (R_i/R^*)\ X\Big/\sum_{i=1}^{n} (R_i/R^*).$$

Now $X/\Sigma\,(R_i/R^*) = \bar{X}$ is the average intake per consumer unit, if the reference individual is assigned one consumer unit and an individual with requirement R_i is considered equivalent to R_i/R^* consumer units. It should be noted that, by definition, R_i incorporates the energy implication of all the relevant differences (i.e. age, sex, body mass, activity) between individual i and the reference person. In practice, the computation of consumer unit conversion does not incorporate all their differences. If we assume that $H(R)$ is proportional to R with a constant of proportionality k, then, if the inequalities $R^* - kR^* < \bar{X} < R^* + kR^*$ hold, the inequalities $R_i - kR_i < X_i < R_i + kR_i$ also hold, since $X_i = \bar{X}\,(R_i/R^*)$. Thus, all members of a household are free from nutritional stress if its average intake per consumer unit is within the homeostatic range of the average person in the population as a whole. Again, if we ignore the upper limit of homeostasis, the extent of undernutrition in the population is $F(\bar{R} - k\bar{R})$ where $F(x)$ is the cumulative distribution of persons by household average intake per consumer unit. This is precisely Sukhatme's estimate, once it is realized that the constant of proportionality k is derived from the coefficient of variation σ_w/R where σ_w is intra-individual variation. Sukhatme sets k as $2\sigma_w/R$. His implicit assumption about intra-household allocation of intakes is a plausible and reasonable one to make in the absence of any other information.

4.3.5 Implications of correlation between intakes and requirements

It is clear that, if one considers a population of healthy individuals differing in age, sex, and activity but in stationary stochastic equilibrium, x and R cannot be independent. If we denote by $\bar{R}$ the mean requirement for the population of such individuals, one can write $x = \bar{R} + u + v$, where $u = R - \bar{R}$ and v represents the deviation of the actual intake of an individual from his requirement R. Thus, the covariance between x and R is $E(x - \bar{R})\,(R - \bar{R})$, where the expectation is taken over the joint distribution of u and v across individuals. Assuming u and v to be uncorrelated, this covariance equals the variance Eu^2. By assumption, this is different from zero, since we are considering a population of individuals who differ in age, sex, and activity levels. If we assume that the intra-individual variance, i.e. Ev^2, is a constant, then the correlation between x and R equals the so-called intra-class correlation, i.e. $(Eu^2/Eu^2 + Ev^2)^{1/2}$.

An interesting implication of the above formulation is drawn in Srinivasan (1981). Suppose we have data on x_{it} for N individuals $(i = 1, \ldots, N)$ on T periods $(t = 1, \ldots, T)$. Then, as long as $Ev^2 \neq 0$, the maximum likelihood estimate of individual i's requirement $R_i = \bar{R} + u_i$ is not his mean intake $\bar{x}_t$ over the T periods, but a weighted average of $\bar{x}_t$ and the overall mean x, the respective weights being the shares of the variance Eu^2 and Ev^2 in the total variance $Eu^2 + Ev^2$ among the individuals and periods. This has the further consequence that the difference in mean takes $\bar{x}_i$ and $\bar{x}_j$ of individuals i and j overstates the difference in their requirements, i.e. $u_i - u_j$.

4.3.6   The nature and consequences of adaptation

In the above discussion attention was focused exclusively on short-term adjustment through homeostasis. Turning now to the longer-term adaptation, it goes without saying that data on intake of an individual referring to a short period can tell us very little about his long-term equilibrium or, indeed, whether there is any tendency of convergence towards an equilibrium at all! As argued earlier, one needs longitudinal data over a sufficiently long period of time to answer this question. It should also be clear that there are possibilities of multiple stochastic steady-state equilibria. For instance, an individual can adapt to the same shock to the mean of his intake process in alternative ways: by adjusting levels of discretionary activities, by allowing the mean body mass to change, etc.[7] Corresponding to each mode of adjustment, there can be a long-term equilibrium. Although, given some overall welfare indicator which is a function, say, of the moments of the steady-state distribution of endogenous variables (e.g. mean body mass, mean level of discretionary activities, etc.) characterizing each equilibrium, one may be able to rank alternative equilibria, it is likely that such an indicator will be quite insensitive within a wide range to some of the moments. For example, for an adult of a given height and body frame, mean body mass could vary over a range of 5 kg or more without affecting his health status or functioning in any way.

There is substantial evidence of several modes of adaptation to severe shocks to the intake process, although the precise pathways (metabolic and other) through which it takes place are not well understood. H. L. Taylor *et al.* (1945) carried out metabolic, physiological, and psychomo-

---

[7] According to conventional wisdom (e.g. FAO/WHO/UNU 1985), additional energy intakes have to be provided to pregnant or lactating women to allow for satisfactory foetal growth and secretion of milk. But there is evidence to suggest that energy needs of pregnancy and lactation may be accommodated by a fall in basal metabolic rate and changes in energy expenditure on physical activity (McNeill and Payne 1985; Laurence *et al.* 1984). This is an example of adaptation.

Sukhatme (1987) attributes to Waterlow (1984) the notion of adaptation at three levels—biological/genetic, physiological, and social/behavioural—and the suggestion that the genetic make-up determines the extent to which physiological adaptations are possible and that the capacity for physiological adaptation influences the necessary social or behavioural adaptations. While this is consistent with the definition of adaptation in this paper, it is somewhat restrictive in suggesting a hierarchy in the three levels running from biological/genetic to social/behavioural. My own concept of adaptation is more general; for instance, it does not rule out conscious changes in social or behavioural patterns in response to shocks thereby affecting the burden of adaptation thrown on the other two levels.

tor measurements on four men who performed hard work under rigidly controlled conditions during five two-and-a-half-day fasts, successive fasts being separated by five- to six-week intervals. They found that repeated exposure to the fasting state resulted in more effective adaptation to fasting, although the mechanism remains obscure. During the second and third days of fasting all men were able to maintain their blood sugar in work at a significantly higher level in the fifth as compared with the first fast. Motor speed and co-ordination deteriorated less during the fifth fast. Reaction time and pattern tracing showed a statistically significant improvement, while two other psychomotor tests showed trends in the same direction. Danforth *et al.* (1978) argues that the metabolic changes that take place during starvation, in addition to the reduction in basal metabolic rate, allow the essential functions of life to continue for longer periods than would be predicted if such an economy were not part of the adaptation. Edmundson (1979) concludes, from his study of individual variations in basal metabolic rate (BMR) and mechanical work efficiency in East Java, that low energy intakes there may be related to both long-term genetic adaptation and short-term phenotypic adaptation, with a decrease in BMR playing a major role in facilitating a higher level of metabolic efficiency for energy stress subjects. Apfelbaum *et al.* had reached a similar conclusion earlier:

The change in energy expenditure constitutes an adaptation phenomenon—an environmental change (intake) provokes a reaction (change in expenditure), which maintains the organism as constant as possible (energy stores). The fact that this adaptation is progressive . . . shows that it must be realized through an integrating system such as energy stores and also, as the number of adipose cells does not vary in adults, the adipose cell volume. How this information is transmitted or by which mechanism the thermogenic yield is modified by metabolic pathways is not known. (Apfelbaum *et al.* 1971:1408)

One of the most controversial issues relating to adaptation concerns growth retardation in early childhood. Payne points out that:

A young child will respond in a relatively reversible fashion to dietary changes and may, for example, follow a period of reduced growth by a fast 'catch-up'. With increasing age, this potential for fully reversible responses is reduced, and growth becomes more and more 'programmed' on to a relatively less flexible course. This means that adjustments to changes can be both short-term and reversible, but also long-term and relatively irreversible, and that we can expect to find groups of people who have on average different patterns of physical characteristics and capacities from those of other groups and environments. (Payne 1989)

For example, if we compare children of the same age from developed countries, growing in an environment in which dietary intake is not a constraint and infectious diseases are infrequent, with those growing in

the disease-ridden and intake-constrained environment of poor countries, the former are taller and heavier than the latter. On the other hand,
if, instead of comparing weight or height for age, we compared weight-
for-height, the difference in the two groups tends to narrow substantially.[8] To some, such as Seckler (1982), this suggests that the adaptation
to their environment of children in poor countries has led them to be
shorter and lighter than their developed country counterparts, but that
they are just as healthy in a functional sense. In other words, the more
serious health issue is not *stunting* (i.e. relatively low height-for-age) but
wasting (i.e. relatively low weight-for-height). On the other hand, to
those such as Gopalan (1983*b*), who seem to identify meeting height and
weight standards for age as a *sine qua non* for health, stunting is a serious
nutritional problem. Unfortunately, empirical evidence on the functional
consequence of mild and moderate malnutrition as measured by the
failure to meet the anthropometric standards (height, weight, skinfold
thickness, etc.) is scanty.

Payne (1985*a*) reports on a food intervention trial in Guatemala where
food supplements were made available to women during pregnancy and
lactation and subsequently to their offspring on a voluntary basis, with
subjects being given food on request at health centres. The results
showed that, on average, the growth and behavioural performance,
measured in terms of spontaneous exploratory levels, competitiveness,
persistence, etc., of the children, was poorer for the group whose uptake
of supplementary food was smaller. Given that the decision to ask for
food supplementation was voluntary, Payne argues that it would be
unwise to conclude from the results that nutrition is the causal agent
and hence that food supplementation of whole populations would greatly
increase social performance and productivity. He rightly suggests that
one has to look for unobserved or unmeasured common factors, such as
the children's physical, psychological, and social environment, for an
explanation of their low voluntary uptake of food, smaller body size, and
poor performance.

4.3.7 *Measurement errors*

A few remarks are in order on the errors of measurement in data-sets
used for estimating the extent of undernutrition. The sensitivity of the
estimates to the errors, depending on the method used with respect to
the average energy intake of a population, can be substantial. For in-

---

[8] Ryan *et al.* (1984) report that, if one used international standards for weight-for-age,
the proportion of children in the 1–6 year age group classified as suffering from moderate
to severe malnourishment varied from about 22 per cent to 49 per cent in four south Indian
villages. If the standards for weight-for-height were used instead, the same proportion
varied 12 per cent to 19 per cent depending on social class.

stance, consider the crudest method of classifying persons as undernourished if their energy intakes are below the average requirement for
the population. If intakes are distributed normally with a mean of 2700
kcal per day and a standard deviation of 200, the proportion deemed
undernourished will be 50 per cent if the average requirement is also
2700. If, because of measurement error, the true mean intake is 2650
(an error of about 2 per cent) with no error in the standard deviation,
the true proportion deemed undernourished will be 60 per cent instead
of 50 per cent, an error of 20 per cent. Since very often intake data are
put together from food balance sheets and estimates of population, both
being subject to significant measurement error, the resulting estimates
of proportion of undernourishment are subject to substantial error, even
if we accept the methodology of estimation of undernourishment.

Table 4.1. Calorie distribution among rural households: India, 1971–1972

Monthly expenditure per capita (Rs)	Average energy intake per day per consumer (k cals)	Number of Households		
		Total	With intakes *below 1500 k cals* per day per consumer unit	With intake *above 4000 k cals* per day per consumer
0–15	1493	444	267	5
15–21	1957	1207	218	16
21–24	2287	813	55	19
24–28	2431	1174	45	37
28–34	2734	1748	33	112
34–43	3127	2028	16	281
43–55	3513	1655	5	433
55–75	4016	1318	5	578
95–100	4574	598	5	341
100+	6181	482	2	337
All Classes	2724	11 468	651	2159

Source: National Sample Survey (1976), Vol.1, tables 0.0R–0.10R.

Consider, for example, the data in Table 4.1 on energy intakes,
derived from a sample survey of households in rural India in 1971–2.
The average energy intake per consumer unit varied from 1493 kcal per
day in the poorest class to 6193 kcal per day in the richest. If we take
1500 kcal as the bare minimum for survival, nearly 6 per cent of the
sample households had average intakes below this level, and 75 per cent
of these households belonged to the two poorest classes and 83 per cent
to the three poorest classes. At the other extreme, nearly 19 per cent of
sample households had intakes exceeding 4000 kcal, of which 51 per
cent came from the richest three classes. If there is anything to the theory

of energy requirement, and if these data are taken at face value, 6 per cent of rural households in India are at the verge of death and nearly 20 per cent were pushing towards serious problems of obesity! There is no independent evidence to corroborate this. Indeed, the crude death rate in 1984 for India as a whole was only 12 per 1000 of population.

Part of the explanation for this puzzle lies in measurement errors. Although the enumerators were instructed to record the value of food consumed by each household rather than the value of food produced by the household, there are reasons to believe that this instruction was not observed. For example, meals provided by employers as part of wages and consumed by agricultural workers were sometimes recorded as consumption of the employer households and not as that of the employee households, thereby overstating their consumption and understating the consumption of the worker households. Another example is the food served on ceremonial occasions, such as marriages, funerals, and religious functions. These are recorded in the consumption of the 'host' household, although many invitees also partake of the meals. Here again, it is likely that this overstates the consumption of richer households as they are more likely to spend lavishly on feasts. But poor also spend on ritual feasts. Interestingly, five households in the poorest class had intakes exceeding 4000 kcal and two in the richest had intakes below 1500 kcal which is consistent with the former hosting a feast and latter partaking of a feast hosted by some other household! If agricultural workers belong to the poorest classes and the land-owning employer households belong to the richest classes, the figures reported in Table 4.1 are plausible; the error in recorded consumption as compared with true consumption will bias the estimated extent of undernutrition. There are other possibilities of measurement error arising from differential wastage of food across income classes (it is likely that the poor waste less than the rich), errors in conversion to energy intake using Atwater conversion factors, etc. It is not possible to determine how widespread measurement errors are and whether they are quantitatively significant without undertaking a specially designed study.

It is not the case that consumption survey data from developing countries are the only ones subject to serious measurement error. Bhalla (1980) analysed data from the Health and Nutrition Evaluation Survey of over 20,000 individuals in the USA during the period 1971–4. The intake data related to one day only and were obtained through recall. The data showed that 67 per cent of US males and 80 per cent of US females had intakes below recommended daily requirements! In a society where obesity is a more serious problem than undernutrition, these figures do not make sense. This demonstrates the weakness of the methodology and the data-base. Clearly, either intake data have a downward bias, or requirements are overstated—or both.

4.4 POLICY ISSUES

I have addressed elsewhere (Srinivasan, 1981, 1983*a*, 1983*b*, 1986) some of the issues relating to policies for combating undernutrition. Lipton (1983) provides an exhaustive and excellent discussion of many of the nutrition- and poverty-related issues. Also, Gittinger *et al.* (1985) provide an analytical and empirical discussion of food policy in a unified framework involving production, consumption, and distribution. I will add only a few brief remarks here. In designing public policy intervention, it is essential to keep in mind the fact that intakes and activities of individuals, in particular children and dependent adults, are largely determined by household decisions regarding consumption, participation in the labour force, choice of occupation, etc. And these decisions are constrained by opportunities available to the household in the market, its asset endowments, and public policies. Two examples will suffice to illustrate the implications of this fact for nutrition-oriented policy intervention.

Consider a policy of providing subsidized food rations to a part or whole of the population of a country, a policy that is very common in the developing world. If the rations can be resold with no transaction cost in the open market, and if the introduction of the policy does not significantly affect the market price of food, the provision of the ration is equivalent to the provision of an income supplement equal to the subsidy value of the ration. If the marginal propensity to spend on food is c, the additional consumption of food induced by a ration of R kg will be only cRs, where s is the *ad valorem* subsidy per kilogram of food. Except in the extremely unlikely case of $c = 1$ (unitary marginal propensity) *and* $s = 1$ (free rations), the additional consumption will be less than the ration R. If the open-market price were to rise, as is likely with the introduction of a rationing scheme, the additional consumption will be even less. Thus, to induce an additional consumption of R kg, the ration may have to be substantially higher than R. The situation gets further complicated if high transaction costs or strict enforcement precludes resale. Since any subsidy has to be financed in some fashion, the alternative ways in which it is financed may have different implications for the consumption of different socioeconomic groups and for the long-term growth of the economy.

Sah and Srinivasan (1988) provide a theoretical analysis of the distributional implication of an urban ration scheme supplied by procurement at below-market prices from rural producers. They show that, in an economy in which there are inequalities in the distribution of land in rural areas (with a sizeable landless class) and in incomes in urban areas, an intervention that involves no net subsidy from the budget makes urban residents who do not supplement their rations with open-market purchases better off and landless workers and small peasants worse off. There exist a critical land-holding size and an urban income level such that, if urban consumers with incomes above the critical limit are made better off, then rural residents with lands below the critical size (including the landless) are necessarily made worse off by the intervention. Thus, a scheme involving no net budget subsidy that is oriented towards improving the nutritional status of the urban poor may succeed in doing so only at the expense of the nutritional status of the rural poor.

Narayana et al. (1988) explore empirically alternative rationing and financing schemes for India using an applied general equilibrium model. Their main findings are that, if the cost of the subsidy needed can be financed through substantial increases of the tax rates on incomes of the rich, a massive redistributive programme involving the distribution of 100 kg of wheat per person per year to every Indian *free of cost* results in a substantial reduction in poverty and undernourishment. However, if the tax rates cannot be raised and the subsidy has to be financed by reduction in public investment, such a programme introduced in 1980 results in a 10 per cent lower gross domestic product (GDP) in year 2000 as compared to a situation with no programme. The loss in GDP is modest, while the gains in the form of reduction in poverty and undernourishment are substantial.

Taylor et al. (1983) review the operation and effectiveness of food subsidy and food-for-work schemes in several countries. They concluded that all schemes involved a substantial degree of leakage in various ways. There was reshuffling of household expenditures and intra-family allocation of food in response to the price changes, and (the implicit) income effects of a subsidy. For poor countries, the subsidies involved a substantial share of government expenditure and in many cases generated demand for additional food imports. Administrative costs of the programmes were also not negligible, and it was costly, if not administratively infeasible, to restrict access to such programmes through a means test. It is more difficult to reach some target populations (e.g. pregnant and/or lactating women) than others. On the other hand, some schemes, by their design, placed the control over the access to subsidized food directly in the hands of the women members of the household and thus had a greater nutritional impact (on children, particularly) than other schemes. They suggest that the effectiveness of subsidy schemes in reaching the poor can be enhanced by subsidizing foods that make up a larger share of the consumption of the poor and locating outlets for such food in the areas where they live. Unfortunately, the design of many of the existing programmes tends to increase rather than reduce the direct costs as well as opportunity costs that the poor have to incur in participating.

Another widely implemented policy is that of providing free, or at least heavily subsidized, meals or food supplements to schoolchildren. Unlike the rationing schemes discussed above, meals provided in the school cannot be directly converted into equivalent income. However, indirect conversion is possible: by reducing the food eaten at home by the child that will be fed at school, a household can reduce its expenditure on food and use the amount saved for other purposes. Of course, whether or not there will be full compensation—that is, whether the child's food intake at home will be reduced by the amount supplied at school, so that its total intake will remain unchanged compared with the situation before the introduction of the policy—depends once again on the household's preferences. This is one of the main reasons why the evaluations of this type of intervention policy mostly show no improvement in the nutritional status of children not receiving such meals. Another major drawback of such a scheme is that it cannot reach children who are not in school, although the possibility that the introduction of such a scheme may induce poor parents who may not have otherwise done so to send their children to school has to be taken into account. However, in many poor countries the opportunity cost of sending children to school can be very high for very poor parents in rural areas: first, because, their children supply labour to income-earning activities of the household, and second, because the direct cost of schooling may also be high relative to their incomes. In such situations the prospect of a free meal for one's children may not in itself be sufficiently attractive to induce parents to send them to school, even taking full account of the enhanced future earnings of the child arising from better nourishment and schooling.

It was mentioned earlier that episodes of illness can affect intakes. In poor societies where clean water is a scarce commodity, water-borne infectious diseases are endemic. Unless these and other prevalent infectious diseases are tackled, attempts to improve the health of the population through nutrition interventions may not be cost-effective, and possibly may prove completely unsuccessful.

There is considerable evidence (Behrman and Deolalikar 1987) that even extremely poor households do not choose their food basket so as to maximize energy intake from the amount they spend on food; i.e., not only energy content but also taste of food is important. This means that as incomes increase even poor households may shift to foods that simply have a better taste and total energy intake may not rise very much; i.e., the income elasticity of energy intakes is low. Thus, to increase energy intakes significantly, households' incomes have to be raised substantially. Although this blunts the effectiveness of an income-based approach to undernutrition, given the problems associated with policies of direct nutrition intervention, not many cost-effective alternatives to improving the income-earning opportunities of the poor may in fact exist for bringing about a long-term sustained improvement in the nutritional status of the poor.

4.5 SUMMARY AND CONCLUSIONS

The conceptual and empirical bases underlying most of the available estimates of the extent of undernutrition in the world are weak. The most appropriate conceptualization of the complex system of health and nutrition in humans is to view it as an ongoing process in which the internal metabolic processes (e.g. those governing circulation, respiration, growth) and acts of volition (e.g. intake, activity) by the individual interact, with the effects of such interaction being spread over time. Homeostasis was defined as that feature of the metabolic process that keeps the system along a stable equilibrium path in response to fluctuations in some of the exogenous processes. Adaptation was defined as a combined response of metabolic processes and those subject to individual choice to shifts in exogenous processes. It was argued in particular that energy intakes of an individual can vary within the homeostatic range without impairing the person's health and activities and without changes in body mass. If this is so, it is misleading to compare the average intake of an individual over a relatively short period, as most empirical studies do, with a long-term average requirement to determine whether the individual is adequately nourished.

A model for implementing the process approach is proposed. It draws on some recent work on 'error correction' models of economic time-series in which short-run dynamics and the process of adjustment in moving from one long-run equilibrium to another are consistently formulated. However, empirical estimation of such models needs longitudinal data, which are typically unavailable in the nutrition field.

A number of thorny statistical problems arise in moving from an individual to a population of individuals, in inferring properties of a long-run equilibrium from data relating to short periods, in assessing energy intakes and their distribution across individuals from data that often relate to expenditure on food (and that, too, at the household or even higher levels of aggregation), and in allowing for measurement errors in data. Even if the weak conceptual base of the available methodologies of estimation of undernutrition is ignored, the statistical problems alone are enough for the resulting estimates to be viewed with extreme caution.

A brief discussion of policy issues relating to nutrition intervention raised a number of problems involved in reaching the targeted population in an effective way. The experience with direct nutrition intervention policies appears to be mixed. From a long-run perspective, it would appear that rapid economic development that succeeds in lifting the poor out of their poverty, rather than food subsidies or nutrition supplements, is the surest way of eradicating undernutrition.

5

On Some Controversies in the Measurement of Undernutrition

S. R. Osmani

5.1 INTRODUCTION

This paper attempts to evaluate two related debates which have figured prominently over the last decade in the literature on the measurement of undernutrition.[1] One of them has arisen from the controversial views of P. V. Sukhatme, and the other from those of David Seckler. Both have argued that the traditional methods of measuring undernutrition give a highly exaggerated picture by placing the 'norm' of adequate nutrition at a much higher level than is warranted by theories and facts.

Their views have indeed much in common—so much so that their critics often attribute the views of one to the other, although not always with justice. They are actually concerned with two rather different measures of undernutrition, and the theories they invoke in support of their cases are by no means the same. Therefore, although Seckler and Sukhatme find common ground in berating the orthodox methods of estimating undernutrition, their arguments need to be evaluated separately and independently of one another. This is what I intend to do in this chapter.

Sukhatme is concerned primarily with the intake-based measure of undernutrition, in which the proportion of undernourished people is usually estimated by comparing observed calorie intake with a norm of average calorie requirement. Seckler, on the other hand, is concerned with anthropometric measures of undernutrition among children, in which measurement of actual body size is compared with some desirable standard. Both, however, claim that the standards of comparison used in either case are much too high, and that, furthermore, the reason why the standards are too high is not that the architects of these standards made a ghastly measurement error in an empirical sense, but that they got the theory wrong—the theory of how the human body responds to nutritional environment. Therefore, what lies at the heart of these controversies is a difference in theory, or hypothesis, about human's biological response to nutritional stimulus.

I am grateful to Jean Drèze, R. Floud, and T. N. Srinivasan for useful comments.

[1] 'Undernutrition' refers to the phenomenon of deficiency in energy intake. The broader phenomenon of 'malnutrition', referring to the deficiency of some or all of different kinds of nutrients, is not addressed in this paper.

However, the aspects of biological response to which Sukhatme and Seckler draw our attention are quite different from one another. Sukhatme's arguments rest on the hypothesis that costless variation in the efficiency of energy utilization allows a person to maintain the same state of health within a fairly wide range of intake. If this hypothesis were true, then the standard practice of comparing observed intake with a fixed average norm of requirement would clearly overestimate the magnitude of undernutrition; and this is what Sukhatme contends is the case. For Seckler, however, the crucial response mechanism is not the variation in energy utilization, but variation in the rate of growth of body size: he argues that different rates of growth can be equally consistent with a desirable state of health, so that the use of fixed anthropometric standards (usually based on very high rates of growth) overestimate the magnitude of undernutrition.

Thus, following rather different routes, both Sukhatme and Seckler are led to advocate much lower standards of comparison for the assessment of undernutrition than are usually employed. The resulting difference in the magnitude of measured undernutrition can be enormous. In the case of India, for example, traditional methods indicate that nearly half the rural population is undernourished, whereas the lower cut-off points yield a figure of only 15–20 per cent. Not surprisingly, the theories of Seckler and Sukhatme have generated a heated controversy, with supporters of their theories blaming the mainstream tradition for grossly overstating the magnitude of undernutrition, and being blamed in turn for dangerously underplaying the extent of human misery.

I shall not, however, be concerned in this paper with the exact numerical magnitudes that are generated by the opposing theories. My aim is to assess the logical and empirical validity of the claims made by Sukhatme and Seckler for their respective theories. I begin in Section 5.2 by explaining the concept of the 'requirement standard for a reference individual', and indicate exactly where Sukhatme's views depart from the mainstream. The foundations of his theory are then critically examined in Section 5.3 and those of Seckler in Section 5.4. Finally, some concluding remarks are offered in Section 5.5.

5.2 THE ENERGY REQUIREMENT OF A 'REFERENCE' ADULT

5.2.1 The concept of a 'standard'

The human body requires energy for performing both internal functions (chemical as well as mechanical works within the body) and external work on the environment. The required energy is supplied mostly by the food consumed; but, if necessary, additional supplies can be obtained by burning up reserve stores of energy from within the body. Conversely, when the ingested food yields more energy than is expended by the body, the excess energy is stored. Any imbalance between intake and expenditure thus causes an equivalent variation in energy stores. This is reflected mainly in a corresponding change of body weight, but also in the composition of the body, i.e. in the proportion of different forms of energy stores such as fat (adipose tissue) and lean body mass.

When a person is in a state of 'energy balance', i.e. when intake equals expenditure at a given level of physical activity, his body weight and composition remain unchanged; as such, he can be said to be in a state of equilibrium. Most people in the world are in a state of equilibrium, in the sense that very few are continually losing or gaining weight. However, different persons are found at different levels of equilibrium, and the same person can move from one equilibrium to another over time.

Now one way of approaching the concept of 'energy requirement' may be to ask, How much energy is required to maintain an equilibrium? The answer obviously is, The intake associated with the lowest possible equilibrium level. Clearly, if 'requirement' is defined in this way, then most people will be found to be meeting their requirement: only the miniscule proportion who are continually losing weight will be considered to be failing to do so. But is the maintenance of equilibrium an adequate criterion for defining the requirement 'standard'? The answer depends on what meaning we wish to vest in the notion of a 'standard'. If it is merely intended to mean a level of adequacy that will ensure the survival of an organism, then certainly, an intake that can sustain the lowest equilibrium will qualify as a standard. But when nutritionists talk about 'standards', they usually aim at levels of adequacy that will ensure something more than survival. And quite rightly so: after all, the objective of being nourished is not merely to survive, but to achieve satisfactory levels of various functional capabilities (e.g. the ability to avoid disease or to perform physical activities) which depend upon the level of nutrition. If a 'standard' is supposed to ensure all these capabilities, then obviously, mere maintenance of equilibrium will not do. One will have to ask, 'Which equilibrium?', because different levels of equilibrium may be associated with different levels of functional capabilities. The 'standard' must then be defined as that level of intake which is associated with the minimum level of equilibrium at which all the nutrition-related functional capabilities can be maintained at desirable levels.

Since an equilibrium is associated with a specific body weight at a given level of activity, the 'requirement standard' can also be defined in terms of the levels of body weight and activity that are consistent with full functional capabilities. Accordingly, the latest expert committee on nutritional standards offers the following definition:

The energy requirement of an individual is that level of energy intake from food which will balance energy expenditure when the individual has a bodysize and composition and level of physical activity consistent with long-term good health and which will allow for the maintenance of economically necessary and socially desirable physical activity. (FAO/WHO/UNU 1985: 12)

In actual practice, the 'requirement standard' is first postulated for a hypothetical 'reference person' who is defined as an adult male of a given age living in a given environment. The requirements of all the real people (or, more precisely, all *types* of people) are then obtained by applying appropriate conversion factors. According to the definition given earlier, the requirement of a reference adult will of course depend on what we specify to be a desirable body weight and on the adult's level of activity.[2] But once these are specified, do we know how to go about estimating his requirement? This is the point where a major controversy begins to emerge; for there does not appear to exist a commonly accepted theoretical framework for estimating the requirement of a reference adult. There is, of course, a dominant 'establishment' view, but there is also a strong 'heretic' view which differs fundamentally from the prevailing orthodoxy.[3]

5.2.2   The parting of ways: variable efficiency of energy utilization

The establishment view can be described as the 'fixed-requirement' model, which postulates that, once body weight and the level of activity have been specified, the energy requirement of a reference adult can be uniquely determined. It is of course granted that different individuals of the reference type may have different requirements (for reasons to be explained below), but it is believed that for any given individual there is only one level of intake that can maintain equilibrium at given body-weight and activity levels. The heretics, on the other hand, argue that requirement is not fixed for any given person, but can vary intra-individually; that is to say, there is supposed to be a *range* of intake within which a person can maintain his body weight and activity.

The crucial issue is whether or not energy expenditure can vary when body weight and activity remain fixed. If expenditure also remains fixed, then obviously, there is only one level of intake that can maintain equilibrium, and hence requirement can be said to be fixed. On the other hand, if expenditure can vary, then so can equilibrium intake, so require-

---

[2] In practice, the desirable bodyweight is obtained by first taking the average height of adult males in a given community and then applying some norm of weight–height ratio. Note that in doing so, requirement gets related to *desirable* weight but *actual* height. This does not, however, mean that the nutritionists regard height to be a matter of indifference from the point of view of functional capability (as we shall see in Section 5.4). It merely reflects the recognition that height cannot be changed in adult life so that there is little point in basing requirement on a norm of desirable height.

[3] P. V. Sukhatme is the leading exponent of the 'heretic' view.

ment can be said to be variable intra-individually. But how can expenditure vary?

Note that total expenditure of energy is made up of three components: (1) the energy expended in doing essential internal works, called the basal metabolic rate (BMR); (2) energy expended in the performance of external physical activity; and (3) a small component called the 'thermic effect of food' which accounts for the energy expended in absorbing the ingested food. Now the amount of internal work depends partly on age and sex; but it depends mainly on the amount of body mass, because more work is obviously involved in a body of greater mass. It also depends to some extent on body composition, since the metabolic activities of different types of tissues are not the same. The amount of external work, on the other hand, depends on the nature of physical activity, but it also depends partly on body mass, especially in activities involving movement of the body, for the simple reason that more energy has to be expended in moving a greater mass. Thus, the total amount of work done by the body would seem to depend on age, sex, body weight, body composition, and the level of physical activity. But all these parameters are specified at given levels while defining a reference person who, therefore, must be assumed to be doing the same amount of work all the time.

How then does the question of variable expenditure arise? It arises simply from the proposition that the amount of energy expended per unit of work need not remain fixed, so that total expenditure of energy can vary even if the amount of work does not.[4] Underlying this proposition, and the controversies surrounding it, is a deep theoretical dispute on the process of 'energy metabolism', i.e. the biochemical process of converting food into various forms of work done by the body. To clarify where the difference of opinion lies, it is perhaps best to begin with the common core that is not in dispute.

It is generally agreed that, in order to obtain energy in usable form, the body has to convert food through a series of transformations, from one kind of 'energy store' to another. To give a simplified picture, when food is ingested there first occurs what is known as intermediate metabolism. At this stage energy is stored temporarily in several alternative forms, such as glycogen, lipid (fat), and protein. When the body needs energy for work, these intermediate stores are further metabolized into high-energy bonds, like ATP (adenosine tri-phosphate), which are finally

---

[4] Strictly speaking, even the amount of work need not remain constant for a reference person. This is partly due to the fact that, even when physical activity is specified in terms of given tasks, the amount of 'work' (in the thermodynamic sense) may still vary because of subtle differences in the manner of performing a task. This possibility gives rise to the notion of variable 'ergonomic' efficiency. In internal work, too, there is room for variation, e.g. in mechanical work such as sodium pumping and chemical work such as protein turnover, although to what extent such variation does in fact occur is strictly in the realm of speculation (Blaxter 1985).

converted into work.[5] In each of these stages of transformation
(food → intermediate stores → ATP → work) some energy is inevitably
lost, in accordance with the second law of thermodynamics. Therefore
it is necessary to make a distinction between the energy *involved* in a
work and the energy *expended* in doing the work. In an overall accounting, total energy expended (which includes the energy lost in the process
of transformation) is always greater than the energy actually involved in
a work. The proportion of energy that actually gets utilized is called the
'efficiency of energy metabolism'.[6]

All this is common ground between opposing theories. Where the
difference lies is on the issue of whether, and to what extent, the efficiency of energy utilization can vary for a given individual. According to
the establishment view, efficiency remains more or less fixed when body
weight is held constant, as is the case with a reference person. As
mentioned before, the amount of work done by a reference person may
also be assumed to be fixed. Now if a fixed amount of work is done with
a constant efficiency, then obviously, total expenditure of energy must
remain constant. Hence the notion of a fixed requirement.

The heretics accept that the amount of work may remain constant for
a reference person, but they believe that efficiency can vary, so that total
expenditure of energy can vary while equilibrium is maintained.[7] Hence
the notion of variable requirement.

This difference in theoretical perspective leads naturally to different
empirical estimates of energy requirement. Historically, the requirement
of a reference adult has been estimated by two alternative empirical
procedures.[8] The most common procedure, which may be called the
'intake-based approach', is to observe the intakes of a group of healthy
individuals of the reference type over a period of time and to take their
average intake as the standard of requirement. The underlying assumption here is that, since these people are apparently healthy, their intakes
must be matching their requirements. In the alternative procedure,
called the 'factorial approach', total requirement is estimated by adding
up different components of energy expenditure (BMR, physical activity,
the thermic effect of food); in this approach too, the 'average' value of
each component is estimated for a group of reference-type individuals.

The idea of taking 'average' is partly to smooth out random errors of
measurement. But partly also it follows from the recognition that, while

[5] A brief exposition of the process can be found in Flatt (1978).

[6] As it happens, this efficiency is rather surprisingly low—no more than 33% for physical
work and even less for internal work (Blaxter 1985).

[7] Hegstead (1974) and Sims (1976) describe a number of possible ways in which
efficiency can vary.

[8] A brief historical sketch of the evolution of nutritional standards can be found in
Harper (1985).

efficiency, and hence requirement, is fixed for any particular individual, it may vary inter-individually among different individuals of the reference-type. Such variation is deemed to arise from inherent genetic differences in the efficiency of energy utilization.

The heretics, on the other hand, argue that the observed variation in requirement among individuals is due not so much to genotypic variation in efficiency as to phenotypic variation within the same individual over time. In other words, it is suggested that, if different people of the reference-type are seen to be maintaining equilibrium at different levels of intake and expenditure, it is mainly because each of them is occupying a different point within the range of intra-individual variation of requirement.

From this perspective, Sukhatme has gone on to argue that, if one is interested in setting a cut-off point for identifying inadequate intake, it should be set not at the average value, but at the lower end of what he calls the 'range of homeostasis' (which means the range of variation in the requirement of the same individual). He postulates this lower limit to be 2σ below the 'average' (μ), where σ stands for the standard deviation of intra-individual variation in requirement.[9] Using this cut-off point, Sukhatme was able to show that the incidence of nutritional poverty in India was less than half of what Dandekar and Rath (1971) had estimated earlier by using the 'average' norm. By sheer reconceptualization of the requirement norm, the magnitude of poverty was cut down at a stroke from an enormous 46 per cent to a more innocuous-looking 15–20 per cent. Hence the furore over the concept and measurement of requirement.

In order to form a proper judgement on this matter, it is necessary to look very closely at the manner in which Sukhatme reached his remarkable conclusions. I shall try to do this in two steps. First, I shall examine the foundations of Sukhatme's hypothesis that requirement varies intra-individually owing to variable efficiency of energy utilization. Next, I shall explore the logic of using the particular cut-off point $\mu - 2\sigma$, given the hypothesis of variable requirement.[10]

5.3   THE THEORY OF AUTOREGULATORY HOMEOSTASIS

It will be helpful to bear in mind at the outset that the theory from which Sukhatme draws his conclusions is not primarily a theory of requirement

[9] Sukhatme has developed his argument through a series of papers: see Sukhatme (1977a, 1978, 1982a, 1982b), Sukhatme and Margen (1982) and Sukhatme and Narain (1982), among others.

[10] Perhaps I should mention that I have found Sukhatme's style of reasoning eminently obscure and his arguments often difficult to follow. What is presented below is a strictly personal interpretation of what I believe to be the logical core that lies beneath his writings.

at all: it is a theory of how long-term energy balance is maintained by free-living healthy individuals, and is called the theory of autoregulatory homeostasis.

One of the interesting facts of life which has intrigued applied nutritionists over the years is the way so many people manage to keep body weight within a fairly narrow range even in the developed world, where energy intake is practically unconstrained by the limitations of purchasing power (James 1985). Various explanations have been offered to account for this remarkable phenomenon of weight homeostasis. Some nutritionists consider physiological mechanisms of appetite control to be the principal regulatory system (James 1985). Many othersbelieve that the answer lies in conscious control of energy expenditure (Beaton 1984). Alternatively, Payne and Dugdale (1977) have postulated an internal feedback mechanism whereby random fluctuations in intake and expenditure lead to transient and self-correcting changes in body weight. But the most relevant in our present context is the old idea of 'luxusconsumption', which has recently been revived by Miller *et al.* (1967), Sims (1976), and others, by the name of 'dietary-induced thermogenesis' (DIT). According to this hypothesis, bodyweight is maintained by burning off excess calories i.e., by producing more heat (thermogenesis) than usual. Presumably, the opposite occurs when intake is in deficit. Such variation in thermogenesis is simply the mirror image of variation in the efficiency of energy utilization.

Sukhatme and Margen (1982) endorse the 'thermogenesis' view that weight homeostasis is maintained through variation of efficiency, but in doing so they go one step further. They postulate a model to describe the manner in which efficiency varies over time. The essence of the model can be stated in the form of the following proposition.

Efficiency of energy utilization varies over time in an autocorrelated manner. If a healthy person is economically or otherwise unconstrained in his intake of calories, and if he remains engaged at a fixed level of activity while maintaining his body weight, then his intake will also be seen to vary over time in an autocorrelated manner.

Formally, let I' denote the intake on any day t consumed by an unconstrained healthy person maintaining body weight and engaged in fixed activity. Then, according to this theory, the temporal pattern of intakes can be shown by the following equation:[11]

$$I'_t = \rho \, I'_{t-1} + e_t \qquad\qquad (1)$$

[11] There seems to exist a good deal of confusion as to how Sukhatme actually deduced this equation. A brief account is given in the Appendix of what I believe to be the basis of this deduction.

where ρ is the co-efficient of first-order autocorrelation and e_t is a random error.

Recall that the intake of a healthy person (maintaining body weight and activity) is by definition equal to his requirement. Therefore equation (1) can also be interpreted as stating that the energy requirement of a person is not fixed, but varies from day to day in an autocorrelated manner.

Now the phenomenon of autocorrelation has three very important implications.

1 An autocorrelated variable is generated by a stochastic stationary distribution, i.e. a distribution with constant mean and variance. This implies that we cannot exactly predict what the value of I'_t will be on any particular day, but we know that the distribution from which it comes will remain unchanged, and in particular will have a constant mean, over time. Because of the constancy of mean, it can be expected that, if a large number of observations are taken over time, the observed average of I'_t will approach the theoretical mean μ of the distribution. But what does μ stand for? Since variation in I'_t arises solely from variation in efficiency (with body weight and activity being fixed, and no constraint operating on the intake of calories), μ must stand for the level of intake and expenditure based on average efficiency. One can therefore say that the observed average intake of a healthy individual maintaining body weight and engaged in a fixed level of activity will be equal to the theoretical average expenditure (based on average efficiency). This is the theory of autoregulatory homeostatis. The idea of autoregulation consists in the fact that, although efficiency varies from day to day, it does so in an autoregulated manner so as to keep average intake equal to average expenditure. We can thus see how autocorrelation—a statistical concept—implies autoregulation—a physiological concept.[12]

2 Autocorrelation also implies that the variance of the mean of intakes I'_t does not decline rapidly to zero as the period over which the mean is taken is increased. Therefore if mean is taken over a relatively short period, say a week, then the mean intake will have a significantly non-zero variance. In other words, the weekly mean intake will not as a rule be equal to μ, the 'true' mean. From Edholm et al.'s (1970) data, Sukhatme has estimated that the coefficient of variation of weekly mean is in the order of 12–15 per cent. Recalling that intake equals requirement for the reference-type people, one could therefore say that

[12] This inference has at times met with considerable scepticism; see e.g. Dandekar (1982) and Waterlow (1985a). However, very often the source of scepticism is a misunderstanding about the nature of the argument. For example, Dandekar (1982) has argued that, if intakes are autocorrelated because of extraneous constraints, it would not indicate autoregulation. This is of course true, but beside the point. It has not been suggested that *any* autocorrelation implies autoregulation: only that autocorrelation is relevant which is observed in the intakes of reference-type people who have an unconstrained access to food intake.

requirement varies intra-individually with a coefficient of variation of about 12–15 per cent (when the reference period is a short span of time, such as a week).

3   The variation of intake in Edholm's data is due apparently to both inter- and intra-individual variation. But when the data were subjected to hierachical analysis of variance, taking note of autocorrelation in time series, it was found that most of the observed variation was actually due to intra-variation. This is the basis of Sukhatme's contention that intra-individual (or phenotypic) variation overwhelms any truly inter-individual (or genotypic) variation. In physiological terms, it means that, if requirements are found to vary in a population of reference-type individuals, it is not because each has a fixed but mutually different level of metabolic efficiency (as assumed in the establishment view), but because each happens to occupy a different point in the range of intra-individual variation at the time of enquiry.

Of these three implications of autocorrelation, the first one, deducing the theory of autoregulatory homeostasis, constitutes the specific contribution of Sukhatme and Margen in the theory of weight regulation by healthy unconstrained individuals. Their theory can also be described as the model of *stochastic regulation*, to denote the idea that body weight is regulated over time through stochastic variation of efficiency. The last two implications are by-products of this theory, which Sukhatme utilizes in the process of justifying his cut-off point of $\mu - 2\sigma$ in the debate over assessment of undernutrition. I should, however, point out at this stage that there are really two Sukhatmes when it comes to justifying $\mu - 2\sigma$: I shall refer to them as mark I and mark II versions. The mark I version follows straight from the model of stochastic regulation just described; but the mark II version virtually abandons this model and embraces what may be called the model of adaptive regulation. This mutation is defended on the ground that the latter model follows from the former, but as we shall see, this is not quite so.[13]

5.3.1   Mark I rationale of $\mu - 2\sigma$: stochastic regulation

In the conventional approach, a person is identified as undernourished if his mean intake (m) over a sample period (say, a week) falls short of some norm of average requirement (μ), i.e. if $m < \mu$. But this inequality can be shown to be a poor criterion of undernutrition if the theory of stochastic regulation is accepted. Recall that μ is obtained in practice from *inter*-individual average of requirements over a sample period. But

[13]   Mark I is of chronologically earlier vintage, being most visible in the publications of 1977 and 1978. Mark II is more a product of the 1980s, developed largely in response to the criticisms of mark I.

according to the third implication of autocorrelation mentioned above, these inter-individual differences are really the reflection of underlying intra-individual variation. Therefore μ can be taken to be an estimate of intra-individual average requirement over the long term.[14] Accordingly, the inequality $m < \mu$ can be interpreted as a person's weekly intake falling below his long-term requirement. Now we know from the second implication of autocorrelation that the weekly intake of a healthy unconstrained person may easily deviate from his long-term requirement. Therefore, it will be wrong to treat everyone whose m is less than μ as undernourished.

One really has to distinguish between two separate cases that may generate the inequality $m < \mu$: (1) the case of unconstrained healthy people eating less in the sample period simply because their requirement has fallen below μ in the normal course of intra-individual variation; and (2) the less fortunate case where the inequality reflects some constraint on intake. The first case is evidently not one of undernutrition; for, although the observed intake is less than μ, the 'expected' intake over the long term will be equal to μ (by the first implication of autocorrelation). In the words of Sukhatme, the variation in intake is in 'statistical control'. However, in the second case, where the intake is constrained, there is a possibility of failure in 'statistical control'; i.e., 'expected' intake may turn out to be less than μ. Only such cases should be treated as undernutrition.[15] We therefore need a criterion for determining who are and who are not in 'statistical control' of intake variation over time. But how can we find such a criterion?

Sukhatme's strategy was to look for a characteristic feature of the intake of healthy unconstrained people—a feature that could be used as a criterion for distinguishing the well-nourished people from the undernourished ones. The particular feature that he used for this purpose was the 'range of homeostasis', i.e. the range of variation, within which the intake of a healthy person can be expected to lie. As it happens, 95 per cent of the healthy people can be expected to have intake within the range $\mu \pm 2\sigma$, assuming that efficiency varies as a normal distribution. If an observed intake falls outside this range, one can be reasonably confident that it is not the intake of a healthy person. Thus, argues Sukhatme (1978: 1383), 'Clearly, most individuals in health in the framework of this model will have an intake between $\mu \pm 2\sigma$. It follows that the proportion of individuals below the lower critical limit may be taken to represent the estimate of the incidence of undernutrition.' This is the mark I rationale for using $\mu - 2\sigma$ as the criterion of undernutrition.

---

[14] Assuming of course that the distribution of requirements is the same for everyone.

[15] 'Clearly, undernutrition must be defined as the failure of the process to be in statistical control' (Sukhatme 1978: 1383).

There is, however, a flaw in this logic. In order to claim that the incidence of undernutrition is to be estimated as the proportion of people whose intake falls short of $\mu - 2\sigma$, it must be established that *everyone* with intake in the range of homeostasis is well nourished. But Sukhatme's premiss (the first proposition in the quotation above) does not ensure this: it only ensures that if a person is healthy his intake will lie in the range $\mu \pm 2\sigma$. From this it does not follow that anyone who has intake within this range is necessarily healthy. For example, if some extraneous constraint on intake rather than variable efficiency brings down someone's intake in the sample period below μ (albeit above $\mu - 2\sigma$), and if the nature of the constraint is such that it is going to persist over time, then clearly, average intake will not equal μ even in the long run. Such people must be considered undernourished by Sukhatme's own criterion, viz. the failure of 'statistical control'. Consequently, the cut-off point of $\mu - 2\sigma$ will in general lead to an underestimate of total undernutrition.

The mistake lies basically in the failure to see that to have one's intake within the range of homeostasis is only a *necessary* condition for being well nourished: it is by no means a *sufficient* condition. Yet it is sufficiency that is needed to justify the claim that everyone with intake above $\mu - 2\sigma$ should be considered well nourished. The failure of 'mark I' justification is thus seen to lie in an elementary confusion between 'necessity' and 'sufficiency'.

Elementary as it is, this flaw in logic has seldom been noticed, perhaps because Sukhatme's rationale for advocating $\mu - 2\sigma$ has often been misunderstood by friends and foes alike.[16] As a result of this misunderstanding, his proposals have usually been indicted for the wrong reasons. In particular, instead of being criticized for making a logical mistake, he has been attacked for allegedly holding a socially reprehensible kind of value judgement.

One strand of such misguided critique has arisen from the mistaken belief that the cut-off point of $\mu - 2\sigma$ was intended to take care of the problem of *inter*-individual variation in requirement.[17] The argument is, briefly, as follows.

When requirement varies from person to person, the choice of any single cut-off point will give rise to two opposite kinds of errors. Some

---

[16] One exception is Mehta (1982: 1935).

[17] Dandekar (1981: 1248), for one, seems to commit this error. In all fairness, however, it ought to be pointed out that Sukhatme himself sowed the seeds of confusion when he initially described σ to be composed of both inter- and intra-variation (Sukhatme 1978: 1383). Later, however, in response to the criticisms of Dandekar (1981), Krishnaji (1981), and others, he tried to salvage the matter by invoking the third implication of autocorrelation mentioned above, which states that apparent inter-variation is due almost entirely to intra-variation, so that all of σ could be taken to reflect intra-variation (Sukhatme 1981a: 1321 or 1981b: 1035).

people whose intake is less than the cut-off point but greater than their respective requirements will be wrongly classified as undernourished (type I error); on the other hand, some people whose intake is greater than the chosen point but less than their respective requirements will be wrongly classified as well nourished (type II error). Clearly, there is a trade-off between the two types of error; a cut-off point that reduces one type of error inevitably raises the other. Therefore the choice of a cut-off point must depend on the relative importance one wishes to attach to avoiding the two types of error. If one's value judgement were such as to attach a high premium on capturing the truly undernourished people, one would use a high cut-off point even though it meant wrongly counting some well-nourished people as undernourished. On the other hand, the choice of a low cut-off point like $\mu - 2\sigma$ would imply a strong desire to avoid calling a person undernourished when he is not so, even though it raises the probability that we shall fail to call a person under-nourished when he is so. The value judgement implicit in this latter choice does seem to betray a lack of social concern for the problem of undernutrition. And Sukhatme has been accused of this sin because of his advocacy of $\mu - 2\sigma$; but quite unjustly so, because his choice is based not on the logic of inter-individual variation but that of *intra*-individual variation in requirement.[18]

But even when it has been understood that intra-individual variation is what Sukhatme is concerned with, the exact rationale behind $\mu - 2\sigma$ has not always been correctly understood. For example, Dandekar (1981), writing in a critical vein, and Srinivasan (1981), taking a sympathetic view, have both interpreted Sukhatme to be posing the problem in the framework of a statistical test of hypothesis. They conceive the problem as follows: given that a person's weekly intake (m) varies over time, how can we judge whether or not his long-term average intake $\overline{m}$ is equal to his requirement μ? The usual statistical procedure is to assume that $\overline{m}$ is in fact equal to μ, and to reject this hypothesis only if the probability of its being correct is very low. Now the probability of its being correct will be as low as 5 per cent or less if m happens to be below 'μ minus two standard deviations' (assuming that intake is normally distributed). Therefore, those with intake below this critical limit could be treated as undernourished. It is in this way that the cut-off point of $\mu - 2\sigma$ is supposed to have been derived.

[18] However, this criticism does apply to an earlier incarnation of Sukhatme when σ actually referred to *inter*-individual variation among reference individuals (Sukhatme 1961). Curiously, he now refers to this earlier work too as implicitly using the notion of *intra*-variability (Sukhatme 1982b: 14–16). This is strange, because the value of σ was derived in 1961 entirely from the differences in requirements arising from activity differences among individuals. It had nothing to do with *intra*-individual variation, or even with genotypic *inter*-individual variation owing to different efficiencies of energy utilization. Why, nevertheless, Sukhatme likes to hark back to bygone days to conjure up a thematic continuity that does not exist remains a source of abiding mystery.

Once this interpretation is accepted, it is not difficult to see how the criticism of 'reprehensible value judgement' becomes a natural one to make. The test-of-hypothesis framework starts with the premiss that there is no undernutrition (i.e. that $\overline{m} = \mu$), and rejects it only if the probability of its being true is extremely small. This means, as Dandekar (1981:1248) rightly points out, that 'we shall not accept the existence of undernutrition unless the evidence is overwhelming'. This would indeed appear to be a rather odd kind of value judgement, especially when one notes the deep social concern with the problem of undernutrition that motivated the search for cut-off points in the first place.

But we do not believe that Sukhatme was using the test-of-hypothesis framework. There are at least two reasons for this belief. First, in this framework the critical limit of 'μ minus two standard deviations' must be derived by using the standard deviation of *intake distribution*, whereas the entity σ in Sukhatme's criterion of $\mu - 2\sigma$ refers to the standard deviation of *requirement distribution*. It is true of course that σ will also stand for the standard deviation of intake of the healthy unconstrained people, but this is not true for everyone. For those whose intake is somehow constrained, σ will in general be different from the standard deviation of intake. Thus, the criterion $\mu - 2\sigma$ does not emerge from the test-of-hypothesis framework.[19]

Second, the problem of variable requirement, which is so central to Sukhatme's concern, is not relevant to this framework at all. Everyone could have the same requirement Θ, constant over time, and yet if intake is based on a short sample period it will be necessary to ask whether $\overline{m}$ can be expected to equal Θ, knowing only the sample observation m. In short, the test-of-hypothesis framework is essentially concerned with the general problem that intake may vary over time for a variety of reasons, so that one week's data may not reveal the average intake of anyone; whereas Sukhatme's concern lies in the specific case that variation in efficiency will create a divergence between weekly intake and long-term requirement of healthy unconstrained people. His problem was to ensure that such people do not get counted as undernourished. That is why he was looking for a distinguishing feature of healthy people. He thought he had found one in the range of homeostasis ($\mu \pm 2\sigma$), and used the lower limit to set apart the well-nourished people from the under-nourished ones.

As we have seen, this was a mistake; but it has to be seen for what it is—a logical error rather than a consequence of holding an unappealing value judgement. The error consisted in thinking that a necessary condition for being a healthy person could be used as a sufficient condition

---

[19] Srinivasan (1981: 7) recognizes that σ will not be appropriate for everyone, but he does not apparently see this as rendering the 'test-of-hypothesis' framework an incorrect interpretation of Sukhatme.

for identifying healthy people. Specifically, the error lay in the failure to see that, if the theory of autoregulatory homeostasis is accepted, then it would indeed follow that the intake of a healthy person would vary within the range $\mu \pm 2\sigma$; but it would not follow that *anyone* whose intake lies above $\mu - 2\sigma$ is healthy.[20]

At this point enters the mark II version. Sukhatme brings in the notion of 'adaptation' to justify the proposition that *everyone* with intake above $\mu - 2\sigma$ should indeed be considered well nourished.

5.3.2   Mark II rationale of $\mu - 2\sigma$: adaptive regulation

Before coming to the structure of this argument, it is necessary to make a few remarks about the concept of adaptation. This is one of the most elusive concepts in the whole of nutrition science, as different people seem to use it to mean quite different things.[21] It is, therefore, essential to be completely clear about the sense in which the word 'adaptation' is used in the present context.

In the broadest possible sense, adaptation can be described simply as an organism's strategy to survive in response to an adverse environment, for example a reduction in food intake. In this general sense, adaptation may take various forms covering time spans of varying lengths. It may, for example, involve long-term *genetic adaptation* through the Darwinian process of natural selection in which only the genotypes less demanding in their energy requirement come to survive. But individuals can also adapt in their own life-span (*phenotypic adaptation*). This may again involve a relatively long-term somatic adaptation in which the rate of growth of body is reduced in response to lower food intake (such adaptation is discussed in Section 5.4), or it may involve fairly short-term responses. These short-term responses may again be of at least three kinds, involving adjustment of physical activity, body weight (and composition), or efficiency of energy utilization.

While all these adaptive mechanisms help an organism to survive in a stressful situation, not all of them are altogether costless in terms of various functional capabilities. There is in fact a great deal of controversy over which of these mechanisms, if any, enables an organism to adapt

[20] Besides this logical error, there is also the problem that the theory of autoregulation may have to be abandoned in any case in the light of recent scientific evidence. For example, the findings of Rand *et al.* (1985) cast serious doubt on the hypothesis of autoregressive variation in both protein and energy requirement. Also, Garby and his colleagues have found that the energy expenditure of subjects at fixed levels of intake and activity remains remarkably constant over time, which contradicts the hypothesis that efficiency varies spontaneously within a stochastic distribution (Garby *et al.* 1984; Garby and Lammert 1984).

[21] A whole conference devoted to clarifying the concept and mechanisms of *Nutritional Adaptations in Man* (Blaxter and Waterlow 1985) has failed to produce a generally agreed definition. Compare the introduction and postscript written by Waterlow (1985*a*, 1985*b*).

in a functionally costless manner, and if so within what limits. Sukhatme proposes that variation in efficiency offers an avenue for costless adaptation to low food intake (up to a point). The idea is that as intake is reduced the body uses the available energy more efficiently than before, i.e. wastes less energy in the process of metabolism, so as to maintain the 'effective' availability of calories. It is this specific notion of adaptation that Sukhatme invokes in defence of his mark II rationale. But a great deal of needless controversy has arisen from the failure of some of his critics to appreciate that his argument is based exclusively on pure adaptation in efficiency, unaccompanied by any other adaptive mechanism.

Thus, Gopalan (1983a) bases his critique on the wrong premiss that a person permanently subsisting at the lower end of Sukhatme's range of adaptation would have exhausted all adaptive possibilities. In particular, he believes that body weight will have been reduced to such a low level that, unlike a healthy person, an 'adapted' person will no longer be able to take further advantage of the important regulatory mechanism of adjustment in body weight when faced with temporary shortfall in intake. He further argues that such adaptation 'may help the victim to avoid the catastrophe of death, but . . . will not help him to live a normal life of activity and productivity' (p. 598). Not surprisingly, he considers the idea of calling such people well nourished an unacceptable 'policy of brinkmanship'.

But this criticism is off the mark. It is based on the presumption that a person who adapts at Sukhatme's reduced intake level of $\mu - 2\sigma$ does so by reducing his body size. But reduction of body size cannot be the adaptive mechanism that Sukhatme has in mind, and it is not difficult to see why. Recall that Sukhatme's concern is to find the energy requirement of a reference adult who is maintaining given levels of body weight and activity. And the level of body weight he takes as given is precisely the one that is used by his critics. If that agreed level of body weight is to be maintained, then obviously, he cannot be allowing for any adaptation in body weight.[22]

Perhaps the confusion arises from Sukhatme's show of solidarity with Seckler's 'small but healthy' hypothesis (which I discuss in Section 5.4). But it should be noted in the first place that even Seckler's hypothesis is not concerned with adaptive changes of body weight in a person's adult life: it has to do with adaptation in the rate of growth among children. Second, while it is true that Sukhatme combines Seckler's hypothesis with his own to present a grand vision of what he calls 'the process view of nutrition', his own methodology for the measurement of

[22] The failure to see this point completely misleads Zurbrigg (1983), who launches a rather spiteful ideological critique from the premise that Sukhatme's theory was all about reducing requirement because reduction in body weight did not matter.

undernutrition does not allow for Seckler's hypothesis. Thus in Sukhatme's own estimates of undernutrition, the 'conversion factors' between adults and children were calculated on the basis of the same requirement norms for children that everybody else used for India, instead of being scaled down to take note of adaptation in physical growth *à la* Seckler.

In fact, adaptation in body size plays no role in Sukhatme's mark II rationale for $\mu - 2\sigma$. The rationale derives solely from adaptation in efficiency, using the following kind of argument.

If efficiency increases adaptively as food intake is decreased, then the body can do the same amount of 'work' as before without drawing upon energy stores. This will enable a 'reference' person to maintain body weight and activity within a range of energy intake. Accordingly, no single intake can serve as *the* requirement of a reference person. In fact, he could be said to be meeting his requirement at any intake within the 'range of adaptation'. Only when intake falls below the range of adaptation can a person be said to be undernourished. As Sukhatme (1982*b*: 38) explains, 'However, a point is reached in the intake of food below which BMR gets depressed and the body is forced to part with its fat in favour of the vital need to maintain body heat. This is the point of minimum physiological requirement or clinical undernutrition.' Then he suggests that the range of adaptation is given by $\mu \pm 2\sigma$, which he had earlier described as the range of autoregulation, and hence argues that $\mu - 2\sigma$ is the appropriate cut-off point for measuring undernutrition.

Now the description of $\mu \pm 2\sigma$ as the range of adaptation, and not merely as the range of autoregulation, is a particularly significant departure. We have seen that in the autoregulation framework one could only say that the intake of healthy people would fall within the range of $\mu \pm 2\sigma$. One could not assert the converse, i.e. that an intake above $\mu - 2\sigma$ was sufficient for a person to be healthy, and that is what created a logical problem in accepting $\mu - 2\sigma$ as the cut-off point. But it is different if $\mu \pm 2\sigma$ is viewed as the range of adaptation. For now one can assert that, if a man is given any intake within this range, his efficiency will adapt accordingly to bring expenditure into equality with his intake without any effect on body weight and activity. If that is so, then everyone with intake (m) above $\mu - 2\sigma$ must be considered adequately nourished.[23] In other words, the inequality $m > \mu - 2\sigma$ is now both necessary and sufficient for a person to be well nourished. The logical flaw in the mark I rationale thus seems to be neatly avoided in the mark II version.

But this achievement is more apparent than real. It is true of course that, if $\mu - 2\sigma$ could be established as the limit of adaptation, it would

[23] 'It follows that a person *must* be considered in energy balance *whenever* his intake falls within homeostatic limits of balance' (Sukhatme, 1982*b*: 39; emphasis added).

indeed be the correct cut-off point. But as we have noted, $\mu \pm 2\sigma$ was originally described as the 'range of autoregulation', i.e. the range within which the intake of a healthy unconstrained person can be expected to lie. In contrast, the 'range of adaptation' refers to a range within which anyone can costlessly adapt, even if his intake is constrained to deviate from the average. One is obviously dealing here with two different phenomena, and there is no apparent reason why the two ranges should coincide. But Sukhatme assumes that the two ranges are exactly the same; and in doing so, he takes recourse to the argument that autoregulation implies adaptation.[24] I shall argue that autoregulation does not imply adaptation and that, a fortiori, the range of autoregulation cannot be identified with the range of adaptation.

Sukhatme makes the transition from autoregulation to adaptation by focusing on the fact that both phenomena are characterized by a common mechanism: namely, variation in the efficiency of energy utilization. But this transition is not logically valid, because the qualitative nature of 'efficiency variation' is not the same in the two cases. In particular, the causal relationships between intake and efficiency are exactly the opposite. In autoregulation, 'a healthy individual varies his or her intake, increasing it when wastage is larger and decreasing it when it is lower' (Sukhatme and Margen 1982:109); in other words, causation runs from efficiency to intake. But in adaptation the line of causation is completely reversed: 'When total energy is less, the body wastes less, thus using the intake with greater efficiency. As intake increases, wastage also increases and the energy is used with decreased efficiency' (Sukhatme 1982b: 38); in other words, causation runs from intake to efficiency. The contrast is therefore obvious: in autoregulation efficiency varies in a spontaneous manner and intake merely follows suit, whereas adaptation is by definition a phenomenon in which variation in efficiency is induced by prior variation in intake.

This distinction between 'spontaneous' and 'induced' variation in efficiency is crucial for our argument, so let us see more closely how the model of autoregulation is based solely on the notion of spontaneity. In describing this model, Sukhatme and Margen repeatedly remind us that efficiency varies 'as a matter of course' within a stochastic stationary distribution. This leads to corresponding variation in requirement, so that in the case of an unconstrained person 'intake is regulated in autoregressive manner to meet his needs' (Sukhatme 1981a:1318; emphasis added). The causation thus runs from variation of efficiency to change of requirement and finally to intake ('to meet his needs'). It all starts with prior spontaneous variation in efficiency as a stochastic process.

---

[24] 'It is apparently the autoregressive mechanism in daily expenditure in maintaining bodyweight which enables a man to adapt his requirement to intakes without affecting the net energy needed for maintenance and physical activity' (Sukhatme 1982b: 39).

The idea of spontaneous variation comes out most clearly when one considers the analogy drawn by Sukhatme and Margen (1978, 1982) between their models for energy and protein. They found autocorrelation in both models and claimed that these are similar biological phenomena. It is, however, significant to note that intake was kept *fixed* in the protein model, and yet expenditure varied in an autocorrelated manner presumably because of similar variation in the efficiency of protein absorption. There was thus no scope for efficiency to vary in response to intake. If the analogy is to be retained, one must then admit that efficiency of energy utilization varies in a spontaneous manner: intake merely follows suit when it is free to vary (see Mehta 1982: 1335).

Indeed, unless one assumes that spontaneous variation in efficiency is the driving force, it becomes impossible to explain why intake *must* be autocorrelated for free-living healthy individuals. If efficiency merely responded to intake, a healthy person could vary his intake in any way he liked (within limits of course) and still maintain weight homeostasis. Therefore, instead of observing that 'low intake is followed by a low intake and high intake followed by a high intake' (Sukhatme 1981*a*: 1319), one could as well observe low intake being followed by high intake, and vice versa. It is only because efficiency is supposed to vary spontaneously within a stochastic stationary distribution and intake is supposed to follow suit that intake must vary in a similar manner and exhibit autocorrelation in its time series.

It is thus clear that autoregulation and adaptation envisage two entirely opposite lines of causation between intake and efficiency. Sukhatme, however, tends to ignore this fact. He keeps on changing direction in the mid-course and moves back and forth along the opposite lines of causation, while giving the impression of talking about the same thing.[25] But this impression is misleading, because 'induced' and 'spontaneous' variation in efficiency cannot be the same biological phenomenon.

Autoregulation, therefore, cannot imply adaptation, which means that the range of adaptation cannot be equated with the range of autoregulatory homeostasis. It follows that Sukhatme's mark II rationale for $\mu - 2\sigma$ remains unconvincing so long as the value of $\mu - 2\sigma$ is derived from the model of autoregulation. If adaptation is to be the rationale for lowering the norm of energy requirement, then this norm must be

---

[25] Here is an interesting example. In explaining the autoregressive model, Sukhatme writes, '[1] On current evidence this means that intake in man will vary as a matter of course . . . in a manner that is self-regulated . . . [2] It implies that when intake is low the body uses energy more efficiently . . . [3] In other words the body adapts requirement to intake by varying the efficiency of utilization' (Sukhatme 1981*a*: 1319; numbering added). Note the mode of transition: the first part is clearly about autoregulation; in the second part causation gets blurred and gives way to 'association'; then, hinging on this association, causation is reversed in the final part.

derived from independent evidence on the limits of adaptation. So, what is the evidence on this?

5.3.3 Is there adaptation in energy efficiency?

The idea that efficiency of utilization can adapt to different levels of intake is not a novel one; nor is it claimed to exist for energy alone. Several nutrients such as protein and iron are known to possess this attribute. In fact, the established practice of calculating protein requirement is based on this notion. It is accepted that there exists a 'safe range' of intake within which the effective absorption of protein is maintained at a constant level by varying the rate of utilization. Accordingly, the lower limit of the range is defined as the minimum protein requirement; and it is this 'minimum' rather than 'average' requirement that is used to judge whether a person consumes adequate protein or not (Scrimshaw and Young 1978; Munro 1985; FAO/WHO/UNU 1985).[26]

The idea of 'adaptation' to a range of energy intake is an exactly analogous one, and so is the plea to use the 'minimum' rather than the 'average' requirement as the cut-off point. The problem, however, is that the biological evidence on adaptation is not as clear-cut in the case of energy as in the case of nutrients such as protein or iron. As a result, the paradigm of 'fixed' energy requirement still holds sway over much of nutrition profession, although the weight of discordant notes cannot be ignored.

There is a vast literature on the subject and we cannot attempt to review it here.[27] However, several salient features of the accumulating evidence may be pointed out.

The adaptationists draw evidence from both cross-sectional and longitudinal studies. There is by now a considerable body of cross-sectional evidence to show that people at different levels of habitual intakes can maintain similar body weight while remaining engaged in apparently similar activities. In fact, as high as twofold range in the variation of energy intake is quite common (Rose and Williams 1961; Widdowson 1962; Edmundson 1977, 1979). This could be interpreted as an *a priori*

---

[26] It is, however, recognized that the 'minimum' requirement may vary from person to person. Accordingly, the 'recommended' protein allowance for population groups is set at two standard deviations above the average of 'minimum' requirements, with a view to providing adequate protein for as many people as possible, even if it means overproviding for some of them in the process.

[27] Several useful reviews have come out in the recent years, some more dismissive of the adaptationist view than others. The comprehensive reviews of James and Shetty (1982) and Norgan (1983) belong to the dismissive category, while that of Apfelbaum (1978) is much more sympathetic. Somewhat less comprehensive reviews can be found in Grande (1964), Durnin (1979), Edmundson (1980), Garrow (1978a) and D. S. Miller (1975). See also Srinivasan (1983b) and Dasgupta and Ray (1990).

evidence that people can adapt to low food intake by using energy more efficiently.

But there are at least three problems with this interpretation: (1) 'apparently similar' activities may conceal important differences in energy expenditure, specially in the so-called 'discretionary' (leisure-time) activities; (2) the reported 'low intakes' may not really be low: for example, when some of the 'reportedly' low-intake subjects were experimentally fed their 'reported' diet, most of them were found to be losing weight (Ashworth 1968; Durnin 1979); (3) most importantly, the observed inter-individual differences may simply reflect genotypic differences in the efficiency of energy utilization between individuals, rather than phenotypic adaptation within the same individual.

The last argument is sometimes countered by invoking Sukhatme's finding that 'apparent' inter-individual variation can be ascribed almost entirely to intra-individual variation. But this is just a misapplication of an argument in the wrong context. Sukhatme's argument referred to short-run variations in intake and to the implication of autocorrelation in such variations around the mean level; it does not obviously apply to the case of long-term 'habitual' intakes with which these cross-sectional studies are concerned. Edmundson, whose own studies are relatively free from the first two problems mentioned above, is keenly aware of the third, and readily admits that one cannot be sure how much of intake variation is due to genotypic differences and how much, if any, to genuine phenotypic adaptation (Edmundson 1980).

In fact, this difficulty of disentangling the phenotypic from the genotypic variation is inherent in all cross-sectional studies (Prentice 1984). What one really needs is longitudinal evidence on the same person experiencing deviation from habitual intakes. A striking evidence of this kind was provided long ago by Neumann (1902), who found over a period of two years that he could increase his intake by as much as 800 calories per day without significant change of body weight. He described this phenomenon as 'luxusconsumption', and provided probably the first scientific evidence that human efficiency of energy utilization can adapt to a wide range of intake.

But subsequent laboratory experiments, under more controlled conditions and covering a larger sample of subjects, have failed to provide unambiguously corroborative evidence. In this respect, one can draw upon both underfeeding and overfeeding experiments, the principal findings of which may be summarized as follows.[28] (1) Under severe caloric restriction, BMR per kilogram of body mass decreases, thus showing an

[28] Some of the best-known underfeeding experiments are reported in Benedict et al. (1919), Keys et al. (1950), Grande et al. (1958), and Apfelbaum et al. (1971). Among the overfeeding experiments, one may mention inter alia Miller et al. (1967), Apfelbaum et al. (1971), Sims (1976), and Norgan and Durnin (1980).

increase in the efficiency of energy utilization; but it is necessarily accompanied by a reduction in body mass as well. (2) The findings of overfeeding experiments are more controversial: not all experiments show that weight gain can be contained by adaptive decrease in efficiency (i.e. through 'dietary-induced thermogenesis'). Even when thermogenesis occurs, it seems to be triggered only after some weight gain has taken place.

There is thus some evidence to show that phenotypic adaptation of a kind may take place in the efficiency of energy utilization, but it seems almost always to be accompanied by alteration of body weight. This is not, therefore, the kind of adaptation that is relevant for determining the intra-individual range of requirement, for the latter ought to be based on a given level of body weight. What is relevant for this purpose is 'pure' adaptation in efficiency, i.e. adaptation that occurs without any change of body weight. But the existing evidence does not indicate that such adaptation is possible.

It should, however, be borne in mind that in all these experiments calorie intake was either severely reduced or grossly blown up. The possibility has not, therefore, been ruled out that at moderate levels of deviation 'pure' adaptation in efficiency may still occur.[29] Future experiments may throw light on this possibility; but at present there is no scientific basis for arguing that a significant scope for 'pure adaptation' exists, far less for making a quantitative assessment of the limits of adaptation.

Thus, the hypothesis of intra-individual adaptation in requirement is not yet substantiated by scientific evidence, although the possibility cannot be altogether ruled out. It is, therefore, fair to conclude that Sukhatme's advocacy of $\mu - 2\sigma$ cannot be justified in the light of current scientific evidence.

However, this does not mean that we can happily return to the use of the 'average requirement' as the cut-off norm. I have noted that there is a good deal of evidence in support of inter-individual variation in requirement; and we have also seen that in the presence of inter-individual variation the use of 'average' gives rise to two opposite kinds of errors, which may or may not cancel each other out. Whether to use the 'average' or some other norm becomes a matter of value judgement in this case. A value-neutral way of tackling this problem would be to shun the 'cut-off point approach' altogether and use instead a joint distribution of intake and requirement. Armed with this distribution, one can determine the proportion of people whose intake is actually less than

[29] Rand et al. (1985) have produced evidence which shows that, even at moderate levels of deviation, adaptive thermogenesis does not seem to operate without an accompanying change in body weight. But as the authors point out, there are problems of interpretation. One difficulty is that the levels of physical activity were not monitored, which makes it difficult to ascertain if the failure to maintain weight was due to failure of thermogenesis or to alteration in activity.

their respective requirements. Unfortunately, however, there are serious informational constraints in the practical application of this approach.[30]

5.4   PHYSICAL GROWTH AND ANTHROPOMETRIC STATUS: THE 'SMALL BUT HEALTHY' HYPOTHESIS

The debate to be reviewed in this section relates to the measurement of undernutrition among children by the anthropometric method. In this method, observed measurements of body size (as measured by height, weight, etc.) are compared with what are considered to be 'desirable standards'. If the observed measurement falls short of the standard, the child is presumed to be undernourished. The debate is about how to specify the standards of comparison. This is analogous to the debate reviewed earlier, in which the question was how to specify the standard of comparison while judging whether or not observed intake is adequate. And as in that debate, here too there is a deep division between a widely held 'establishment' view, dubbed the 'genetic potential' theory, and a small but influential group expounding a 'heretic' view.

The difference between these views may be best clarified by referring to the actual practice of how 'desirable standards' are determined in the traditional approach. This is done by observing the growth curves of well-nourished children growing normally in the developed world. These curves are then used to determine desirable rates of growth, as well as optimal anthropometric standards, for application in the rest of the world. The underlying principle is as follows: since the children in the reference group are unhindered by nutritional deprivation and hence are enjoying the maximal growth permitted by their genetic potential, they constitute an ideal standard against which to judge the nutritional adequacy of all other groups. Two assumptions are implicitly made in this procedure: (1) there is no difference in the genetic potential of different races in the world; and (2) anything less than the achievement of full genetic potential must be deemed to constitute 'inadequate' nutrition.

The first assumption is based on fairly strong empirical grounds, as can be seen from the recent reviews by Martorell (1984) and D.F. Roberts (1985). Numerous studies have shown, for example, that children in poor developing countries can in general grow at the Western rates if adequate intake and environmental hygiene can be ensured. The assumption of the same genetic potential is, therefore, a fairly safe one.[31]

---

[30] The papers by Kakwani and by Anand and Harris (Chs. 6 and 7 below) address the issue of how best to deal with the problem of inter-individual variation in the absence of knowledge about the joint distribution of intake and requirement.

[31] Some exceptions are noted, e.g. in respect of a few tribal communities and the people of the Far East (D. F. Roberts 1985).

But the second assumption is deeply controversial: it constitutes the essence of 'genetic potential' theory and is the prime target of attack by its critics. The problem centres on *why* nutrition should be deemed inadequate when genetic potential is not achieved. It is, of course, quite clear that the concept of genetic potential has an obvious appeal as the normative target of growth which every community could aspire to achieve. In this normative sense, the failure to achieve genetic potential is indeed a case of 'inadequate' nutrition. But the scientific concept of 'undernutrition' refers not to the failure to meet some normative target, but to the failure to maintain the functional capabilities that depend on the level of nutrition. In the context of assessing undernutrition, therefore, the second assumption must imply that *any* deviation from the genetic potential necessarily entails some functional impairment. But this is precisely where the problem lies. Historically, the studies of functions were confined to cases of severe shortfall from genetic potential; and there is no doubt that functional impairment does occur in such cases. However, the evidence on what happens in the case of moderate shortfall is only beginning to emerge; yet the paradigm of genetic potential has always assumed that in practice any shortfall is a sign of undernutrition.

The critics who challenge this paradigm argue that, within limits, deviation from genetic potential does not entail any functional impairment; i.e., people can be 'small but healthy', to use a popular phrase coined by Seckler. The origin of this hypothesis can be traced to a group of eminent biologists who have been much concerned with the processes of human growth. For instance, J. M. Tanner, who is one of the leading authorities on human growth and whose influence Seckler acknowledges, explicitly warns against assuming that being small is necessarily bad. In fact, he coins the phrase 'bigger not better' and argues that, 'Though rate of growth remains one of the most useful of all indices of public health and economic well-being in developing and heterogenously developed countries, it must not be thought that bigger, or faster, is necessarily better. From an ecological point of view smallness has advantages' (Tanner, 1978: 4; see also Goldstein and Tanner 1980). The advantage consists in the fact that a small body enables a person to survive and to sustain his level of activity in a world of nutritional constraint, because a smaller body requires less energy both for maintaining itself and for performing external work. Seckler extends this point further and argues that, while maintaining itself and the level of activity, the small body, unless it is too small (in a sense to be defined below), can also avoid all kinds of functional disabilities (Seckler 1980, 1982, 1984a, 1984b).[32] Accordingly, he suggests that the appropriate

---

[32] More precisely, the hypothesis can be stated as follows: if two persons of different heights (one having achieved his genetic potential and the other falling short by a margin to be specified below) are both living in the same environment and receiving an intake that

reference standard for the assessment of undernutrition should be lower than the maximal growth path permitted by genetic potential.

Before assessing the merit of the hypothesis, it should be noted that Seckler's initial formulation of the hypothesis suffered from a lack of rigour which has given rise to a good deal of confusion. He defined as 'small but healthy' (SBH) all those who are suffering from mild to moderate malnutrition (MMM) according to conventional standards (Seckler 1980, 1982). But this is imprecise, because the set of MMM may be different for different types of anthoropometric measurements, of which there are quite a few. The most widely used measures are weight-for-age (Gomez classification), height-for-age, and weight-for-height (Waterlow classification).[33] Weight-for-height is a measure of 'wasting' and height-for-age is a measure of 'stunting', whereas weight-for-age may reflect both wasting and stunting. It is clear from Seckler's writings that the domain of SBH was meant to be confined to the case of pure 'stunting' unaccompanied by 'wasting'. Thus, for instance, he claimed that 'about 90% of all the malnutrition found in these countries involved people with low height for age *but with the proper weight for height ratio*' (Seckler 1980: 223; emphasis in original), and wondered 'if there is anything wrong with these small people other than their smallness' (p. 233). Yet he often talked of mild to moderate malnutrition as if it were an undifferentiated category. The imprecision has since been rectified, and Seckler (1984a, 1984b) has recently defined SBH explicitly as referring to the mild to moderate degrees of pure stunting (i.e. between 80 and 100 per cent of the 'Harvard median standard' for height-for-age with normal weight–height ratio). In other words, his hypothesis is that only those who are '*moderately* stunted' but '*not at all* wasted' are 'small but healthy'. It follows that any empirical judgement on the validity of Seckler's hypothesis must be based on samples that satisfy these twin criteria of 'moderate' stunting and 'no' wasting. In practice, much of the critique of SBH has gone astray by picking out samples which were either 'severely' stunted or where wasting went hand in hand with stunting.

The distinction between wasting and stunting is in fact quite a crucial one. Both are indicative of retarded growth in a general sense, but of two quite different kinds. 'Wasting' represents depletion of body tissue, whereas 'stunting' indicates slower rate of new tissue deposition. They thus represent two distinct biochemical processes whose functional consequences need not be the same. It is generally recognized that 'wasting'

---

is commensurate with their respective body size and (desirable) activity, then the smaller person will enjoy the same level of functional capability as the bigger person, despite his having failed to achieve his genetic potential; smallness *per se* (within a range) does not matter.

[33] An excellent account of the alternative measures and their relative usefulness can be found in Waterlow (1972).

is much more harmful than 'stunting'. But Seckler goes a step further and suggests that moderate stunting is not harmful at all.

This proposition is based on the following kind of reasoning. If the level of nutrition is not consistent with normal body weight at the genetically permissible maximal height, and if such height is yet to be attained, then equilibrium will have to be achieved by depleting body tissue (i.e. 'wasting') in order to supply additional energy. This will admittedly have adverse functional consequences. But 'stunting' offers an adaptive mechanism to avoid these consequences by reducing height and thereby reducing nutrient demand in keeping with supply. At this low-level equilibrium, existing tissues need not be depleted to supply additional energy, and normal body weight for height can be maintained. Therefore, it is argued, if stunting is within a moderate range, 'There are no impairments because this range represents an adaptive response of bodysize to adverse conditions *in order to avoid these impairments*' (Seckler 1980:224; emphasis in original).

But this argument is not entirely convincing. Just because adaptation is designed to avoid some adverse consequences, it does not follow that it has no adverse effects of its own. It is at least conceivable that more severe consequences are averted at the cost of less severe ones. There is thus no *a priori* reason to believe that an adapted state, such as 'stunting', is necessarily costless.

Thus, on the purely conceptual grounds, the plausibility of Seckler's theory remains wide open. It is now necessary to evaluate the existing empirical evidence on the relationship between stunting and functional impairment.

We shall presently review some of the evidence in this regard. But prior to that, I wish to point out some of the unfair criticisms that have been made from both sides of the debate based on misunderstandings of each other's position.

First, the precise content of Seckler's hypothesis has not always been correctly appreciated. Seckler does not propose that good health consists in being small (as opposed to being big), but that being small (up to a point) may be just as healthy as being big. The operative phrase is, therefore, 'small *but* healthy' and not 'small *is* healthy', as has sometimes been misconstrued. This confusion seems to permeate much of the critique by Gopalan (1983*b*), who even goes so far as to use evocative phrases like 'small is beautiful' in presenting a caricature of Seckler's views, and to take him to task for 'pleading the virtues of smallness'. The confusion seems to arise from a failure to distinguish between two quite different issues: one relates to the relative desirability of different body sizes in a given situation of nutritional constraint, and the other relates to looking at body size as an indicator of health. It is in the first context that Seckler pleads the virtues of smallness, but then, nobody questions that smallness has advantages in a situation of constraint. On the other hand, when it comes to indicating health, Seckler shows no particular preference for smallness, because in his view the same level of health is maintained within a range of body sizes.

On the other side of the fence, the 'genetic potential' theory too has faced a couple of unfair criticisms. One of them has been raised by Payne and his colleagues, and the other by Seckler himself.

Payne and his colleagues interpret the genetic potential theory in quite a novel way. In the usual interpretation, all functions are assumed to be maximized when the full genetic potential is achieved. In their novel interpretation, however, no diet maximizes all aspects of health at the same time; and one particular aspect that is not maximized by diets permitting realization of genetic potential is longevity.[34] The argument is that such diets usually give rise to obesity, and the cardio-vascular diseases associated with obesity tend to reduce longevity. The state of 'full genetic potential' is thus seen to represent a particular trade-off between longevity and other functions, so that a belief in the virtue of 'genetic potential' would imply an acceptance of this particular trade-off. In other words, the genetic potential theorist is supposed to view the human body as a self-optimizing mechanism which, if faced with no constraint, will choose an optimum configuration using 'a set of built-in relative value weightings or trade-offs between different kinds of function . . . ' (Payne and Cutler 1984: 1486); he is thus supposed to have an axiomatic faith in the self-optimizing capacity of the human body, in much the same way as a neoclassical economist assumes optimizing behaviour on the part of an individual consumer. But it is argued that this faith is misplaced, because, while 'It is reasonable to believe that evolution through natural selection has given rise to some built-in system of priorities, . . . it is quite another thing to believe that these priorities are those we might choose' (Payne and Cutler 1984: 1490). In other words, what the body chooses for itself is not necessarily what we as scientists should accept as best for the body.

As a matter of historical fact, however, the 'genetic potential' theorists have not in general viewed the 'state of full potential' as one involving a trade-off between conflicting functions, simply because they do not admit of any such conflict. Obesity, and its effect on longevity (or any other function such as work capacity), is not seen as a necessary concomitant of achieving genetic potential. It is true that *ad libitum* feeding, while permitting the expression of full genetic potential, will also tend to increase obesity. But the argument for allowing full genetic potential to blossom is not an argument for *ad libitum* feeding. Nobody suggests that we should achieve the full genetic potential for accumulating fat.

[34] See Payne (1985: 87), Payne and Cutler (1984: 1490), and Pacey and Payne (1985: 71). See also Martorell *et al.* (1978: 142) for a similar view.

The plea is for achieving the potential for height with a body composition that does not veer towards obesity. It is believed that it is possible to achieve such balance, and it is this balanced state that is implied by the achievement of full genetic potential. In reality, of course, what we often observe in the Western societies is an unbalanced state, where obesity prevails because of overeating. This calls for a careful selection of samples when deriving nutritional standards from the Western world. If the prevailing 'standards' have failed to take such care, as it is sometimes alleged, it is a problem with the practice, not the principle, of the genetic potential theory.

Seckler (1984a) launches his own critique from a more philosophical plane. He invokes the Popperian criterion of falsifiability to judge whether or not a theory is scientific, and argues that, while his own theory yields falsifiable predictions and is hence scientific, the genetic potential theory is in principle non-falsifiable and hence non-scientific. In making this claim, he interprets the 'genetic potential theory' as one that defines 'health' without any regard for functional implication, as if definitionally equating good health with the achievement of genetic potential. Thus, a person below the potential would by definition be called 'unhealthy', 'even if he or she has no observable signs or symptoms of "unhealth" '(Seckler 1984a: 1886). Such a definitional theory would indeed be non-scientific, as it would be even in principle non-falsifiable.

However, this does not seem to be a correct interpretation of the establishment view. Leading modern advocates of the genetic potential theory such as Beaton (1983), Gopalan (1978), Thomson (1980), and others have always emphasized the functional concept of health; and the latest testament of the establishment view embodied in the form of FAO/WHO/UNU (1985) enshrines this concept in unequivocal terms. Their hypothesis is that all functions are simultaneously maximized when and only when full genetic potential is achieved. It is certainly falsifiable in principle, the falsifiable prediction being that any deviation from potential would impair at least some function. Their theory is, therefore, as much scientific by the Popperian criterion as Seckler's own theory is.

The trouble, however, is that the hypothesis has been accepted and put into practice without sufficient demonstration of its validity, which has encouraged the emergence of the 'small but healthy' hypothesis in the first place. But the latter hypothesis too has so far been based on inadequate empirical evidence, drawing mainly upon studies on only one kind of function, viz. immunocompetence among the children, when there are other functions that also need to be studied. Moreover, the studies of children alone will not suffice. Since stunted children very often grow into small adults, it must be asked what adverse effects small adult size might have in later life. I shall consider below four functions that are usually singled out for this purpose.[35] Two of them—immuno-competence and cognitive development—relate principally to the children; the other two—physical work capacity and reproductive efficiency—become more relevant in adult life.

5.4.1 Evidence on the relationship between moderate stunting and nutritional functions

Immunocompetence The effect on immunocomptence can be studied at least at two levels: (1) epidemiological studies on mortality and morbidity resulting from reduced immunocompetence, and (2) clinical studies of impairments in the immunological system of the human body.

Studies of both kinds abound in the literature. But they suffer from at least two limitations for our present purpose. First, most studies relate to severe cases of malnutrition, while our interest here is with the mild to moderate category. Second, the most frequently used nutritional indicator is weight-for-age, which does not serve our purpose, unable as it is to distinguish between wasting and stunting; moreover, even when height-for-age is used it is not always clear that weight-for-height is normal for the sample, and that is the kind of sample we need.[36] However, some tentative conclusions can still be reached.

In a celebrated study among Bangladeshi children, Chen *et al.* (1980, 1981*b*) have found that the rates of morbidity and mortality among children with mild to moderate deficit in terms of height-for-age were no different from those of normal children. A more recent study by Heywood (1983) has also shown that, when weight-for-height was normal, stunting by itself made no difference to the incidence of mortality among the children of Papua New Guinea.

The general nature of these findings is confirmed by Martorell and Ho (1984) who have recently reviewed the literature on the relationship between anthropometric indicators and the risk of infection. They have in fact found no evidence that poor nutritional status, as measured by anthropometric indicators, is associated with greater incidence of infection; as Martorell (1985:22) concludes, "nutrition seems to have little to do with who gets sick". On the other hand, there does appear to exist an association between nutritional status and the severity of infection; but it is the weight-for-height index (wasting) rather than height-for-age (stunting) that seems generally to predict well the severity of infection.

---

[35] I should point out that this is not intended to be a comprehensive review, which is clearly beyond my competence. However, I do draw upon a number of authoritative reviews by experts in their respective areas, though I do not always agree with them fully.

[36] Recall the twin criteria of defining 'small but healthy'. These limitations apply equally to the evaluation of other functions.

It may be argued that in some sense a direct study of the immunological system would be a better way of identifying functional impairment. In fact, clinical studies have shown that all the major components of the immunological system (viz. the cell-mediated immune system, immunoglobulines (antibodies), phagocytes, and complements) may be damaged in the event of severe undernutrition, the first component being the most visibly damaged (Chandra 1980, 1982; Suskind 1977). But no such conclusion can be drawn about moderate levels of nutritional stress. For example, Reddy et al. (1976) found that the cell-mediated immune system as well as the phagocytic function were damaged only when weight-for-age fell below 70 per cent of the standard. It is true that the index used here was weight-for-age rather than height-for-age, which is more relevant for our purpose. But note that the set of people above 70 per cent of the standard weight-for-age fully subsumes the SBH-relevant set (i.e. those with height-for-age above 80 per cent of standard and with normal weight-for-height). Thus, the findings of Reddy et al. would seem to indicate that no part of the immune system is visibly impaired in the case of *pure moderate* stunting. A more direct evidence is provided by Bhaskaram et al. (1980), who actually used the height-for-age indicator. They studied the immunocompetence of adolescents who had experienced growth retardation in their early childhood. No impairment was found in any component when stunting was within moderate limits, and just one component (cell-mediated immunity) was found damaged in the case of severe stunting.

Thus, both epidemiological and clinical studies would seem to suggest that pure moderate stunting does not entail any visible loss of immunocompetence.

Reproductive efficiency It has been suggested that shorter women produce more vulnerable babies. The suggestion is based on the following kind of reasoning. First, it is well known that shorter women generally bear smaller babies (DDH/INCAP 1975). Second, it has been repeatedly shown that low-birthweight babies have a higher risk of mortality (H. C. Chase 1969; Martorell 1979). By combining these two facts, Martorell et al. (1978) argue that maternal height can be said to be related 'logically to infant mortality as well'(p. 150).[37]

However, it may not be entirely logical to combine the two facts mentioned above. There are two reasons for this. First, the critical concept here is that of a low-birthweight (LBW) baby, which is defined as a normal-term newborn weighing less than 2.5 kg. It is among such babies that higher mortality has been observed compared with babies weighing more than 2.5 kg. In the context of the SBH hypothesis, it

---

[37] See also Thomson (1980) for a similar mode of reasoning.

should therefore be shown that moderately stunted (but not wasted) women tend to bear a higher proportion of LBW babies; a simple association between maternal height and birthweight will not do. While the oft-quoted DDH/INCAP (1975) study has indeed shown that shorter women bear a larger percentage of LBW babies than taller women, the difference becomes striking only when the extreme ranges of height are compared; between the tallest two groups, spanning a range of 147–65 cm, the difference is negligible. Thus, the effect of moderate stunting is not yet established.

Second, it is not at all clear at the theoretical level why stunting in a mother's own childhood should retard the growth of her foetus in adult life. In a comprehensive review of the etiology of low-birthweight infants, Battaglia and Simmons (1979) do not mention a single factor that can be unequivocally attributed to stunting *per se* on the basis of existing biological knowledge.[38]

Yet researchers are often persuaded by the existence of empirical association alone. A case in point is the pioneering study by Thomson (1966), which gave currency to the view that short mothers produce more vulnerable babies. Based on a study of women belonging to the more developed part of the world (Scotland), he concluded that low maternal stature is associated with higher risk of infant mortality. His own explanation was in terms of physical and physiological malfunctions presumably caused by maternal short stature. But as Calloway (1982: 739) has pointed out, Thomson reflects a 'bias' here in *assuming* that 'height and birthweight are related through inherent physical/physiological processes', for he does not spell out what these processes could conceivably be or what their theoretical basis is. A more logical explanation can be found in some other information supplied by Thomson himself. The shorter women came generally from a lower socioeconomic status and had on the average a lower health status which may have been due to lower socioeconomic status itself. Ill-health, possibly combined with a lower level of nutrition, may have meant early damage to foetal life and hence the subsequent risk of mortality of their babies compared with those of taller women who mostly came from a higher socioeconomic group. Stunting as such may not have had anything to do with this.

The same argument applies *a fortiori* to the stunted women in the developing world. The deprivation experienced by them in their childhood may have made them stunted. When they grow into adults, the same deprivation at the time of pregnancy may retard the growth of their foetuses. But here it is the lack of nutrition during pregnancy, rather

---

[38] It has been pointed out by Thomson (1980) that, if stunting is caused by 'rickets', a woman may suffer from a kind of pelvic distortion which may seriously damage the foetus. But here we are concerned with the more general case of stunting caused by calorie deficiency.

than stunting *per se*, that is responsible for retardation in foetal growth. Much of the association between short maternal stature and low-birth weight babies in poor societies may perhaps be explained in this manner.

In any case, when small mothers are seen to produce small babies, for whatever reason, that in itself need not be a cause for worry. It may even be an advantage in a situation of nutritional constraint. Smaller babies have a lower maintenance requirement than the larger ones and hence carry a better chance of survival in an adverse condition (unless of course they happen to be low-birthweight babies in the technical sense). This was noted by Thomson (1966: 211) himself, who found that when only the *low* socioeconomic group was considered it was the taller women whose infants were subject to a higher incidence of mortality. A subsequent study by Frisancho *et al.* (1973) confirmed this observation among a poor population group in Peru: the shorter women were found to have a higher 'offspring survival ratio'. Against this, however, there is a counter-example recently provided by Martorell *et al.* (1981), who found among a group of poor Mayan women that the taller women had a lower rate of infant mortality and a higher rate of surviving offspring. Also, unlike in Thomson's study, the poor performance of shorter women cannot be explained by worse socioeconomic condition, as the samples came from a particularly homogeneous group. However, as the authors point out, the group as a whole was very short, 'among the shortest in the world'. The comparison was thus between short and very short mothers in an exceptionally short population. The question of moderate stunting, therefore, remains wide open.

Work capacity and productivity Does small stature in men lead to reduced work capacity and productivity? Gopalan (1983*b*), Spurr (1983, 1984), and several others have argued that it does. To understand the theory behind this claim, it is necessary to be familiar with an important physiological concept called 'physical work capacity' (PWC).

Physical activity is performed through the mediation of skeletal muscles which generate energy with the help of oxygen and produce work. The maximal volume of oxygen uptake ($VO_2(\text{max})$) is, therefore, an indicator of the maximum amount of energy that can be liberated by skeletal muscles, and hence the maximal amount of work that can be done. This maximal work potential is called physical work capacity, also known as the maximal aerobic capacity.

The amount of $VO_2(\text{max})$ depends in the first place on the total amount of muscle cell mass (MCM), sometimes proxied by lean body mass (LBM) or simply body weight. It also depends partly on the health of the circulatory system as measured by the level of blood haemoglobin and cardiac efficiency. Furthermore, it is known to have a positive association with sustained training (as in the case of athletes) as well as with the level of habitual physical activity. But body size is the most important determinant, accounting for over 80 per cent of the difference in VO_2(max) between subjects suffering from varying degrees of protein-calorie deficiency (Spurr 1983: 7).

Viteri (1971) has noted that cell function does not seem to be impaired in mild to moderate cases of nutritional deficiency; i.e., aerobic capacity per unit of cell mass remains intact. It is the difference in the amount of cell mass that makes the difference in absolute VO_2(max). One can thus argue that, since the stunted adults have less body mass than adults of normal height, they would also have a proportionately lower VO_2(max) and hence a lower level of physical work capacity.

But does a lower level of PWC matter? After all, it is well known that in actual work conditions people do not exert at more than 35–40 per cent of VO_2(max) even when engaged in heavy work for a eight-hour day (Astrand and Rodahl 1977). So what is wrong if stunting leads to the lowering of a ceiling that is never reached in real life anyway? Spurr (1983, 1984) has argued that stunting will nevertheless lead to lower productivity, especially in occupations involving heavy physical work. He postulates a theoretical model to explain the logic and also cites evidence in support of his contention. I shall argue that neither the theory nor the evidence is entirely convincing.

The logic of Spurr's theory is deceptively simple. In heavy physical work everyone may be assumed to be expending energy at the maximum sustainable rate (say, 40 per cent of VO_2(max)). Since a shorter man has lower VO_2(max) than a taller man, he will be spending a lower absolute amount of energy while working at this rate. Assuming that energy cost per unit of task is the same for everyone, it must then follow that the shorter man will produce less.[39]

The trouble with this argument lies in the assumption of the same (per unit of task) energy cost for everyone. Note that the energy cost per unit of task (as measured by oxygen consumed while doing the work) has two components: the energy cost of basal metabolism that goes on during the period of work, and the energy required for the work itself. The first component, as noted in Section 5.2, depends directly on body mass. The same will be true also for the second component, especially in typical heavy work involving body movement, because the energy involved in work is directly proportional to the mass that is moved. Thus, the gross energy cost per unit of (heavy) task can be assumed to be roughly

---

[39] The unit of 'task' is given by a set of physical dimensions (e.g. moving an object of a given mass to a certain distance along a given direction). Note that we speak here of 'task' rather than 'work'. This is intended to avoid terminological confusion: in thermodynamics, the concept of 'work' is measured in terms of energy so that it does not make sense to speak of energy cost per unit of 'work'.

proportional to body mass. It means that, while lower VO_2(max) (owing to lower body mass) will constrain a shorter man to spend a lower absolute amount of total energy, his energy cost per unit of task will also be proportionately lower.[40] As a result, his productivity need not suffer.[41]

The preceding argument relates to productivity per unit of time. Total productivity will obviously depend also on stamina, i.e. on the length of time a person can sustain a heavy workload. But then, there is no evidence that smaller men have less stamina. When Spurr and his colleagues conducted endurance tests on subjects with different body weights (but none severely malnourished) they found no difference in the time for which a subject could sustain a workload at 80 per cent of VO_2(max) (Barac-Nieto et al. 1978).

There is thus no a priori reason to assume that stunted men would be less productive, even in doing heavy physical work. Yet empirical evidence is often cited to prove the disadvantage of being small. Two kinds of evidence are marshalled in this respect, one indirect and the other direct.

The indirect evidence is drawn from a number of studies that have shown that productivity is positively related to VO_2(max). Coupled with the observation that smaller men must have lower VO_2(max), this evidence is then taken to imply that smaller men would be less productive (Spurr 1984). But this inference is not necessarily valid. Note that the difference in VO_2(max) can arise because of differences in residual factors such as haemoglobin, habitual activity, etc. When these residual factors, rather than lower body mass, bring down VO_2(max) there is no reason to expect a corresponding reduction in energy expenditure per unit of work. Therefore, if lower VO_2(max) constrains total energy expenditure, as in heavy physical work, there is every reason to suspect that productivity will suffer. One can thus accept the finding that lower VO_2(max) leads to lower productivity without accepting that smaller men produce less. For the latter to follow, it must be shown that the difference in VO_2(max) occurred in the first place because of differences in body size, and not because of residual factors.[42]

This means that nothing short of direct evidence will do. In this respect, two studies are often quoted: Spurr et al. (1977), and Satyana-

[40] In technical jargon, a shorter man will have a higher 'gross mechanical efficiency'. Note that this conclusion does not depend on the assumption of higher metabolic or ergonomic efficiency on the part of the smaller men. Spurr based his assumption of the same energy cost on the premiss that smaller men are not known to be more efficient users of energy. In respect of metabolic or ergonomic efficiency, he may well be right. But surely, the 'gross mechanical efficiency' must still be lower for smaller men simply by virtue of lower body mass, and that alone would given them a lower energy cost per unit of task.

[41] See Ferro-Luzzi (1985: 65) for a similar argument.

[42] As it happens, in several of the studies cited by Spurr, the 'high productivity' group did not differ from the rest in respect of height and weight; see Hansson (1965) and Davies (1973b). This suggests that it was the residual factors that were responsible for differences in VO_2(max) and hence in productivity.

rayana *et al.* (1977). Both demonstrate that productivity is positively related to height, but care is needed in interpreting the results.

Spurr *et al.* (1977) have shown, through a multiple regression analysis, that $VO_2(max)$, height, and body fat are all significantly related to productivity. In other words, even when the effect of $VO_2(max)$ is eliminated, height still remains positively associated with productivity. Now that seems somewhat surprising. According to theory, height is supposed to affect productivity by limiting $VO_2(max)$. So if $VO_2(max)$ is controlled, what physiological mechanism remains through which height is supposed to affect productivity? One cannot but suspect that height happens to be a proxy here for some unknown non-physiological variable. Therefore the physiological theory that stunting *leads to* lower productivity remains open to question.

The study by Satyanarayana *et al.* (1977) is free from this particular problem. When weight was controlled, height did not seem to have any independent effect, as should be the case if height is to limit productivity through body mass and $VO_2(max)$. This study is, therefore, more relevant to the issue at stake. However, two points must be noted. First, the correlation between height and productivity was pretty weak at the individual level, and non-existent at the group level. Second, and most significantly for our present purpose, almost all the subjects had a below-normal weight-height ratio, and hence do not constitute a SBH-relevant set.

On the whole, then, there is as yet no compelling reason to suspect that 'pure' moderate stunting hampers productivity in adult life.

Cognitive development Cognitive ability is a catch-all phrase that denotes a number of separate functions (such as motor development, intersensory co-ordination, intelligence, learning skill) which depend on the health of the neurological system. Scientific research on the effect of nutrition on these functions, though at a very nascent stage, has already identified a number of possible pathways through which severe protein-calorie deficiency may damage cognitive ability (H. P. Chase 1976; Balazs *et al.* 1979). However, it is not yet established whether the biochemical processes involved in moderate stunting can produce similar results.

Nevertheless, empirical studies have almost always found a positive association between height and mental development. In a survey of studies on mild to moderate undernutrition, Pollitt and Thompson (1977) have come to the generalization that, among populations where malnutrition is endemic, indicators of human growth (stunting) as well as socioeconomic variables correlate significantly with measurements of mental development. Some of the studies are not exactly relevant for our purpose, since they compared only severe stunting with normal height.

But the same cannot be said about a study by Klein *et al.* (1971), who looked for an association across the spectrum and found a correlation coefficient that was small (0.23) but statistically significant.[43]

These studies have given currency to the view that 'big is smart'. Seen merely as an association, this view is probably right. But to interpret it causally would be rather premature. One complication arises from the fact that the development of the brain and the central nervous system as a whole depends on both nutrition from within and stimulus from outside. Furthermore, in actual socioeconomic conditions in which malnourished children live, both nutrition and stimulus are often simultaneously deficient. It is therefore, difficult, and often impossible, to determine to what extent, if at all, nutrition *per se* is responsible for slow mental development.[44]

In spite of this difficulty, it has been possible to show fairly conclusively that episodes of acute undernutrition in early life do retard mental development. This has been shown, for example, by comparing children with a history of acute undernutrition with siblings (from the same family) without such a history but who presumably have been exposed to similar environmental stimulus. This convenient strategy cannot, however, be pursued in the chronic case (the case of moderate stunting), because marked difference in chronic undernutrition (as opposed to acute episodes) can seldom be found within the same family. Comparisons are, therefore, necessarily made across different environmental conditions, thus creating the problem of identification.

When this observation is combined with our lack of knowledge of how the biochemical processes involved in moderate stunting might affect cognitive development, it may seem tempting to defend the 'small but healthy' hypothesis by arguing that the observed mental retardation cannot be ascribed to nutritional deprivation. In other words, one might argue that the small may still be called healthy from the nutritional point of view (Pacey and Payne 1985: 113).

There is, however, a difficulty with this argument. One may accept that the nutrition-induced biochemical processes that are involved in stunting do not cause impairment of cognition, and that stimulus is the culprit: but that does not eliminate the role of nutrition. It is important to realize that nutrition and stimulus are not two independent factors. Stimulus depends a great deal on a child's exploratory activities, of which play is a very important medium; and such activity is very much a function of nutrition. This means that, unlike other nutritional func-

---

[43] For some recent evidence, see Jamison (1986) and Moock and Leslie (1986).

[44] This is a general conclusion reached by several reviewers of the state of the art; see e.g. Lloyd-Still (1976*a*), Martorell *et al.* (1978), Cravioto and Delicardie (1979), and Brozek (1982).

tions, cognitive development need not be affected by the pathways of biochemical processes alone. An alternative pathway exists in the form of: nutrition → activity → stimulus → cognitive development. In this way, the very same phenomenon of nutritional constraint that leads to stunting through the pathway of biochemical processes may also retard mental development through the pathway of activity. In that event, the mental retardation of a stunted child cannot but be viewed as a loss of nutritional capability.

In view of the preceding discussion, we find it necessary to make a distinction between two possible interpretations of the 'small but healthy' hypothesis: (1) moderate stunting *per se* does not impair any nutritional capability; and (2) a moderately stunted child can be assumed not to suffer from any impairment of nutritional capabilities, provided it has a normal weight-for-height.

The first is a causative statement, and I feel inclined to treat it sympathetically in view of our consideration of all the functions mentioned above. The second is an associative statement, and here our discussion on cognition points to the need for caution. Recall that the same nutritional deprivation that causes stunting may also impair cognitive development (not *because of* but *simultaneously with* stunting). This means that, even if it is right to say that moderate stunting does not cause any functional impairment, it will not be right to say that a moderately stunted child is necessarily healthy from a nutritional point of view. In other words, the validity of the causative statement (1) does not ensure the validity of the associative statement (2).

The doubt over the associative statement leaves one in bit of a quandary. While one cannot accept that a stunted child is necessarily healthy, neither can one go back to embrace the genetic potential theory, because the falsity of the associative statement does not imply the truth of the converse. In other words, one cannot assume that a stunted child has necessarily suffered from nutrition-constrained cognitive retardation. That would depend on whether the child had actually reduced his activity at the same time that it became stunted. For all we know, it may not have done so and may have actually absorbed the entire nutritional constraint through adaptive stunting. By looking at anthropometry alone, one cannot be sure. The moral, if there is any, is simply that the anthropometric approach to the assessment of nutritional status ought to be supplemented by observations on the activity level of the population concerned.[45]

---

[45] This of course begs the question of how to judge the adequacy of activity levels. This is by no means a simple matter, and a fair amount of controversy has grown over this issue. Some of the relevant concerns are discussed in Osmani (1990).

5.5 SUMMARY AND CONCLUSIONS

This chapter set out to review the debates surrounding the views of Sukhatme and Seckler on the measurement of undernutrition. The conclusions that have emerged from our review can be summarized as follows.

The claim that the norm for energy requirement should be set at two standard deviations below the average cannot be sustained. Sukhatme tried to justify this claim by using two quite different models of variable efficiency, one stochastic and the other adaptive. In the stochastic model, efficiency of energy utilization varies in a spontaneous manner and intake varies *pari passu*, whereas in the adaptive model variation of efficiency is induced by prior variation in intake. The justification of the lower cut-off point in terms of the stochastic model is logically wrong, because this model only ensures that having one's intake above the point is a necessary condition for being well nourished, but it does not ensure sufficiency. On the other hand, if the adaptive model is accepted, then it would be logically correct to set the norm at the lower limit of adaptation rather than at the average value. But the limit of adaptation cannot be identified with Sukhatme's cut-off point, which was derived from the stochastic model. This is because stochastic variation is not the same thing as adaptation, for the simple reason that spontaneous and induced variation in efficiency cannot be the same biological phenomenon. The limit of adaptation must be found from independent scientific evidence on 'pure' adaptation in efficiency, unaccompanied by any change in body weight. However, existing scientific knowledge does not provide any evidence in support of pure adaptation of this kind.

On the controversy over the possibility of costless adaptation in physical growth, I found it useful to distinguish between two interpretations of the 'small but healthy' hypothesis, one causative and the other associative. The causative interpretation was found difficult to refute in the light of existing evidence. But the associative interpretation was found difficult to sustain because physical retardation may easily be associated with the loss of one kind of nutritional function (i.e. cognitive skill) even within the range in which retardation itself does not cause any functional impairment.

Much, of course, remains to be resolved on the scientific front. For instance, while I have concluded that the current scientific evidence does not support the hypothesis of costless adaptation in the efficiency of energy utilization, I cannot claim that the hypothesis has been refuted, either. This is simply because the right kind of scientific experiments (involving longitudinal observations on individuals subjected to moderate caloric restriction and engaged in a fixed level of activity) have not yet been performed. To take another case, while I have concluded that the causal interpretation of the 'small but healthy' hypothesis is a highly plausible one, a lot more experiments are needed (on different kinds of functions involving different samples of moderately stunted people) for it to command general confidence. In any case, even if the hypothesis is taken to be valid, the range of growth rates within which the full range of nutrition-related functions can be sustained at a desirable level is still not known with any measure of scientific precision. Seckler's identification of this range with the conventional definition of 'moderate' stunting is an *ad hoc* one, based on casual empiricism rather than controlled scientific experiment.

These and many other issues remain to be resolved before undernutrition can be measured with the desired scientific accuracy.[46]

Meanwhile, disagreements are inevitable. However, the most disturbing spectacle one notices in these debates is how so many of the disagreements originate from sheer misunderstanding of positions rather than from basic differences in scientific perspectives. I have pointed out some of these misunderstandings in the course of reviewing the debates. I shall conclude the paper by showing how vacuous some of the policy debates have been.[47]

One of the reasons why the debate over adaptation has generated so much heat is the fear that, by showing the magnitude of undernutrition and the related phenomenon of poverty to be much less than what it is believed to be, the adaptationists might encourage a potentially dangerous complacence on the policy front. A typical expression of this fear can be found in Zurbrigg's (1983) statement that 'Sukhatme's argument can lead to politically expedient redefinition of poverty' (p. 2083). Now, politicians do, of course, manipulate academic ideas if they find it expedient to do so. But ideas must be judged on their own merit; and in this particular case they do not logically warrant the kind of fears expressed.

The adaptationists have generally been careful in drawing a distinction between nutritional poverty (i.e. undernutrition caused by poverty) and general socioeconomic poverty. A person who has adapted to a low level of intake may have avoided nutritional poverty; but in doing so he does not become non-poor in a general sense, for it is his general poverty that has forced him to adapt in the first place. In other words, the necessity to adapt is itself an indication of poverty. By this criterion, Sukhatme reckons that most of the people in rural India could be counted as poor, although undernutrition arising from poverty may be no more than

[46] Another set of unresolved issues relates to the quantitative magnitudes of the interactions between food and environmental hygiene in precipitating undernutrition. These issues are discussed in Osmani (1990).

[47] For a more comprehensive discussion of the implications of nutritional conversies for policy and other concerns of economics, see Osmani (1990).

15–20 per cent (Sukhatme 1982c: 248).[48] One may disagree with the second part of the statement, but there is certainly nothing in it to encourage a complacent view of poverty.

Similar confusion has surrounded the views of Seckler. Because he considers the stunted children to be 'healthy', he has often been interpreted as implying that stunting is not a matter of policy concern. Thus Martorell (1985:25) interprets him as arguing that 'planners should concern themselves with wasting and not with stunting'; and Gopalan (1983b:34) raises the alarm that to accept Seckler's views 'is to acquiesce (however unwittingly) in the preservation of the status quo of poverty, ill-health, undernutrition and socio-economic deprivation'. Once again, what the critics fail to notice is the distinction between undernutrition and general deprivation that the adaptationists are trying to highlight. Seckler (1984a) in fact states quite categorically that, whether or not we call stunted children undernourished, the fact that they have been forced to become small indicates that they are generally deprived; and as such they are certainly a cause for policy concern.

Encouraging complacence on the policy front would therefore hardly seem to be a necessary consequence of the views espoused by the adaptationists. Both camps can agree that general socioeconomic poverty is a serious problem in the developing world (they may even agree on its magnitude) without agreeing on the magnitude of prevailing undernutrition.

Let us now turn to one of the principal charges made by the adaptationists against their opponents. One recurring theme running through the writings of all the leading adaptationists, including Sukhatme, Seckler, and Payne, is the claim that acceptance of their view will lead to a more equitable allocation of resources. The argument runs briefly as follows. Those who have successfully adapted are indeed deprived, but those who have failed to adapt and become undernourished are even more so. Thus, the people identified as 'truly undernourished' by their criterion would usually belong to the neediest section of the population; by identifying them, it is claimed, one is helping to channel scarce food and other resources to those who need them most. By implication, it is suggested that the non-adaptationist view does not make any distinction between degrees of need and is not concerned with priorities. This point is made most explicitly by Payne and Cutler (1984), who claim that in the genetic potential theory, as in Paretian neoclassical economics, one is not concerned with whether the benefit goes to the severest or the

---

[48] By the same token, Sukhatme (1982c) also questions the usefulness of the traditional dietary approach for the measurement of poverty (quite apart from questioning its usefulness for the measurement of undernutrition).

least severe cases of deprivation as long as somebody benefits without worsening anyone else's condition.[49]

This is clearly a rather curious argument. The desire to concentrate on the most deprived cases has nothing to do with the nutritional phenomenon of adaptation. It arises simply from the value judgement that the gain of the neediest should be valued most. A devout non-adaptationist can equally hold this value judgement, and may decide to give top priority to those farthest from the genetic potential, even though he may believe that anyone below the potential is undernourished to some extent. Obviously, the difference of opinion on the possibility of adaptation does not entail any difference of policy as far as ranking of priorities is concerned.

Avoidance of such false debates is the first prerequisite for sharpening the genuine differences in scientific perspectives. And only with such sharpening can one expect a speedy resolution of the unresolved scientific issues.

APPENDIX: DEDUCING AUTOCORRELATION IN THE CALORIE INTAKE OF A REFERENCE-TYPE PERSON

Some critics (e.g. Mehta 1982; Rand and Scrimshaw 1984) seem to believe that autocorrelation in calorie intake was deduced by Sukhatme by analogy with the protein model, in which similar autocorrelation was earlier noticed by Sukhatme and Margen (1978). But this is not quite so: the autocorrelation in energy intake was actually deduced by a statistical analysis of intake and expenditure of energy reported for a group of subjects by Edholm *et al.* (1970).[50] But then, there is a problem here too. The variable for which autocorrelation was studied was neither intake nor expenditure, but the difference between the two, or 'energy balance', as it is called by the authors. And, as Mehta (1982) rightly notes, it is not immediately clear how autocorrelation in 'energy balance' implies autocorrelation in either efficiency or intake or expenditure.

---

[49] Elsewhere, Pacey and Payne (1985) take the precaution of pointing out that this is not a necessary implication of the genetic potential model, but that it could be interpreted in this way by unscrupulous policy-makers. But this really amounts to setting unduly restrictive rules of the game. Besides, if one wants to play the game this way, one should also face the retort that the unscrupulous policy-makers can misinterpret the adaptationist model, too, to feel complacent about the 'adapted'.

[50] It is true, however, that the deduction was made only indirectly, as the nature of data prevented a direct test of autocorrelation by actually fitting an autoregressive model. It was this lacuna that made it necessary to draw analogy with the protein model for which an autoregressive model was actually fitted. However, the purpose of the analogy was to spell out the full implications of the autoregressive model, not to deduce the model in the first place.

Note that Sukhatme's objective was to show that efficiency varies from day to day and intake varies *pari passu*, even when a person is maintaining body weight and activity at the same levels. This he could not do simply by looking at actual variations in intake, because these could reflect the combined effects of three different factors: variable efficiency, change in the amount of activity, and change in the bodily stores of energy (i.e. change of body weight).[51] It was, therefore, necessary to eliminate the last two factors in order to isolate the effect of variable efficiency. The use of 'energy balance' was intended to do precisely that. I shall show that 'energy balance' as defined by Sukhatme reflects that part of the variation in intake which results solely from variation in efficiency.[52]

Exactly how the use of 'energy balance' data does that has tended to remain obscure, owing to a pervasive confusion about the nature of 'expenditure' data reported by Edholm. The confusion is best illustrated by an apparent conundrum noted (but not resolved) by Mehta (1982). If 'expenditure' refers to actual total expenditure of energy in a day, then by the first law of thermodynamics the difference between intake and expenditure (i.e. 'energy balance') must be equal to the change in energy stores within the body, i.e. to the change in body weight. However, Edholm's data show, and Sukhatme lays much emphasis on it, that cumulative 'energy balance' over a week does not equal the weekly change in body weight. The first law is thus seen to be violated. On the other hand, if 'expenditure' refers only to a part of total expenditure (for instance, the part actually used by the body, excluding the part dissipated as heat), then of course the first law is no longer violated; but it then becomes impossible to sustain Sukhatme's proposition that average intake equals average expenditure in the long run, for a part can never be equal to the whole.[53] Thus, if Sukhatme's analysis is to make any sense, the expenditure in Edholm's data cannot refer either to actual total expenditure or to a part of it.

What then does it stand for? I suggest that it stands for the presumed total expenditure based on average efficiency. In other words, 'expenditure' was computed by multiplying the total amount of each kind of activity with a constant value of energy cost (per unit of each activity) based on average efficiency.[54]

---

[51] Although Edholm's subjects were engaged in broadly similar activities from day to day, their level of activity did not remain exactly constant. Similarly, they maintained body weight within a narrow range, but not at a fixed level. Thus, all three factors mentioned here could account for the observed variation in intake.

[52] I am concerned here with the autoregulatory model (Sukhatme mark I), where intake adjusts to efficiency, and not with the adaptive model (Sukhatme mark II), where efficiency adjusts to intake.

[53] See the discussion in the text on the implications of autocorrelation.

[54] That 'total' expenditure rather than a part of it was measured is evident from Edholm *et al.* (1970): 'The total energy expenditure was computed from midnight to midnight' (p. 1095), covering all kinds of activities including sleep. On the other hand, although it is nowhere mentioned explicitly that 'presumed' rather than actual expenditure was being measured, it seems to be implicit in the methodology of calculating expenditure. In fact, Garrow has noted this point explicitly while referring to Edholm's data in his comments on Beaton: 'The energy costs of each activity were assumed to be constant. The variability was in the amount of activity' (Beaton 1985: 232).

Once this interpretation is accepted, it becomes easy to see how the variation in 'energy balance' reflects pure variation in efficiency.[55]

Note first of all that Sukhatme measured both intake and expenditure *per unit of body weight* so as to eliminate the effect of weight change over time.[56] Let this normalized 'energy balance' on any day t be expressed as $\beta_t = I_t - E_t$, where I_t and E_t refer respectively to intake and expenditure per unit of bodyweight. Next note that since expenditure is measured in terms of constant efficiency, daily variation in E_t is due *solely* to variation in the amount of activity; but the variation in I_t is due to variation in *both* activity and efficiency.

Let us now eliminate from I_t and E_t the common component Δ_t of daily variation which results from the deviation of actual activity in a day from the mean activity level. We are then left with (i) $I'_t = I_t - \Delta_t$, which can be defined as the daily intake when activity, but not efficiency, is held at the mean level, and (ii) $\mu = E_t - \Delta_t$, which is the average expenditure when both efficiency and activity are at the mean level; i.e., μ is simply the average requirement of calories at a given level of activity. Since average requirement equals average intake for healthy individuals (as Edholm's subjects are presumed to be), μ can also be interpreted as the intake corresponding to the average values of efficiency and activity. Thus, the intake of an unconstrained individual would be represented by μ when neither efficiency nor activity varies, and by I'_t when only efficiency varies. Therefore, the difference $(I'_t - \mu)$ reflects the variation in intake which arises solely from variable efficiency. However, the difference $(I'_t - \mu)$ is nothing but the 'energy balance' (β_t) as defined earlier, because

$$\beta_t = I_t - E_t$$
$$= (I_t - \Delta_t) - (E_t - \Delta_t) \qquad (A1)$$
$$= I'_t - \mu.$$

Therefore, the observed variation in 'energy balance', as defined by Sukhatme, can be taken to reflect pure variation in efficiency.

The next step in the argument consists in showing that (1) Edholm's 'energy balance' data reveal autocorrelation, which is interpreted, in view of the preceding argument, as revealing autocorrelation in the daily variation of efficiency; and (2) autocorrelation in efficiency implies autocorrelation in the intake and expenditure of an unconstrained healthy person maintaining body weight and engaged in a fixed level of activity.

The first step in this argument, i.e. the existence of autocorrelation in 'energy balance', was established through the following chain of reasoning:

[55] Surprisingly, Sukhatme himself never spells out this interpretation. On the contrary, he often gives the impression that he is talking about *actual* total expenditure. To get around the conflict with the first law of thermodynamics that such an interpretation involves, he suggests that, in a biological system, the law need not hold at every instant, but can operate with a lag. But it is very difficult to justify this view. There are, of course, some theoretical problems in interpreting the laws of thermodynamics in a disequilibrium system, as the biological system happens to be (Morowitz 1978); but the notion of a lag does not emerge from all this.

[56] 'Since we are essentially concerned with the analysis of intake and expenditure in man *maintaining bodyweight* and engaged in defined tasks, both intake and expenditure are expressed per kilogram bodyweight basis' (Sukhatme 1982b: 26; emphasis added).

1 If the apparent 'balance' was due to measurement error alone, the cumulative 'balance' over a period of time would have been close to zero. But the cumulative weekly 'balances' are actually very large, which indicates that the variation in 'balance' reflects genuine variation in efficiency.

2 If the variation of daily 'balance' were purely random, the variance of mean 'balance' would decline inversely as the length of the period over which mean is taken. However, the data show that the variance declines much more slowly than the inverse of the length of period. This indicates that the daily 'balances' are autocorrelated with each other.[57]

3 When hypothetical variances of 'mean' energy balance were calculated by assuming a first-order autocorrelation coefficient of 0.3, these hypothetical values corresponded fairly closely to the values estimated from Edholm's data. Evidences 2 and 3 thus together provide an indirect proof that daily 'energy balances' are related to each other through first-order autocorrelation. One can thus postulate the model,

$$\beta_t = \rho \beta_{t-1} + u_t \tag{A2}$$

where ρ is the coefficient of autocorrelation and u_t is a random error with zero mean and constant variance.

Now since $\beta_t = I'_t - \mu$ (i.e. (A1)) and μ is a constant, it follows that I'_t is also serially correlated; i.e.,

$$I'_t = \rho I'_{t-1} + e_t \tag{A3}$$

Recall that I'_t is the energy intake when both body weight and activity (but not efficiency) are held constant. Therefore, I'_t can be interpreted as the energy intake of a reference person maintaining body weight and engaged in a fixed level of activity (set at the average activity level). Also, recall that the intake of a reference person is by definition equal to his requirement. It follows, therefore, that the intake and requirements of healthy individuals maintaining body weight and engaged in fixed activity are not fixed but vary from day to day in an autocorrelated manner.

To sum up, the chain of deduction goes as follows. (1) The observed autocorrelation in 'energy balance' in Edholm's data implies that the efficiency of energy utilization varies from day to day in an autocorrelated manner. (2) Since the intake of a reference person (i.e. an unconstrained healthy person maintaining body weight and engaged in a fixed level of activity) can vary only in line with variation of efficiency, it follows from (1) that his intake will also vary in an autocorrelated manner. (3) Since the intake of a reference person is by definition equal to his requirement, it follows from (2) that requirements too vary with similar autocorrelation.

---

[57] For the mathematical details of this inference, see Srinivasan (1981: 7).

6

Measuring Undernutrition with Variable Calorie Requirements

N. C. Kakwani

6.1 INTRODUCTION

A major problem involved in estimating the extent of undernutrition in a population is the identification of undernourished persons. The FAO has been concerned with the issue of determining the dietary energy requirements of individuals in different age and sex groups that will allow them to maintain the required physical efficiency; it periodically publishes the average calorie requirement norms for a reference man and woman. Some attempts have been made to measure undernutrition using these norms. This approach, which classifies a person as undernourished if his or her calorie intake is below the required norm, was followed first by Ojha (1970) and Dandekar and Rath (1971) for India and later by Reutlinger and Selowsky (1976) and FAO (1977) at a global level. These studies led to a heated debate among economists and statisticians, the most important among them being Dandekar (1981, 1982), Sukhatme (1981a, 1981b, 1982b), and Srinivasan (1981).

Much of this debate centres on the problems arising in using the 'average' requirement norm in a situation where requirements are known to vary both inter-personally—i.e. from person to person even of the same age, sex, and physical activity level—and intra-individually—i.e. for the same individual at different points in time. This chapter is concerned with the problem of inter-individual variation. In his recent writings, Sukhatme has tended to play down the significance of inter-individual variation by arguing that intra-individual variation is by far the most important source of variation in requirement. Nutritionists, however, are deeply divided on this issue, many of them holding the opposite view that intra-individual variation is of a minor order of magnitude.[1] Furthermore, it is important to recognize that, even if Sukhatme were to be proved right on this point, the problem of inter-individual variation will continue to persist. As is well known, Sukhatme refuses to accept

This paper is a modified version of Kakwani (1988). I am grateful to S. R. Osmani and Amartya Sen for their comments on an earlier draft. Juhani Holm of WIDER provided me with expert computational assistance, for which I am indebted to him.

[1] These controversies are discussed in the papers by Gopalan, Payne, Srinivasan, and Osmani in this volume (Chs. 2–5 above).

'average' requirement as the norm and suggests instead that the norm should be set at the lower limit of the range of intra-individual variation in requirement. In his writings, he tends to assume that this lower limit is the same for all individuals. But this need not be so. The lower limit is determined by an individual's metabolic ability to regulate his energy expenditure; since there is no reason to expect all individuals to have the same capacity for metabolic regulation, the lower limit need not be the same for every individual. Thus, the problem of inter-individual variation in requirement cannot be avoided after all.

When requirements vary inter-individually, the use of an 'average' norm leads inevitably to two types of error. Some well-nourished people will be classified as undernourished just because their intake falls below the average requirement, even though their own requirements may lie below their intakes. This is known as the type I error. Conversely, some undernourished people will be classified as well nourished on the grounds that their intake is higher than average requirement, even though their own requirement may be higher still. This is the type II error.[2]

These two errors will exist whenever we take a single requirement level as the norm, be it average requirement or something else. The ideal solution is to look at the joint distribution of intakes and requirements, and to estimate the number of people whose intakes fall below their respective requirements. But unfortunately, the distribution of requirement is not known, so the ideal solution is beyond our reach.

A major objective of this paper is to suggest sensible ways of estimating undernutrition in the absence of the ideal solution. To that end, methodologies are developed to deal with different levels of information available on the distribution of requirement. Obviously, the less we know about requirements, the less we can tell about the state of nutrition. But it is our contention that we can still say something of value; the objective of our methodologies is to enable us to do so by making the most of the available information, and without committing either a type I or a type II error.

A second objective of the paper is to develop a new class of undernutrition measures. Most of the recent literature is centred around estimating the proportion of population that is undernourished, without taking note of the degree of severity of their undernutrition. A proper measure of undernutrition should take into account not only the proportion of people undernourished, but also the gap between the calorie requirement and intake of each individual. I shall develop a class of such measures.

[2] For further discussion of these two types of error, see Ch. 5 above by Osmani.

The paper is organized as follows. First, the usual 'average norm' approach is discussed in Section 6.2. Then in Section 6.3 the new class of severity-sensitive measures of undernutrition is developed. Next, I develop methodologies for comparing undernutrition across populations under different levels of information on requirements, viz. (1) where both mean and variance of requirements are known (Section 6.4), (2) where only mean is known (Section 6.5), and (3) where nothing is known about requirements (Section 6.6).

Finally, in Section 6.7 the methodologies developed in this paper are applied to the Indian data (National Sample Survey of 1971–2) which formed the basis of earlier computations carried out by Sukhatme (1978, 1981a, 1982b) and Dandekar (1981). The estimates of undernutrition have been obtained here by utilizing the entire distribution of calorie requirement rather than using single threshold points.

6.2 THE AVERAGE CALORIE NORM APPROACH

Suppose that the calorie intake x of an individual is a random variable with mean μ and the probability density function $f(x)$. If the calorie requirement of an individual is a given number R and his calorie intake is x, then the person is said to be suffering from undernutrition if $x < R$.

Since the energy requirement of an individual is not fixed, it can be assumed that requirement follows a probability distribution with density function $g(R)$ with mean $\bar{R}$.

Let $P(x)$ be the probability that a person with calorie intake x suffers from undernutrition. This probability must depend on $g(R)$ and is given by

$$P(x) = \int_x^b g(R) \, dR = 1 - G(x),$$

where $a \leqslant R \leqslant b$ and $G(x)$ is the probability distribution function of calorie requirement. An index of undernutrition is then given by

$$M = \int_0^\infty [1 - G(x)] f(x) \, dx, \tag{1}$$

which is interpreted as the probability that a randomly selected person in the population suffers from undernutrition. This index is referred to as the head-count of the measure of undernutrition.

An approximate procedure to estimate the extent of undernutrition is to calculate the proportion of population with energy intake less than $\bar{R}$, i.e.

$$F(\bar{R}) = \int_0^{\bar{R}} f(x)\,dx, \tag{2}$$

where $F(x)$ is the probability distribution function of calorie intake. This approach will be referred to as the average calorie norm (ACN) approach.

As already pointed out, Sukhatme (1978) and also Srinivasan (1983a) have questioned the ACN approach on the grounds that it leads to considerable overestimation of the degree of undernutrition in the population. Their charge of overestimation is based on the grounds of both inter- and intra-individual variation. In this section I argue that, so far as the problem of inter-individual variation is concerned, the extent of overestimation is small.[3] In order to assess the extent of overestimation, let us integrate (1) by parts:

$$M = \int_0^\infty F(x)\,g(x)\,d(x). \tag{3}$$

Then using Taylor's expansion gives

$$F(x) = F(\bar{R}) + (x - \bar{R})\,f(\bar{R}) + \frac{1}{2}(x - \bar{R})^2\,f'(\bar{R}), \tag{4}$$

where $f'(x)$ is the first derivative of $f(x)$ and the terms of higher order of smallness have been omitted. Hence (4) is an approximate relationship. Combining (3) and (4) gives an approximate relationship

$$M = F(\bar{R}) + \frac{1}{2}\,\sigma_R^2\,f'(\bar{R}), \tag{5}$$

where σ_R^2 is the variance of the requirement distribution.

Like any income distribution, we may assume that the distribution of calorie intake is a skewed distribution with a single mode. One characteristic of such distributions is that the mean is greater than the mode. If $\bar{R}$ (the average calorie requirement) is greater than the mode of the calorie intake distribution, which will generally be the case, $f'(\bar{R})$ (the slope of the calorie intake density function) will be negative. Thus, equation (5) implies that $F(\bar{R}) > M$; i.e., the average calorie norm approach tends to overestimate the extent of undernutrition. The extent of such overestimation depends on the second term in the right-hand side of (5). It is expected that $f'(\bar{R})$ will be of smaller order of magnitude than σ_R^2; thus, we conjecture that the degree of overestimation is not large. The validity of this conjecture is examined with the help of a simulation exercise on the Indian data in Section 6.7.

[3] Note that this result is based on the assumption of independence between intake and requirement distributions. Once this assumption is relaxed, as in Section 6.4, there can be either overestimation or underestimation, and its extent may be large or small, depending on the nature of correlation between intake and requirement.

6.3 A NEW CLASS OF UNDERNUTRITION MEASURES

The aggregate measure of undernutrition M given in (1) is interpreted as the probability that a randomly selected individual in the population suffers from undernutrition. This measure provides an estimate of the proportion of population that is undernourished. Thus, it may be called a head-count measure of undernutrition (the term used in the measurement of poverty literature).[4]

Most of the recent debate on undernutrition is entirely centred around the head-count measure. The proportion of individuals suffering from undernutrition, as such, does not reflect the intensity of undernutrition suffered by those who are undernourished because it does not make any distinction between mild and severe forms of undernutrition suffered by individuals. The measurement of the degree of undernutrition must take into account the gap between the calorie requirement and intake for each individual. If it does not, it can lead to perverse results.

Suppose the distribution of requirements is given by a vector $\mathbf{R} = (1, 1.5, 10)$, which is fixed for a population. Suppose further that there are three individuals in the population whose calorie intakes are given by the vector $\mathbf{x} = (2, 2.5, 3)$. It can be easily verified that $M = \frac{1}{3}$; i.e., the proportion of population suffering from undernutrition is 33.3 per cent.

Let us now suppose that there is a threefold increase in the individuals' calorie intake. It can be verified that M is still equal to $\frac{1}{3}$ despite the fact that intensity of hunger (or undernutrition) is considerably reduced. In order to rectify such a defect, I have developed below a class of undernutrition measures that take into account the proportion of undernourished individuals as well as the extent of their deprivation.

Let $h(x, R)$ be the degree of undernutrition suffered by an individual with calorie intake x and requirement R. Since R follows a probability distribution, the expected undernutrition suffered by an individual with intake x is given by

$$E(U/x) = \int_0^\infty h(x, R) g(R) \, dR. \tag{6}$$

Since the individual suffers from undernutrition only if $R > x$, we must have

$$H(x, R) = 0 \quad \text{if} \quad x \geqslant R$$

$$> 0 \quad \text{if} \quad x < R.$$

Then (6) should be written as

---

[4] Sen (1976) calls the head-count ratio a very crude index of poverty because 'an unchanged number of people below the "poverty line" may go with a sharp rise in the extent of the short-fall of income from the poverty line'.

$$E(U/x) = \int_x^\infty h(x, R)g(R)\,dR.$$

In order to make this idea empirically operational, it is necessary to specify the function $h(x, R)$. One simple specification in terms of one parameter is given by

$$h(x, R) = \left(\frac{R - x}{\bar{R}}\right)^\alpha,$$

R being the average calorie norm, which gives

$$E(U/x) = \int_x^\infty \left(\frac{R - x}{\bar{R}}\right)^\alpha g(R)\,dR.$$

The average undernutrition suffered by the population is then given by

$$K(\alpha) = \int_0^\infty \left[\int_x^\infty \left(\frac{R - x}{\bar{R}}\right)^\alpha g(R)\,dR \right] f(x)\,dx, \tag{7}$$

where α is the parameter to be specified. If $\alpha = 0$, $K(\alpha)$ is equal to the measure M, and when $\alpha = 1$, $K(\alpha)$ becomes

$$K = \frac{\bar{R} - \mu}{\bar{R}} + \frac{1}{\bar{R}} \int_0^\infty x\,G(x)f(x)\,dx - \int_0^\infty G_1(x)f(x)\,dx, \tag{8}$$

where

$$G_1(x) = \frac{1}{\bar{R}} \int_0^x R\,g(R)\,dR.$$

It can be proved that the sum of the two integrals in the right-hand side of (8) is non-negative, which implies that $K > (\bar{R} - \mu)/\bar{R}$.

A common procedure to determine undernutrition at aggregate level is to compare the average per capita availability of energy with per capita energy needs. When requirement exceeds availability, the country or region is classified as inadequately nourished. Such a measure may be given by $(\bar{R} - \mu)/\bar{R}$ which, of course, has many well-known limitations (mainly because populations are not homogeneous with respect to intakes and requirements of individuals belonging to them).

Since the measure K derived above takes into account the distribution of calorie intake among different individuals as well as the distribution of calorie requirements, it may be considered a suitable measure of undernutrition at aggregate level. It can be seen that the commonly used measure, i.e. $(\bar{R} - \mu)/\bar{R}$, underestimates the degree of undernutrition, which implies that, even if the average per capita calorie intake of a country is exactly equal to its per capita calorie requirement, undernutrition will still exist.

This observation was made at the United Nations World Food Conference held in Rome in 1974, where it was considered that energy supplies in the developing regions should be at least 10 per cent above aggregate requirements to allow for maldistribution. The figure of 10 per cent was arrived at on an *ad hoc* basis, but now equation (8) can be used to estimate the magnitude of underestimation. I performed these calculations on the Indian data presented in Section 6.7 below and found that the average energy supply for the rural areas should be about 20.6 per cent above the average energy requirement, and the corresponding figure for the urban areas was found to be 11 per cent. This means that in the rural areas the average calorie intake per consumer unit must increase from 2952 to 3353 calories, an increase of 13.6 per cent, in order for undernutrition (as measured by K) to be completely eliminated. Similarly, in the urban areas the calorie intake per consumer unit must increase by 19.2 per cent from 2588 to 3086 calories. These calculations are, of course, based on the assumption that the distribution of calorie intake does not change when the average calorie intake is increased in the population.

Further, note that when $\alpha = 1.0$ the degree of undernutrition suffered by an individual is given by the exact amount of his calorie shortfall. It would be more appropriate to give a higher weight to the larger calorie shortfall, which implies that α should be greater than unity. How much greater it should be is a matter of value judgement.

If the distribution of $g(R)$ collapses at the mean $\bar{R}$, it can be proved that $K(\alpha)$ becomes

$$K(\alpha) = \int_0^\infty \left(\frac{R-x}{\bar{R}}\right)^\alpha f(x)\,dx,$$

which is an expression for the class of decomposable poverty measures proposed by Foster *et al.* (1984) with poverty line $\bar{R}$. Thus, $K(\alpha)$ provides a generalization of their poverty measure when the poverty line is not a fixed number but follows a probability distribution.

6.4 ESTIMATION WHEN ONLY THE MEAN AND VARIANCE OF REQUIREMENTS ARE KNOWN

When only the mean and variance of requirements are known, we may try to make a range of estimates by using alternative forms of two-parameter distributions. I performed the computations on the basis of two distributions, namely uniform and normal.

6.4.1   Uniform distribution

First I assume that $g(R)$ is uniformly distributed with mean $\bar{R}$ and standard deviation σ_R. It can be shown that

$$1 - G(x) = 1 \qquad\qquad \text{if} \qquad x < \bar{R} - \sqrt{3}\sigma_R$$

$$= \frac{\bar{R} + 3\sigma_R - x}{2\sqrt{3}\sigma_R} \qquad \text{if} \qquad \bar{R} - \sqrt{3}\sigma_R \leq x \leq \bar{R} + 3\sigma_R$$

$$= 0 \qquad\qquad \text{if} \qquad x > \bar{R} + \sqrt{3}\sigma_R$$

which, on substituting in (1), gives

$$M = F(\bar{R} - \sqrt{3}\sigma_R) + \frac{\bar{R} + \sqrt{3}\sigma_R}{2\sqrt{3}\sigma_R} [F(\bar{R} + \sqrt{3}\sigma_R) - F(\bar{R} - \sqrt{3}\sigma_R)]$$

$$- \frac{\mu}{2\sqrt{3}\sigma_R} [F_1(\bar{R} + \sqrt{3}\sigma_R) - F_1(\bar{R} - \sqrt{3}\sigma_R)], \tag{9}$$

where $F(x)$ is the probability distribution function of the distribution of calorie intake and

$$F_1(x) = \frac{1}{\mu} \int_0^x xf(x)\,dx$$

is the first-moment distribution function, which is interpreted as the proportion of calories consumed by the people who have calorie consumption less than or equal to x.

Further, it can be verified that the class of undernutrition measures $K(\alpha)$ derived in (7) is given by

$$K(\alpha) = \frac{1}{2\sqrt{3}\sigma_R(\alpha + 1)} \int_0^{\bar{R} + \sqrt{3}\sigma_R} (\bar{R} + \sqrt{3}\sigma_R - x)^{\alpha + 1} f(x)\,dx$$

$$- \frac{1}{2\sqrt{3}\sigma_R(\alpha + 1)} \int_0^{\bar{R} - \sqrt{3}\sigma_R} (\bar{R} - \sqrt{3}\sigma_R - x)^{\alpha + 1} f(x)\,dx, \tag{10}$$

which leads to M when we substitute $\alpha = 0$.

6.4.2   Normal distribution

Assuming that $g(R)$ is normally distributed with mean $\bar{R}$ and standard deviation σ_R, then

$$G(x) = Q\left(\frac{x - \bar{R}}{\sigma_R}\right), \tag{11}$$

where

$$Q(x) = \frac{1}{\sqrt{2\pi}} \int_{-\infty}^{x} e^{-\frac{1}{2}t^2} \, dt.$$

Thus, M will be given by

$$M = \int_{0}^{\infty} \left[1 - Q\left(\frac{x - \bar{R}}{\sigma_R}\right) \right] f(x) \, dx,$$

which can be readily computed given the distribution of calorie intakes.

K given in (8) can be computed if we know $G(x)$ and $G_1(x)$. $G_1(x)$ for a normal distribution is given by

$$G_1(x) = \frac{1}{\bar{R} \sqrt{2\pi} \, \sigma_R} \int_{0}^{x} R e^{-\frac{1}{2}\left(\frac{R - \bar{R}}{\sigma_R}\right)^2} \, dR,$$

and $G(x)$ is derived in (11). So, substituting (11) and this equation in (8), we can obtain an estimate of K given the distribution of calorie intake.

All the measures of undernutrition presented so far are based on the assumption that the calorie intake x and the calorie requirement R, both measured per consumer unit, are independently distributed. This was the suggestion given by Sukhatme (1961), who argued that, since the available evidence indicates small correlation between the two variables, x and R can be assumed to be independently distributed for practical evaluation. Despite this evidence, it may be useful to see how the value of correlation coefficient affects the estimates of undernutrition. So let us consider a bivariate density between intake x and requirement R, $f(x, R)$. Then the head-count measure of undernutrition, which is the probability that a randomly selected person in the population suffers from undernutrition, is given by

$$M^* = \iint_{R < x} f(x, R) \, dx \, dR. \tag{12}$$

In practice, the bivariate density function $f(x, R)$ is not known. One common procedure is to assume that it is a bivariate normal density. This approach has two major limitations. First, the distribution of calorie intake is expected to be skewed whereas the bivariate normal distribution implies that it is symmetric. Second, the entire distribution of calorie intake is characterized by only two parameters, i.e. μ and σ^2; therefore, it cannot provide good fit to the entire distribution of calorie intake.

In order to solve this difficulty, let us write

$$f(x, R) = g(R/x) f(x),$$

where $g(R/x)$ is the conditional density of R given x, and $f(x)$ is the marginal density of x. Then M^* can be written as

$$M^* = \int_0^\infty \int_x^b g(R/x)f(x)\,\mathrm{d}R\,\mathrm{d}x,$$

where the density function $f(x)$ can be obtained from the given data on calorie intakes. To compute M^*, it will be necessary to specify the density function $g(R/x)$. So let us assume that $g(R/x)$ follows a univariate normal distribution with mean and variance as

$$E(R/x) = \bar{R} + \rho \frac{\sigma_R}{\sigma}(x - \mu)$$

and

$$\mathrm{var}\,(R/x) = \sigma_R^2(1 - \rho^2),$$

respectively, where ρ is the correlation coefficient between x and R. Then M^* will be given by

$$M^* = 1 - \int_0^\infty Q\left[\frac{x - \bar{R} - \rho \frac{\sigma_R}{\sigma}(x - \mu)}{\sigma_R\sqrt{(1 - \rho^2)}}\right]f(x)\,\mathrm{d}x, \qquad (13)$$

where $Q(x)$ is defined in (11) and $f(x)$ can be derived from the actual data on calorie intakes.

The numerical estimates of M^* for alternative values of ρ are presented in Section 6.7.

6.5 ESTIMATION WHEN ONLY MEAN REQUIREMENT IS KNOWN

When only mean requirement is known, we may still obtain upper and lower bounds on the measure of undernutrition, provided we can assume symmetry of the requirement distribution.

Let us write M as

$$M = \int_0^{\bar{R}} [1 - G(x)]f(x)\,\mathrm{d}(x) + \int_{\bar{R}}^\infty [1 - G(x)]f(x)\,\mathrm{d}(x).$$

It is obvious that

$$\int_0^{\bar{R}} [1 - G(x)]f(x)\,\mathrm{d}(x) \geqslant [1 - G(\bar{R})] \int_0^{\bar{R}} f(x)\,\mathrm{d}(x) = [1 - G(\bar{R})]\,F(\bar{R}) \qquad (14)$$

and

$$\int_{\bar{R}}^{\infty} [1 - G(x)] f(x) \, \mathrm{d}(x) \geq 0, \tag{15}$$

which are derived from the fact that the distribution function $G(x)$ is a non-decreasing function in its domain.

Combining (14) and (15), we obtain

$$M \geq [1 - G(\bar{R})] F(\bar{R}),$$

and if we assume $g(R)$ to be symmetrically distributed around its mean $\bar{R}$, $G(\bar{R}) = \frac{1}{2}$, which gives

$$M \geq \tfrac{1}{2} F(\bar{R}),$$

which provides a lower bound on M and can be obtained by knowing $\bar{R}$ and the distribution of calorie intake.

Similarly, it can be seen that

$$\int_{\bar{R}}^{\infty} [1 - G(x)] f(x) \, \mathrm{d}x \leq [1 - G(\bar{R})] [1 - F(\bar{R})] \tag{16}$$

and

$$\int_{\bar{R}}^{\infty} [1 - G(x)] f(x) \, \mathrm{d}x \leq F(\bar{R}), \tag{17}$$

which gives

$$M \leq F(\bar{R}) + [1 - G(\bar{R})] [1 - F(\bar{R})];$$

and if $g(R)$ is symmetric around its mean, we obtain an upper bound on M as

$$M \leq \tfrac{1}{2} + \tfrac{1}{2} F(\bar{R}).$$

This leads to the following proposition:

PROPOSITION 1   If the distribution of calorie requirement is symmetric around its mean, then

$$\tfrac{1}{2} F(\bar{R}) \leq M \leq \tfrac{1}{2} + \tfrac{1}{2} F(\bar{R}).$$

6.6 PARTIAL RANKING OF POPULATIONS ACCORDING TO THE DEGREE OF UNDERNUTRITION

In this section we deal with the question, If the distribution of calorie requirement is completely unknown (including its mean), is it possible to say, on the basis of distribution of calorie intake alone, whether one population has greater or less undernutrition than another ? This issue is of considerable practical importance for two reasons. First, the average calorie norms published by FAO are derived from studies on healthy young men in the developed world and are of questionable applicability for other populations (FAO 1978). Second, if, as it is argued by Sukhatme, the body possesses a self-regulatory mechanism, then the mean of the distribution of 'true' calorie requirements will be less than the average calorie norm $\bar{R}$, and that is very much an unknown quantity.

I derive below a criterion for ranking any two populations with respect to the degree of undernutrition, provided it can be assumed that both populations have an identical distribution of requirements, even though it is unknown. This criterion will be particularly useful in comparing the degree of undernutrition of a population at different time periods, given the fact that the distribution of individual requirements does not change that much over a short period.

Suppose we are interested in comparing undernutrition in populations 1 and 2 which have density functions of calorie intake $f_1(x)$ and $f_2(x)$, respectively. Let $g(R)$ be the common density function of the requirement distribution; then the indices of undernutrition for the two populations are

$$M_1 = \int_0^\infty [1 - G(x)] f_1(x) \, dx$$

and

$$M_2 = \int_0^\infty [1 - G(x)] f_2(x) \, dx,$$

which on integration by parts become

$$M_1 = \int_0^\infty F_1(x) g(x) \, dx$$

and

$$M_2 = \int_0^\infty F_2(x) \, g(x) \, dx$$

respectively, where $F_1(x)$ and $F_2(x)$ are the distribution functions of the calorie intake distributions of populations 1 and 2 respectively. It can be seen that, if $F_1(x) \geq F_2(x)$ for all x, then $M_1 \geq M_2$. This leads to the following proposition:

PROPOSITION 2   If $F_1(x) \geq F_2(x)$ for all values of x, then the undernutrition in population 1 will always be greater than or equal to that in population 2.

This proposition provides a criterion of ranking the two populations according to the head-count measure of undernutrition, provided the two curves $F_1(x)$ and $F_2(x)$ do not cross. If, however, these curves cross, one cannot say whether one population has greater or less undernutrition than the other population. Thus, this criterion provides only a partial ranking of populations.

Next, we consider the ranking of populations according to undernutrition as determined by the class of measures derived in (9) above. These measurements for populations 1 and 2 may be written as

$$K_1(\alpha) = \int_0^\infty E(U/x) f_1(x) \, dx \qquad (18)$$

and

$$K_2(\alpha) = \int_0^\infty E(U/x) f_2(x) \, dx \qquad (19)$$

respectively, where

$$E(U/x) = \int_x^\infty \left(\frac{R-x}{R}\right)^\alpha g(R) \, dR. \qquad (20)$$

Using Leibniz's rule for differentiating an integral, the first and second derivatives of $E(U/x)$ with respect to x are derived as[5]

$$\frac{\partial E(U/x)}{\partial x} = \frac{-\alpha}{\bar{R}} \int_x^\infty \left(\frac{R-x}{\bar{R}}\right)^{\alpha-1} g(R) \, dR < 0 \qquad (21)$$

$$\frac{\partial^2 E(U/x)}{\partial x^2} = \frac{\alpha(\alpha-1)}{\bar{R}^2} \int_x^\infty \left(\frac{R-x}{\bar{R}}\right)^{\alpha-2} g(R) \, dR > 0 \qquad (22)$$

for $\alpha \geq 1$, respectively. Integrating (18) and (19) twice by parts gives

$$K_1(\alpha) = \int_0^\infty \varphi_1(x) \frac{\partial^2 E(U/x)}{\partial x^2} \, dx \qquad (23)$$

and

$$K_2(\alpha) = \int_0^\infty \varphi_2(x) \frac{\partial^2 E(U/x)}{\partial x^2}, \qquad (24)$$

where

$$\varphi_1(x) = \int_0^x F_1(x) \, dx \qquad \text{and} \qquad \varphi_2(x) = \int_0^x F_2(x) \, dx.$$

It can be readily seen that, since $\partial^2 E(U/x)/\partial x^2 \geq 0$ for $\alpha > 1$, if $\varphi_1(x) \geq \varphi_2(x)$ for all values of x, then $K_1(\alpha) \geq K_2(\alpha)$, which leads to the following proposition:

PROPOSITION 3 If $\varphi_1(x) \geq \varphi_2(x)$ for all values of x, then undernutrition in population 1 will be greater than or equal to that in population 2 when undernutrition is measured by the entire class of undernutrition indices $K(\alpha)$ (except $\alpha = 0$).

Note that $F_1(x) > F_2(x)$ and $\varphi_1(x) > \varphi_2(x)$ for all values of x are the first- and second-order dominance conditions in the field of decision-making

[5] Note that the term arising from differentiating the lower limit of the integral is zero.

under uncertainty, respectively.[6] The first-order dominance condition always implies the second-order dominance condition, but the converse is not true.

The graphs for $F_1(x)$ and $F_1(x)$ can be drawn without any difficulty from the data on the distribution of calorie intakes. However, values of $\varphi_1(x)$ and $\varphi_2(x)$ are not directly obtainable from these data. In order to tackle this problem, we utilize the idea of Lorenz curve $L(p)$ (which is interpreted as the proportion of calories consumed by the bottom $100 \times p$ per cent of the population, where p lies in the range $0 \leq p \leq 1$.

The relationship between the Lorenz curve ranking and the ranking implied by $\varphi(x)$ is given by the following lemma (Atkinson 1970):

LEMMA The following statements are equivalent:

(A) $\varphi_1(x) \geq \varphi_2(x)$ for all x;

(B) $\mu_1 L_1(p) \leq \mu_2 L_2(p)$ for all p;

where μ_1 and μ_2 are the average calories consumed by populations 1 and 2, and L_1 and L_2 are their Lorenz curves, respectively.

Following Kakwani (1984), the product of mean calorie intake and the Lorenz curve may be called the generalized Lorenz curve, which is directly observable from the data of the distribution of calorie intake. Thus, the following proposition, which follows immediately from proposition 3 and the above lemma, provides an empirically operational criterion to rank any two distributions of calorie intakes:

PROPOSITION 4 If the generalized Lorenz curve for population 2 is higher than that for population 1 at all points, then undernutrition in population 1 will be higher than that for population 2 when undernutrition is measured by the entire class of indices $K(\alpha)$ (except $\alpha = 0$).

Note that we can rank the populations only if the generalized Lorenz curves for the two distributions do not intersect. If they do intersect then it is not possible to say which of the two distributions has a greater degree of undernutrition. In order to obtain the complete ranking, we have to specify a distribution of calorie requirements.

6.7 NUMERICAL ESTIMATES OF UNDERNUTRITION

This section presents the numerical estimates of undernutrition based on the Indian data (National Sample Survey of 1971–2) which formed

---

[6] See Rothschild and Stiglitz (1970), and Hadar and Russell (1969).

the basis of earlier computations carried out by Dandekar (1981) and Sukhatme (1977*a*, 1981*a*, 1982*b*).

Table 6.1.   Calorie distribution by consumer units : all-India rural areas 1971–1972

Monthly expenditure per consumer unit (Rs)	No. of households	Av. no. of consumer units per household	Av. calorie intake per day per consumer unit	Distribution of consumer units (%)
0–15	444	4.99	1493	4.6
15–21	1207	4.74	1957	11.8
21–24	813	4.78	2287	8.0
24–28	1174	4.51	2431	11.0
28–34	1748	4.44	2734	16.0
34–43	2028	4.20	3127	17.6
43–55	1655	4.08	3513	14.0
55–75	1319	3.70	4016	10.1
95–100	598	3.31	4574	4.1
100+	482	2.84	6181	2.8
All classes	11468	4.29	2724	100.0

Source: National Sample Survey (1976).

First, I shall outline the computing procedures adopted by Dandekar and Sukhatme. Their estimates were derived from the data given in Table 6.1, which gives the distribution of calorie intake by households. The households have been arranged in ascending order by their per-consumer-unit monthly expenditure. The average calorie requirement for India as developed by FAO/WHO is 2780 kcal at the retail level. Dandekar used the average calorie norm approach to estimate undernutrition, i.e. the proportion of population that has a calorie intake of less than 2780 kcal.

Instead of estimating the proportion of individuals suffering from undernutrition, Dandekar estimated the proportion of consumer units having a calorie intake of less than 2780. Using the method of linear interpolation in the fifth expenditure group (28–34), he arrived at a figure of 4.6 + 11.8 + 8.0 + 11.0 + 16.0; i.e., 46.4 per cent of consumer units were suffering from undernutrition.

Both Dandekar and Sukhatme derived their estimates of undernutrition on the basis of grouped data which were obtained by ranking households according to their per-consumer-unit monthly expenditure. Their estimates will be correct only if there is a monotonic relationship between calorie intake and total expenditure. Such a relationship may not exist, owing to differences in tastes and habits of different individuals. In order to investigate this empirically, I computed the average calorie intake of various household deciles when households are ranked by both energy intake and monthly expenditure per consumer unit. The numerical estimates are presented in Table 6.2.

Table 6.2. Average calorie intake by household deciles when households are ranked according to daily energy intake per consumer unit and monthly expenditure per consumer unit: all-India rural areas, 1971–1972

Household deciles	Average calorie intake	
	Ranking by daily energy intake per consumer unit	Ranking by monthly expenditure per consumer unit
1	1333	1675
2	1818	2094
3	2093	2331
4	2341	2541
5	2586	2745
6	2849	2960
7	3145	3197
8	3508	3482
9	4040	3880
10	5843	5058
Total population	2956	2996

Source: National Sample Survey (1976).

It can be seen from these results that the average calorie intake in lower deciles is higher when households are ranked by monthly expenditure than when they are ranked by energy intake. This clearly indicates that the number of undernourished will be underestimated when calculated from the data based on expenditure ranking. This is an important observation, because it casts doubt on the estimates of global undernutrition obtained by FAO (1977) and the World Bank (Reutlinger and Selowsky 1976) based on the income or expenditure distribution data. To determine the extent of underestimation, I ranked households by their energy intake per consumer unit.

Using these rankings, the average calorie norm (ACN) approach yielded a percentage of consumer units suffering from undernutrition of 52.3 for the rural areas and 66.5 for the urban areas. These results clearly suggest that substantial underestimation occurs when the estimates of undernutrition are derived from data based on expenditure or income ranking instead of the ranking by calorie intake. This conclusion will hold if even the Engel curve, relating calorie intake to total expenditure, is estimated with a high value of R^2 (the coefficient of determination). The occurrence of a high R^2 is a common phenomenon when Engel curves are estimated from grouped data, and may lead to a belief that there is a one-to-one correspondence between calorie intake and total expenditure. This is clearly shown to be untrue.

Table 6.3. Head-count measure of undernutrition based on the distribution of individuals: India, 1971–1972

Head-count measure	Av. calorie norm approach	Uniform distribution	Normal distribution
Rural areas	52.4	51.3	51.4
Urban	67.5	64.2	64.5
Ratio of rural to urban undernutrition	0.776	0.799	0.797

It is interesting to note that both Sukhatme and Dandekar measure the incidence of undernutrition by estimating the percentage of consumer units, rather than individuals, suffering from undernutrition. This approach runs into serious conceptual problems because it measures the sufferings of hypothetical consumer units rather than the sufferings of individuals within households. Consider for instance two households with the same number of consumer units but differing with respect to the number of individuals belonging to them—one household has more children than the other. The above approach will give equal weight to the sufferings of individuals in both households despite the fact that one household comprises a larger number of individuals than the other. This is clearly unwarranted, because it implies that the suffering of children and female adults is less important than that of adult males. Any two individuals suffering from the same degree of undernourishment must be given exactly equal weight: there exists no justification for discriminating between individuals with respect to their sufferings. Since our utmost concern is with individuals, the aggregate index of undernutrition should be defined in terms of the distribution of individual sufferings only.

Various estimates of the head-count measure of undernutrition based on the distribution of individuals are presented in Table 6.3. These estimates are derived by assuming the average calorie norm of 2780 per consumer unit with coefficient of variation of 15 per cent around this value. It is interesting to note that the ACN approach provides estimates quite close to those obtained by using the entire distribution of calorie requirements. Further, the estimates of undernutrition obtained by uniform and normal distributions are almost identical, implying that it makes little difference what form of calorie requirement distribution is chosen.

Table 6.4. Head-count measure of undernutrition for diffferent values of coefficient of variation: India, 1971–1972

Coefficient of variation	Rural		Urban	
	Uniform distribution	Normal distribution	Uniform distribution	Normal distribution
0.0	52.4	52.4	67.5	67.5
2.5	52.4	52.4	67.4	67.4
5.0	52.3	52.3	67.1	67.1
1.5	52.1	52.1	66.6	66.6
10.0	51.9	51.9	66.0	66.0
12.5	51.6	51.6	65.2	65.3
15.0	51.3	51.4	64.2	64.5
17.5	50.9	51.1	63.3	63.7
20.0	50.5	50.8	62.2	62.9
22.5	50.2	50.5	61.2	62.1
25.0	49.8	50.3	60.3	61.3
27.5	49.5	50.0	59.4	60.6
30.0	49.2	49.8	58.6	59.7

Since the coefficient of variation of the distribution of requirements is not known exactly, it may be useful to examine the sensitivity of estimates of undernutrition with respect to the coefficient of variation. Table 6.4 presents these estimates for different values of the coefficient of variation varying from 0 to 30 per cent. It is remarkable that estimates do not vary as much as might be expected, particularly in the rural areas. This is an important observation because of the uncertain knowledge about the exact value of the coefficient of variation in the distribution of calorie requirements.

Table 6.5 presents estimates of the class of severity-sensitive undernutrition measures proposed in Section 6.3. These estimates show a pattern quite similar to that from the head-count measurements. Although the ratio of the degree of undernutrition in the rural area to that in urban area increases monotonically with α, the differences are not all that large.

The estimates of undernutrition that have been presented so far were computed on the assumption that the calorie intake x and the calorie requirement R, both measured in per-capita consumer units, are independently distributed. This is an unrealistic assumption, because, although in a healthy active population of reference age, sex, and weight, the intake may be expected to equal the average energy expenditure, the population under consideration consists of both healthy and unhealthy (undernourished) individuals, so that the correlation between x and R will be small and therefore, for all practical purposes, can be assumed to be zero. But this procedure will provide only an approximate value of the extent of undernutrition. It is interesting to see how good this approximation will be when the correlation coefficient between x and R is not small. Table 6.6 presents the values of the head-count measure of undernutrition for alternative values of the correlation coefficient ρ.

Table 6.5. Class of severity–sensitive undernutrition measures $K(\alpha)$: India, 1971–1972

	Uniform distribution α			Normal distribution α		
	0.0	1.0	2.0	0.0	1.0	2.0
Rural	51.3	14.4	6.07	51.4	14.3	—
Urban	64.2	17.9	7.30	64.5	17.9	—
Rural–urban ratio	0.799	0.804	0.831	0.797	0.800	

Table 6.6. Head-count measure of undernutrition when the calorie intake and requirement are correlated: India, 1971–1972

Coefficient of correlation	Rural areas	Urban areas
0.00	51.40	64.50
0.10	51.07	64.64
0.20	50.79	64.86
0.30	50.50	65.16
0.40	50.21	65.56
0.50	49.93	66.09
0.60	49.65	66.79
0.70	49.37	67.73
0.80	49.12	69.02
0.90	48.90	70.88

It is interesting to observe that the degree of undernutrition decreases monotonically with ρ in the rural areas but shows a monotonic increase in urban areas. I did some further simulations and arrived at the conclusion that, if $\mu > \bar{R}$, the degree of undernutrition decreases monotonically with ρ and the reverse is the case when $\bar{R} > \mu$. Anyway, these results indicate that the estimates of undernutrition will not be too biased if ρ is assumed to be zero.

Finally, Table 6.7 presents estimates of the generalized Lorenz curve $[L(p)]$ for different values of ρ. It can be seen that the generalized Lorenz curve for calorie intakes is higher for rural areas than for urban areas for all values of ρ. From proposition 4 above, it follows that undernutrition in rural areas will be lower than that in urban areas for all distributions of calorie requirements when undernutrition is measured by the entire class of indices $K(\alpha)$ (except $\alpha = 0$); but if undernutrition is measured by the head-count ratio, we require the stronger condition of first dominance, viz. $F_1(x) > F_2(x)$ for all x. The numerical results showed that the probability distribution function for urban areas is higher than that for rural areas for all values of calorie intakes. Thus, proposition 2 leads to the conclusion that undernutrition in rural areas is unambiguously lower than that in urban areas.

Table 6.7. Generalized Lorenz curve for rural and urban areas: India, 1971–1972

p	Rural areas		Urban areas	
	$L(p)$	$\mu[L(p)]$	$L(p)$	$\mu[L(p)]$
0.10	0.0451	133.3	0.0516	133.3
0.20	0.1072	316.8	0.1200	309.9
0.30	0.1786	527.9	0.1967	508.0
0.40	0.2583	163.4	0.2803	123.9
0.50	0.3462	1023.2	0.3707	957.4
0.60	0.4427	1308.5	0.4681	1208.9
0.70	0.5490	1622.7	0.5734	1480.9
0.80	0.6673	1972.3	0.6885	1778.2
0.90	0.8033	2374.3	0.8180	2112.6
1.00	1.0000	2955.7	1.0000	2582.7

6.7   SUMMARY AND CONCLUSIONS

The objective of this chapter was twofold: (1) to develop sensible methodologies for comparing the nutritional status of different populations, given the fact that within each population nutritional requirements vary from person to person, and (2) to develop measures of undernutrition which would take account not only of the number of people undernourished but also of the severity of their undernutrition. These methodologies were illustrated with the help of Indian data. Some of the major findings of the study are summarized below.

1   The average calorie norm approach that has been used by the World Bank and the FAO to estimate undernutrition at global level overestimates the degree of undernutrition (in the event of independence between intakes and requirements), but the extent of the overestimation may be small.

2   A common procedure to determine undernutrition at aggregate level is to compare the average per-capita availability of energy with the average per-capita energy needs. It has been demonstrated that this procedure underestimates the degree of undernutrition, which implies

that, even if the average per-capita calorie intake of a country is exactly equal to its average per-capita calorie requirement, undernutrition will still exist. Using the Indian data for 1971–2, I found that the average energy supply for the rural (urban) areas should have been about 20.6 (11) per cent above the average energy requirement if undernutrition were to be eliminated with the existing pattern of distribution.

3   This paper establishes a procedure for partial rankings of populations according to the degree of undernutrition which does not require any knowledge of the distribution of calorie requirements, including its mean. Using this procedure, it is shown that undernutrition in rural areas of India is lower than that in urban areas for all distributions of calorie requirements.

4   The study also explores the measurement of undernutrition when calorie intake and requirement are correlated. It is shown that the estimates of undernutrition are not too biased if the correlation is assumed to be zero.

7

Issues in the Measurement of Undernutrition

S. Anand and C. J. Harris

7.1 INTRODUCTION

One way of attempting to alleviate chronic undernutrition is through the use of economic policies. In order to design such policies, it is important to understand the relationship between economic and social characteristics on the one hand, and undernutrition on the other. At a minimum, it is important to determine which socioeconomic groups suffer most from undernutrition; at a maximum, it would be desirable to discover how an individual's economic and social conditions affect his nutritional opportunities, and vice versa.

Two types of data source seem to be particularly relevant to these questions: (i) medically intensive surveys, designed to identify symptoms of clinical undernutrition; and (ii) household budget surveys, designed to obtain a wide variety of economic and social data. The first type of survey provides an accurate assessment of whether or not a particular individual in the sample is undernourished. But the number of individuals sampled in such surveys tends to be small, and the design of the surveys insufficiently random; moreover, they collect very few economic data, and those they do collect are often not precise. The second type of survey usually involves a comprehensive coverage, an adequately random sample design, and the canvassing of rich socioeconomic information; but it does not provide reliable medical information.

Evidently, then, neither type of survey is ideally suited to the purpose at hand. One obvious response would be to design and conduct a special survey that is dedicated to this purpose. This response deserves to be taken seriously, but it does raise a number of issues. First, a large number of surveys of the types described have already been conducted, and still more are likely to be conducted in the future. So it is useful to discover what use, if any, can be made of such existing and potential data sources in order to address our purpose. Secondly, both of the existing types of survey have a specific rationale and objective. A survey ideally suited to our own purpose might not serve either of these two

For helpful comments and suggestions in preparing this paper, we should like to thank Jean Drèze, Jeya Henry, Siddiq Osmani, and especially Amartya Sen.

objectives adequately. Hence it might be more practical to consider whether the existing surveys can be adapted to give adequate answers to the questions we have posed without compromising their rationale. Thirdly, considerable expertise in the design and conduct of the existing types of survey has been accumulated. Adapting one of these types might therefore have a better chance of success than embarking upon a new type which is dedicated to the purpose at hand.

The main aim of this chapter is to try and determine what can be learned about undernutrition from household budget surveys as they currently exist. But we also hope that our investigation will shed light on the question of how such surveys might be adapted in order to provide better information on undernutrition, and on the limits to the scope for adapting them.

The potential relevance of household budget surveys to the estimation of the incidence of undernutrition derives from the fact that they often contain data on the amount and type of food consumed by households. These data are usually used to calculate quantity weights for indices of the cost of living. However, since the data are available at the level of household, it is tempting to try and use them to assess whether individual households have adequate food. This has often been done, the most common method being to classify as undernourished those individuals who belong to households with a per-capita food intake below a given population norm.

The major problem with this approach is that it neglects the variation in nutritional requirement across individuals. This variation will lead to the familiar two types of classification error (see Anand 1983: 117–18). The first occurs when a household's per-capita intake lies above the norm but its requirement is larger than its intake; the second occurs when a household's per-capita intake lies below the norm but its requirement is smaller than its intake. By analogy with statistical concepts, these errors are usually referred to as being of type I and type II, respectively (relative to the hypothesis of undernourishment). Because of these errors, the individuals identified as 'undernourished' by the population norm may not be representative of those who are actually undernourished—with intake less than own requirement. Any attempt to relate economic variables to 'undernourishment' identified in this way may well lead to biased results. Worse still, there is no reason why type I and type II errors should be equal. So the approach may not even give a reliable estimate of the *number* of truly undernourished.

One possible response to these difficulties is to exploit other information contained in a household budget survey. For example, data on the age, sex, and occupation of an individual, and the number of days that he works, are often available. These can in principle be used to improve one's estimate of the individual's requirement, and thereby to reduce the error in one's estimate of the adequacy or otherwise of his intake. Household budget surveys do not, however, collect data on all variables relevant to the determination of an individual's requirement. For example, they do not collect data on metabolic efficiency, and they seldom contain data on height. Moreover, the data they do include that are relevant to activity (such as occupation and days worked) at best give a rough indication of the activity level of an individual. Hence, while the error in one's estimate of the adequacy of an individual's intake can be reduced by such means, it cannot be eliminated.

A second response is not to attempt to determine which individuals are undernourished, but to concentrate on finding a criterion or set of criteria that is sufficient for undernutrition. The set of individuals who satisfy these criteria will then constitute a subset of the undernourished, and their number will give an underestimate of the number of the undernourished. The main contribution that this strategy can make is to show that the problem of undernutrition is non-negligible. If the set of individuals who satisfy the criteria possess characteristics not shared by the remainder of the sample, it may also enable policies to be targeted to the undernourished that are reasonably free from the problem of leakage. But it does not provide a reliable means of tracking the course of undernutrition over time within a country, or of comparing undernutrition across countries.

A third response is to make supplementary use of variables that are not standard in the analysis of undernutrition. One possibility here is that certain economic variables may help to capture the extent to which resources are available to meet an individual's food needs. For example, an individual whose calorie intake is less than the norm but who has a high food expenditure is unlikely to be undernourished. The individual's high food expenditure clearly and directly reveals that he disposes of the resources necessary to obtain a higher calorie intake; the fact that he does not opt for a higher intake suggests strongly that he has a low requirement.

A fourth response—which also exploits economic information—is to argue that, for poor individuals at least, decreasing economic welfare (measured, for example, by income or total expenditure) and increasing undernutrition go hand in hand. This is a powerful, and in our view plausible, assumption. If true, it has correspondingly powerful implications. After all, household budget surveys are well suited to the measurement of economic welfare. Hence, if economic welfare and undernutrition are closely related, the bottom 10 per cent (say) of individuals ranked according to economic welfare should provide a reasonable proxy for the 10 per cent most undernourished individuals in the population. Equally importantly, the use of measures of economic welfare may allow us to circumvent the difficulties in estimating an individual's requirement mentioned above. Put very crudely, the basic difficulty in estimating an individual's requirement is that the estimate will be noisy, and that this noise will lead to classi-fication errors. If, however, one averages the estimates over individuals within a welfare group, then the effects of noise should be sharply reduced. (In particular, variations in metabolic efficiency would average out.) So one can obtain an estimate of the number of undernourished by finding that level of economic welfare at which, on average, intake and requirement are equal, and counting the number of individuals whose welfare falls below this level.

The structure of this chapter is as follows. Section 7.2 sets out the framework for our discussion of undernutrition, and sketches a simple model to help explain our concept of requirements. (A formal treatment is given in Appendix A.1.) Section 7.3 investigates the conventional approach of using a calorie cut-off to identify the undernourished. The issues are introduced by considering first the case of perfect correlation between intake and requirement (Section 7.3.1), which is then generalized to the case of imperfect correlation (Section 7.3.2); Section 7.3.3 considers the problems with this approach in identifying the most undernourished people in the population. Section 7.4 suggests a novel approach to identifying the undernourished—one that improves upon the calorie cut-off method by exploiting supplementary economic data to obtain information about indi-vidual requirements. Section 7.5 approaches undernourishment directly via economic welfare, and thus also utilizes supplementary information (but in a different way). Section 7.6 is in conclusion.

7.2 THE FRAMEWORK

The question under consideration in this chapter is easy to state in the abstract. Suppose that Y is the nutritional intake, and X the nutritional requirement, of an individual. Then, by definition, the individual is undernourished if and only if $Y < X$ or $Y/X < 1$. So, if one had data on both Y and X, it would be a simple matter to determine whether an individual was undernourished. However, often one will have data on Y and various data relevant to the determination of X, but no data on X itself. To what extent can one determine which individuals are undernourished, or even how many individuals are undernourished, in such cases?

We hope that much of what we have to say on these questions will be robust to the exact interpretation given to X and Y. It may, none the less, be helpful to give a somewhat more concrete indication of the kind of interpretation that we have in mind.

The first difficulty that arises is this. There are many dimensions to nutrition, including calories, essential amino-acids, vitamins, and so on. Yet by taking X and Y to be scalars, we are effectively treating nutrition as a one-dimensional variable. One way of justifying this would be to argue that it is possible to aggregate the various dimensions into a single meaningful measure. Another would be to argue that, in practice, the various dimensions of nutrition are closely linked, and that a valid first approximation is therefore to treat just one of the dimensions. We are inclined to adopt the second position, and to focus on calorie intake and calorie requirements. In this we follow, *inter alia*, Poleman (1981*b*) and Lipton (1983).[1]

There are some difficulties in defining and measuring even calorie intake. For example, amino-acids can be used to build up tissue and also can be broken down to provide energy; and it is hard to disentangle the calorie intake of an individual from that of the household to which he belongs. But these are relatively minor compared with the issues that arise when one tries to define and measure calorie requirements. So we concentrate on the latter.

Suppose that one tries to adopt a purely positive definition of requirements: X is a measure of the energy required by the individual to undertake his various activities (including physical and metabolic). What then would it mean to say that $Y < X$? After all, Y is simply a measure of the energy consumed by the individual, and as such must be equal to the energy expended, by the first law of thermodynamics (the law of the conservation of energy).[2] One obvious response is to point out that the energy deficit $X - Y$ is drawn from bodily reserves. Unfortunately, if one adopts this point of view, undernutrition must be seen as a purely short-run phenomenon. To put it crudely, an individual is undernourished if he is currently losing weight. But it is not possible to obtain a concept of long-run, or chronic, undernutrition. To put it crudely once again, an individual for whom $Y < X$ permanently wastes away and eventually dies. Put another way, periods in which $Y < X$ must be balanced by others in which $Y > X$; otherwise the individual cannot build up the bodily reserves on which he is supposed to draw.

Yet we would argue that chronic undernutrition is a perfectly meaningful concept. One must therefore define requirements in such a way that it can occur. In view of the preceding discussion, this must involve introducing a normative element into the definition of requirements.

In order to see what might be involved here, it is helpful to consider the following very simple model. An individual's body has an essential fixed component, which we call his *frame*, and a 'non-essential' variable component, which we call his *reserves*. He incurs a *metabolic energy cost*[3] proportional to his body size, and a *physical energy cost* proportional to

---

[1] See also McLaren (1974), Reutlinger and Alderman (1980), World Bank (1986), Osmani (1987), and Dasgupta and Ray (1990).

[2] We are grateful to Philip Payne for drawing our attention to the importance of bearing the first law in mind when considering questions of requirements.

[3] We deliberately avoid the word 'requirement' here.

the product of his body size and his activity level.[4] Finally, the rate of change of his reserves is proportional to the difference between his total energy cost (metabolic and physical) and his energy intake. (His frame does not change.)

As it stands, this model is purely positive. But one can introduce a normative element as follows. First, one decides on a minimum acceptable level of reserves. Then one defines an individual's calorie requirement to be that level of intake which would allow him to maintain the desired level of reserves while maintaining his existing level of activity. This definition is perfectly consistent with chronic undernourishment: a chronically under-nourished individual's reserves fall until they reach a point at which the saving on the physical and metabolic energy cost associated with his reserves compensates for the shortfall in intake. One thus obtains a theory which corresponds well to the common-sense idea that undernourishment and wasting go hand in hand. (The model and the definition of requirements are set out more formally in Appendix A.1. This appendix can be viewed as an attempt to flesh out the model of nutrition implicit in the recent FAO/WHO/UNU (1985) Expert Consultation Report.)

The model is, none the less, too simplistic as it stands. For instance, it is often emphasized that one way in which individuals facing a shortfall in food respond to their predicament is by cutting back on activity; and reducing activity to too low a level is harmful to the organism—it can, for example, result in the atrophy of muscles and cartilages. The simplest response to this criticism is to introduce a minimum acceptable level of activity, and to define an individual's calorie requirement to be that level of intake which would allow him to achieve either his current or this minimum level of activity, whichever is higher, while maintaining the desired level of reserves.

Another respect in which the model may be too simplistic is that, while the activity level of an individual who is engaged in income-earning efforts may easily exceed the minimum acceptable, he may none the less be forced to cut back on what might loosely be described as social activity (using 'social' in a sufficiently broad sense); and this could be deleterious psychologically. This criticism can also be accommodated by incorporating a target level for social activity into the formula for re-quirements in the obvious way.

Such adjustments should, however, be limited in both size and scope. The general reason for this is that, by broadening the set of ends that nutrition is deemed to serve, one runs the risk of 'undernutrition' ceasing to reflect the elementary idea of 'not having enough to eat'—while failing to capture the more general notion of deprivation by which the broader set of ends is presumably motivated. We give two examples.

[4] This formulation is based on the 'factorial' approach to requirements recommended by the FAO/WHO/UNU (1985) Expert Consultation Report.

Suppose one argues that a substantial degree of physical fitness is important for an individual's health, and accordingly sets a minimum acceptable level of activity. Then one might easily be forced to classify an overweight individual as undernourished because his intake, while excessive for his chosen level of activity, is insufficient for the minimum level of activity specified. Suppose, next (to take a more controversial example), that one specifies an individual's calorie requirement to include the energy necessary to search for work. Then one would run into an analogous problem: one might be forced to classify as undernourished an individual who *chooses* not to search for work and is adequately fed by his family for the amount of activity that he does undertake.[5, 6]

There are, however, two more serious oversimplifications. One of these is the assumption that frame is fixed. This assumption is blatantly false for children! One can begin to accommodate children within the model by choosing a minimum acceptable rate of growth instead of a minimum acceptable level of reserves. However, the choice of rate of growth is likely to be controversial in practice. Also, the size that a child can potentially attain will depend on its genes. (Genetic differences are also relevant in the case of adults, but would seem more serious in the context of children.) The other oversimplification is the absence of any consideration of health and disease.

7.3 USING A SIMPLE CALORIE CUT-OFF

In this section we shall suppose that people are distinguished by the pair (X, Y) of their nutritional requirement and nutritional intake, respectively. Although X and Y could in theory be independently distributed across people, we would in practice expect them to be positively related. Without even considering activity, a person with a high metabolic energy cost—say, because he has a large frame or a high basal metabolic rate—is likely, *ceteris paribus*, to have a high energy expenditure and intake. Choice of activity—in which a physical energy cost is incurred—is only likely to help strengthen the positive relationship.

---

[5] The case for making such an allowance would seem to derive its force from examples such as the following. A poor individual stays at home because he does not have the energy to look for work. If he could only have a good meal, then he could go and search for work. Having found work, he would be able to feed himself, and thus break the vicious circle in which he is trapped. But such an individual would be classified as undernourished on our approach anyway; for if his reserves were at or above their target level, he would have the energy necessary to look for work.

[6] The basic problem in both these examples is that the ends that nutrition is deemed to serve do not coincide with the ends the individual actually pursues.

One popular approach to identifying the undernourished consists in specifying a calorie cut-off y_c, and counting the number of individuals who fall below it. Often y_c will be set equal to $\bar{X}$, the population mean of X. Two questions arise naturally in relation to this approach: (i) When is it appropriate to use a calorie cut-off y_c? (ii) How should y_c be chosen? In particular, should y_c be set equal to $\bar{X}$?

7.3.1   The case of perfect correlation

In trying to assess undernutrition, the question of interest is whether $Y - X < 0$. On the other hand, the variable used when applying a calorie cut-off is Y. So a sufficient condition that *some* calorie cut-off exactly identify the undernourished is that $Y - X$ be perfectly rank-correlated with Y.[7] This condition is, needless to say, very strong. But that is only as one would expect when it is required that a second, potentially non-equivalent, variable substitute exactly for the first.

A special case of perfect rank correlation is perfect correlation in the ordinary sense. This case suffices to illustrate the points we wish to make. It is equivalent to Y being perfectly correlated with X. Thus suppose that

$$Y = a + bX, \tag{1}$$

where $b > 1$. This case might be motivated by thinking of requirements X as being determined largely by work, and assuming that an individual will increase his X by working only if he can more than compensate for the increase by the calories he can obtain with the extra wages he is thereby paid.[8] It is illustrated in Fig. 7.1(a). In terms of that figure, the undernourished are precisely those individuals for whom (X, Y) falls below the 45° line. Since the realizations of the random variable (X, Y) are confined to the line $y = a + bx$, these individuals can be identified equivalently as those for whom $Y < y_c$; in other words, y_c is an upper-bound cut-off.[9]

---

[7] The model in Appendix A.1 suggests that, to a first approximation, Y/X is more appropriate as an (ordinal-level-comparable) indicator of nutrition than $Y - X$. This being the case, it might be more natural to treat perfect rank correlation between Y/X and Y as a sufficient condition for a calorie cut-off to identify the individuals for whom $Y/X < 1$. The discussion of the present section already casts some light on the problem when it is rephrased in this way—one need only interpret X as the logarithm of requirement, and Y as the logarithm of intake.

[8] Once again, the reader may prefer to reinterpret X and Y as the logarithm of requirement and intake, respectively. The argument would then be that an individual will increase his requirement only if he thereby obtains a more than proportionate increase in intake. Or, to put it differently, he will change his behaviour in such a way as to increase his requirement only if he thereby reduces his degree of undernutrition.

[9] Such an upper-bound cut-off can be used to identify the undernourished in the case both of $b > 1$ *and* $b < 0$.

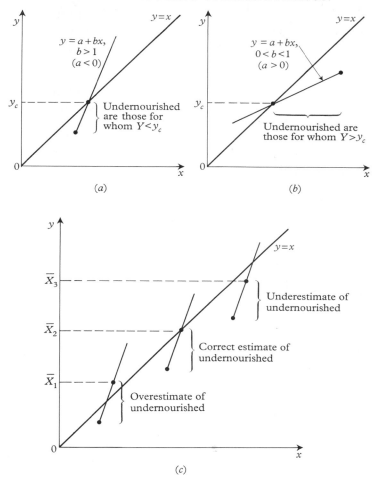

Fig. 7.1. Simple calorie cut-off: the case of perfect correlation

The case of perfect correlation must, however, be treated with care. Consider Fig. 7.1(b), which is analogous to Fig. 7.1(a) except that now $0 < b < 1$. Once again, the undernourished can be identified using a calorie cut-off y_c, but this time the undernourished are those whose intake Y *exceeds* y_c; i.e., y_c is a lower-bound cut-off. Lest this situation be regarded as an irrelevant pathology, note that it is possible to conceive of situations where individuals with high intake and requirement are undernourished—one such group is the tea estate workers in Sri Lanka.[10]

[10] Indeed, close examination of the argument to the effect that $b > 1$ shows that it really applies to the behaviour of a single individual faced with an expanding range of opportunities; but, once account is taken of the fact that, in practice, the joint distribution can consist of individuals facing disparate ranges of opportunities, the argument need not apply.

Returning to the case where $b > 1$, we know that some cut-off y_c is appropriate, but we do not know which. The basic problem here is that in practice one has only limited information on the distribution of X, such as the mean requirement $\bar{X}$. And this information is not sufficient to determine y_c.[11] In particular, setting $y_c = \bar{X}$ may lead to overestimation, correct estimation, or underestimation of the number of undernourished. These possibilities are illustrated in Fig. 7.1(c), where three different populations with respective mean requirements $\bar{X}_1$, $\bar{X}_2$, and $\bar{X}_3$, are depicted.

As a result, it is not possible to answer even the less ambitious of the two questions with which we began Section 7.2, namely, How many individuals are undernourished?[12] It may, however, be possible to provide an underestimate of the number of undernourished, and even to identify a group of individuals who are unambiguously undernourished. Stated in the abstract, the idea is to set $y_c = \underline{x}$, where $\underline{x}$ is the lowest requirement level in the population. Any individual for whom $Y < y_c$ must then be undernourished, since his intake is less than the minimum possible requirement, and hence less than his own requirement. We return to this idea in the next subsection.

7.3.2   The case of imperfect correlation

In practice, $Y - X$ and Y, and X and Y, will not be perfectly correlated. So it is important to consider explicitly the general case of imperfect correlation.

With imperfect correlation, there is no real possibility that a calorie cut-off will correctly identify the undernourished.[13] Associated with any given cut-off there will be either type I error (rejecting the hypothesis that an individual is undernourished when in fact it is true), or type II error (accepting the hypothesis of undernourishment when it is false), or both. This situation is illustrated in Fig. 7.2(a). (In this figure (X, Y) is taken to be uniformly distributed over an ellipse. This is a convenient expositional device which we shall exploit throughout the remainder of this section. When (X, Y) is distributed in this way, the conditional expectation of X given Y is linear in Y, the conditional expectation of Y

---

[11] More generally, the fundamental problem is that one may know the (marginal) distributions of X and Y, but not their joint distribution. In the special case of perfect rank correlation, however, one can reconstruct the joint distribution provided one knows whether the rank correlation is $+1$ or -1.

[12] In the special case of perfect rank correlation, the questions of how many individuals are undernourished, and of which individuals are undernourished, are equivalent, provided one knows whether the rank correlation is $+1$ or -1.

[13] Suppose that Y has density $f_Y(y)$ on $[\underline{y}, \bar{y}]$, X has conditional density $f_{X|Y}(x|y)$, $f_Y(.)$ and $f_{X|Y}(.\,|\,.)$ are continuous, and $f_Y(.) > 0$ on $[\underline{y}, \bar{y}]$. Suppose also that the fraction of the population that is undernourished lies strictly between 0 and 1. Then *no* cut-off y_c correctly identifies the undernourished.

given X is linear in X, and the percentage of the population falling into any region is proportional to the area of the region.[14])

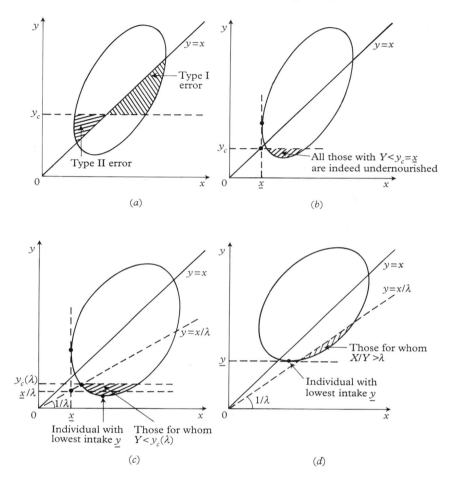

Fig. 7.2. Simple calorie cut-off: the case of imperfect correlation

Because at least one type of error occurs, no matter what the cut-off y_c, there is no possibility of identifying the undernourished by use of the cut-off. However, it is possible to define a group that forms a subset of the set of undernourished individuals. Indeed, if $\underline{x}$ is the lowest

[14] For linearity of the conditional expectations, we do not require that (X, Y) be distributed uniformly over the ellipse. In fact, the level curves of the density of (X, Y) could be concentric ellipses. For example, (X, Y) could have a suitably truncated joint normal distribution.

possible requirement level in the population, then any individual for whom $Y < \underline{x}$ must be undernourished. This idea is illustrated in Fig. 7.2(*b*).

There is no theoretical difficulty with this method. Indeed, $\underline{x} \le X$ for *any* individual, by definition of $\underline{x}$. Hence if $Y < \underline{x}$, it follows at once that $Y < X$. The potential difficulty is practical: it could happen that the number of individuals for whom $Y < \underline{x}$ is very small.

In order to implement the method, one can consider a hypothetical individual with the following characteristics:

(i)   He undertakes only the minimal level of activity necessary to maintain long-term health; in particular, he is unemployed.
(ii) He is of small stature; for example, his height is two standard deviations below the population mean.[15]
(iii) His weight is low for somebody of his stature; for example, it is two standard deviations below the mean weight of individuals of his height.

One can then apply the 'factorial approach' adopted by the FAO/WHO/UNU (1985) Expert Consultation Report to arrive at an estimate of the requirement of this individual. This estimate provides the calorie cut-off. We have conducted preliminary calculations along these lines using the Consumer Finance Survey 1981/82 of the Central Bank of Ceylon.[16] Our results suggest that at least 12 per cent of the population of Sri Lanka may be undernourished.[17]

These results are reassuring, since they suggest that the method is not vacuous. But one caveat should be mentioned. In implementing the approach, we did not actually use $\underline{x}$, the lowest conceivable requirement, but used instead the requirement of an individual of small stature and small weight-for-height—two standard deviations below the mean in each case. Consequently it is conceivable that some of the individuals identified are in fact adequately nourished. None the less, it seems certain that the number of individuals identified is an underestimate of the number of undernourished individuals.

---

[15]   In the preliminary calculations reported below, we have used the data on heights from Stoudt (1961).

[16]   The published report on this survey is Statistics Department, Central Bank of Ceylon (1984). We converted food quantity data from the CFS 1981/82 household files into calories by use of food value tables prepared by the Medical Research Institute, Sri Lanka (MRI 1972)—subsequently published as World Health Foundation of Sri Lanka (1979). Our cleaning of the CFS 1981/82 food quantity data is described in Anand and Harris (1987); for an item-by-item account, see Anand and Harris (forthcoming).

[17]   In making these calculations, we actually took account of the age and sex of individuals. It would be interesting to see whether failure to do so results in a lower (and therefore worse) underestimate for undernutrition.

7.3.3   On identifying the most undernourished

Since one can identify a subset of the undernourished by lowering y_c sufficiently, it is tempting to ask whether one can identify a subset of those undernourished to a given degree by the same means. In this subsection we investigate this possibility.

In order to proceed, we need to give a meaning to the 'degree of undernutrition'. In practice, this is a subtle question. The points that we wish to make, however, can be illustrated adequately in terms of the simple model of Section 7.2. Indeed, in that model it seems reasonable to define one individual as more undernourished than another if the ratio of his target reserves to actual reserves is higher than for the other individual. In other words, the ratio of target to actual reserves is a correct ordinal-level-comparable indicator of undernutrition. If, more-over, the target level of reserves is proportional to frame, then it can be shown that this ratio is monotonic increasing in X/Y. It follows that X/Y will be an *equivalent* ordinal-level-comparable indicator of under-nutrition. (Details of the argument can be found in Appendix A.1. The relationship is strictly convex.) In particular, if the set of individuals for whom $X/Y > \lambda > 1$ constitutes a fraction p of the population, then that set consists precisely of the $(100p)$ per cent most undernourished individuals in the population.

Suppose therefore that we concentrate on those individuals for whom $X/Y > \lambda > 1$. For reasons similar to those we have already discussed, if $y_c = \underline{x}/\lambda$, then, for all individuals for whom $Y < y_c$, it is also the case that $X/Y > \lambda$. This suggests that we can identify a subset of the set of individuals undernourished to any given degree.

There is, unfortunately, an important caveat. This relates to the size of the set of individuals for whom $Y < \underline{x}/\lambda$. That this set should get smaller as λ rises is only to be expected. After all, the set of individuals for whom $X/Y > \lambda$ is also getting smaller. But the situation can turn out to be much worse than this: the ratio of the number of individuals for whom $Y < \underline{x}/\lambda$ to the number for whom $X/Y > \lambda$ can fall as λ rises. Indeed, if λ is too large, the method can break down altogether and, even though the set of individuals for whom $X/Y > \lambda$ is non-empty, it may be impossible to obtain a non-empty subset of this set by using a calorie cut-off alone.

The problem can easily be illustrated. Suppose that, for each λ, $y_c(\lambda)$ is the maximum y_c such that, for all individuals for whom $Y < y_c(\lambda)$, it is also the case that $X/Y > \lambda$. (Setting y_c in this way will not be feasible in practice. But, from the purely theoretical point of view, it gives the method the best chance of success. In particular, it is always the case that $y_c(\lambda) \geq \underline{x}/\lambda$.) Then, when λ is near 1, we expect a positive overlap between the sets $\{Y < y_c(\lambda)\}$ and $\{X/Y > \lambda\}$. This is illustrated in Fig.

7.2(c). However, once λ rises above the value that X/Y takes on in the case of the individual with the lowest intake in the population, it may turn out to be impossible to find such a y_c. This is illustrated in Fig. 7.2(d).

In conclusion, it should be emphasized that this difficulty is not special to the way we have chosen to draw our figures. It stems, rather, from the fundamental observation that the variables Y and X/Y are simply not equivalent in general.[18] Consequently, if one does choose to investigate the group for whom $Y < \underline{x}/\lambda$, one must bear in mind that, the higher is λ, the less likely it is that the group is representative of those undernourished to degree λ. Similarly, if the group for whom $Y < \underline{x}/\lambda$ constitutes a fraction p of the population, there is no reason why it should be representative of the ($100p$) per cent most undernourished individuals in the population. Moreover the higher is λ, the less representative it is likely to be.

Remark 1. In this section we have tried to identify the undernourished group, consisting of those individuals whose calorie intake Y falls below their calorie requirement X. The actual group that we have identified consists of those whose calorie intake Y falls below a common calorie cut-off y_c. Ideally, one would like the two groups to coincide. However, in practice this is unlikely to happen. One is therefore led to consider other less stringent, but none the less desirable, properties that the actual group might possess. One such property is 'purity', which we define to be the proportion of individuals in the actual group who also belong to the undernourished group. Another property is 'comprehensiveness', which we define as the ratio of the size of the actual group to the size of the undernourished group.

Remark 2. When X is unknown, it is unlikely to be possible to achieve both purity and comprehensiveness. It may, however, be possible to achieve one at the expense of the other. Indeed, setting $y_c = \underline{x}$ is designed to achieve purity at the expense of comprehensiveness. It would be helpful to have a method that achieved comprehensiveness of unity at the expense of purity. (Note that purity never exceeds 1. Comprehensiveness, on the other hand, may exceed 1. The ideal value for comprehensiveness is 1.)

Remark 3. We have already noted that, by setting y_c at a particular low level, one can ensure high purity. It is tempting to try to show more generally that purity increases as y_c is lowered. A simple sufficient condition for this is that the proportion of the cross-section of individuals at $Y = y$ who are adequately nourished (i.e. for whom $X < Y$) is increasing with y. More formally, let $f_{X|Y}(x|y)$ be the density of X conditional

[18] Let $\underline{y}$ be the minimum intake observed in the population, and let $\bar{\lambda}$ be the highest value of X/Y. Then the basic problem is that the groups $\{Y = \underline{y}\}$ and $\{X/Y = \bar{\lambda}\}$ will not necessarily intersect.

on Y, and let $F_{X|Y}(y|y) = \int^y f_{X|Y}(x|y)\,dx$. Then purity $\pi(y_c)$ increases as y_c is lowered if $dF_{X|Y}(y|y)/dy > 0$ for all y. (See Proposition A.2 in Appendix A.2.)

Remark 4. It is easy to find cases in which this condition is fulfilled.[19] Suppose, for example, that as y changes only the location of the conditional distribution of $(X|Y=y)$ changes. That is, suppose that there exists a density $g(.)$ and a function $l(.)$ such that $f_{X|Y}(x|y) = g(x - l(y))$. Suppose furthermore that $l'(y) < 1$ for all y (in other words, that the conditional distribution of $(X|Y=y)$ shifts rightwards at rate less than unity with y). Then $dF_{X|Y}(y|y)/dy = (1 - l'(y))\,g(y - l(y)) > 0$. In particular, if X and Y are jointly normally distributed, then we obtain $l(y) = (\rho\sigma_X/\sigma_Y)y$, where σ_X and σ_Y are the standard deviations of X and Y, respectively, and ρ is their correlation coefficient. Hence if $\sigma_X < \sigma_Y$, as seems likely, then $l'(y) < 1$ and purity $\pi(y_c)$ increases as y_c is lowered.[20]

Remark 5. If, as in Remark 4, the conditional distribution of $(X|Y=y)$ for different y is a translation along the curve $l(y)$, then up to a constant the conditional regression of X on Y will also be a translation along $l(y)$. In other words, if $f_{X|Y}(x|y) = g(x - l(y))$, then $E(X|Y=y) = l(y) + \text{constant}$. If $l(y)$ is now proportional to y, which we can write as $l(y) = (1/b)y$ for some b, and writing the constant as $(-a/b)$ for some a, then $E(X|Y=y) = (1/b)y - (a/b)$. Written in this form, the analogy with the earlier case of perfect (linear) correlation between X and Y, stated as $Y = a + bX$ in equation (1) above, becomes apparent. There the regression of X on Y is simply given as the straight line $x = (1/b)y - (a/b)$. Hence the condition $l'(y) < 1$ in the imperfect correlation situation of Remark 4 is equivalent to the condition $(1/b) < 1$, i.e. $b > 1$ or $b < 0$, in the perfect correlation situation in equation (1) of Section 7.3.1.

Remark 6. The condition $l' < 1$ can be motivated in much the same way as the condition $b > 1$ in Section 7.3.1: on average, individuals will increase their requirement only if this increase is more than compensated by an increase in intake, in other words $\partial E(X|Y=y)/\partial y < 1$. But once again, we must point out that this motivation for the shape of the joint

[19] An obvious case in which this condition holds is when X and Y are independently distributed. Then $f_{X,Y}(x,y) = f_X(x)f_Y(y)$, and $f_{X|Y}(x|y) = f_X(x)$ for all y. In this case, $dF_{X|Y}(y|y)/dy = f_X(y)$, which being a density function is non-negative everywhere and strictly greater than 0 on the support of X. In particular, X and Y will be independently distributed if $f_{X,Y}(x,y)$ is a joint uniform density over a rectangle whose sides are parallel to the axes. For this distribution it is easy to verify geometrically (through a diagram) that purity $\pi(y_c)$ increases as y_c is lowered.

[20] This analysis acquires added relevance when X and Y are interpreted as the logarithm of requirement and intake, respectively. The assumption of normality in this case then corresponds to an assumption that requirement and intake are jointly *lognormally* distributed.

distribution can break down when the range of opportunities open to a group of individuals is radically different from the range open to the rest of the population, and that an example of such a group is the tea estate workers of Sri Lanka.

Remark 7. If it does transpire that $l'(y) > 1$ in the imperfect correlation situation, then $dF_{X|Y}(y|y)/dy = (1 - l'(y))f_{X|Y}(y|y) < 0$. In this case, purity $\pi(y_c)$ increases as y_c is *raised* [21] rather than lowered (as in Remark 4). Condition $l'(y) > 1$ in the imperfect correlation situation is equivalent to condition $0 < b < 1$ in the perfect correlation situation, and corresponds to the regression line of X on Y having a slope greater than unity (in the y-direction). Here, as in the perfect correlation case depicted in Fig. 7.1(b), y_c should be used as a *lower* rather than upper bound in identifying the undernourished, and y_c should be *raised* rather than lowered in order to improve purity.

Remark 8. There seem to be two main benefits from achieving high purity. First, if the actual group is pure, then its size will be an underestimate of the true number of undernourished individuals. Such an underestimate may serve to show that the problem of undernutrition is non-negligible. Secondly, if one is concerned primarily to avoid leakage of resources that are intended for the undernourished, then one will be much more concerned about purity than about comprehensiveness. But this approach also has significant limitations. These stem mainly from the fact that a pure actual group that is not comprehensive may not be representative of the undernourished group.

Remark 9. One important aspect of representativeness is the degree of undernutrition. To what extent is the degree of undernutrition of individuals in the actual group representative of that of the undernourished (to degree λ) group? One way of answering this question is to calculate the average degree of undernutrition of the individuals in the actual group, and that of those in the undernourished (to degree λ) group. But this raises a new issue: which (if either) of the two ordinally equivalent indicators of undernutrition should we use for the purpose of calculating the average? Put another way, what is the correct level- and *unit*-comparable indicator of undernutrition? The ratio X/Y does not seem to have much to recommend it. For, if this indicator is used, then we must conclude that an individual for whom $X/Y = 2$ is only twice as undernourished as one for whom $X/Y = 1.5$, yet the former is probably nearly dead from starvation. The ratio of target to actual reserves seems a better measure, for it assigns a large weight to individuals who are near starvation. In particular, if one tried to minimize undernutrition according to

---

[21] With $dF_{X|Y}(y|y)/dy < 0$, it follows from Lemma A.1 in Appendix A.2 that $\pi'(y_c) > 0$.

this measure, one's first priority would be to eliminate starvation itself. We therefore adopt this measure in the ensuing discussion.[22]

Remark 10. The discussion of Section 7.3.3 suggests that, if the actual group is comprehensive, then the average degree of undernutrition of individuals in it will understate the degree of undernutrition of individuals in the undernourished group.

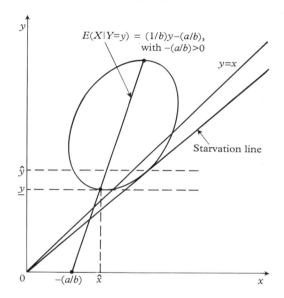

Fig. 7.3. Trade-off between purity and representativeness

Remark 11. We have already argued that purity is likely to increase as y_c is lowered. It is tempting to ask whether the same is true of the average degree of undernutrition. To answer this, it is natural to consider how the average degree of undernutrition of the cross-section of individuals for whom $Y = y$ varies as y varies. There are at least two factors at work here. To understand them, let $D(.)$ be the convex function relating the ratio X/Y to degree of undernutrition, so that the degree of undernutrition is $D(X/Y)$. (The formula for D is given in Appendix A.1.) Then the first factor involves the change in the mean level of X with y. Indeed, $E[(X/Y) \mid Y = y] = E(X \mid Y = y)/y$. If $E(X \mid Y = y)$ rises with y but less than in proportion, i.e. $l'(y) < 1$ or $b > 1$ in Remark 5 (which is what we have tended to regard as the leading case), then this factor will tend to

[22] This measure actually assigns infinite weight to individuals for whom reserves are zero. While quite reasonable in theory, this might lead to practical difficulties. (Where exactly is the point at which reserves can be taken to be zero?) So in practice one might adopt some other, more suitable, convex function of (X/Y).

lead to a fall in $E[D(X/Y) \mid Y = y]$ as y rises. The second factor, on the other hand, involves the change in the variance of X as y rises: this seems likely to rise for low values of y, tending, via the convexity of D, to lead to an increase in $E[D(X/Y) \mid Y = y]$ as y rises.

Remark 12. A simple example, in which both factors are at work, is given in Fig. 7.3. In that figure, (X, Y) is uniformly distributed over an ellipse. The ellipse is oriented in such a way that the linear function $E(X \mid Y = y)$ has an intercept which implies that $E[(X/Y) \mid Y = y]$ is decreasing in y.[23] Thus, the first factor is unambiguously at work. Indeed, it can be shown that $E[D(X/Y) \mid Y = y]$ decreases as y increases from $\underline{y}$ up.[24] However, $E[D(X/Y) \mid Y = \hat{y}]$ is infinite; so eventually the second factor dominates, and $E[D(X/Y) \mid Y = y]$ increases with y. This result could be expressed roughly by saying that, if there is a significant amount of extreme undernutrition in the population, then lowering the calorie cut-off too far will make the actual group identified seriously unrepresentative of the undernourished group.[25]

7.4 SUPPLEMENTATION

In Section 7.3 we asked how much one can hope to learn using data on individuals' calorie intakes only. A major possibility explored was setting a calorie cut-off equal to the minimum level of requirements in the population. And we argued that, while the group of individuals identified by this method would probably not be representative of the undernourished as a whole, the size of the group would provide an underestimate of the number of undernourished. In practice, however, although data on X itself will not be available, various data relevant to its estimation may be. In this section and the next we discuss the supplementary use that can be made of such data.

Obvious examples of variables relevant to the estimation of X are age, sex, occupation, and number of days worked. In terms of the simple

[23] For example, if $E(X \mid Y = y) = (1/b)y - (a/b)$, then $E[(X/Y) \mid Y = y] = E(X \mid Y = y)/y = (1/b) - (a/b)(1/y)$, and this is decreasing in y if and only if $-(a/b) > 0$. Assuming $b > 0$, this corresponds to the *intercept* $a < 0$ in equation (1). See Figs. 7.1(a) and (b). (Note that, by contrast, the 'calorie gap' measure $E(X - Y \mid Y = y) = [(1/b) - 1]y - (a/b)$ in this case, and this is decreasing in y if and only if $(1/b) < 1$. This corresponds to the *slope* b in equation (1) being *either* > 1 *or* < 0.)

[24] Actually a more general result is available. Suppose that (X, Y) is uniformly distributed over a region; let $\underline{y}$ be the lowest value of y achieved in that region, and suppose that there is a unique $\hat{x}$ associated with $\underline{y}$; and suppose that the boundary of the region is described near $(\hat{x}, \underline{y})$ by the equation $y = k(x)$, where $k(\hat{x}) = \underline{y}$, $k'(\hat{x}) = 0$, and $k''(\hat{x}) > 0$. Then, provided that the rate of change of $E(X \mid Y = y)$ with y is at most unity, i.e. $(1/b) < 1$ in Remark 5 of Section 7.3, $E[D(X/Y) \mid Y = y]$ will be decreasing in y.

[25] This discussion glosses over a technical problem. Although $E[D(X/Y) \mid Y = \hat{y}]$ is infinite, $E[D(X/Y) \mid Y \leqslant \hat{y}]$ is not. Hence we cannot in fact be sure that the average degree of undernutrition of the group $\{Y \leqslant y\}$ increases as y approaches $\hat{y}$ from below. This problem is easily patched up: one need only assume that the starvation line actually cuts the ellipse rather than simply touching it.

model of Section 7.2, age and sex might be thought of as helpful in estimating frame, and occupation and number of days worked as helpful in estimating activity. Taken together, the four variables could be used to obtain an estimate $\hat{X}$ of X. The estimate $\hat{X}$ could be used in turn to obtain an improvement in the method of Section 7.3. To picture this improvement, one can compare the joint distribution of $X/\bar{X}$ and $Y/\bar{X}$ with that of $X/\hat{X}$ and $Y/\hat{X}$. If the estimate $\hat{X}$ is a good one, the latter joint distribution will be narrower and more vertical than the former.[26] (In the extreme case where $\hat{X} = X$, the latter will be confined to the vertical line $x = 1$.) As a result, applying a cut-off to $Y/\hat{X}$ should work better than applying a cut-off to $Y/\bar{X}$.[27]

In this section we shall, however, be concerned with the role that other—monetary—variables can play in alleviating the difficulties associated with a calorie cut-off. The basic problem with a calorie cut-off is that some individuals' intakes fall below it not because they are undernourished, but because their requirements are low. Others' intakes lie above it because their requirements are high, not because they are adequately nourished. The relevance of a monetary variable like food expenditure derives from the fact that it may help to identify such individuals. Indeed, an individual's revealed food expenditure provides a measure of the resources that the individual is prepared or able to devote to food. If, despite having a high food expenditure, an individual's calorie intake is low, the presumption must be that his requirement is low: had his requirement been high, then with the same resources devoted to food, he would have exploited cheaper calorie sources and increased his intake. On the other hand, a low food expenditure but high calorie intake suggest that the individual has a high requirement. Thus, calorie intake data supplemented by food expenditure data provide indirect information on an individual's requirement.

In order to explore the potential relevance of food expenditure to such cases, we need to consider the economic context within which an individual operates. Very crudely, one can conceive of an individual as facing a number of employment opportunities among which he must choose. His final choice of employment has direct implications both for his income and, through its effect on his activity level, his calorie requirement. It may also have implications for his expenditure pattern. For

---

[26] In other words, the variance of $X/\hat{X}$ will be smaller than the variance of $X/\bar{X}$. This will help reduce both type I and type II errors associated with a given calorie cut-off.

[27] For example, in applying the method of minimum requirements to the joint distribution of $X/\bar{X}$ and $Y/\bar{X}$, one would use as cut-off the minimum value m_0 attained by $X/\bar{X}$. This is a measure of the degree to which one might overestimate the requirement of an individual if one estimated it using $\bar{X}$. (In fact, $m_0 = x/\bar{X}$.) In applying the method to the joint distribution of $X/\hat{X}$ and $Y/\hat{X}$, one would use as cut-off the minimum value m_1 attained by $X/\hat{X}$. If $\hat{X}$ is a good estimate of X then m_1 will be greater than m_0, and less than but close to 1.

example, there may be travel expenses. So, overall, the process by which his final food expenditure and calorie requirement are determined is a complex one. However, once they are determined, it seems reasonable to regard them as exogenous determinants of his calorie intake: his food expenditure determines the resources available to meet his needs, which are themselves determined by his requirement.

Suppose therefore that intake is a function of food expenditure and requirement, and that this function is linear; i.e.,

$$Y = a_1 + b_1 X + c_1 \Phi \qquad (2)$$

where Φ is food expenditure. Suppose too that $0 < b_1 \leq 1$ and $c_1 > 0$. This relationship is undoubtedly extreme in two respects: (i) the dependence of Y on X and Φ is linear;[28] and (ii) there is no noise. We return to these problems below. But it serves to illustrate very clearly the kind of role that food expenditure could play. The coefficient c_1 is positive because a greater availability of resources to devote to food makes it easier, *ceteris paribus*, to attain a given calorie intake. The coefficient b_1 is positive because, for given Φ, a higher requirement will drive the individual to exploit cheaper calorie sources, possibly at the expense of the variety or palatability of the food that he consumes. It is at most unity because of the implied costs in terms of variety and palatability.[29]

In this case one can improve on the degree to which a group identified by a calorie cut-off is representative of the undernourished, as follows.[30] Suppose that y_c is given (not necessarily equal to $\underline{x}$); let p be the fraction of the population for whom $Y < y_c$, and let φ_p be the value of food

---

[28] As with the earlier linear equation (1) linking Y and X, one might want to interpret equation (2) as holding in the logarithms of the variables.

[29] The coefficient b in equation (1) being greater than the coefficient b_1 in equation (2) (we have assumed $b > 1$ and $b_1 \leq 1$) will imply a positive sample covariance between X and Φ given that $c_1 > 0$. From (1) and (2) we have $(b - b_1) \operatorname{var}(X) = c_1 \operatorname{cov}(X, \Phi)$.

[30] One might also in this case be able to improve upon the underestimate of the number of undernourished obtained by using the simple calorie cut-off $\underline{x}$ in Section 7.3.2. With $\underline{x}$ the lowest requirement level in the population, let $\Phi = \varphi_{\underline{x}}$ be the constant food expenditure line which passes through the point $(\underline{x}, \underline{x})$ in (X, Y) space; i.e., $\varphi_{\underline{x}}$ is defined by

$$\underline{x} = a_1 + b_1 \underline{x} + c_1 \varphi_{\underline{x}}.$$

Since $0 < b_1 \leq 1$ and $X \geq \underline{x}$, it is not hard to see that

$$\{Y < \underline{x}\} \subseteq \{\Phi < \varphi_{\underline{x}}\} \subseteq \{Y < X\}.$$

Unfortunately, $\varphi_{\underline{x}}$ cannot be estimated because a_1, b_1, and c_1 are unknown. However, we can obtain a lower bound for $\varphi_{\underline{x}}$ by taking the expectation of equation (2) conditional on Y, and evaluating this at $Y = \underline{x}$:

$$\underline{x} = a_1 + b_1 E(X | Y = \underline{x}) + c_1 E(\Phi | Y = \underline{x}).$$

Subtracting this from the above equation defining $\varphi_{\underline{x}}$, we get

$$c_1 [\varphi_{\underline{x}} - E(\Phi | Y = \underline{x})] = b_1 [E(X | Y = \underline{x}) - \underline{x}]$$
$$\geq 0 \qquad \text{since } E(X | Y = \underline{x}) \geq \underline{x}.$$

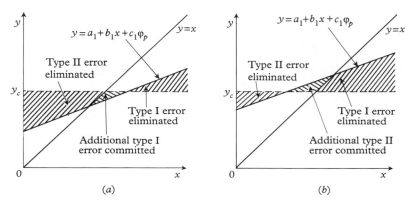

Fig. 7.4. Using food expenditure to reduce type I and type II error

expenditure such that precisely $(100p)$ per cent of the population has $\Phi < \varphi_p$. Then the group $\{\Phi < \varphi_p\}$ involves less type I error and also less type II error than the group $\{Y < y_c\}$, and thus is more representative of the undernourished.[31]

Indeed, because the size of the two groups is the same, the change in type I error in moving from the group $\{Y < y_c\}$ to the group $\{\Phi < \varphi_p\}$ must be equal to the change in type II error. Moreover, the change in both must be negative, because the lines of the form $\Phi = $ constant are upward-sloping and with a slope no more than unity, whereas those of the form $Y = $ constant are horizontal. This result is illustrated in Fig. 7.4, which depicts the two main possibilities for the line $\Phi = \varphi_p$. In Fig. 7.4(a) this line passes below the point (y_c, y_c). It follows that type II error is unambiguously reduced, and therefore there must also be an equal net reduction in type I error. In Fig. 7.4(b) the line passes above (y_c, y_c), and type I error is unambiguously reduced; hence there must be an equal net reduction in type II error. We have not assumed any particular joint distribution for X and Y in order to emphasize that the result is completely general.[32]

Hence since $c_1 > 0$, we have $\varphi_{\underline{x}} \geqslant E(\Phi | Y = \underline{x})$, and therefore $\{\Phi < E(\Phi | Y = \underline{x})\} \subseteq \{\Phi < \varphi_{\underline{x}}\}$. It follows that $\#\{\Phi < E(\Phi | Y = \underline{x})\} \leqslant \#\{\Phi < \varphi_{\underline{x}}\} \leqslant \#\{Y < X\}$. Now, the underestimate $\#\{\Phi < E(\Phi | Y = \underline{x})\}$ of the number of undernourished may be better (i.e. larger) than $\#\{Y < \underline{x}\}$. Note that the food expenditure cut-off $E(\Phi | Y = \underline{x})$ can be read off directly from the regression of Φ on Y.

[31] We are using a crude measure of representativeness here, i.e. the percentage of the group identified as undernourished that really is undernourished.

[32] If the joint distribution of X and Y is continuous, then the reduction in both types of error must be non-negative. (The assumption of continuity is needed only to ensure that φ_p is well defined.) If the assumptions of n. 13 above are satisfied, then the reductions must be strictly positive (except in the pathological case where the group $\{Y < y_c\}$ is either empty or the entire population).

Remark 1. The result that the group identified by Φ is purer than that identified by Y generalizes to a nonlinear, but still deterministic, formulation. If $Y = \chi(X, \Phi)$, $0 < \partial\chi/\partial X \leqslant 1$, and $\partial\chi/\partial\Phi > 0$, then the group $\{\Phi < \varphi_p\}$ is purer than the group $\{Y < y_c\}$. But this generalization is perhaps of less interest than an appropriate generalization to a stochastic formulation.

Remark 2. If we retain linearity but allow noise, then we obtain the relationship $Y = a_1 + b_1 X + c_1 \Phi + \varepsilon$, where ε is an error term. For this model a result as clear-cut as that of the previous paragraph does not appear to be available. However, some use of Φ as a supplementary criterion is certainly desirable. For example, if ε is bounded and φ_c is chosen large enough, then the group $\{Y < y_c$ & $\Phi < \varphi_c\}$ will involve less type II error and no more type I error than the group $\{Y < y_c\}$. But it is no longer clear that exclusive use of Φ is justified.

Remark 3. Our motivation for making supplementary use of Φ carries over to other indicators of the resources available to an individual, such as income and total expenditure. But Φ is probably superior since it reveals most directly an ability to obtain calories. By contrast, an individual may not be free to translate a high income or total expenditure into calories; for he might have a high rent or high costs of travel to work, neither of which is alterable in the short-run.

Remark 4. One can motivate supplementary use of Φ on a different ground. In Anand and Harris (1985, 1990) it is argued that Φ is a good welfare indicator, and it seems unlikely that individuals with a high welfare or standard of living will be undernourished. Given this motivation, one might once more wish to explore the possibility of using total expenditure or income, this time as alternative welfare indicators.

Remark 5. Another supplementary variable that one might employ is foodshare. In this case our criterion for undernourishment would be very close to Lipton's (1983, 1988) criterion for ultra-poverty, in the sense that it would make simultaneous use of foodshare and calorie intake. But there are two problems. First, foodshare cannot be motivated as a measure of the resources available to an individual to spend on calories. Secondly, as we have argued in Anand and Harris (1990), foodshare is a poor welfare indicator. While these considerations mean that foodshare is not suitable to be used as a supplementary variable in identifying undernourishment, they amount to a critique of Lipton's criterion for ultra-poverty only inasmuch as one believes that poverty and undernutrition are closely related.[33]

---

[33] Lipton's (1983) own position on this particular question is not entirely clear. Certainly he believes that food adequacy should play an important role in defining poverty: 'We shall define "moderately poor" and "ultra-poor" by food adequacy' (p. 7). Also, 'Although a few people receive too few dietary calories despite high incomes and outlays, and a few receive enough despite exceptionally low income and outlays, the vast majority are receiving too few calories because they are poor. Very few non-poor are hungry or undernourished'(p. 8).

Remark 6. The use of two variables to try to identify the under-nourished can be regarded as a special case of a more general approach. The general problem is to identify those individuals for whom $Y < X$. Although Y is directly observable, X is not. Hence we need to resort to indirect methods. Supplementation using Φ exploits the fact that it is probably reasonable to regard X as an exogenous variable in an individual's choice of food consumption pattern. A more general approach would exploit further interactions between X and other observable variables. The most obvious candidate for such a variable is probably total expenditure. The problem is that we need to know more about the interactions between X and other economic variables in order to use such additional information sensibly. The only really reliable way to arrive at such information is by conducting a survey incorporating both nutritional and economic variables. Since much more intensive work is needed to measure nutritional variables, it would be impractical to incorporate them into a household budget survey. However, we offer as a serious policy recommendation the idea that a smaller-scale intensive survey should be conducted. The results of such a survey could be invaluable in allowing one to interpret large-scale household budget surveys.

Remark 7. In Section 7.3 we sought to improve the purity of the group identified by means of a simple calorie cut-off y_c by lowering that cut-off. Such an improvement, however, can be achieved only at the expense of comprehensiveness (i.e. the numbers identified relative to the size of the undernourished group). The approach of this section allows one to improve purity without sacrificing comprehensiveness. For a group of any given size identified by means of a calorie cut-off alone, one can improve purity by supplementary use of food expenditure. In other words, using both a calorie cut-off and a food expenditure cut-off while keeping the numbers identified constant will yield an unambiguous improvement in purity. (This entails raising y_c and introducing a φ_c.)

7.5 APPROACHING THE UNDERNOURISHED VIA ECONOMIC WELFARE

It can be argued that an individual's economic welfare and the degree to which he is undernourished will be closely related. After all, his economic welfare is determined largely by his command over resources, and his command over resources includes command over food resources. Moreover, this relationship is likely to be particularly strong for poorer individuals, for whom food concerns will be uppermost. If such a rela-

On the whole, we are inclined to think that Lipton (1983: 4–9) does regard undernutrition and poverty (especially ultra-poverty) as being quite closely related.

tionship does exist, and if economic welfare is observable, then we know that some welfare cut-off will determine the undernourished precisely. This is reminiscent of Section 7.3.1, and leads one to hope that it might be possible to identify a subset of the undernourished. This is indeed the case. But there is an important difference. In Section 7.3.1 we obtained a subset by using an extremely conservative level of require-ment in our calculations. In the present case, by contrast, it is possible to increase this level in two mutually reinforcing ways.

In order to describe the reasons for which one can reasonably use a higher level of requirement, it is helpful first to set out our problem rather more formally. Suppose that welfare is W, and suppose for the moment that W is observable. Then the claim that an individual's wel-fare and the degree to which he is undernourished are closely related can be modelled by requiring that there exist a strictly increasing func-tion $\psi(.)$ such that

$$\frac{Y}{X} = \psi(W). \tag{3}$$

In this relationship, X is unobservable and the exact form of $\psi(.)$ is unknown.

Now (3) can be re-expressed in the form $Y = \psi(W)X$. This in turn implies, on taking expectations conditional on W, that $E(Y|W) = \psi(W)E(X|W)$. Let $r(.)$ and $s(.)$ be the theoretical regressions of Y and X, respectively, on W. By definition, this means that $E(Y|W) = r(W)$ and $E(X|W) = s(W)$. Since both Y and W are observable, one can regress Y on W to obtain an estimate $\hat{r}(.)$ of $r(.)$. However, since X is not observ-able, we cannot estimate $s(.)$ in this way. But it is still possible to obtain an underestimate $\underline{\hat{s}}(.)$ for $s(.)$.

The idea is then to find $\underline{w}_c$ to satisfy $\hat{r}(\underline{w}_c)/\underline{\hat{s}}(\underline{w}_c) = 1$. Such a $\underline{w}_c$ will be an underestimate of the true cut-off w_c, which satisfies $\psi(w_c) = 1$ by definition. Indeed,

$$\psi(w_c) = 1 = \frac{\hat{r}(\underline{w}_c)}{\underline{\hat{s}}(\underline{w}_c)} \qquad \text{(by the definitions)}$$

$$= \frac{r(\underline{w}_c)}{\underline{s}(\underline{w}_c)} \qquad \text{(in a large sample)}$$

$$\geq \frac{r(\underline{w}_c)}{s(\underline{w}_c)} \qquad \text{(because } \underline{s}(.) \leq s(.))$$

$$= \psi(\underline{w}_c) \qquad \text{(because } r(w) = \psi(w)s(w) \text{ for all } w),$$

where $\underline{s}(.)$ is the asymptotic value of $\underline{\hat{s}}(.)$. Hence $\underline{w}_c \leq w_c$ by the strict monotonicity of $\psi(.)$.

From this formal description of the problem, it is evident that the main focus must be on the estimate $\underline{\hat{s}}(.)$. The most conservative approach would simply note that $X \geq \underline{x}$ and that therefore $E(X \mid W) \geq \underline{x}$ too. Hence one can safely set $\hat{\underline{s}}(.) \equiv \underline{x}$. But the value $\underline{x}$ is extreme in two important respects: it involves an individual with (i) the lowest reasonable level of activity and (ii) the smallest reasonable frame. And it is possible to improve on $\underline{x}$, and therefore on $\hat{\underline{s}}(.)$, in both these respects.

Let us begin with activity. Most household budget surveys include some information relevant to the estimation of activity. For example, a survey might include an individual's occupation, the industry in which he works, and the number of days he worked during a reference period. Such data provide at best a very imperfect indication of the activities in which an individual engaged, and the length of time in which he engaged in them. Hence, in using them to make an estimate of his activity level, one must bear in mind an important trade-off. Each time one adjusts one's estimate of an individual's activity level by exploiting an additional variable, one reduces the bias of the estimate, but increases its variance because of the noise inherent in the new variable. This trade-off may not always affect the estimate favourably. In particular, the mean-square error of the estimate may actually increase.[34]

Such difficulties impose strict limits on the accuracy of one's estimate of the activity level of a single individual. However, they can be mitigated if one can find a way of working with *groups* of individuals instead of with single individuals, and then *averaging* over these groups. And this is precisely what the variable W allows us to do: we can divide individuals into welfare groups and then average over welfare groups. (The formal counterpart to this is to take expectations conditional on W.) For example, from the Consumer Finance Survey 1981/82 of the Central Bank of Ceylon, one finds that in the bottom welfare (food expenditure per capita) decile of the estate sector in Sri Lanka, men work on about 41 per cent of days on average, and women work on about 37 per cent of days on average.[35] And a significant amount of information on the nature of a typical day's work of a male or female estate worker is available from other sources.[36] *Averaging over welfare groups should also eliminate the problems created by inter- and intra-personal variations in metabolic efficiency.*

---

[34] A second difficulty is that the more detailed the information one has on the individual's occupation, the less well understood will be the implications of this information for his energy requirements. This is an instance of a general problem known as over-conditioning.

[35] In the top decile, they work respectively 63% and 62% of days on average.

[36] In the preliminary calculations reported below, information on occupational activity was translated into energy requirements by use of WHO (1974, 1978) and FAO/WHO/UNU (1985). No allowance, however, was made for discretionary (leisure and other socially desirable) activity; in other words, non-working time (out of bed) was valued at the minimum BMR factor for waking hours.

Let us turn now to frame. Household budget surveys do not usually contain information on the heights of individuals.[37] On the other hand, information on the distribution of heights is often available independently. This information can be exploited as follows. Let $t(.)$ be the theoretical regression of height H on welfare W; i.e. $E(H \mid W) = t(W)$. Then there are strong reasons for believing that $t(.)$ is non-decreasing in W (and probably that $t(.)$ increases quite significantly). Also, let $h(p)$ and $w(p)$ denote the $(100p)$th percentiles of the height and welfare distributions, respectively. Then the smallest possible value that $E(H \mid W)$ can take on, given the constraint that $t(.)$ is non-decreasing, is $E[H \mid H \leqslant h(w^{-1}(W))]$. And this increases from $\underline{h}$, the minimum possible value of height in the population when W is at its minimum level, to $\bar{H}$, the average height in the population when W reaches its maximum level. In particular, it is greater than $\underline{h}$ once W rises above its minimum. (Note that $\underline{h}$ was the value of height used in arriving at $\underline{x}$.)

Overall, then, by exploiting the variable W one can increase estimated activity and estimated frame significantly above the levels assumed in the calculation of $\underline{x}$. Since requirement depends, roughly, on the product of activity and frame, these increases will tend to reinforce one another. So a tighter underestimate of requirement is obtained. But how significant is the improvement in the underestimate of undernutrition? In order to answer this question, we have again undertaken preliminary calculations using the Consumer Finance Survey 1981/82 of the Central Bank of Ceylon.[38] Our results suggest that at least 18 per cent of the population of Sri Lanka is undernourished.

Remark 1. In general, one might expect $E(X \mid W)$ to be increasing in W for low values of W, and then beyond a certain point to be decreasing. For initially the attainment of higher welfare is dependent upon obtaining employment, and this will increase requirements. But beyond a certain point more remunerative jobs actually entail less physical activity. This is consistent with the assumptions of this section which require that Y/X, not X, be monotonic in W.

Remark 2. Actually, one could argue that the monotonicity of Y/X in W breaks down for high values of W, perhaps because very wealthy people will be more health-conscious. The approach of this section will continue to work in this case provided that Y/X remains above 1 for

---

[37] This may be because investigators would have to round up all the members of a household to obtain it, whereas they can obtain the remainder of the information from just one or two individual members.

[38] For these calculations we used food expenditure per capita as the variable W, and obtained the estimates $\hat{s}(.)$ and $\hat{r}(.)$ by non-parametric regression. Note that $\hat{s}(.)$ is an underestimate of $s(.)$ because, while we took account of occupational activity and percentage of days worked, the energy requirements for non-occupational activity were underestimated. Details may be found in Anand and Harris (forthcoming).

such values of W. This is likely to be true if one works with a sufficiently tight concept of requirements.

Remark 3.   So far we have not said anything about how the theoretical regression $r(.)$ should be estimated. We believe the best method is to use non-parametric regression.[39] For it is very difficult to arrive at a satisfactory parametric functional form; and if an inappropriate form is inadvertently used, then the estimate of $w_c, \underline{w}_c$, can be seriously biased by observations on Y for values of W nowhere near w_c. This is particularly serious if one is motivated by Remark 2 above.

Remark 4.   Nor have we said much about the nature of the variable W. It might be either of the standard welfare indicators, i.e. income and total expenditure; or it might be the welfare indicator proposed more recently in Anand and Harris (1985, 1990), namely food expenditure.

Remark 5.   The use of a welfare indicator does however raise a new issue. How noisy an indicator of welfare is the variable chosen? Broadly speaking, there are two possible effects. To understand these, suppose that the indicator U is simply welfare W measured with error ε. That is, $U = W + \varepsilon$ where $E(\varepsilon \mid W) = 0$ (almost surely). Then the regression of Y on U suffers from errors-in-variables. As a result, $\hat{r}(w)$ will overestimate $r(w)$ for low values of w. Hence the cut-off obtained will be smaller than the true value. If the cut-off could be applied directly to welfare W, then an underestimate of the number of undernourished would result. But obviously, W is no more observable for the purposes of applying the cut-off than it was for conducting the regression. The indicator U must be used instead. This is likely to increase the estimate of the number of undernourished. For the cut-off is likely to lie at a point at which the density of W is upward-sloping, which suggests that there will be more type II error than type I error when U is used to estimate the number of individuals for whom W lies below the cut-off. In practice, the first effect can be expected to dominate.

Remark 6.   The approach suggested in this section is similar in form but not in spirit to that used by Reutlinger and Selowsky (1976).[40] They wanted to know the percentage of individuals in a country who had a calorie intake below a given calorie norm. Unfortunately, they did not have data on the distribution of intake. But they did have data on the distribution of income in the country. In order to make use of these data, they selected a group of countries similar to the country in question. They then regressed the per-capita calorie intake of the countries in this group on their per-capita income. In this way they obtained a relationship between calories and income. Applying this relationship to the calorie norm, they obtained an income norm. The percentage of individuals in

[39] For general discussion on non-parametric regression, see Prakasa Rao (1983) and Silverman (1986).

[40] See also World Bank (1986).

the country with income falling below this income norm was then deemed to be the percentage of undernourished. By contrast, we actually have both calorie and income data for all individuals. Yet we in effect replace actual calorie intake with 'predicted' calorie intake to arrive at our estimate. Our non-parametric approach also avoids a problem encountered by Reutlinger and Selowsky. They tried four functional forms, and then picked the only one that gave remotely sensible calorie predictions. While this one was certainly the best of the four they tried, there is no guarantee that it is appropriate. Since the results vary widely with the functional form chosen, it seems preferable to use a non-parametric approach, thereby allowing the data to determine the functional form.

7.6 CONCLUSIONS

Several points emerge from our analysis. First, in the analysis of poverty it is often emphasized that a simple head-count of the number of individuals who fall below a poverty line is inadequate; this index needs to be supplemented by a measure of how far below the poverty line the individuals fall (see Sen 1976, Anand 1977). By analogy with this point of view, some authors (e.g. Dasgupta and Ray 1990) have recently suggested that the number of individuals falling below a calorie norm should be supplemented by a measure of how far below it they fall. We endorse this general idea. We would, however, take issue with their specific suggestion, namely that the 'calorie gap' $X - Y$ be the focus of attention. For, while we would not wish to place excessive reliance on our formal model of requirements, it does bring out clearly the importance of the *ratio* X/Y, as well as the need to use a sufficiently 'undernutrition-averse' (i.e. *convex*) transformation of this ratio.

Secondly, the limited defence that can be made of the use of a calorie norm to identify undernourished individuals seems to rest on a basic argument, according to which an individual will not change his behaviour in such a way as to raise his calorie requirement unless in the process he obtains an increase in calorie intake that more than compensates. But this argument clearly breaks down when one tries to compare the calorie intakes of two individuals who face significantly different ranges of opportunities. The example we gave here was that of an estate worker in Sri Lanka. The opportunities open to, say, a rural worker are simply not available to an estate worker. As a result, there is no reason to consider an estate worker, whose calorie intake is higher than that of a rural worker, to be less likely to be undernourished than the rural worker. But the same logic applies to any comparison between groups which are not closely similar in respect of the opportunities they face. In particular, caution must be exercised when comparing aggregate calorie intake data across countries.

Thirdly, we pointed out that, when a population is reasonably homogeneous, lowering the calorie cut-off can be expected to increase the probability that an individual whose intake falls below the cut-off really is undernourished. This is a benefit of lowering the cut-off. But it must be balanced against the costs of doing so. One danger is that by employing too low a cut-off one may classify as adequately nourished too many individuals who are in fact undernourished, and thus sacrifice the numbers identified excessively. A second is that, as the cut-off is lowered, the group identified as undernourished may become less and less representative of the undernourished themselves. In particular, the average degree of undernutrition of the group identified by means of a calorie cut-off might actually fall as the cut-off is lowered.

Fourthly, once the difficulties created by the variation of calorie requirements within the population are recognized, it is no longer clear that calorie intake is the best single indicator to use for the purpose of identifying the undernourished. For example, applying a cut-off to food expenditure might yield better results than applying a cut-off to calorie intake. Better still might be to make simultaneous use of more than one indicator, in particular, both food expenditure and calorie intake.

APPENDIX

A.1 The Model of Requirements

Let B be body size, F frame, R reserves, M metabolic energy cost, P physical energy cost, A activity, X requirement, Y intake, and $\bar{R}$ the target level of reserves. Then, according to our model,

$$B = F + R$$
$$M = \alpha B$$
$$P = \beta AB$$
$$\frac{dB}{dt} = -\gamma(M + P - Y)$$

for suitable $\alpha, \beta, \gamma > 0$. For given A, F, and Y, the long-run level of R will be determined by these equations and the condition that $dB/dt = 0$. Similarly, for given A and F, requirement X is that value of Y such that these four equations and the condition $dB/dt = 0$ are satisfied when $R = \bar{R}$. It is easy to check that

$$R = \frac{Y - (\alpha + \beta A)F}{\alpha + \beta A}$$

and

$$X = (\alpha + \beta A)(F + \bar{R})$$

are the resulting formulae for R and X.

Now suppose that $\bar{R}$ is proportional to F, i.e. that $\bar{R} = \delta F$ for some $\delta > 0$. And define an individual's degree of undernutrition to be $\bar{R}/R$. Then it turns out that we can infer the individual's degree of undernutrition from (X/Y) alone. Indeed,

$$\frac{\bar{R}}{R} = \frac{\delta F(\alpha + \beta A)}{Y - (\alpha + \beta A)F}$$

(by definition of $\bar{R}$ and using the formula for R), whereas

$$(\alpha + \beta A)F = X/(1 + \delta)$$

(by definition of $\bar{R}$ and using the formula for X). Hence

$$\frac{\bar{R}}{R} = \frac{\delta}{(1 + \delta)(Y/X) - 1}$$

$$= \frac{\delta(X/Y)}{(1 + \delta) - (X/Y)}.$$

That is,

$$\bar{R}/R = D(X/Y),$$

where the degree of undernutrition D is a monotonic increasing and convex function of (X/Y) for $0 \leqslant (X/Y) < (1 + \delta)$. It is easy to verify that $D'(X/Y) > 0$ and $D''(X/Y) > 0$ in this case. The degree of undernutrition D tends to infinity as (X/Y) tends to its upper limit of $(1 + \delta)$. Considering D as a family of functions parameterized by δ, D as a function of (X/Y) becomes less convex for higher δ, and tends in the limit to the linear function (X/Y) as δ tends to infinity.

A.2   The Effect of Lowering the Calorie Cut-Off

Let X be requirement, Y intake, $f_{X,Y}(x,y)$ the joint density function of (X, Y), $f_Y(y)$ the marginal density of Y, $f_{X|Y}(x|y)$ the conditional density of X given Y, $F_Y(.)$ the distribution (cumulative density) function of Y, $F_{X|Y}(.|y)$ the distribution function of $X|Y$, and $\pi(y_c)$ the proportion of those below the calorie cut-off y_c who are correctly classified as undernourished. (Thus, $\pi(y_c)$ is by definition the *purity* of the group $\{Y < y_c\}$.)

Then

$$\iint f_{X,Y}(x,y)\,dx\,dy = 1, \int f_Y(y)\,dy = 1, f_{X,Y}(x,y) = f_{X|Y}(x|y)f_Y(y), \int f_{X|Y}(x|y)\,dx = 1$$

for all y, $F_Y(y_c) =$ proportion of the total population with $Y < y_c$, and $F_{X|Y}(y|y) =$ proportion of the population at $Y = y$ for whom $X < Y$.

The proportion of the population below y_c that is misclassified as undernourished (i.e. the proportionate type II error for cut-off y_c) is

$$1 - \pi(y_c) = \frac{\int^{y_c} \left[\int^y f_{X|Y}(x|y)\,dx \right] f_Y(y)\,dy}{\int^{y_c} f_Y(y)\,dy}$$

$$= [1/F_Y(y_c)] \int^{y_c} F_{X|Y}(y|y)\,f_Y(y)\,dy.$$

LEMMA A.1 $\pi'(y_c) = -[f_Y(y_c)/F_Y(y_c)^2] \int^{y_c} \dfrac{dF}{dy}_{X|Y}(y|y)F_Y(y)\,dy.$

Proof   Differentiating $\pi(y_c)$, we obtain

$$\pi'(y_c) = \left[f_Y(y_c)/F_Y(y_c)^2 \right] \left[\int^{y_c} F_{X|Y}(y|y)\,f_Y(y)\,dy - F_{X|Y}(y_c|y_c)F_Y(y_c) \right]$$

Now integrate by parts the expression $\int^{y_c} F_{X|Y}(y|y)\,f_Y(y)\,dy$ in brackets assuming that the lower limit of integration is, for example, 0 at and below which all densities vanish. This yields

$$\int^{y_c} F_{X|Y}(y|y)\,f_Y(y)\,dy = F_{X|Y}(y_c|y_c)\,F_Y(y_c) - \int^{y_c} \frac{dF}{dy}_{X|Y}(y|y)\,F_Y(y)\,dy.$$

Substituting this in the above expression for $\pi'(y_c)$ gives the desired result.   □

PROPOSITION A.2   *Given any joint density function $f_{X,Y}(x,y)$, a sufficient condition for $\pi'(y_c) < 0$ for any y_c is that $dF_{X|Y}(y|y)/dy > 0$ for all y.*

Proof   Sufficiency follows directly from Lemma A.1.   □

COROLLARY A.3   *Given any joint density function $f_{X,Y}(x,y)$, lowering y_c will reduce the proportionate misclassification of the group undernourished to degree λ (i.e. those for whom $X/Y > \lambda$) if $dF_{X|Y}(\lambda y|y)/dy > 0$ for all y.*   □

The condition in Proposition A.2 (and Corollary A.3) is also necessary in the following sense:

PROPOSITION A.4   *If $dF_{X|Y}(y|y)/dy \leq 0$ for some y, then there exists a y_c and a joint density function $f_{X,Y}(x,y)$ such that $\pi'(y_c) \geq 0$.*

Proof   By appropriate choice of y_c and marginal distribution $F_Y(.)$, one can use Lemma A.1 to show that $\pi'(y_c) \geq 0$.   □

8

Anthropometric Measures of Nutritional Status in Industrialized Societies: Europe and North America since 1750

R. Floud

8.1 INTRODUCTION

In the less developed countries of the world today, the association between human physical growth and the physical, economic, and social environment is clear for all to see. Poverty, malnutrition, and disease shape the bodies of the people from birth to death. Both at the micro level, where the health of individual children is monitored, and at the macro level, where group or population means are calculated, physical growth is clearly seen to be responding to changes in the environment and to social and medical intervention.

For these reasons, the study and monitoring of physical growth is of particular interest in developing countries. It is also worth considering, however, whether physical growth is of interest in the industrialized and more developed societies, and how far insights from the developing countries can reasonably be applied to countries where levels of income and of health are far different. This chapter therefore first considers the meaning of anthropometric measures of physical growth; it then describes the history of physical growth in the industrialized world and suggests some explanations for the patterns that can be observed.

8.2 WHY SHOULD WE STUDY HUMAN PHYSICAL GROWTH?

Human physical growth is studied for many reasons. To paediatricians and other medical researchers, the primary focus is on the impact of the environment on the individual or the small group and the aim is the cure or alleviation of ill-health or distress. To human biologists, growth is a central concern in understanding the complex of nutritional and hor-

I am most grateful to all the participants at the WIDER conference and in particular to Robert Pringle, Philip Payne, and Amartya Sen for their comments. Siddiq Osmani also made invaluable suggestions which led to extensive revisions in the order of the argument.

monal mechanisms that control change in the human body. To the epidemiologist, growth is of interest as a summary measure of environmental influences and increasingly as a proxy for environmental influences during childhood and adolescence which may affect later health. To the practical nutritionist, growth is a measure of the success of intervention in diet. To the economist, physical growth and strength help to determine individual labour productivity. To the anthropologist, growth is a measure of man's adaptation to his physical environment. To the historian, growth is a measure of changing nutritional status which is closely related to the concept of the 'standard of living', the subject of many historical controversies.

These different concerns of social and biological scientists are naturally reflected in their modes of investigation of the phenomena of physical growth. The different aims determine the questions that are asked, the variables that are measured, and the period of growth that is studied. Thus, the vast majority of medical investigations are concerned with the first years of life, few with adolescence, and fewer still with the later phases of growth and then shrinking in middle and old age. Studies of nutritional intervention and of the impact of malnutrition on growth are concerned almost entirely with the less developed countries, studies of height differences between occupational groups almost entirely with the more developed countries. Economists concentrate on contemporary societies, historians and some anthropologists on societies of the past.

In addition, auxologists (as students of human growth are called) study many aspects of growth and use many indicators—height, weight, height-for-age, weight-for-height, and skinfold thickness, to name but some. The most frequently used indicator, however, is height; and, since that is also the indicator most commonly available from historical sources, it is height that is the focus of this chapter.

It is useful to distinguish at the outset between two ways in which height may be viewed. First, it can be seen as an indicator of the past and present; second, it can be seen as an indicator of the future. In both cases, height links a group of people to the environment in which they have grown up and in which they are to live.[1]

8.2.1   Height as an indicator of the past and present

There is ample evidence from history, from both the developing world and the industrialized world, of the value of height as an indicator of the past or present environment of an individual or of a group of people.

---

[1] It has been suggested that height as an indicator of the past should be described as 'indicative' and as an indicator of the future described as 'intrinsic'. I prefer, for reasons that will appear in the discussion below, to think of height as indicative both of the past and the future rather than to seem to imply that height has a definite intrinsic value.

Studies of the efficacy of nutritional supplements provide striking evidence of the rapidity of response of growth to an improved environment. Martorell *et al.* (1980) found that children provided with a high-protein, high-calorie beverage grew significantly taller and heavier than a control group; moreover, 'the higher the supplement category, the larger are the children in all four dimensions (supine length, weight, head circumference and arm circumference)' (pp. 224–5). As they commented,

the results of the present study suggest that simple and well-known measures such as weight and supine length (height) should be utilised in evaluating public health programs. These are not only among the most sensitive of measures but also among the most reliable. (Martorell *et al.* 1980: 229)

At the level of whole societies, Eveleth and Tanner introduced their monumental study within the International Biological Programme of *Worldwide Variation in Human Growth* with the following words:

A child's growth rate reflects, better than any other single index, his state of health and nutrition; and often indeed his psychological situation also. Similarly, the average values of children's heights and weights reflect accurately the state of a nation's public health and the average nutritional status of its citizens, when appropriate allowance is made for differences, if any, in genetic potential. *This is especially so in developing or disintegrating countries.* Thus a well designed growth study is a powerful tool with which to monitor the health of a population, or to pinpoint subgroups of a population whose share in economic and social benefits is less than it might be. Indeed as infant mortality rate goes down during a country's development, so the importance of monitoring growth rate increases. (Eveleth and Tanner 1976:1; my emphasis)

The link between environment and physical growth was also plain in the developing countries of the past. As today, the connection was often clearest to visitors, who see with fresh eyes distinctions that have become so familiar as to be invisible to residents. In 1833, for example, one of the British Factory Commissioners, Dr Bisset Hawkins, commented that:

I believe that most travellers are struck by the lowness of stature, the leanness and paleness which present themselves so commonly to the eye at Manchester, and, above all, among the factory classes. I have never been in any town in Great Britain nor in Europe in which degeneracy of form and colour from the national standard has been so obvious. (Parliamentary Papers 1833:xxi)

It was also clear, as in Guatemala and other less developed countries today, that social intervention in the form of feeding programmes and medical programmes could have significant effects. The trustees of the Marine Society, a London charity, described in the late eighteenth century how the boys in their care, drawn from the slums and stews of London, grew rapidly when given food and shelter; while, later in the nineteenth century, enquiries into recruiting for the army were told of the rapid physical growth of recruits after their induction into the army and the receipt of regular meals.

It was, no doubt, because he could see with his own eyes the correlation between environment and physical growth that L. R. Villermé could produce, in 1829, one of the earliest but also one of the most complete and perceptive accounts of the link:

Human height becomes greater and growth takes place more rapidly, other things being equal, in proportion as the country is richer, comfort more general, houses, clothes and nourishment better and labour, fatigue and privation during infancy and growth less: in other words, the circumstances which accompany poverty delay the age at which complete stature is reached and stunt adult height. (Villermé 1829: 385–6; trans. and quoted by Tanner 1981:162)

Despite these early comments, and despite the modern experience of physical growth and deprivation in the less developed countries, many people in the more developed countries instinctively reject the association between height and the environment which Villerme observed. Either they are incredulous at the suggestion that there are significant differences in physical growth between distinct groups in the community, or they are unwilling to accept that such distinctions have an environmental origin. Why is this so?

In part, as I have argued elsewhere, it stems from the Darwinian inheritance which has predisposed us to accept genetic or at least pseudo-genetic explanations for human differences (Floud 1986). In part, also, it must stem from the fact that, as I shall show below, differences in the patterns of physical growth and their results in terms of height and weight are now much less dramatic than they were, both within and between the more developed countries.

In part, however, the difficulty stems from the lack of an adequate scientific model of the causation of growth. Summaries of the literature present a lengthening list of the correlates of physical growth; in summarizing studies made before 1974, Eveleth and Tanner identified, among environmental influences on variation in growth, the following: nutrition and disease, socioeconomic level, urbanization, seasonal and climatic variation, psychosocial stress, and the 'secular trend' for which 'factors such as improved nutrition, control of infectious disease through immunisations and sanitation, more widespread health and medical care, and population mobility (both geographically to urban areas and socially upwards) appear to be responsible' (1976: 261). More recently, studies such as that by Rick Steckel have emphasized economic variables such as per capita income and the level of inequality, while sociologists have emphasized the possible effects of education and 'health behaviour' in relation to diet (Steckel 1983; Power et al. 1986).

Despite the much more sophisticated techniques on which individual studies of this kind are now based, in many ways we have not advanced very much further than Villermé in understanding, for any particular population or point in time, the relative contribution of each of these multifarious factors to human growth. Some progress has been made; Martorell has convincingly shown, for example, that illness now seems to play little role in determining growth in the developed countries, while studies 'from developing nations report that common childhood ailments, in particular diarrhoeal diseases, are clearly associated with poor physical growth' (Martorell 1980: 89).

But such cases are rare, and the absence of a general causal model vitiates many of the individual studies that have been made: they make use of a variety of statistical methods and do not report the results in a consistent form. Moreover, in the absence of a comprehensive model linking all the variables, the correlations that have been reported are necessarily misleading, since the functional relationships that have been estimated do not take account of other variables that have been shown or at least alleged to be of relevance. The separate correlations are not equivalent to partial correlations, since they are not controlled for other relevant variables. In addition, there is a strong likelihood of collinearity between some of the variables; the well documented synergistic relationship between nutrition and some diseases is an obvious and highly relevant example (Rotberg and Rabb 1983). If both malnutrition itself and diseases such as infantile diarrhoea cause stunting in growth, and if malnutrition predisposes children to diarrhoeal diseases and exacerbates their effects, then the statistical disentangling of their separate contribution to growth is likely to be a task of monumental difficulty.

In one sense, this problem of identifying the contribution of various environmental factors to human physical growth can be disregarded— finessed might be a better word—by invoking the concept of growth as an index of nutritional status. Height is probably best seen as an indicator of a complex of environmental factors that affect the human body and together determine the nutritional status of a person at a moment in time. For obvious reasons, height is not an indicator of such status at each moment: rather, it sums up the successive states of the human body during the growth period from conception to the cessation of height growth in adulthood. As Robert Fogel puts it,

In considering the relationship between nutrition and height, it is important to keep in mind that height is a net rather than a gross measure of nutrition. Moreover, although changes in height during the growing years are sensitive to current levels of nutrition, mean heights reflect the accumulated past nutritional experience of an individual over all of his growing years including the fetal period. . . .

The measure of net nutrition represented by mean heights depends on the intake of nutrients, on the amount of nutrients available for physical growth after the necessary claims of work and other activities (including recovery from infections), and on the efficiency with which the body converts nutrients into outputs. The body's ability to generate a surplus for growth will vary with such factors as age, the climate, the nature of the available food, clothing and shelter, the disease environment, the intensity of work, and the quality of public sanitation. In other words, the same nutritional input can have varying effects on physical growth, depending upon environmental conditions. Consequently, mean height . . . is a measure of the balance between food consumption and the claims on that consumption. (Fogel 1986c:29)

Such a generalized index of human welfare is well worth having. In *Measuring the Condition of the World's Poor*, Morris David Morris discusses objections to all the conventional measures of socioeconomic performance and sets out six criteria that a composite measure of such performance must satisfy:

1. It should not assume that there is only one pattern of development.
2. It should avoid standards that reflect the values of specific societies.
3. It should measure results, not inputs.
4. It should be able to reflect the distribution of social results.
5. It should be simple to construct and easy to comprehend.
6. It should lend itself to international comparison. (Morris 1979: 21)

Morris himself advocates, as satisfying these criteria, the 'physical quality of life index' with three components: infant mortality, life expectation at age 1, and basic literacy. Each component is scaled and then combined with equal weights. It would appear, however, that height as an indicator of nutritional status meets all six of Morris's criteria without the need for any scaling or weighting, which, as Morris himself admits, is inevitably somewhat arbitrary.

Height and nutritional status are therefore analogous to measures of welfare. Indeed, to many economic and social historians, the interest of anthropometric measures of nutritional status lies primarily in the light that they can shed on variation in the standard of living of populations in the past. There are important ways, however, in which measures of height differ from conventional measures of welfare such as real income levels, and even from conventional measures of health such as are collected in surveys of the health of a population.

First, as Fogel has frequently emphasized, nutritional status is itself a net rather than a gross measure: it reflects not the gross value of inputs in the form of consumption of food, warmth, and shelter, but the balance between those inputs and demands on the body for maintenance, growth, and work effort, including the defeat of disease. 'Moreover, although changes in height during the growing years are sensitive to current levels of nutrition, adult height reflects the accumulated past nutritional experience of an individual over all of his growing years including the fetal period' (Fogel 1986c: 26). Similarly, the mean height of a population represents the cumulated nutritional status of that population during the periods of height growth of its members.

Cumulated nutritional status, represented by height, is thus very unlike conventional measures of welfare which describe the welfare of an individual or a nation at one moment in time, irrespective of past experience or, indeed, of the likely future welfare of that person or nation. Height, by contrast, is closer in many ways to a measure of human capital. First, it represents accumulated experience, the balance between inputs and outgoings up to the time of measurement. Second, however, it represents future potential.

8.2.2 Height as an indicator of the future

Military recruiters in the past explicitly sought tall recruits; they did so on the grounds that such men would be healthier and better able to withstand the stresses and strains of military life. Slave-owners, too, were prepared to pay more for taller slaves and selected relatively tall slaves for elite tasks:

other things being equal, a male who was three inches taller than the typical adult male was 62 percent more likely to be a driver than one who was three inches shorter than the typical male. On average, drivers were an inch-and-a-half taller than the men (and five inches taller than the women) who labored in the gangs.

Advantage in height also increased the likelihood that men would be selected as craftsmen and that women would be chosen as domestics. (Fogel 1989)

As Fogel points out, increased height in this instance gave both a physical and a psychological advantage. The same seems to be true in modern developed societies. First, psychological advantage is suggested by a number of studies which have shown that relatively tall men and women are more likely to be upwardly socially mobile, whether by occupational mobility or through marriage. This relationship has been shown by Illsley (1955) in studies based on women in Aberdeen and by Knight and Eldridge (1984) in their survey of British adults. It has also very recently been demonstrated in an analysis of the British National Child Development Study by Power et al. (1986): they show that there is a clear class gradient in height at age 23, and that this persists even after controlling for the social class of the parents.

Thus, social mobility between birth and 23 was selective with respect to height, but mobility did not account for the social class gradients in height; indeed, there was some suggestion that the differences in the proportions short might be wider by social class at birth than by social class at 23. (Power et al. 1986: 409)

The exact mechanisms relating social mobility to height, and thus to cumulated nutritional status, have not yet been explored within this or other studies. But it seems likely that the health of the child and young adult must be an important factor; that is, healthier and (probably) richer children have a better chance of achieving upward social mobility than their poorer, less healthy peers, perhaps because relative poverty and ill-health detract from education. It is even possible that such poverty affects brain development and thus intelligence, although such a connection is highly speculative at the income levels that are achieved in the more developed countries.

Second, physical advantage has been suggested in a number of studies which have shown that, after controlling for other variables, height has an independent effect on life expectation and, probably, on morbidity (Waaler 1984; Marmot et al. 1984). Marmot et al., in a study of the British civil service, found that height was a significant predictor of cardio-vascular mortality, even after controlling for social class, smoking behaviour, and other variables; and Waaler demonstrated the same relationship for both cardio-vascular and respiratory diseases, while showing that it did not hold for accidental death. Waaler is prepared to argue that the increased height of the Norwegian population, betokening higher nutritional status during the growth period, is likely to result in declining mortality levels in the future.

If, as these studies suggest, cumulated nutritional status as represented by height exerts a long-term influence on life chances in a variety of ways, then the analogy between height and human capital seems close. On the other hand, height has an aspect that differentiates it both from conventional measures of welfare and from measures of human capital: once growth has ceased, or (in most developed societies) much earlier, nothing can be done to increase it. Nor, in fact, given the economic and general dependence of most children upon their parents, can any individual do anything to increase his height, though it is conceivable that the parents might be able to do so. There is little evidence, however, that food supplementation programmes or even protection from disease can make any difference to height or growth in the developed world. It remains possible, of course, for nutritional status to be maintained or improved after the period of growth ceases, but such improvements will no longer be reflected in anthropometric measures.

The measurement of height thus offers great potential for the description and exploration of the changing nutritional status of peoples in the past and in the present; if also offers the potential to contribute to the explanation of many changes, in morbidity, mortality, and even in social and occupational mobility, which have long intrigued social scientists. But can height in the past be adequately measured?

8.3 THE MEASUREMENT OF HEIGHT IN THE PAST

The measurement of height is not straightforward. First, there are numerous documented sources of measurement error; although methods of measurement have been improved and standardized over the years, early methods were crude in the extreme (Tanner 1981). Second, there are problems that arise from the sources of information that are available to us. Our primary source of evidence on height during the past two centuries stems from the operations of military forces and in particular from military recruitment, whether voluntary, as was characteristic of the English-speaking nations, or by conscription, as was the case in most of the rest of Europe. Other sources do exist; the slave trade to the Americas, and in particular the effort to regulate and then abolish the trade and slavery itself, provides evidence of the heights and other physical characteristics of Africans forcibly transplanted to the new world. Finally, there exist a number of surveys of the heights of populations carried out mainly in the twentieth century, either explicitly for commercial use or by governments interested to provide information useful to designers of clothing and furniture.

However, the primary source of data on changes in the physical growth of populations remains the recruitment records. This gives rise to some pitfalls and difficulties of interpretation. It was normal for volunteers to be recruited between the ages of 15 and 30, although preponderantly between the ages of 18 and 22; with volunteer data, therefore, it is usually possible to build up a description of the last years of physical growth and to estimate the age at which growth typically ceases. Conscripts, on the other hand, were typically recruited only at a single age, normally 18, 19, or 20, although it varied between countries and over time within countries.

Such conscript data can give only a snapshot, at one moment in time, of the complex process of human growth and, moreover, of a moment at which the process of growth in those measured has largely but not entirely ceased. Ideally, one should be able to observe the whole growth process from birth to maturity, since it is known that environmental factors affect not only the absolute height achieved at a given age but also the tempo of growth. It is well known, for example, that the age at menarche in girls has become earlier since the nineteenth century, and the same applies to the timing of the adolescent growth spurt in boys and girls and to the age at which final height is achieved. This last point is highly relevant to conscription data; whereas in the past an 18-year-old might well not have achieved his final height when he was measured for military service, today he would almost certainly have done so. A comparison of the mean height of a cohort of 18-year-olds today with a cohort of 18-year-olds from one century ago will therefore probably overestimate the change in final height. On the other hand, even if we knew the change that had occurred in final height, that change would itself be an underestimate of the effect of changing environment on growth, since some of that impact would have been reflected in the earlier maturity—perhaps at the same absolute height—of the modern cohort as compared with that of the past. The problem arises because, although the tempo of growth and the final height are linked, the two phenomena are to some extent independent of each other; there are some fast-growing, early maturing groups who are short, and some slow-growing, late maturing groups who are tall (Tanner 1982: 574–5). I will return to this problem below.

Military conscription data must, therefore, be interpreted with great care. Nevertheless, they offer by far the largest and the most consistent set of evidence available for the description of changes in mean height; they therefore form the principal source that is used below, although they have been supplemented by survey data and, most importantly, by data from volunteer recruiting in Britain, in its American colonies, and in the USA. Such data have their own problems of statistical estimation and interpretation, stemming from the frequent omission of those shorter than the prevailing height standard required by the army, which have been discussed and largely resolved in a number of papers (Wachter 1981; Floud and Wachter 1982; Wachter and Trussell 1982).

While this is probably not a serious problem in the calculation of mean heights from large samples, more severe difficulties arise from cases in which particularly short recruits were excluded altogether from measurement; as mentioned above, it has been necessary to develop special statistical procedures to cope with this problem (Wachter 1981; Wachter and Trussell 1982).

Even more problematic, however, is the difficulty, referred to briefly above, that there is no single appropriate summary measure of the height of a person or a group. Absolute height can be measured at a particular age—in late teenage years as it normally was in the case of conscription—or at birth, at age 2, or when growth can be assumed to have ceased entirely. But the interpretation of the result of that measurement can only be made within the context of the whole profile of growth relevant to that person or group. As Tanner puts it,

within a given, well-nourished population, there is no correlation between tempo and final height; tall men are as likely to have been late as to have been early maturers. Even between populations at different levels of nutrition, the correlation is far from close. A population which is short at age 14 may be so either because its children are delayed in growth (in which case they may reach a considerable height as adults) or because they are simply short—before, then and later with average tempo. As for trends within a single population, in historical data increasing mature size usually is accompanied by increasing tempo of growth. But the two should certainly not be regarded as inseparable; at least in theory, a trend in tempo might continue beyond the point at which a trend in mature size finished, or even vice versa. (Tanner 1982: 575)

Since this is so, no single measure of height can be relied upon to summarize the entire growth experience, as it might be required to do when entering as the single dependent variable into an estimation of the determinants of nutritional status. It is probable that, as Tanner indicates, final height in adulthood comes closest to serving as such a summary measure. On the other hand, differentials in adult height between populations and between groups within populations are typically much smaller than are differentials in height at, for example, the time of the adolescent growth spurt; evidence from maximum likelihood estimates of socioeconomic differentials in the heights of male adults in Britain in the early nineteenth century suggest a range of not more than 3–4 inches in adult heights, but the range at age 14 between boys from the London slums and boys from the upper classes who entered the Royal Military Academy was as much as 10 inches (Floud *et al.* 1990).

Faced with this situation, it is possible to argue that final height provides the most conservative estimate of height differences and that it is, therefore, the safest indicator of nutritional status. It is tempting to dismiss adolescent height differences as 'merely' the product of differences in the timing of the adolescent growth spurt. But the height at adolescence is not a spurious indicator: differences in tempo do reflect differences in nutritional status, and, by implicitly subsuming them within adult height, we may be not only substantially underestimating the changes in nutritional status that have occurred, but also depriving ourselves of variance which should be of use in statistical analysis. It is true that in practice we rarely have the luxury of choice, since the data usually do not permit us to observe the whole growth profile or even more than one part of it; but we should not therefore forget how partial or inadequate one single measure of height may be.

Despite these difficulties, it is sensible to try. What can we discover about heights in the past?

8.4 HUMAN HEIGHT IN THE INDUSTRIALIZED WORLD, 1750–1980

It is unfortunately necessary, because of the availability of data, to confine our attention to the countries of western Europe and North America. Evidence from military records shows that the average height of European male populations at the age of conscription has varied, during the last two hundred years, between 159 and 181 cm. The shortest mean height yet recorded or computed for conscripts recruited on a national basis is that of 159.1 cm for recruits aged 18 to the Habsburg armies in the eighteenth century (Komlos 1985), while Kiil (1939) estimated that the height of recruits aged 18.5 to the Norwegian army in 1761 was 159.5 cm; the *Historical Statistics of Italy 1861–1965* (Italy 1978) shows that the mean height of 20-year-old recruits born in 1854 was 162.39 cm; Spanish recruits, as late as 1913, had a mean height of 163.6 cm (Rodriguez n.d.).

Since growth would probably have continued after the age at which these recruits were measured, it is likely that these measurements are a slight underestimate of final adult heights for those communities. On the basis of modern populations in the less developed world, who have similar mean heights, it is reasonable to add an estimate of about 3 per cent for further growth after the age of 18, giving an estimated minimum mean final height for European national populations of about 165 cm.

Measurement of the upper end of the observed range can rely on modern data. Army recruits aged 17.5 in the Netherlands had a mean height of 180.7 cm in 1982 (Netherlands 1983). These men, the tallest recorded in Europe, were closely followed by Norwegians with a mean of 179.4 cm in 1983 (Norway 1984). In the absence of survey data, it is not clear how much further growth before final height is reached should be assumed for such tall populations, but it is unlikely that more than 1 per cent more could possibly occur, giving an estimate for final height of not more than 182.5 cm.

The range of final heights for whole national populations observed in Europe has thus been between about 165 and 183 cm during the past two hundred years. As would be expected, the range over sub-groups of national populations has been somewhat wider. The shortest geographical group of all appears to have been recruits from the town of Murcia in Spain, whose mean height was only 158.8 cm in 1895 (Carrion 1986: 7). At the upper end of the scale, the tallest geographical group yet recorded within Europe appears to be the inhabitants of Aust-Agder in Norway at 180.8 cm (Norway 1986), although it seems likely that some Dutch areas would have higher means; the Dutch statistical yearbook unfortunately ceased to record regional height data after the Second World War. If we again allow 3 per cent further growth after conscription for the shortest recorded group and 1 per cent further growth for the tallest, we can estimate the range for large geographical sub-groups of national populations to have been between 163.6 and 182.6 cm.[2] There is, unfortunately, too little evidence to make similar statements about the range across different socioeconomic groups, al-

[2] Distributions of heights are approximately normal and typically have standard deviations in the range of 5.8–6.9 cm.

though, once again, one would expect the range to widen somewhat if economic and occupational factors could be taken into account. Some variation of this type is, presumably, proxied by geographical variation, and I have used height material to discuss inequality within Europe in another publication (Floud 1989).

All the European and North American societies for which evidence on physical growth is available have experienced increases in mean height during the past two centuries, or at least since records have become available. So ubiquitous is this phenomenon that it has simply been called 'the secular trend' by auxologists and human biologists. Study of the evidence, however, shows that different societies have approached their modern mean heights by very different routes. It is possible to distinguish three broad groups, although the divisions between them are often slight.

Fig. 8.1. Adult Height: America and Britain, 1740–1940

The first group (Fig. 8.1) consists of Britain, its North American colonies, the USA, and, probably, Australia. Estimated height means for North America and Britain are shown in the figure. These countries exhibited heights that were relatively great, both by modern standards and, as we shall see, by the standards of Europe as a whole as early as the eighteenth century; thereafter heights followed a cyclical path without a marked upward trend until the twentieth century (Sokoloff and Villaflor 1982). Substantial increases in height then took place, particularly after the Second World War, with some evidence that mean heights ceased to rise during the 1960s, although this is still in dispute.

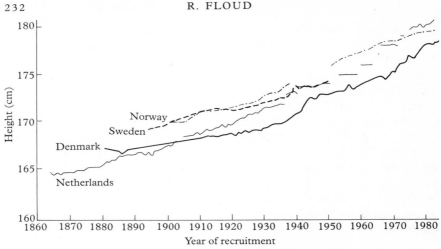

Fig. 8.2. Height at Conscription Age: Sweden, Norway, Denmark, and the Netherlands, 1860–1980

The second group (Fig. 8.2) consists of a number of northern European nations, in particular Denmark, Norway, the Netherlands, and probably Sweden. These countries all had significantly lower mean heights than the English-speaking nations in the eighteenth and early nineteenth centuries but grew rapidly, particularly in the twentieth century, and have now become among the tallest peoples in the world.

The third group (Fig. 8.3) consists of a number of southern European nations, in particular France, Italy, and Spain, which have had mean

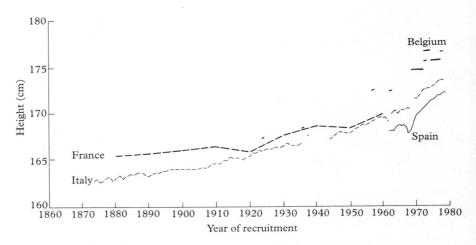

Fig. 8.3. Height at Conscription Age: Belgium, France, Italy, and Spain, 1860–1980

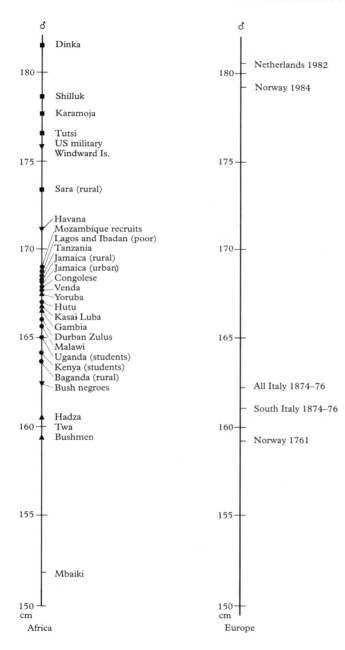

Fig. 8.4. The Contrast between the Range of European Heights over Time
and of African Heights Today
Source: Eveleth and Tanner (1976)

heights consistently below those of northern Europe, but have seen increasing growth, particularly since the Second World War.

The difference between the second and the third group is of particular interest, since it shows that, despite the common growth overall, the process has not so far been one of convergence to a common European mean height. Indeed, the gap between the mean height of Italian and Dutch male conscripts, for example, has grown consistently, both in absolute and in relative terms, over the last century. In 1874 Italian recruits averaged 162.4 cm and Dutch 164.9 cm, a difference of 2.5 cm, while in 1982 the averages were respectively 172.8 cm and 180.7 cm, a gap of 7.9 cm. Although Italians are now growing taller at a rapid rate, it would be rash to predict when, if at all, the gap will be closed.

It is important to put the growth in European heights over the last two hundred years in perspective. It is a matter of considerable psychological interest—although it is not a subject that seems to have received explicit attention from psychologists—that apparently small differences in height, of the order of a centimetre or two, are very clearly perceived as significant differences by observers. As a consequence, and because we presumably carry in our minds a concept of the usual range of human heights that we are likely to encounter, we also tend to overestimate the actual size of height differences between different groups. Figure 8.4 therefore reproduces a diagram from Eveleth and Tanner (1976: 103) of the modern heights of African adults and juxtaposes this with the range of European heights over the last two hundred years. It can be seen that the European range over time spans almost the whole of the African range over space, with the exception of some, though not all, bushmen and pygmy tribes.[3]

As a specific example, the Norwegian recruits of the 1760s were as short as African bushmen, while today they are as tall as the Dinka of the Sudan. This comparison is not meant to imply that it is to be expected that, given adequate nutrition, bushmen will ultimately grow as tall as the Dinka, for we do not know whether this will be so, but rather to emphasize by analogy how different the Norwegians of the eighteenth century would have looked from the Norwegians of today.

Despite the overall increase in heights in Europe and America, there is abundant evidence of the persistence of differences in mean heights

[3] Eveleth and Tanner (1976:338) report the Mbaiki as having an average adult height of 151.8 cm and the Bunia as 145.0 cm. The sample sizes were, however, only 15 and 14 respectively (Rimoin et al. 1976; Mann et al. 1962). The shortest other African groups were Bushmen of Botswana (157.8 cm with an N of 15 and 159.4 cm with an N of 292: Wyndham 1970; Tobias 1962), the Fulero of the Congo (159.1 cm with an N of 100: Hiernaux 1965), the Twa pygmies of the Congo (160.0 cm with an N of 23: Ghesquiere 1972), and the Hadza of Tanzania (160.5 cm with an N of 36, at ages 25–34: Barnicot et al. 1972). Only in the case of the Hadza was the age reported. (All cases reported in Eveleth and Tanner.)

within national populations, related both to geography and to socioeconomic status, and to the interaction of these two influences with each other and with other environmental factors. Such differences persist even in the countries with the greatest mean height; in Norway in 1985, for example, the region of Troms had a mean height of 178.1 cm while that of Aust-Agder averaged 180.8 cm. In other countries the differentials are still wider; in France in 1960 there was a gap of 6.35 cm between the shortest department, Morbihan at 166.2 cm, and the tallest, Seine at 172.55 cm (Chamla 1964:211–12). Survey evidence also shows that in Britain there is still a significant difference in mean height not only by region but also by social class; as the authors of the government survey comment,

it is clear that there is a class effect on height independent of age and sex. In almost every age group people from households headed by a manual worker were shorter, on average, than people from non-manual worker households. Overall, the average height of men was 175.5 cm (5′ 9″) in Social Classes I and II but 172.3 cm (5′ 8″) in Social Classes IV and V. Similarly, female height in Social Classes I and II was 162.5 cm (5′ 4″) compared with 159.6 cm (5′ 3″) in Classes IV and V. (Knight and Eldridge 1984)

It is however often asserted that in countries such as Sweden, which have less marked income and wealth inequality than Britain, such class gradients have now disappeared.

The evidence of change in the heights of Europeans thus presents social scientists with a number of problems. What has caused, first, the overall increase in heights; second, the differing patterns seen in different national countries; and, third, the persistent height differences that are still found even in countries that have very high levels of income and correspondingly low levels of mortality and morbidity?

8.5 AN INTERPRETATION OF THE INCREASE IN EUROPEAN HEIGHTS

The thousand or more studies reported by Eveleth and Tanner (1976), together with the many more performed since 1974, make it clear that height variation is a reflection of a multiplicity of possible environmental influences interacting with genetic factors. In the less developed countries, it is possible to assert that the primary causes of heights that are low by the standards of the more developed countries are poverty and disease, associated in the familiar synergistic relationship.

In addition, it seems likely that the overall disease environment, worsened by the extreme poverty of the bulk of the population, accounts for a phenomenon that Robert Fogel has named the 'peerage paradox'. This stems from the observation, first made of the British peerage in the eighteenth and nineteenth centuries, that high-wealth and high-income groups in society—presumably able to command whatever food and comfort they wished to consume—nevertheless had life expectations significantly worse than similarly wealthy groups in developed countries today (Fogel 1989). I have observed a similar phenomenon in the case of height: the sons of the aristocracy who attended the Royal Military Academy in the nineteenth century, although far taller than working-class boys, were yet shorter than the modern mean for the entire British population and shorter still than the modern upper-class mean (Floud *et al.* 1990). Although it is possible that both life expectation and height could be accounted for by poor treatment of aristocratic children in the nursery, it seems much more likely that the general level of infectious disease, from which they could be only partially isolated, was responsible for the poor nutritional status of the upper classes. Similar conclusions have been drawn from modern studies of high-income families in the developing world today (Rea 1971).

Thus there is little mystery about the causes of the poor nutritional status and low height of the bulk of the population of less developed countries or of their relatively low average nutritional status; the low average income and the extreme inequality in the distribution of incomes experienced in those countries is bad both for those suffering from poverty, malnutrition, and disease and for those who, though apparently rich enough to avoid such deprivation, yet suffer from living in such a society.

But can the same be said of the more developed, industrialized countries that are the focus of this paper?

The most striking feature of the change in mean height in Europe and North America shown in Figs. 8.1–8.3 is clearly the overall increase in all countries in the twentieth century, compared with a stable rate, a much slower rate of increase, or even a temporary decline in the nineteenth century. As I have shown elsewhere, height growth in the countries of western Europe, excluding Britain, during the late nineteenth and twentieth centuries is highly correlated with movements in GDP per capita and the rate of infant mortality (Floud 1984). I have not yet attempted a similar analysis of British and North American data, but it seems reasonable to expect that the same ecological relationship would apply. Since we know that, in most of the countries studied, infant mortality has fallen to low levels since the beginning of this century, it seems likely that movements in GDP have recently been a more significant influence. This is particularly so if one includes within those movements changes in the distribution of national income and wealth (Steckel 1983).

The situation in the nineteenth century is much more complex. Although the movement of gross domestic product per capita in Britain and the USA in the eighteenth and nineteenth centuries is still the subject of hot debate, it seems almost certain that, in terms of the conventional measures of welfare, both Britain and its American colonies, later the USA, were the wealthiest countries in the world. This is, indeed, borne out by the height data. It is somewhat surprising that, between those two countries, the American colonies should have exhibited such an advantage in mean heights over Britain in the eighteenth century, but this can probably be accounted for by very high levels of food consumption in the rural colonies. It appears that this advantage disappeared during the first quarter of the nineteenth century, perhaps as a result of the early stages of British industrialization and the rising real incomes which it and the agricultural revolution brought to the British working class.

What is most puzzling, however, is the failure of either the American or the British mean heights to rise significantly during the nineteenth century, when it is commonly thought that the impact of industrialization, after some lags, led to an increase in the real incomes of the populations. Indeed, in both countries mean heights appear to have fallen from the levels reached early in the second quarter of the century, and not to have regained those levels until almost a century later. This is despite the fact that conventional measures of real income show very marked increases in both countries.

While it is impossible to be certain, it seems highly likely that this check or reverse in height growth can be attributed to the later stages of the impact of industrialization, when the growth of industry led to massive urbanization and a worsened disease environment. Both Fogel and Komlos, in work so far unpublished, have suggested that the American evidence is compatible with such an explanation, particularly since there seems to be some ground for thinking that the reverse came first in the urban areas and then spread to the countryside. In Britain it is known that infant mortality and life expectation, which had improved in the latter part of the eighteenth century, show little significant change for much of the nineteenth century: while child and adult mortality declines from the 1870s, infant mortality, which is particularly relevant to growth, does not improve markedly until the twentieth century. There is also abundant impressionistic evidence of the poverty, disease, and degradation of the urban areas of industrializing Britain. Moreover, detailed analysis of British military records shows clearly that birth and residence in the urban areas, in particular London, was associated with shorter height, and that the positive association between urban residence and tallness that is a feature of twentieth-century data was negative in the eighteenth and nineteenth centuries (Floud *et al.* 1990).

It also seems possible, although much more detailed research would be needed to confirm this, that differences in the disease environment contributed to the differences between northern and southern European countries seen in Figs. 8.2 and 8.3, although both Italy and Spain also had, until recently, much lower income levels than the northern European countries. It seems likely that the very rapid recent increase in mean heights in Italy and Spain represents the recent increases in the wealth of those countries and the conquest of endemic and epidemic disease.

Another feature of the western European data deserves more discussion. In the several countries for which annual data are available, the growth in heights appears extremely smooth, a rising trend undisturbed by the various cataclysms that have affected Europe during this century. By contrast, both British and American data for the eighteenth and nineteenth centuries show marked fluctuations. It is possible, of course, that the contrast reflects in some way the different methods of military recruitment used in each group of countries. It is unlikely, however, that statistical procedures used on the British recruitment data, to compensate for the effects of the lower height limit, could be at fault. Such procedures are of little importance in the North American case, where the distributions were little affected by the rejection of the shortest potential recruits. Sampling variability may be a problem, since much of the British and most of the North American data are based on samples; but in most cases the sample sizes are large.

It seems likely, however, that one major distinction between the European and, at least, the British data may be of importance. As mentioned above, the conscription data include most if not all of the male populations, while in Britain recruits were drawn almost entirely from the working class, many of whom were living in or brought up in poverty, and who would exhibit more fluctuation in mean height as a result of environmental variation than would recruits drawn from the upper and middle classes. It may be, therefore, that variations in height in the European countries have been dampened by the inclusion of upper- and middle-class recruits in their height statistics, and that this leads to the relatively smooth pattern of change over time in those countries. Only detailed research in the military archives, as opposed to the use of published statistics, can settle this issue.

Even if the overall trend in European heights is not too difficult to explain, some problems remain. In the industrialized countries extreme poverty has long been avoided by income support schemes of various kinds, infant mortality and morbidity has been enormously reduced, and the general income level of the population is both far higher and more equally distributed than in less developed countries. It thus seems clear that, although the overall trends in height over time may indeed reflect the elimination of much poverty and disease in the developed world, neither the current variation in height and nutritional status within that world nor, to some extent, the trend in the most recent past can owe much to the traditional causes of such variation. These countries are today so rich, and they have been so rich for so long, that malnutrition and epidemic or endemic disease seem unlikely determinants of height variation. One is faced, in fact, with the modern version of the 'peerage paradox'; instead of needing to explain the low heights of the rich within a poverty-stricken society, we now need to explain the low heights of the poor within an affluent society.

It can be argued that the matter is one for empirical study; after all, the statistical estimation of the determinants of height will presumably reveal the most influential variables. In principle this is so, but such estimation is likely to be extraordinarily difficult because of problems of measurement of many of the variables and of multicollinearity. In addition, such studies as that of Martorell on the relationship between disease and growth emphasize the view that, as Steckel puts it in discussing his modern cross-sectional study,

it is likely that different coefficients would be obtained from data for earlier time periods. Improved medical technology probably shifted the relationship between average height and per capita income. Knowledge of the germ theory of disease, for example, enabled individuals to improve health, and therefore increase height, with no change in income. (Steckel 1983: 4)

Nevertheless, there are persuasive arguments for the view that, even in the more developed countries, differences in income, wealth, and health still exert a measurable and significant influence on nutritional status and therefore on height. The strongest support comes from the analysis of differentials in height by social class, which are clear in Britain but greatly attenuated, if present at all, in Sweden. The survey by Knight and Eldridge (1984) shows these differentials for adults in Britain, but numerous studies of children demonstrate their pervasiveness and the early age at which they become established. Rona et al. (1978), for example, showed that there is an association in British children between height and parental social class, sibling size, and the unemployment of parents; while Smith et al. (1980) showed that such associations and the resulting differentials are established before children enter school at the age of 5. By contrast, Lindgren (1976) found for Sweden that 'No significant differences between socio-economic strata defined by father's occupation and family income were found either for height and weight or for ages at PHV, PWV and menarche' (p. 501).

It is possible, of course, that income differences are not responsible for such class differences in height; other possibilities might be the extent of psychological and emotional support for children, differences in the amount of work effort or other physical activity required in different classes, or even inherited characteristics. But, of these, only the last could conceivably affect children as young as the age of 2, when class differences in height can be found, and it seems most unlikely that genetic inheritance could explain marked class differences in countries such as Britain which have high levels of social mobility. The evidence of Sweden, where income differences have been much reduced but where behavioural differences between white-collar and manual workers are still evident, also suggests the primacy of income as a determinant. But exactly how income exerts its influence—whether through the quality or quantity of diet, warmth, housing density, or other mechanism—still remains undetermined.

If we look forward rather than back, the main implication of Figs. 8.1–8.3, so far as the contemporary developed world is concerned, is that we have not yet experienced the full effects of the improvement in nutritional status which is shown by measurements of height to have occurred in recent decades. If, as Waaler's work suggests, such improvements have direct consequences for mortality levels, in particular for mortality from respiratory and cardio-vascular diseases, then it is likely that significant improvements in mortality and associated morbidity have still to occur in most of the countries of western Europe. This is particularly so if such improvement is combined with the independent effects of reductions in tobacco consumption and an increase in exercise, which are both known to affect such diseases.

Further improvement in the overall nutritional status of the populations in the more developed world is unlikely, however, without a decrease in inequality. Steckel (1983) found that, in a cross-sectional analysis of contemporary societies, the extent of inequality was a significant determinant of mean height, and this is confirmed by the evidence, quoted above, which links height to class structure in Britain and, presumably, in other developed countries. Unfortunately, in Britain at least, the combined effects of fiscal measures to increase income and wealth inequality and the increase in unemployment are militating against such an improvement: it may indeed be true that, for the first time since the nineteenth century, a developed nation is experiencing a decline in the mean height of its population.

8.6 CONCLUSIONS

Anthropometric data thus set us many puzzles. Yet the exploration of those puzzles takes us into central areas of the social and biological sciences, for there is little that is more fundamental than long-term influences on the health and welfare of human populations. The purpose of this chapter has been to set out some of the evidence that puzzles us, to suggest some methods of approach, and to stimulate further investigation. It is clear, at the least, that anthropometry is as relevant to an understanding of the industrialized world as it is vital as a diagnostic tool amid the malnourished populations of the developing world. It was for this reason that Galton, while developing in his study of anthropometry many of the basic tools of the modern statistician and econometrician, called for a regular anthropometric survey of countries in the developed world; his plea, still unheeded, is as relevant today as it was a century ago.

9

Second Thoughts on the European Escape from Hunger: Famines, Chronic Malnutrition, and Mortality Rates

R. W. Fogel

> Most of the people in the world are poor, so if we knew the
> economics of being poor we would know much of the economics
> that really matters.
>
> T. W. Schultz (1980)

9.1 INTRODUCTION

During the late 1960s a wide consensus emerged among social and economic historians regarding the causes of the decline in the high European death rates that prevailed at the beginning of the early modern era. The high average mortality rates of the years preceding the vital revolution were attributed to periodic mortality crises which raised 'normal' mortality rates by 50–100 per cent or more. It was the elimination of these peaks, rather than the lowering of the plateau of mortality in 'normal' years, that was believed to be principally responsible for the much lower mortality rates that prevailed at the end of the nineteenth century (Helleiner 1967:85; Wrigley 1969:165; Flinn 1970:45). These crises, it was held, were precipitated either by acute harvest failures or by epidemics (Flinn 1970:45). Some scholars argued that, even if the diseases were not nutritionally sensitive, famines played a major role because epidemics were spread by the beggars who swarmed from one place to another in search of food (Meuvret 1965:510–11). Whatever the differences on this issue, it was widely agreed that many of the

This paper stems from research connected with the project on 'Secular Trends in Nutrition, Labor Welfare, and Labor Productivity', which is jointly sponsored by the National Bureau of Economic Research and the Center for Population Economics of the University of Chicago. The findings reported here were supported by grants from the Walgreen Foundation and the University of Chicago. I am especially indebted to E. A. Wrigley, who called to my attention a number of the key issues discussed below, and whose criticisms of my early work on these issues pushed my research in new directions. I have also benefited from the comments of George Alter, Jere Behrman, Ronald D. Lee, R. Floud, Patrick Galloway, John Komlos, S. R. Osmani, James Riley, J. M. Tanner, and Amartya Sen on an earlier draft, and from the discussion at the WIDER Conference on Poverty, Undernutrition, and Living Standards.

mortality crises were due to starvation brought on by harvest failure (Wrigley 1969; Flinn 1970, 1974).

A mechanism by which a harvest failure was transformed into a mortality crisis was proposed by Hoskins in two influential papers published in the 1960s (1964, 1968). Noting that it was possible to identify harvest failures by looking at the deviations in grain prices from their normal level, Hoskins computed the annual deviations of wheat prices from a 31-year moving average of these prices. Normal harvests were defined as those with prices that were within ± 10 per cent of the trend. He found that, over the 280 years from 1480 to 1759, good harvests (prices 10 per cent or more below trends) were about 50 per cent more frequent than deficient harvests (prices 10 per cent or more above trend). His most important finding, however, was that good and bad harvests (as shown by prices) ran in sequences, so there were frequently three or four bad years in a row. These sequences, he argued, were due primarily not to weather cycles but to the low yield-to-seed ratios, which he put at about 4 or 5 for wheat at the beginning of the sixteenth century. Thus, one bad harvest tended to generate another because starving farmers consumed their reserve for seeds. The consequence of several bad harvests in a row was a mortality crisis.

The interpretation of the European escape from hunger and high death rates embodied in this train of research was brought into question with the publication of The Population History of England, 1541–1871: A Reconstruction by E. A. Wrigley and R. S. Schofield (1981). Using data from 404 parish registers widely distributed throughout England, these scholars and their associates constructed monthly and annual estimates of the English population over a 331-year period, as well as monthly and annual estimates of the national birth rates, mortality rates, and nuptiality rates. Although important issues have been raised about various assumptions employed in the analytical procedures that transformed the information on baptisms and burials contained in the Anglican registers into national estimates of birth rates and death rates, it is widely agreed that the reconstruction was carried out with meticulous care, and that the various adjustments for deficiencies in the record were judicious. Whatever the shortcomings of the reconstructions, the new time series produced by Wrigley and Schofield have become the foundation for all further research into the demographic history of England (Flinn 1982; Lindert 1983).

In addition to presenting their basic time series and describing the complex procedures employed to produce them, Wrigley and Schofield began the processes of relating these demographic rates to underlying economic and social phenomena. They determined that both fertility rates and marriage rates were strongly correlated with measures of real wages and the cost of living, but that mortality rates were not.[1] A chapter of the book contributed by Lee (1981) reported a statistically significant but weak relationship between short-term variations in death rates and in wheat prices; but Lee, as well as Wrigley and Schofield, concluded that short-run variations in English mortality were 'overwhelmingly determined' by factors other than the food supply (R. Schofield 1983: 282). In so far as the long-term trend in mortality was concerned, Wrigley and Schofield reported that they were unable to find even a weak statistical correlation between mortality rates and the food supply (Wrigley and Schofield 1981:325–6).

Since the findings of Wrigley, Schofield, and Lee appear to be so sharply in conflict with the train of research that has linked the escape from high mortality rates to the escape from hunger, it is tempting to declare that one of the research trains must be wrong, and to choose sides. I believe that such a conclusion is not only premature but very likely wrong. The aim of this chapter is to reconsider the older line of research in the light of the findings of Wrigley, Schofield, and Lee in order to see where they are compatible and where the evidence tilts towards one or the other side.

In the next section, I present evidence indicating that the elimination of crisis mortality accounted for only a small part of the decline in national mortality rates during the nineteenth century. Section 9.3 argues that some previous attempts to infer the extent of the shortfall in the quantity of foodgrains harvested from movements of prices have exaggerated that shortfall because of overestimates of the elasticity of demand for foodgrains. Section 9.4 presents an alternative hypothesis which makes sharp changes in the distribution of foodgrains, resulting from relatively small shortfalls in output, the principal cause of periodic famines. A mechanism underlying such distributional changes is proposed. It is then argued in Section 9.5 that famines could have been avoided, and apparently were avoided during 1600–40 in England, by proper government policies. Section 9.6 deals with the effects of chronic malnutrition on mortality rates. It presents evidence which suggests that most of the secular decline in mortality in England, France, and Sweden before 1875, and about half of the decline between 1875 and 1975, was due to the reduction of chronic malnutrition. Section 9.7 presents the principal findings of the paper and briefly comments on their implications for current debates on policy.

---

[1] The analysis of Wrigley and Schofield is cast in terms of crude death rates rather than age-standardized rates because the counts of vital events in their 404 parishes do not give the specific ages at which these events occurred; consequently they were not able to examine the effects of famines on the age structure of mortality.

9.2 THE NEW FINDINGS ON MORTALITY CRISES

One of the most important aspects of the *The Population History* is the new light it sheds on mortality crises over the 331 years it covers. Wrigley and Schofield are the first scholars who have had a sample of parishes large enough in number and wide enough in geographic coverage to permit an estimate of the national impact of mortality crises on the annual crude death rates in early modern England. Following established procedures, they measure mortality crises as deviations from a 25-year moving average, and define a crisis year as one with an annual CDR (crude death rate) that is more than 10 per cent above trend. That criterion yielded 45 crisis years, a bit less than 14 per cent of the years in their study (Wrigley and Schofield 1981:333). They also computed national crisis months (months with monthly death rates at least 25 per cent above trend), and found that 94 years contained at least one such crisis month (pp. 338–9). Their analysis confirmed many of the findings of scholars working with less complete data. The year 1558/9, for example, emerged as by far the worst year for mortality in the entire period. They also found that the most severe mortality crises were concentrated during 1544–1658, although there was a lethal recurrence during the late 1720s.

Perhaps the most important aspect of the new time series on mortality, however, is that these data drastically diminish the role of crisis mortality as an explanation for the high mortality rates that generally prevailed between 1541 and 1800. This conclusion emerges from two tables in *The Population History*, which together provide the data needed to compute the crisis component of total mortality. The results of the computation are presented in Table 9.1 by quarter-centuries (or fractions thereof) as well as by centuries (or fractions thereof). In no quarter-century did crisis mortality account for as much as 10 per cent of the total mortality. Even after crisis mortality is factored out, the 'normal' mortality remains above 25 per thousand for the sixteenth, seventeenth, and eighteenth centuries. Indeed, the 'normal' mortality rate of the eighteenth century was as high as the total mortality rate of each of the two preceding centuries, despite their many crises. Consequently, the escape from high mortality rates was due primarily not to the elimination of crises, as many have previously argued, but to the reduction in so-called normal mortality levels. Nearly three-quarters of the decline of mortality between 1726–50 and 1851–71, despite the relatively high level of crisis mortality at the beginning of this period and its negligible level at the end of it, was due to the reduction of 'normal' mortality.

It follows that, even if every national mortality crisis identified by Wrigley and Schofield was the result of a famine, the elimination of periodic famines cannot be the principal explanation for the secular decline in mortality. This is not to deny that famines in particular localities at particular times produced great increases in local mortality rates: too much evidence of local disasters induced by food shortages has accumulated to rule out such phenomenon. However, in light of the Wrigley–Schofield data, it now seems clear that, dramatic as they were, mortality crises, whether caused by famines or not, were too scattered in time and space to have been the principal factor in the secular decline in mortality after 1540.[2]

Table 9.1. The impact of crisis mortality on the average crude death rate: England, 1541–1871

Period	(1) CDR per 1000 person–years	(2) Crisis mortality per 1000 person–years	(3) CDR after factoring out crisis mortality (per 1000)	(4) Crisis mortality as % of average mortality	(5) Crisis mortality as % of 'premature' mortality
By quarter–centuries					
(1) 1541–50	30.33	2.25	28.08	7.42	9.64
(2) 1551–75	28.28	2.35	25.93	8.31	11.04
(3) 1576–1600	24.21	1.22	22.99	5.04	7.09
(4) 1601–25	24.61	2.05	22.56	8.33	11.64
(5) 1626–50	26.36	0.99	25.37	3.76	5.11
(6) 1651–75	28.07	1.58	26.49	5.63	7.50
(7) 1676–1700	30.29	1.66	28.63	5.48	7.13
(8) 1701–25	27.79	0.06	27.73	0.22	0.29
(9) 1726–50	30.57	2.34	28.23	6.40	9.93
(10) 1751–75	27.28	0.40	26.88	1.47	1.97
(11) 1776–1800	26.85	0.55	26.30	2.05	2.77
(12) 1801–25	25.40	0.15	25.25	0.59	0.82
(13) 1826–50	22.58	0.13	22.45	0.58	0.83
(14) 1851–71	22.42	0.13	22.29	0.58	0.84
By centuries					
(15) 1541–1600	26.93	1.87	25.06	6.92	9.38
(16) 1601–1700	27.33	1.57	25.76	5.74	7.72
(17) 1701–1800	28.12	0.83	27.29	2.95	3.93
(18) 1801–1871	23.53	0.14	23.39	0.59	0.85

Notes
Lines (1)–(4): col. (1) Each entry is the average of the quinquennial rates for the period given in Wrigley and Schofield (1981:528–9). *Col. (2)* Each entry (contd.)

---

[2] It is, however, still possible that mortality crises were a much larger part of total mortality before 1541 than they were afterward, both because of differences in the nature of the prevailing diseases in the two periods and because food supplies were probably more inadequate in medieval times.

9.3 MEASURING THE VARIABILITY OF FOOD SUPPLY

The Population History does not provide the same challenge to previous thought on the scope of subsistence crises as it does on the question of mortality crises. Indeed, the periods that Wrigley and Schofield identified as the major subsistence crises (1981:321) generally coincide with those identified by Hoskins (1964: figure facing p. 29; 1968: figure facing p. 15). That outcome is not surprising, since the procedures used in the identification and measurement of subsistence crises by Wrigley, Schofield, and Lee are quite similar to those of Hoskins. Wrigley and Schofield used annual deviations in an index of real wages from a 25-year trend to identify subsistence crises. Because of the procedure for smoothing the wage series, as they pointed out, nearly all the variability in the index came from the price deflator which was dominated by grains (broadly defined). Lee, like Hoskins, relied on wheat prices alone, on the grounds that the price of wheat was so highly correlated with other food prices that wheat was 'a good proxy for food prices in general' (Lee 1981: 357).

The tradition of judging the shortfall in the food supply by price is an ancient one dating back at least to Gregory King, who first formalized

(Note to Table 9.1 contd.)
is the difference between the corresponding entries in col (1) and (3). *Col (3)* Wrigley and Schofield (1981: 333) give the CDR (D_{cc}) for each of the 45 years they identify as a crisis year, as well as the percentage deviation of the crisis CDR from a 25–year moving average, which is taken to be the normal CDR for that year. Hence, by dividing 1 plus the percentage deviation into the crisis CDR, it is possible to obtain the 'normal' CDR for the crisis year (D_{nc}). It is also possible to solve the following equation for the normal CDR in non–crisis year (D_{nn}):

$$D = \theta D_{cc} + (1 - \theta) D_{nn}$$

Where D is the average CDR for the time period (as shown in col. (1)) and θ is the share of crisis years during the time period. The average CDR with the crisis mortality factored out (D_n) is then given by

$$D_n = \theta D_{nc} + (1 - \theta) D_{nn}.$$

The entries in col. (3) are the values of D_n. *Col. (4).* Each entry is 1 minus the ratio of the col. (3) entry to the col. (1) entry.

Lines (15)–(18): cols (1) and (3)   The entries for each period are average of the corresponding figures for the sub-periods in lines (1)–(14), weighted by the number of years in the sub-periods. *Col. (2)* Each entry is the difference between the corresponding entries in col. (1) and (3). *Col. (4)* Each entry is 1 minus the ratio of the col. (3) entry to the col. (1) entry. *Col. (5)* 'Premature' mortality is defined as the crude death rate of a given period minus the English death rate of 1980 standardized for the English age structure of 1701–5 (see Fogel 1986a: Table 1).

the systematic relationship between the yield of a harvest and the subsequent price of the grain. Called 'King's Law', his schema (see Table
9.2) has been employed as an estimate of the elasticity of demand for
wheat. Later economists, such as Jevons and Bouniatian, formulated
quite similar laws in equations (Slicher von Bath 1963:118–19). All
three laws are closely approximated by constant elasticity demand curves
with ε ranging between 0.403 and 0.422. As Table 9.2 shows, the
equation

$$Q = 1.00P^{-0.403} \tag{1}$$

gives a very close fit to King's Law in the specified range of prices.[3] It
seems quite reasonable, therefore, to use the deviation in price to infer
the deviation in the yield of a harvest from its normal level, as numerous
analysts have done ever since King's time.

Table 9.2.   A comparison between King's Law and a
constant elasticity of demand equation
(1 = normal price and yield)

King's Law		$Q = 1.00P^{-0.403}$	
Q	P	Q	P
1.0	1.0	1.00	1.0
0.9	1.3	0.90	1.3
0.8	1.8	0.79	1.8
0.7	2.6	0.68	2.6
0.6	3.8	0.58	3.8
0.5	5.5	0.50	5.5

Source: Slicher von Bath (1963:118–19) presents King's
Law and compares it with those of Jevons and Bouniatian.

When King's Law is combined with the proposition that the yield-to-
seed ratios of wheat was about 4—i.e. that one-quarter of the crop was
needed for seeds—the interpretation of harvest failures developed from

---

[3] In a constant elasticity demand equation of the form $Q = DP^{-\varepsilon}$, D represents all of the
variables that might cause the intercept of demand curve to shift (income, prices of
substitutes, prices of complements). The implicit assumption of those who have used King's
Law is that both D and ε are constant. When all variables are standardized on 1, $D = 1$. It
should also be kept in mind that, in applications of King's Law, wheat is generally used as
a proxy for grain or food. Since applications of King's Law generally do not take account
of the possibility that ε shifted during periods of dearth, I have worked within the framework
of that tradition in this section because my aim here is to reveal issues that do not turn on
a shifting demand curve. In Section 9.4 below, an adjustment is made for a shifting
elasticity. However, in both sections it is assumed that the aggregate demand curve is
relatively fixed and that year-to-year fluctuations in price are due primarily to shifts in a
perfectly inelastic short-run supply curve from one harvest to another. See the Appendix
for a further discussion of these points.

price series by Hoskins and numerous other scholars during the past three decades follows immediately. Wheat prices 50 per cent above normal imply a harvest that is 15 per cent below normal, a situation presumed to have put heavy pressure on farmers to dip into their seed reserve. With two such years in a row, even if farmers succeeded in maintaining the normal proportion of the crop for seed reserves, consumption in the second year would be cut by more than a quarter—pushing the average food intake of the lower classes to perhaps 1340 calories per equivalent adult or less per day.[4] How devastating, then, must have been years such as 1555 and 1556, when a 51 per cent deviation of the price of wheat above normal was followed by a 105 per cent deviation above normal—suggesting a decline of lower-class consumption to the neighbourhood of 1180 calories.[5]

The problem is that the implied level of caloric consumption in 1556 is too low to be believable, since it is well below the requirement for basal metabolism. We know, both from controlled semi-starvation experiments and from actual conditions in underdeveloped countries today, that even levels of 1300–1500 calories produce protein-energy malnutrition (PEM) serious enough to incapacitate a large proportion of the population and also lead to so many cases of kwashiorkor that death rates increase significantly among those affected (Scrimshaw 1987; DeMaeyer 1976; Mellor and Gavian 1987; G. Kumar 1987; Foreign Office Commission 1985). A population forced to consume less than basal metabolism for a whole year would have produced noticeable increases in mortality. Yet the Wrigley–Schofield time series, while confirming Hoskin's finding that 1555 and 1556 were years of extreme dearth, report that the mortality rates during these two years averaged about 10 per cent below normal (Wrigley and Schofield 1981:321). Indeed, after searching for a correlation between extreme annual deviations in prices and in mortality rates, they concluded that no significant contemporaneous relationship existed (pp. 325–6), although there was evidence of a weak lagged relationship.[6]

This puzzle is not necessarily without a solution. One possibility is that government intervention prevented a subsistence crisis from turning into a mortality crisis. (Some questions about the role of the government will be explored in Section 9.5.) Another possibility is that defects in the

---

[4] The figure on caloric consumption is derived by applying $(1.5^{-0.403})^2$ to the average caloric consumption of the three lowest deciles of the English distribution in Table 9.8.

[5] The figure is derived in the same way as in n. 4, except that the factor is $(1.51^{-0.403})(2.05^{-0.403})$.

[6] Lee, in his 1981 study (379–82) and in a letter to me (dated 10 July 1989), has pointed out that his analysis of the correlation between wheat prices and mortality revealed a strong simultaneous relationship in the 9 years (out of 287) that the proportional deviation of wheat prices from their trend exceeded two standard deviations: cf. Fogel 1986a: 494–5 and 524, n. 46.

Wrigley–Schofield estimates of mortality may explain the anomalous results. Yet their ingenious procedures for correcting the undercount of deaths, if less than perfect, seems to have produced a series quite adequate for the particular analysis they have undertaken. The problem, I believe, lies not so much in the data but in a series of implicit assumptions that have gradually crept into the analysis of the data, assumptions made so often that they hardened into an unquestioned procedure. It was only with the discovery of the Wrigley–Schofield paradox that the need to reconsider the analytical procedures became evident.

The crux of the problem lies with the application of King's Law which, as has been indicated, is well described by a simple demand equation of the form

$$Q = P^{-\varepsilon}. \tag{2}$$

When P (price) and Q (quantity) are measured as proportional deviations from trend, (2) becomes

$$\overset{*}{Q} = -\varepsilon \overset{*}{P}, \tag{3}$$

where an asterisk over a variable indicates percentage deviations from trend, and ε is the elasticity of demand. Equation (3), which is the definition of that elasticity, is thus a simple linear equation in which the value of the coefficient of the right-hand variable is given by

$$\varepsilon = \frac{\sigma_q}{\sigma_p} r_{pq} = -\frac{\overset{*}{Q}}{\overset{*}{P}}, \tag{4}$$

where σ_q is the standard deviation (s.d.) of $\overset{*}{Q}$, σ_p is the s.d. of $\overset{*}{P}$, and r_{pq} is the correlation coefficient between $\overset{*}{Q}$ and $\overset{*}{P}$. It follows that the value of ε will be greatest when r_{pq} is assumed to equal 1, which is the assumption generally made in the application of King's Law. Since this assumption is not at issue in the analysis that follows, and because a value of r_{pq} less then 1 would strengthen my argument, I will assume that $r_{pq} = 1$ in the balance of the discussion.

It follows from (4) that one can estimate an elasticity for wheat by obtaining estimates of σ_p and σ_q. The estimate of σ_p for wheat is readily available from the wheat prices used by Lee and is about 0.22 for the period 1540–1840 (Lee 1981: 374). The value of σ_q (measured as a proportional deviation from trend), computed for the first 30 years for which data on the physical yield of wheat in England are available (1884–1913), is 0.040.[7] Assuming, as a first approximation, that the

---

[7] The implicit assumption in the literature is that acres planted remained constant and that net importants were zero, so that all of the yearly variation in the quantity of grain was due to variation in yields. In order to avoid complicating the argument further than need be, I have accepted these assumptions. The effect of the assumptions is to bias the result

climatic factors affecting the variability of yield were similar between the seventeenth century and the end of the nineteenth, the preceding figures imply that the demand elasticity for wheat was 0.183 (0.0402 ÷ 0.220), which is more than 50 per cent below the elasticity of the demand for wheat implied by King's Law, or at least by the way that it has been interpreted.[8]

Table 9.3. The effect of allowing for carry-over stocks in the supply of wheat at the end of the new harvest

(1) Deviation from normal yield of current harvest Q_j	(2) Price	(3) Deviation from normal supply if carry-over is 5 months Q'	(4) Deviation from normal supply if carry-over is 4 months Q''
1.0	1.0	1.00	1.00
0.9	1.3	0.93	0.92
0.8	1.8	0.86	0.85
0.7	2.6	0.79	0.78
0.6	3.8	0.72	0.70
0.5	5.5	0.65	0.62

Note: Cols (1) and (2) are from Table 9.2; cols (3) and (4) are computed from

$$Q_j^i = \theta I + (1 - \theta)Q_j,$$

where I is the carry–over inventory, which is assumed to be constant for each value of Q_j (taken from col. (1)), and θ is the share of carry-over inventories after the close of a normal harvest ($\theta = 0.294$ with 5–mo. carry-over and 0.250 with 4–mo. carry-over.

The problem with some previous interpretations of King's Law is that investigators implicitly assumed that carry-over stocks of wheat from the

against the point I am making since the root mean squared errors (RMSEs) around the trend of total production and around the trend of total production plus imports were below the RMSE around the trend of yield during 1884–1913.

[8] Is it valid to use data for 1884–1913 to estimate the variability of per-acre yields in the eighteenth century in view of the marked advances in agricultural technology after 1700? That point needs to be pursued, and it may be possible to estimate the average variance in annual per-acre yields for the eighteenth century from data in estate records. One of the earliest time series is for the USA, which began its system of crop reporting shortly after the American Civil War. These data suggest that, although the technological advances produced large increases in the average yield per acre, they had little effect on the coefficient of variation. For example, the mean wheat yield in the USA during 1961–70 was more than twice the figure for 1871–80; however, the coefficients of variation for the two time periods were virtually identical (computed from US Bureau of the Census 1975: 510–11). Despite irrigation, crop spraying, etc., the principal factors that affect variations around trend (e.g. rainfall, sunshine, temperature) do not seem, even today, to have yielded much to science.

previous harvests were nil. This assumption was an unintended but necessary consequence of treating the deviations from normal annual yields (column (1) of Table 9.2) as the total supply—as when I used the series in columns (1) and (2) of that table to estimate equation (1). However, the annual supply is not just the harvest in a given year, but the harvest plus the carry-over stock from previous years. Davenant (1699:82) estimated that in normal times carry-over stocks varied between four and five months (i.e. between 33 and 42 per cent of a normal crop). Consequently, when estimating the demand curve, the proper quantity is not Q but Q' or Q'' (Table 9.3). When those series are substituted for Q, the estimated values of are given by:

$$Q' = 1.00P^{-0.248} \quad \text{(when carry-overs are five months);} \qquad (2a)$$
$$Q'' = 1.00P^{-0.272} \quad \text{(when carry-overs are four months).} \qquad (2b)$$

Thus, when one corrects for the neglect of carry-over stocks, King's Law implies an elasticity of demand that is not only between 33 and 38 per cent below the level often presumed, but also a good deal closer to the estimate obtained by using the standard deviation of proportional deviations of physical yields from trend at the end of the nineteenth century.

Table 9.4. The normal Distribution of the supply of grain (new crop plus carry–over inventories) at the close of harvest

	%
(1) Carry–over stocks	29.4
(2) Animal feed	8.5
(3) Seed for the next crop	17.6
(4) Human consumption	44.5

Source: lines (1) and (2) Davenant (1699 : 71–4, 82); line (3) Hoskins (1968: 25–6).

Before pursuing the implications of this finding, one other implicit assumption needs to be made explicit. This stems from the neglect of grains fed to livestock as a reserve for human consumption. Although the feeding off of grasses, clover, vetches, turnips, lentils, other meadow crops, and hay provided the bulk of animal feed, Davenant (1699:71–2) estimated that about 12 per cent of annual grain production was normally fed to livestock. In other words, human consumption of grains (see Table 9.4) normally constituted only about 45 per cent of the available supply at the close of a harvest. Even if we add the 17.6 per cent reserved for seeds, there was still normally a reserve of 37.9 per cent (carry-over plus feed) that could serve as a buffer before a deficient harvest required a restriction of human consumption or an encroachment on the seed reserve.

It follows from (3) that not even a 100 per cent deviation of wheat price above trend, which occurred only once in the entire period examined by Hoskins, implied a physical shortfall of wheat (standing here for a typical grain) so large as to eliminate carry-over stocks, let alone the combination of carry-over stocks and animal feed. Even the worst pair of years identified by Hoskins (1555 and 1556) would still have left more than 10 per cent of the normal carry-over inventory as a buffer without encroaching on feed, seed, or human consumption in either year.[9]

The point of the preceding exercise is that, even for a single grain, and even assuming a low yield-to-seed ratio, the physical shortfall in the worst pair of years was not so great as to require a general encroachment on seeds in order to maintain human consumption, although such encroachments undoubtedly occurred in some localities in some years, especially among the poorer farmers. This is not to say that the high prices did not cause sharp reductions in consumption, especially among the lower classes, or to deny the existence of famines. I mean only to call into question the proposition that *nationwide* subsistence crises after 1541 were the consequence of natural disasters.

Indeed, even the preceding discussion overemphasizes the part played by natural factors, since until now I have accepted the common assumption that, because wheat prices were highly correlated with other food prices, wheat prices alone are an acceptable proxy for an index of all food prices. However, when one is attempting to infer the variability of the quantity of food from the variability in wheat prices, the critical question is not the strength of the correlation but the size of the elasticity between these two variables. Since the elasticity (α) of all food prices with respect to wheat prices is given by

$$\frac{\overset{*}{P_f}}{\overset{*}{P_w}} = \alpha = \frac{\sigma_f}{\sigma_w}\, r_{fw}, \tag{5}$$

it follows that, if α is less than 1, σ_f (the s.d. of deviations around the trend in food prices) will be less than σ_w (the s.d. of deviations around the trend in wheat prices) even if correlation between wheat and food prices is perfect ($r_{rw} = 1$). As it turns out, the estimated value of α is 0.346 (and $\bar{R}^2$ is 0.61) over the years 1540–1738, so that use of wheat prices, and their conversion within the context of King's Law into a measure of supply, greatly exaggerates the variability of the food supply during the early modern era (see the Appendix to this chapter).

[9] I do not mean to suggest that farmers actually dipped deeply into carry-over inventories or into feed stores when grain prices rose. Indeed, as I shall argue below, they were quite unwilling to do so. Nevertheless, those inventories were more than adequate to cover the food needs of the destitute without encroaching on reserves for seeds.

If the deviations around trend in the food supply (σ_{fq}) are to be estimated from the deviations in wheat prices, what we need to know is the elasticity of the food supply with respect to wheat prices (ε_{fw}) rather than the King's Law which, even when properly interpreted, gives only the elasticity of the quantity of wheat demanded with respect to wheat price. Unfortunately, the time series needed to estimate σ_{fq} (the s.d. of deviations in the annual quantity of the food supply) for England is not yet available even for recent times, but it is possible to estimate σ_{gq} (the s.d. of deviations from trend in an index of all grain yields) after 1884. With this change, the desired elasticity ε_{fw} can be estimated from equation (6):

$$\varepsilon_{fw} = \frac{\sigma_{gq}}{\sigma_{w}} \, r_{gq,w} \, , \tag{6}$$

where σ_w is the s.d. of proportional deviations from trend on wheat prices. If we assume $r_{gq,w} = 1$, only σ_{gq} needs to be estimated, since as indicated earlier $\sigma_w = 0.220$. When σ_{gq} is estimated from data over the period 1884–1913, it turns out to be 0.0300, which puts ε_{fw} at 0.136.

This provisional estimate of ε_{fw} implies that even the largest deviation of wheat prices above trend in Hoskin's entire 280-year period (or Wrigley and Schofield's 331-year period) involved a manageable short-fall in the supply of food. Although carry-over stocks were diminished, more than two-thirds of the normal amount—more than a three-month supply—remained over and above all claims for feed, seed, and human consumption.

9.4 FAMINES AMID SURPLUSES: A SUGGESTED MECHANISM

There does not, then, appear to have been a single year after *c.*1500 in which the aggregate supply of food was too low to avoid a subsistence crisis. These crises were man-made rather than natural disasters, and clearly were avoidable within the technology of the age, as Davenant (1699:78–88) and other contemporary men of affairs pointed out. Famines amid surpluses remain a phenomenon even today, as Amartya Sen (1981) recently emphasized, not only because foods on a world-wide scale are ample enough to prevent famines, but because famines have broken out in certain under-developed nations despite good harvests. These famines were caused not by natural disasters but by dramatic redistributions of 'entitlements' to grain. The events that promoted the redistributions of entitlements were sharp rises in the price of grain relative to wages or other types of income received by the lower classes. In the 'great Bengal famine' of 1943, for example, the exchange rate between wages and foodgrains declined by 86 per cent, despite an 'exceptionally high' supply of grain. In this case the rise in grain prices had nothing to do with the bountifulness of the harvest, but was driven by forces outside the agricultural sector. The Bengal famine, Sen points out, was a 'boom famine', caused by 'powerful inflationary pressures' unleashed by a rapid expansion of public expenditures (Sen 1981:66, 75).

The relevance of the entitlement approach to the interpretation of the social and economic history of the early modern era does not depend on the source of the rise in grain prices that triggers the redistribution of entitlements. It is the similarity in the structural characteristics of traditional societies of the past and of low-income countries today that makes the entitlement approach pertinent (L. A. Tilly 1983; Hufton 1983; Appleby 1979a; Post 1976; Flinn 1974). At the root of these structural similarities is the highly unequal distribution of wealth and the overarching importance of land as a source of wealth. These twin characteristics lead directly to two other structural features. First, they cause the price elasticity of the total demand for grains to be quite low. Second, they drive a large wedge between the grain demand elasticities of the upper and the lower classes, with the elasticity of the lowest classes having a value that may be 10 or 20 times as large as the elasticity of the class of great land magnates. It is these large class differences in demand elasticities (caused by social organization), rather than wide year-to-year swings in harvest yields (caused by variations in weather or other natural phenomena), that were the source of the periodic subsistence crises that afflicted late medieval and early modern England and the Continent.

The remainder of this section sets forth a mechanism that may have produced a world with famines amid surpluses that were more than adequate to have prevented the famines. I have endeavoured to make the following model conform as closely as possible to the known facts of English society during the early modern era. The Appendix describes my procedures for estimating the key parameters and the sources for these estimates. It also gives the derivations of equations (7)–(11).

Equation (7) is a convenient starting point for the estimation of the relevant elasticities.

$$\varepsilon_i = [\theta(1 - \varepsilon_t) - \beta_i]\,\psi_i - \bar{\varepsilon}_i \qquad (7)$$

where

$\varepsilon_i =$ price elasticity of the demand for grain

$\psi_i =$ income elasticity of the demand for grain

$\bar{\varepsilon}_i =$ income-adjusted price elasticity of the demand for grain

$\beta_i =$ share of grain in total consumption expenditures

$\theta_i =$ share of income arising from the ownership of grain

$\varepsilon_t =$ price elasticity of the total aggregate demand for grain (see (10))

$i =$ subscript designating the ith class

Equation (7) states that the price elasticity of demand for grains of a given class depends not only on $\bar{\varepsilon}_i$ (the income-adjusted price elasticity, which is often referred to as the 'substitution' elasticity) but also on the relative magnitude of $(1 - \varepsilon_t)\theta$ (which is the elasticity of nominal income with respect to the price of grain) and of β_i. It follows from (7) that wealthy landlords would have a much more inelastic demand for grain [because the share of their income arising from the ownership of grain-producing lands equalled or exceeded the share of their income that was spent on the consumption of grains—i.e. because $(1 - \varepsilon_t)\theta_i \geqslant \beta_i$] than landless labourers (for whom $\theta_i = 0$ and β_i is large).

Table 9.5 divides the English population at the middle of the Wrigley–Schofield period ($c.1700$) into four categories or classes, which correspond roughly to the aristocracy and gentry, the yeomanry, artisans and petty shopkeepers, and common labourers (including the unemployed). Out-servants working in the households of the upper classes are included with these classes, since their masters provided the food they consumed. In other words, the population embraced by the landlords (class 1 in the table) includes not only the landlords and their immediate families, but all of their retainers, high and low. The category titled 'farmers and lesser landlords' includes such other owners of food inventories as bakers, brewers, innkeepers, and grain merchants. The categories are thus defined so that virtually all inventories are owned by the two top classes and virtually none by the two bottom ones.

Table 9.5 also presents my estimates of the share of the English population represented by each of the classes, the normal share of each class in the annual consumption of grain (φ_i) and of $\theta_i(1 - \varepsilon_t)$, β_i, ψ_i and ε_i (see the Appendix for sources and procedures). The values of φ_i shown in column (2) imply that landlords consumed nearly two-thirds more, and yeomen about a sixth more, grain per capita than the national average (much of it as ale and spirits); that shopkeepers and craftsmen consumed the national average; and that common labourers and paupers consumed about three-quarters of the national average. These values of φ_i imply that the average caloric intake of the poor was at about the mean level of Ghana or Chad today (World Bank 1984), while that of the landlords was at about the level of US farmers $c.1850$ (Fogel and Engerman 1974).

One important implication of Table 9.5 is that, although labourers comprised about 44 per cent of the population, they accounted for only 33 per cent of the normal consumption of foodgrains. Another implication of the table is that the effect of a rise in grain prices on elasticities was quite different for different classes (see columns (6) and (7)). In the case of landlords and farmers (classes 1 and 2), the rise in prices had two effects: as owners of surpluses, the rise in prices increased their income, while as consumers, it reduced their income. Since the pro-

Table 9.5. Estimates of the 'normal' shares in foodgrain consumption and of the 'normal' price elasticities of the demand for foodgrains, by socioeconomic class in England *c*.1700

Class of household head	(1) Share in population	(2) Normal share in consumption of the foodgrains φ_i	(3) Share of grain in total expenditure of a class β_i	(4) Elasticity of nominal income with respect to the price of grain $\theta_i(1 - \varepsilon_t)$	(5) Income elasticity ψ_i	(6) Income-adjusted price elasticity $\bar{\varepsilon}_i$	(7) Price elasticity ε_i
(1) Landlords (incl. servants and retainers)	0.11	0.18	0.15	0.23	0.10	0.02	0.01
(2) Farmers and lesser landlords (incl. servants)	0.34	0.39	0.15	0.35	0.19	0.05	0.01
(3) Shopkeepers, minor professionals, and craftsmen (incl. servants)	0.11	0.11	0.35	0.00	0.36	0.19	0.32
(4) Labourers and the unemployed (not incl. servants covered in lines (1), (2), and (3))	0.44	0.33	0.70	0.00	0.92	0.41	1.05

Source: see Appendix

ducer's effect is stronger than the consumer's effect, the income component of the price elasticity (i.e. $[(1 - \varepsilon_t)\theta - \beta]\psi$) is negative and so offsets the income-adjusted elasticity ($\bar{\varepsilon}$), making the price elasticities of these two classes quite close to zero. In the case of labourers, however, only the consumption effect operated. In this case the income component of the price elasticity augments $\bar{\varepsilon}$. Although $\bar{\varepsilon}$ is already relatively high, the total price elasticity (ε) is more than twice as high.

The values set forth in Table 9.5 make it possible to estimate the aggregate elasticity of the foodgrain demand for grains (ε_c) by making use of the following relationship:

$$\varepsilon_c = \varphi_1\varepsilon_1 + \varphi_2\varepsilon_2 + \varphi_3\varepsilon_3 + \varphi_4\varepsilon_4. \tag{8}$$

Substituting the appropriate values of φ_i and ε_i into (8) yields

$$\varepsilon_c = (0.18)\,(0.01) + (0.39)\,(0.01) + (0.11)\,(0.32)$$
$$+ (0.33)\,(1.05) \tag{9}$$
$$= 0.387.$$

Thus, the estimates of class elasticities in Table 9.5 imply that the elasticity of the aggregate foodgrain demand was below 0.5, even though common labourers and paupers, who accounted for nearly half the population, had an elasticity in excess of 1. However, as (8) indicates, it is shares in consumption rather than in population that determine the value of ε_c: if it were the population shares that mattered, ε_c would be nearly 30 per cent larger than the indicated size.

Although ε_c is the price elasticity of the aggregate foodgrain demand, it is not the price elasticity of aggregate demand for all grain, which is given by

$$\varepsilon_t = \delta\varepsilon_s + (1 - \delta)\varepsilon_c, \tag{10}$$

where

   $\varepsilon_s =$ the price elasticity of demand for grains used as seed, feed, and carry-over inventories

   $\delta =$ the share of the total supply used as seed, feed, and carry-over inventories.

Since about 55 per cent of the supply of grains was reserved for carry-over, seed, and feed, the estimation of ε_s is critical. If ε_s were 0, ε_t would be only 0.174. There is much commentary in the literature which suggests that that was the case.[10] There was, for example, virtually no long-term variation in the amount of wheat seed planted per acre, which

---

[10] The suggestion that ε_s is close to 0 may appear to conflict with the discussion on pp. 252–4 above, which indicated that carry-over inventories were more than adequate to feed the destitute without impinging on seed reserves. However, the fact that carry-over inventories were adequate to feed the destitute does not mean that the owners of the inventories were willing to release them at prevailing prices, let alone at normal prices.

appears to have stood at about 2.5 bushels from the fourteenth century
to the nineteenth (Wrigley 1987:85; Hoskins 1968:27–8). During the
Irish famine it was noted that many farmers starved to death while
holding on to the stocks of potatoes and grains they had set aside to pay
their rents (Flinn 1981:50). Farmers also were apparently loath to dip
into grain set aside for animal feed.[11] It is not possible with the data
currently at hand to estimate ε_s directly, but it is possible to estimate ε_t,
and then to solve for (10) for ε_s. Using the estimate of σ_{gp} (the s.d. of
deviations in grain prices around trend) for the period 1540–1738, and
of σ_{gq} for 1884–1913, ε_t can be estimated from

$$\varepsilon_t = \frac{\sigma_{gq}}{\sigma_{gp}} r_{gq,\,gp} , \qquad\qquad (11)$$

again assuming $r_{gq,\,gp} = 1$. The resulting value of ε_t is 0.178, which tends
to confirm the belief that during the early modern era the elasticity of
the demand for stocks held in reserve to ensure feed, seed, rental payments, and other contingencies was close to 0.[12]

An important implication of the model set forth in this section is that
a relatively small decline in the supply of grain could have produced a
sharp rise in prices. Because of the highly inelastic demand for inventories, virtually all of the adjustment in entitlements would have taken
place among consumers. As Table 9.6 shows, even a shortfall of supply
as small as 5 per cent triggers significant shifts in the shares of grain
consumed by different classes. In the case of landlords, the rise in their
share largely offsets the decline in output so that their per capita consumption is virtually unchanged. In the case of labourers, however, the
decline in their share reinforces the decline in output so that their per
capita consumption is down by 32 per cent. It is worth noting that,
although output declines by 5 per cent, aggregate foodgrain consumption declines by 11 per cent. Because the demand for grain reserves for
feed, seed, and rentals is so inelastic, virtually the entire shortfall is borne
by foodgrain consumption.

---

[11] We do not yet know what made the feed demand for grain so inelastic. However, it
may be that feedgrains were used primarily for work animals and that farmers believed that
skimping on feedgrains would weaken the horses and oxen on whose well-being the
following year's crop would depend.

[12] See the Appendix for the sources and procedures in estimating σ_{gq} and σ_{gp}. In Fogel
(1986a: 489), I argued that ε_s was only moderately inelastic, despite the fact that English
agricultural historians have implicitly or explicitly maintained that the seed and feed
elasticities of demand were quite low (Hoskins 1964, 1968; Everitt 1967). The same point
was vigorously argued by E. A. Wrigley in an exchange of letters that we had in 1985.
However, it was only after I estimated ε_t from data on yields for the period 1884–1913 that
I reconsidered my earlier judgement and more closely examined the evidence that Wrigley
called to my attention. The weight of that evidence supports Wrigley's position.

Table 9.6. The consequence of shifting 'entitlement' exchange ratios on the share of each class in the reduced crop and on the per capita consumption of each class

		Case where $Q_s = 0.95$		
		Normal share (%) of each class in foodgrain crop $Q_d = Q_s = 1$ $P = 1$ $\varepsilon_t = 0.178$	Share of each class in reduced output of foodgrain at market-clearing price (%)	% decline of each class from normal per capita consumption of foodgrains
		(1)	(2)	(3)
(1)	Landlords (incl. servants and retainers)	0.18	0.201	0.2
(2)	Farmers and lesser landlords (incl. servants)	0.39	0.436	0.2
(3)	Shopkeepers, minor professionals, and craftsmen (incl. servants)	0.11	0.110	10.9
(4)	Labourers and the unemployed (not incl. servants listed under (1), (2), and (3))	0.33	0.252	31.9

Source: see Appendix.

The sharp decline in consumption of the labouring class (when $Q_s = 0.95$) is due to the combination of its high elasticity of demand ($\varepsilon_4 = 1.05$) and the sharp rise in price (P goes to 1.44). It should be noted that about a quarter of the indicated price rise is due not directly to a decline in Q_s from 1 to 0.95, but to the decline in the value of ε_t as the price increases. If ε_t had remained constant, the decline in Q_s would have led to a 33 per cent increase in prices instead of a 44 per cent increase. In other words, one of the effects of the shifting distribution of entitlements is to reduce ε_t, both because ε_c declines and because δ increases. It follows that an initial rise in prices tends to feed on itself, even in the absence of speculative hoarding, by increasing the share of grain entitlements held by classes with a highly inelastic demand.

9.5 THE LONG STRUGGLE TO REPAIR THE SYSTEM OF FOOD DISTRIBUTION

Reductions in the national supply of grain by as much as 5 per cent were rare events during the early modern era, occurring about once a century. However, deficits of 4 per cent in the grain supply were more frequent, occurring about once a generation. When such events occurred, their impact was devastating on labourers and the unemployed, among whom the subsistence crisis was largely confined. Such great events, which reduced a normally poor diet to starvation levels, were social disasters. Whatever their impact on mortality, they could not be ignored by either local or national authorities.

Nor were they. In England during the Tudor and Stuart eras, containing the damage caused by grain shortages was a primary objective of the state. Famines were viewed not only as natural and economic disasters, but also as political ones (Everitt 1967:575). The basic strategy of the Crown was to leave the grain market to its own devices during times of plenty, except to guard against abuses of weights and measures and to foil plots to corner markets. (Even these measures provoked hostility from provincial justices and traders, who resented the attempts of the central government to usurp local rights; as a result of their pressure, the Long Parliament passed legislation which made it impossible for a uniform system of weights and measures to be established up until the nineteenth century: see Everitt (1967:578–9).

In years of grain shortage, however, the state overrode the complaints of traders, merchants, brewers, bakers, and other processors. In 1587 and in subsequent years of dearth, the Privy Council issued a 'Book of Orders' which instructed local magistrates to determine the grain inventories of all farmers, factors, maltsters, and bakers; to force holders of inventories to supply their grain to artificers and labourers at relatively low prices; to suppress unnecessary taverns and unnecessary expenditures of corn in manufacturing; and to prevent all export abroad and limit transportation at home (Everitt 1967:581).

It was, of course, easier to issue such orders than to enforce them. Despite the spectre of popular upheaval that spurred the authorities, they found it difficult to gain control of inventories or to curb the rise of prices. Despite the attempts of magistrates, corn continued to be exported abroad and sold to brewers. Innkeepers who had contracted for their supplies before the harvest insisted on the enforcement of their contracts. When maltsters complied with suppression orders they often found themselves prosecuted by customers who had sent barley to them to be malted. Caught in the middle, many tradesmen and processors were driven to poverty by regulations intended to prevent just that. The procedure enraged farmers and tradesmen who were subject to the inquisitional searches of bailiffs and constables, often for no better reason than the testimony of a common informer (Everitt 1967:583–5).

Because of the resistance of landlords, farmers, merchants, maltsters, and other owners of stock, it has been argued that government efforts to gain control of grain surpluses and to reduce the volatility of prices were a failure. Some hold that the paternalistic restrictions of the government were actually counter-productive, since the effort to uncover hidden stocks of grain served to foster alarm and push prices up. Instead of promoting greater efficiency in the market, these restrictions thwarted the activities of middlemen, whose function was to balance demand and supply by moving grain from places in which it was abundant to those in which it was scarce (Gras 1915:236–6; Everitt 1967:581–5). Others believe that Tudor–Stuart paternalism actually worked. Although it might have taken a while for the scheme to ration grain on behalf of the poor to become effective, numerous instances can be cited during the reigns of James I and Charles I in which concealed grain was brought to market and sold to the poor at reduced prices (Everitt 1967:585–6; Lipson 1971:iii. 444–53; Supple 1964:244–5).

Evidence bearing on this debate can be obtained by relating the variance in deviations of wheat prices from trend to the dominant policies of government in particular periods of time. For this purpose I have defined four periods. The first is 1541–99, which represents the years before the paternalistic apparatus for controlling grain supplies during dearth was in place or became effective. Although precedents for the intervention of the Privy Council during a subsistence crisis may be found during the reign of Henry VIII, it was not until the end of the third decade of Elizabeth's reign that a potentially effective system was spelled out. The *Book of Orders*, published in 1587, listed 33 measures aimed at giving the authorities enough control over the supply to permit the sale of grain for consumption directly to labourers at moderate prices. It set forth a mechanism at the local level for enforcing the regulations, assigned specific roles to sheriffs, justices of the peace, and mayors, and called for special juries of the leaders in each community to oversee the search for surplus stocks (Gras 1915: 236–40; Lipson 1971: iii. 442–5).

Devising a minute system of regulations and making it work are two separate matters, especially since the local justices, who were the lynchpin of the system, were lukewarm to the policy. The system did not become effective until the Privy Council provided the zeal and the administrative pressure required to mobilize local authorities. The turning point came in 1597, with the passage of a series of new laws aimed at alleviating poverty, laws framed in response to three years of turbulence set off by a combination of a depression and severe dearth. Fearing spontaneous insurrections, the Privy Council not only promoted the new legislation but sought to enforce vigorously its 'Book of Orders'.

Beginning about 1600, the Council brought increasingly heavy pressure to bear on the local authorities. Proclamations were much the same as they had been, but the orders were more detailed and the follow-up more systematic. Local authorities responded. In some cities and towns public granaries were established so that stores would be available to sell grain to the poor below market price; the making of malt was regulated by quotas; and searches for surpluses were more thorough. By 1631 the sale of grain to the poor below market prices had become widespread (Leonard 1965:184–99; Jordan 1959:83–108, 126–33; Lipson 1971:iii. 444–53; Supple 1964:244–6, 251–3).

This paternalistic system began to unravel with the Civil War. Indeed, the heavy-handed intervention of the Privy Council with local authorities in order to relieve poverty was one of the grievances of the opposition to Charles I. However, although the victory of Parliament over the King enabled those who sought free markets and the protection of property to have their way, the paternalistic system did not collapse at once. The same inertia at the local level that made it so difficult for Elizabeth and the early Stuarts to effect their reforms now operated in the opposite direction. Although the landholders and merchants who dominated Parliament developed a legislative programme aimed at unshackling farmers, producers, and merchants from the restraints that had been imposed on them, local authorities continued to prosecute those who sought to profit from dearth at the expense of the poor. However, as Parliament implemented its new programme, local authorities veered in the new direction and the paternalistic apparatus atrophied (Chartres 1985).

The motivation for the switch in government policy has been debated by historians but not resolved. Some investigators believe that after the Civil War landowning classes, unrestrained by the bureaucratic paternalism of the Tudors and the early Stuarts, lifted restrictions on producers and merchants and placed a tariff on imports as acts of self-aggrandizement. That process was, in this view, abetted by a grateful William III, who supported export bounties on grain as one of his favours to the class that put him in power (Barnes 1930; R. B. Rose 1961; Lipson 1971, ii). Others, noting that the principal economic problem after the Restoration was economic stagnation and unemployment, believe that new measures were aimed at stimulating a depressed agriculture, promoting the reclamation of the fens and other waste lands, improving the system of marketing and transportation, and promoting industry. According to this view, it was not so much the landlords but the ordinary tenant farmers who would have been impoverished by outworn policies that continued to drive prices down. In the face of an agricultural depression that gripped not only England, but the Continent as well, the key issue was the encouragement of agricultural diversification and the industrial production of agricultural products, including beer and spirits (Everitt 1967; Lipson 1971, ii; Abel 1980; Thirsk 1985; Chartres 1985).

Table 9.7. Analysis of the variance in the deviations of wheat prices from trend during four periods between 1541 and 1745, England

Period		Dates	S^2 (measured as % deviations from trend)
(1)	The years preceding paternalist regulation or during which the machinery for regulation was being put in place	1541–99	935
(2)	The apogee of regulation	1600–40	270
(3)	The dismantling of the regulatory machinery	1641–99	625
(4)	The dominance of government policies aimed at promoting agricultural growth and diversification by raising prices and developing markets	1700–45	633

Source: wheat prices are from Hoskins (1964, 1968).

Whatever the motivation for the switch in policy, it was the abandonment of the Tudor–Stuart programme of food relief, and not natural disasters or the technological backwardness of agriculture, that subjected England to periodic famines for two centuries further. That conclusion is implied by Table 9.7, which shows that during the period 1600–40, when government relief efforts were at their apogee, the variance of wheat prices around trend declined to less than a third of the level of the proceding era. That large a drop cannot be explained plausibly by chance variations in weather, since the *F*-value is statistically significant at the 0.0001 level.[13] Nor is it likely that the sharp rise in the variance of wheat prices during the last six decades of the seventeenth century was the result of chance variations in weather.[14]

In the absence of government action to reduce prices during grain shortages, workers took to the streets and price-fixing riots became a standard feature of the eighteenth century. During the early decade of the eighteenth century the government sought to cope with such out-

[13] The result of the *F*-test would not have changed if equation (11) had been used to obtain the implied values of σ_{gq} (assuming $\varepsilon_t = 0.178$), since $(0.178)^2$ would appear in both the numerator and the denominator of the *F*-statistic and hence would cancel out.

[14] The relevant *F*-values are significant at the 0.004 level.

breaks by enforcing vagrancy and settlement laws and by force (Lipson 1971, iii; Rose 1961). During the late 1750s, however, after food riots of unprecedented scope and intensity, proposals for the government to intervene vigorously in the grain market (to return to the Tudor–Stuart policies), including proposals to re-establish public granaries, re-emerged. As the battle over these questions ebbed and flowed during the next half-century, the government, at both local and national levels, gradually shifted towards more vigorous intervention in the grain market. However, it was not until the nineteenth century that government control over stocks became adequate to reduce the variance in wheat prices to the level that prevailed at the apogee of Tudor–Stuart paternalism. By the middle of the nineteenth century famines had been conquered, not because the weather had shifted, or because of improvements in technology, but because government policy (at least with respect to its own people[15]) had unalterably shifted back to the ideas and practices of commonweal that had prevailed during 1600–40 (Barnes 1930; Post 1977).[16]

9.6 CHRONIC MALNUTRITION AND THE SECULAR DECLINE IN MORTALITY

Had the political will been present, a system of public relief adequate to deal with grain crises could have been in place long before the nineteenth century. So much of the famine-related mortality, and much related suffering short of death between 1640 and 1815, could have been avoided. However, as Table 9.1 shows, even complete success in the struggle to eliminate famines would have left the level of mortality in 'normal' times shockingly high. Indeed, that table undoubtedly exaggerates the extent of famine mortality, since the available evidence suggests that in the English case less than 10 per cent of all crisis mortality between 1541 and 1871 was due to famines (Fogel 1986a:494–5).

Although the possibility that famines might have had only a small impact on aggregate mortality had been anticipated (Le Brun 1971; Flinn 1974, 1981), Wrigley and Schofield provided the data needed to measure the national impact. By demonstrating that famines and famine

[15] The Irish famine makes this qualification necessary. As Mokyr (1985:292) has emphasized, if Ireland had been considered an integral part of the British community, the British government might have felt compelled to intervene much more vigorously than it actually did.

[16] In this connection it is worth noting that famines came to an end early in the 19th c. not only in England, where per capita consumption of calories appears to have reached levels by 18-IV that are comparable to modern-day India, but also in countries such as France, where average caloric consumption was 15–20% lower. This issue is discussed more fully in the next section of the paper.

mortality are a secondary issue in the escape from the high-aggregate mortality of the early modern era, they have indirectly pushed to the top of research agendas the issue of chronic malnutrition and its relationship to the secular decline in mortality. It is clear that the new questions cannot be addressed by relating annual deviations of mortality (around trend) to annual deviations of supplies of food (from their trend). What is now at issue is how the trend in malnutrition might be related to the trend in mortality, and how to identify the factors that determined each of these secular trends.

The new problems require new data and new analytical procedures. In this connection one must come to grips with the thorny issue of the distinction between diet (which represents gross nutrition) and malnutrition (which represents net nutrition: the nutrients available to sustain physical development). I will not dwell on this distinction here (which is set forth in Floud's paper—Chapter 8 above), but will only emphasize that when I mean gross nutrition I will use the term 'diet', and that such other terms as 'malnutrition', 'undernutrition', 'net nutrition', and 'nutritional status' are meant to designate the balance between the nutrient intake (diet) and the claims on that intake.

Malnutrition can be caused either by an inadequate diet or by claims on that diet (including work and disease) so great as to produce widespread malnutrition despite a nutrient intake that in other circumstances might be deemed adequate. There can be little doubt that the high disease rates prevalent during the early modern era would have caused malnutrition even with extraordinary diets, that is diets high in calories, proteins, and most other critical nutrients. I believe that the USA during 1820–80 is a case in point (see Fogel 1986a, 1991b). However, recent research indicates that, for many European nations before the middle of the nineteenth century, the national production of food was at such low levels that the lower classes were bound to have been malnourished under any conceivable circumstance, and that the high disease rates of the period were not merely a cause of malnutrition but undoubtedly, to a considerable degree, a consequence of exceedingly poor diets.

Recently developed biomedical techniques, when integrated with several standard economic techniques, make it possible to probe deeply into the extent and the demographic consequences of chronic malnutrition during the eighteenth and nineteenth centuries. The biomedical techniques include improved approaches to the estimation of survival levels of caloric consumption and of the caloric requirements of various types of labour; epidemiological studies of the connection between stature and the risk of both mortality and chronic diseases; and epidemiological studies of the connection between body mass indexes (BMIs) and the risk of mortality. The economic techniques include various methods of characterizing size distributions of income and of calories, as well as methods of relating measures of nutrition to measures of income and productivity.

9.6.1 Energy Cost Accounting: the case of Britain and France during the Last Quarter of the Eighteenth Century

Historical estimates of mean caloric consumption per capita have been derived from several sources, including national food balance sheets and household consumption surveys. The various problems attendant upon using these sources have been described elsewhere (see Fogel 1987). Despite their limitations, Toutain's (1971) time series of food consumption in France and the household surveys of English food consumption towards the end of the eighteenth century (Shammas 1984) indicate that in each of these countries a majority of the population was malnourished (Fogel 1987).

Toutain (1971), on the basis of a national food balance sheet, has estimated that the per capita consumption of calories in France was 1753 during 1781–90 and 1846 during 1803–12. Converted into calories per consuming unit (equivalent adult male), the figures become about 2290 and 2410 calories. Data in the household budget studies recently re-examined by economic historians indicate that English daily consumption during 1785–95 averaged about 2700 calories per consuming unit (Fogel 1987; Shammas 1984).

One way of assessing these two estimates is by considering their distributional implications. As noted elsewhere, all of the known distributions of the average daily consumption of calories for populations are not only reasonably well described by the lognormal distribution, but also have coefficients of variation that lie between 0.2 and 0.4—a narrow range, which is determined at the top end by the human capacity to use energy and the distribution of body builds, and at the bottom end by the requirement for basal metabolism and the prevailing death rate (Fogel 1987). Consideration of available evidence on mortality rates (Bourgeois-Pichat 1965; Weir 1984), and the findings of Goubert (1960, 1973), Bernard (1975), Hufton (1974), Kaplan (1976), and others on the condition of the lower classes in France during the late *ancien régime*, rule out either 0.2 or 0.4 as plausible estimates of the coefficient of variation and suggest that 0.3 is the best approximation in the light of current knowledge.[17]

---

[17] The main conclusions summarized in this section are robust to any value of the coefficient of variation in the range 0.3 ± 0.1.

Table 9.8. A comparison of the probable French and English distributions of the daily consumption of kcal per consuming unit towards the end of the eighteenth century

Decile	(A) France $c.1785$ $\bar{X} = 2290$ $(s/X) = 0.3$		(B) England $c.1790$ $\bar{X} = 2700$ $(s/X) = 0.3$	
	Daily kcal consumption	Cumulative %	Daily kcal consumption	Cumulative %
(1)	(2)	(3)	(4)	(5)
1 Highest	3672	100	4329	100
2 Ninth	2981	84	3514	84
3 Eighth	2676	71	3155	71
4 Seventh	2457	59	2897	59
5 Sixth	2276	48	2684	48
6 Fifth	2114	38	2492	38
7 Fourth	1958	29	2309	29
8 Third	1798	21	2120	21
9 Second	1614	12	1903	13
10 First	1310	6	1545	6

Source and procedures: see Fogel (1987), esp. Tables 4 and 5 and n.6.

Table 9.8 displays the caloric distribution for England and France implied by the available evidence. Several points about these distributions, which lend support to Toutain's estimate for the French and the estimates derived for the English from the budget studies, are worth noting. First, the average levels are not out of keeping with recent experiences in the less developed nations. Low as it is, Toutain's estimate of the French supply of calories is above the average supply of calories in 1965 estimated for such nations as Pakistan, Rwanda, and Algeria, and only slightly less (by 39 calories) than that of Indonesia. The English estimate is above that for 30 less developed nations in 1965, including China, Bolivia, the Philippines, and Honduras, and only slightly (by 37 calories) below India (World Bank 1987).

Second, the distributional implications of the two estimates are consistent with both qualitative and quantitative descriptions of the diets of various social classes (Hufton 1974, 1983; Goubert 1973; L. A. Tilly 1971; C. Tilly 1975; Frijhoff and Julia 1979; Blum 1978; Cole and Postgate 1938; M. E. Rose 1971; Drummond and Wilbraham 1958; Pullar 1970; Wilson 1973; Burnett 1979). For example, Bernard's study (1975) of marriage contracts made in the Gévaudan during the third quarter of the eighteenth century revealed that the average ration provided for parents in complete pensions contained about 1674 calories. Since the average age of a male parent at the marriage of his first surviving child was about 59, the preceding figure implies a diet of about 2146 calories per consuming unit (Fogel 1987). That figure falls at the 47th centile of the estimated French distribution (Table 9.8, distribution A), which is quite consistent with the class of peasants described by Bernard.

The two estimates are also consistent with the death rates of each nation. The crude death rate in France c.1790 was about 36.1 per 1000, while the figure for England c.1790 was about 26.7 (Weir 1984; Wrigley and Schofield 1981). It is plausible that much of the difference was due to the larger proportion of French than English who were literally starving (Scrimshaw 1987). The French distribution of calories implies that 2.48 per cent of the population had caloric consumption below basal metabolism (the minimum energy required for the functioning of the body);[18] Table 9.8 implies that the proportion of the English below basal metabolism was 0.66 per cent. If a quarter of these starving individuals died each year (see Fogel 1987), they would account for about a fifth (6.6 per 1000) of the French crude death rate, but only about a sixteenth of the English rate (1.7 per 1000) and for about half of the gap between the crude death rates of the two nations.[19]

What, then, are the principal provisional findings about caloric consumption at the end of the eighteenth century in France and England? One is the exceedingly low level of food production, especially in France, at the start of the Industrial Revolution. Another is the exceedingly low level of work capacity permitted by the food supply, even after allowing for the reduced requirements for maintenance because of small stature and reduced body mass (cf. Freudenberger and Cummins 1976). In France the bottom 10 per cent of the labour force lacked the energy for regular work and the next 10 per cent had enough energy for less than 3 hours of light work daily (0.52 hours of heavy work). Although the English situation was somewhat better, the bottom 3 per cent of its labour force lacked the energy for any work, but the balance of the bottom 20 per cent had enough energy for about 6 hours of light work (1.09 hours of heavy work) each day.[20]

---

[18] For a discussion of the concept of basal metabolism and other components of energy requirement, see FAO/WHO/UNU (1985), and the papers by Payne, Srinivasan and Osmani in this volume (Chs. 3, 4, and 5).

[19] This discussion takes account of the incidence of mortality only among those in each country whose consumption of calories was below basal metabolism. However, there were many other individuals who were at increased risk of death because they were malnourished, even though the degree of malnourishment was less extreme: cf. the discussion of Fig. 9.3 below.

[20] Even small amounts of common agricultural or urban manual labour would have put such malnourished individuals on a path towards consuming their own tissue, and if continued long enough would have, sooner or later, resulted in death. These are the people who constitute Marx's 'lumpenproletariat', Mayhew's 'street folk', Huxley's 'substrata', King's

That the English ultra-poor were better off than the French ultra-poor was due partly to the greater productivity of English agriculture (as measured by the per capita production of calories). However, the distribution of income was so unequal in England that, had it not been for the English system of poor relief, the proportion of the English that starved would have been nearly as great as that of the French. In response to the bread riots of the eighteenth century, English authorities substantially expanded the system of poor relief. Between 1750 and 1801 poor relief increased at a real rate of 2.3 per cent per annum, which was nearly three times as fast as the growth of either GNP or the pauper class (Crafts 1985: 45; M. E. Rose 1971: 40–1; Marshall 1968: 26; Mitchell and Deane 1962: 469) Consequently, by c.1790 relief payments to the ultra-poor had become substantial, more than doubling the income of households in the lowest decile of the English income distribution. In pre-revolutionary France, on the other hand, the average annual relief provided to the ultra-poor could purchase daily only about one ounce of bread per person (Fogel 1987, nn. 17 and 18). The responsiveness of the British government to the bread riots of the poor (Barnes, 1930; R. B. Rose, 1961; Marshall 1968), not only kept the English death rate from soaring, but may have spared Britain from a revolution of the French type.

9.6.2 The Implications of Stature and Body Mass Indexes for the Explanation of Secular Trends in Morbidity and Mortality

The available anthropometric data tend to confirm the basic results of the analysis based on energy cost accounting: chronic malnutrition was widespread in Europe during the eighteenth and nineteenth centuries. Furthermore, such malnutrition seems to have been responsible for much of the very high mortality rates during this period. Moreover, nearly all of the decline in mortality rates between 1750 and 1875 appears to be explained by the marked improvement in anthropometric measures of malnutrition. This section summarizes evidence bearing on the relationship between mortality and two anthropometric measures— height at maturity and the body mass index (BMI)—that is discussed in more detail elsewhere (Fogel 1986b, 1987, 1991a, 1991b; Fogel et al. 1992, ch.47; Fogel and Floud 1991).

Height and body mass indexes measure different aspects of malnutrition and health. Height is a net rather than a gross measure of nutrition. Moreover, although changes in height during the growing years are sensitive to current levels of nutrition, mean final height reflects the

'unproductive classes' consuming more than they produced, and the French gens de néant (Himmelfarb 1983; Laslett 1984).

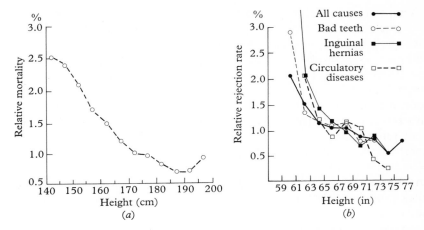

Fig. 9.1. A comparison of the relationship between body height and relative risk in two populations
(a) Relative mortality rates among Norwegian men aged 40–59, 1963–1979
    Source: Waaler (1984)
(b) Relative rejection rates for chronic conditions in a sample of 4245 men aged
    23–49 examined for the US Union army
    Source: Fogel *et al.* (1986)

accumulated past nutritional experience of individuals over all of their growing years including the foetal period. Thus, it follows that, when final heights are used to explain differences in adult mortality rates, they reveal the effect not of adult levels of nutrition on adult mortality rates, but of nutritional levels during infancy, childhood, and adolescence on adult mortality rates. A weight-for-height index on the other hand, reflects primarily the current nutritional status.

A number of recent studies have established the predictive power of height and BMI with respect to morbidity and mortality.[21] The results of two of these studies are summarized in Figs. 9.1 and 9.2. Part (*a*) of figure 9.1 reproduces a diagram by Waaler (1984). It shows that short Norwegian men aged 40–59 at risk between 1963 and 1979 were much more likely to die than tall men. Indeed, the risk of mortality for men with heights of 165 cm (65.0 inches) was on average 71 per cent greater than that of men who measured 182.5 cm (71.9 inches). Part (*b*) of the figure

[21] Many of the issues and some of the evidence regarding the relationship between anthropometric measures, nutritional status, and risk of death are discussed in this volume by Gopalan, Payne, Srinivasan, and Osmani (Chs. 2, 3, 4, and 5). Most of the literature linking anthoropometric measures to morbidity and mortality rates focuses on children aged 5 or less. The literature relating stature and weight to mortality rates at adult ages is more limited. The best study to date is for Norway, reported in Waaler (1984). See Fogel (1986*a*, 1987), Fogel *et al.* (1986), and Fogel (1987) and Fogel and Floud (1991) for a discussion of these matters for the US and several European countries between 1750 and 1975; see Floud *et al.* (1990) on Britain, and Komlos (1990) on Austria and Hungary.

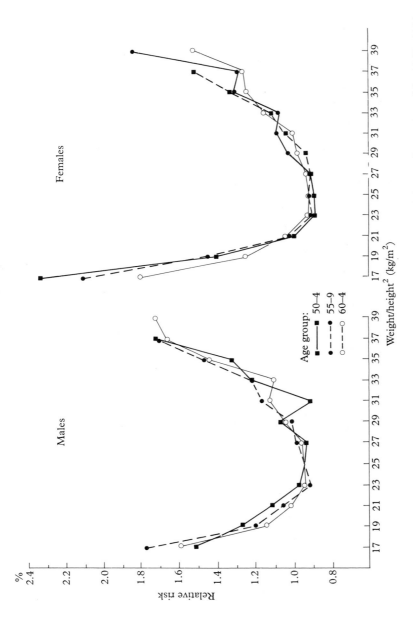

Fig. 9.2. The relationship between BMI and prospective risk among Norwegian adults aged 50–64 at risk, 1963–1979
Source: Waaler (1984)

shows that height was also an important predictor of the relative likeli-hood that men aged 23–49 would be rejected from the US Union Army during 1861–5 because of chronic diseases. Despite significant differen-ces in mean heights, ethnicities, environmental circumstances, the array and severity of diseases, and time, the functional relationship between height and relative risk are strikingly similar. Both the Norwegian curve and the US all-causes curve have relative risks that reach a minimum of between 0.6 and 0.7 at a height of about 187.5 cm. Both reach a relative risk of about 2 at about 152.5 cm. The similarity of the two risk curves in Figure 9.1, despite the differences in conditions and attendant circumstances, suggests that the relative risk of morbidity and mortality depends on the deviation of height not from the *current* mean, but from an *ideal* mean: the mean associated with full genetic potential.[22]

Waaler (1984) has also studied the relationship in Norway between BMIs and the risk of death in a sample of 1.7 million individuals. Curves summarizing his findings are shown in Figure 9.2 for both men and women. Although the observed values of the BMI (kg/m^2) ranged be-tween 17 and 39, over 80 per cent of the males over age 40 had BMIs within the range 21–9. Within the range 22–8 the curve is relatively flat, with the relative risk of mortality hovering close to 1.0. However, at BMIs of less than 22 and over 28, the risk of death rises quite sharply as the BMI moves away from its mean value. It will be noticed that the BMI curves are much more symmetrical than the height curves in Fig. 9.1, which indicates that high BMIs are as risky as low ones.

Although Fig. 9.1 and 9.2 are revealing, neither one singly nor both together are sufficient to shed light on the debate over whether moderate stunting impairs health when weight-for-height is adequate, since Fig. 9.1 is not controlled for weight and Fig. 9.2 is only partially controlled for height (Fogel 1987; Fogel and Floud 1991). To get at the 'small-but-healthy' issue, one needs an iso-mortality surface that relates the risk of death to both height and weight simultaneously.[23] Such a surface, presented in Fig. 9.3, was fitted to Waaler's data by a procedure de-scribed elsewhere (Fogel 1991b). Transecting the iso-mortality map are lines which give the locus of BMI between 16 and 34, and a curve giving the weights that minimize risk at each height.

Fig. 9.3 shows that, even when body weight is maintained at what Fig. 9.2 indicates is an 'ideal' level (BMI = 21), short men are at substantially

[22] For a further discussion of this possibility see Fogel (1987) and Fogel and Floud (1991). It is important to keep in mind that the denominators of the relative risk curves in both parts of Fig. 9.1 are the average mortality or morbidity rate computed over all heights. Consequently, the curves shown here will not necessarily shift merely because of a change in the overall crude death rate or the corresponding morbidity rate.

[23] See Osmani's paper (Ch. 5 above) for a description of the controversy; also cf. Gopalan and Payne (Chs. 2 and 3 above).

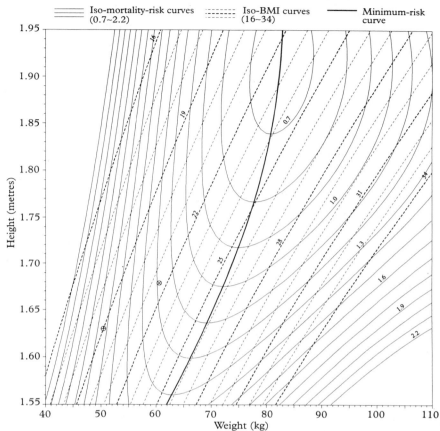

Note:

⊕ = the possible location of adult French males aged 25~34 *c*.1790 on the iso-mortality map. The predicted risk for French males is 1.63.

⊗ = the possible location of comparable English males *c*.1790. The predicted risk for English males is 1.18.

All risks are measured relative to the average risk of mortality (calculated over all heights and weights) among Norwegian males aged 50~64.

Fig. 9.3. Iso-mortality curves of relative risk for height and weight among Norwegian males aged 50–64, 1963–1979

Source: Fogel (1987)

greater risk of death than tall men. Thus, an adult male with a BMI of 25 who is 162 cm tall is at about 55 per cent greater risk of death than a male at 183 cm who also has a BMI of 25. Figure 9.3 also shows that the 'ideal' BMI (the BMI that minimizes the risk of death) varies with height. A BMI of 25 is 'ideal' for men in the neighbourhood of 176 cm, but for tall men (greater than 183 cm) the ideal BMI is between 22 and 24, while for short men (under 164 cm) it is a bit under 26.

Before using Fig. 9.3 to evaluate the relationship between chronic malnutrition and the secular decline in mortality rates after 1750, three issues in the interpretation of that figure need to be addressed. First, since an individual's height cannot be varied by changes in nutrition after maturity, adults can move to a more desirable BMI only by changing weight. I therefore interpret the x-axis as a measure of the effect of the current nutritional status of mature males on adult mortality rates. Moreover, since most stunting takes place below the age of 3 (Tanner 1982; Horton 1985; Martorell 1985; Steckel 1983), I interpret the y-axis as a measure of the effect of nutritional deprivation in *utero* or early in childhood on the risk of mortality at middle and late ages (cf. Tanner 1982; Steckel 1983; Fogel *et al.* 1992, chs. 42 and 47).

Second, in applying Fig. 9.3 to the evaluation of secular trends in nutrition and mortality, I assume that for Europeans environmental factors have been decisive in explaining the secular increase in heights, not only for population means, but also for individuals in particular families. The reasonableness of this assumption becomes evident when one considers the issue of shortness. If shortness is defined as a given number of standard deviations below a changing mean (i.e. if 'short' is 2 standard deviations below the mean, whether the mean is 164 cm or 183 cm), then genetic and environmental factors may be difficult to disentangle. If, however, shortness is defined in absolute terms, say as applying to all males with heights below 168 cm, then it is quite clear that most shortness in Europe and America during the eighteenth and much of the nineteenth centuries was determined by environmental rather than genetic factors.

The point at issue can be clarified by considering the experience of the Netherlands. Shortness has virtually disappeared from that country during the past century and a half. Today, less than 2 per cent of young adult males are below 168 cm, but in *c.*1855 about two-thirds were below that height. Since there has been little change in the gene pool of the Dutch during the period, it must have been changes in environmental circumstances, nutrition, and health that eliminated about 95 per cent of all short males from the Dutch population (van Wieringen 1986; Fogel 1987). Given current growth rates in the mean final height of the Netherlands, the remaining men shorter than 168 cm may yet be virtually eliminated from the Dutch population.

The Dutch case illustrates the general secular pattern of physical growth in the nations of western Europe. The secular increase in mean final heights, which ranged between 10 and 20 centimeters (4 and 8 inches) over the past 200 years, cannot be attributed to natural selection or genetic drift, since these processes require much longer time-spans. Nor can it be attributed to heterosis (hybrid vigour), because the populations in question have remained relatively homogeneous and because the effects of heterosis in human populations have been shown, both empirically and theoretically, to be quite small (Cavalli-Sforza and Bodmer 1971; Damon 1965; van Wieringen 1978; Fogel *et al.* 1983; Martorell 1985; Mueller 1986). Only the top 6 per cent of the Dutch height distribution *c.*1855 overlaps with the bottom 6 per cent of the current distribution of final heights. Since the Dutch mean is still increasing, and we do not yet know the maximum mean genetically obtainable (often referred to as the genetic potential), it may well be that even the 6 per cent overlap between the distribution of final heights in the *c.*1855 generation and that of the latest generation will be cut in the next few decades, perhaps by as much as half.

Third, even if the Norwegian iso-mortality surface is applicable to European populations generally, the surface may not have been stable over time. Since height-specific and weight-specific mortality rates are measured relative to the crude death rate (CDR) for the population as a whole, short-term shifts in the CDR by themselves will not shift the surface. However, fundamental shifts in environment, including changes in medical technology, may shift the risk surface. One way of ascertaining whether there has been a shift in the risk surface is by determining what part of the decline in mortality rates can be explained merely by movements along the surface (i.e. merely by changes in height and weight on the assumption that the surface has been stable since 1750).

The average final heights of men in several European countries over the period from 1750 to modern times are reported in Table 9.9. It will be seen that during the eighteenth century these Europeans were severely stunted by modern standards. The French cohort of 18-IV is the most stunted, measuring only 160.5 cm (63.2 inches). The next two shortest cohorts are those of Norway for 18-III and Hungary for 18-IV, which measured 163.9 cm (64.5 inches). Britain and Sweden were the tallest populations between 1775 and 1875, although by the end of the period Norway nearly matched the leaders.

France was intermediate in its early growth rate, with stature increasing about 0.73 cm per quarter between 18-IV and 19-II. However, the French rate of increase sagged slightly over the next half century and hovered between 165.3 and 166.7 cm until the turn of the twentieth century (Floud 1984). British heights increased more rapidly (1.90 cm per quarter century) and for a longer period than the French. The accumulated increase over the first 75 years (18-III to 19-II) was 5.7 cm, more than three-fifths of the total increase in British heights between 18-III and the current generation of adults. However, British heights declined slightly with the cohort of 19-III and also remained on a plateau for about half a century (Floud et al. 1990). Swedish heights appear to have declined during the last half of the eighteenth century but then to have risen sharply beginning with the second quarter of the nineteenth century, initiating the marked secular increase in Swedish heights that has continued down to the present day.

Table 9.9.   Estimated average final heights of men who reached maturity between 1750 and 1875 in six European populations, by quarter-centuries (cm)

(1) Date of maturity	(2) Britain	(3) Norway	(4) Sweden	(5) France	(6) Denmark	(7) Hungary
(1) 18-III	165.9	163.9	168.1	—	—	168.7
(2) 18–IV	167.9	—	166.7	169.0	165.7	165.8
(3) 19–I	168.0	—	166.7	164.0	165.4	163.9
(4) 19–II	171.6	—	168.0	166.7	166.8	164.2
(5) 19–III	169.3	168.6	169.5	165.2	165.3	—
(6) 20–III	175.0	178.3	177.6	172.0	176.0	170.9

Source: Fogel (1987): Table 7 for all columns except 5. Column 5: rows 3–5 were computed from Meerton (1989) with 0.9 cm added to allow for additional growth between age 20 and maturity (Gould 1869:104–5; cf. Friedman 1982:510 n.14). The entry to row 2 is derived from a linear extrapolation of Meerton's data for 1815–36 back to 1788, with 0.9cm added for additional growth between age 20 and maturity. The entry in row 6 is from Fogel (1987), table 7.

Indeed, over the last century the three Scandinavian countries shown in Table 9.9 and the Netherlands (Chamla 1983) have had the most vigorous and sustained increases in stature in the western world, outpacing Britain and the USA (Fogel 1986a). Hungary's growth pattern differs from that of all the other European nations (Komlos 1990): its cohort of 18-III was taller than that of Sweden, but then Hungarian heights declined sharply for half a century; and, despite a turnabout in the nineteenth century, Hungary remains one of the shortest populations in Europe: its mean height today is below the level achieved by the British cohort of 19-II.

Data on body mass indexes for France and Britain during the late eighteenth and most of the nineteenth centuries are much more patchy than those on stature. Consequently attempts to compare British and French BMIs during this period are necessarily conjectural. It appears that *c*.1790 the average English BMI for males about age 30 was between 21 and 22, which is about 10 per cent below current levels. The corresponding figure for French males *c*.1790 may have been only about 19, which is about 25 per cent below current levels (Fogel and Floud 1991). The conjectural nature of these figures makes the attempt to go from anthropometric data to differential mortality rates more illustrative than substantive. However, Fig. 9.3 indicates the apparent location of French and English males of 18-IV on the iso-mortality map generated from Waaler's data. These points imply that the French mortality rate should have been about 40 per cent higher than that of the English, which is quite close to the estimated ratio of mortality rates for the two countries.[24] In other words, the available data suggest that in 18-IV both France and Britain were characterized by the same mortality risk surface (i.e. the same mortality regimen), and that differences in their average mortality rates are explained largely by differences in their distributions of height and weight-for-height.

This result raises the question as to how much of the decline in European mortality rate since 18-IV can be explained merely by increases in stature and BMIs: that is, merely by movements along an unchanging mortality risk surface. For the three countries for which even patchy data are available—England, France, and Sweden—it appears that nearly all of the decline in mortality between 18-IV and 19-III was due to movements along the Waaler mortality surface, since the estimated changes in height and BMI appear to explain between 80 and 100 per cent of the decline in mortality during this three-quarters of a century. However, movements along the Waaler surface appear to explain only about 50–60 per cent of the decline in mortality rates after 1875. After 1875 increases in longevity involved factors other than those that exercise their influence through stature and body mass (Fogel 1987; Fogel and Floud 1991).

9.7 CONCLUSIONS

Recent findings in economics and demographic history have shed new light on the European escape from hunger and high mortality since 1750. These advances have been stimulated partly by a better integration of biomedical, economic, and demographic analysis and partly by an enormous expansion of the data-base to which these techniques can be applied. Since we are still at an early stage of some of these investiga-

---

[24] The English CDR for 11 years centred on 1790 is 26.7, and 1.40 times that number is 37.3, which is close to the French CDR derived from Weir's data for the 11 years centred on 1790.

tions, current findings must be considered provisional and subject to change.

The seven principal findings of this paper are as follows.

1   Crisis mortality accounted for less than 5 per cent of total mortality in England before 1800, and the elimination of crisis mortality accounted for just 15 per cent of the decline in total mortality between the eighteenth and nineteenth centuries. Consequently, regardless of how large a share of crisis mortality is attributed to famines, famines accounted for only a small share of total mortality before 1800.

2   The use of variations in wheat prices to measure variations in the food supply has led to gross overestimates of the variability of the food supply.

3   The famines that plagued England and France between 1500 and 1800 were man-made—the consequence of failures in the system of food distribution related to an extremely inelastic demand for food inventories, rather than to natural calamities or inadequate technology.

4   Not only was it within the power of government to eliminate famines, but the food distribution policies of James I and Charles I apparently succeeded in reducing the variability of annual wheat prices by over 70 per cent.

5   Although proper governmental policy could have eliminated famines before 1800, it could not have eliminated chronic malnutrition. Elimination of chronic malnutrition required advances in agricultural and related technologies that permitted the per capita consumption of food to increase by about 50 per cent.

6   Improvements in average nutritional status (as indicated by stature and body mass indexes) appear to explain over 80 per cent of the decline in mortality rates in England, France, and Sweden between 18-IV and 19-III but only about half of the mortality decline between 19-III and 20-III.

7   Stunting during developmental ages had a long reach, substantially increasing both morbidity and mortality rates at middle age and later. Small males were at much higher risk of developing chronic diseases during ages 23–40, and were at much higher risk of death above age 49, even if they had optimal BMIs.

These findings indicate that the elimination of chronic malnutrition played a large role in the secular improvement in health and life expectation. They also suggest that the elimination of stunting at early ages is of major importance in the reduction of morbidity and mortality rates in middle age and later. Optimizing the BMI at mature ages may reduce some risks faced by stunted adults, but it does not eliminate the effects of stunting. It also appears that the optimal BMI may be higher for stunted than for tall adults.

APPENDIX

This appendix deals with the assumptions, mathematical derivations, estimation procedures, and sources of data for the analysis and estimates presented in Sections 9.2 and 9.3 above. (For the assumptions, mathematical derivations, and estimation procedures reported in Section 9.6, see Fogel 1987.)

The two principal implicit assumptions that underlie the analysis in Sections 9.2 and 9.3 are traditional in the literature on the pricing of English grain during the early modern era (here taken to be 1500–1750), and are consistent with the available evidence. The first of these assumptions is that the average price each year was established under conditions of a completely inelastic aggregate short-run supply curve. The second is that year-to-year changes in price were due to fluctuations in this short-run supply from one harvest to another around a fixed (or relatively fixed) aggregate demand curve.

The assumption that the demand curve was relatively fixed rests on the flat trend in income and in the relative prices of complements and substitutes for foodgrains (broadly defined), and on the stability of tastes (Mitchell and Deane 1962; Drummond and Wilbraham 1958; Coleman 1977; Grigg 1982; Holderness 1976; Shammas 1983; Wrigley and Schofield 1981).[25] The assumption that the short-run supply curve of grain was completely inelastic rests on (1) the observation that, once the harvest was concluded, the production of grain could not be increased until the next crop was planted and harvested, and (2) the fact that the price wedge between England and the Continent was such that net imports of grain were generally negative even during years of dearth. In the few years when net imports were positive, they were about 1 per cent of annual consumption (Gras 1915; Barnes 1930; Mitchell and Deane 1962).[26]

When the aggregate short-run supply curve is perfectly inelastic, the usual problems of simultaneity disappear, and the estimate of the elasticity of aggregate demand curve can be obtained by regressing price directly on quantity. However, the usual econometric issues of simultaneity remain if one wishes to explain the distribution of the fixed supply between the holders and non-holders

[25] Wrigley and Schofield (1981: 420) present a 25-year moving average of a real-wage index, which they use as a proxy for the trend in real annual per capita income. The average rate of increase in that index between c.1551 and c.1751 is about 0.06 per cent per annum. However, during that period the index trends downward for about 73 years beginning c.1562 and then upward for a longer period beginning c.1635. The average annual rate of decrease in the population index between 1562 and 1635 is about −0.26 per cent, while the average rate of increase between 1635 and 1750 is about 0.25 per cent.

[26] Annual net exports or imports of grain were converted into a percentage of total annual grain consumption on the assumptions that grains provided 80 per cent of caloric intake and that the average daily per capita consumption of all foods yielded about 2100 calories. The total of annual calories obtained from grains in a given year was estimated by multiplying the population of a given year by $1.200 \times 0.8 \times 365$. Net exports of grain were converted into calories on the assumption that 29 per cent of the weight of grain was lost in processing (either milling or using grain to produce beer), so that the flour equivalent of a bushel of wheat was about 44 pounds and each pound of equivalent wheat flour provided 1584 kcal (Mitchell and Deane 1962: 86; McCance and Widdowson 1967). Estimates of the average annual net exports of grain are also provided by Bairoch (1973: 459), Coleman (1977: 121), and Deane and Cole (1969: 65); cf. Chartres (1985: 448–54).

of grain inventories (cf. Fogel and Engerman 1974: ii. 56–8). That task is not undertaken in Section 9.2. When it is undertaken in Section 9.3, the key parameters are not estimated by the econometric procedures since neither the time-series nor cross-sectional data needed for such estimation are available.

A third important implicit assumption for the analysis presented in Section 9.2 is that the distribution of arable land among crops did not vary from year to year but remained fixed by conventions that changed slowly over time. Consequently, all the short-run variation in output from one year to the next in grain crops has traditionally been presumed to have been due to variations in per-acre yields rather than to variations in the number of acres sown (Wrigley 1987; cf. Slicher von Bath 1963; Hoskins 1964, 1968; Abel 1980; Appleby 1978; Grigg 1982).

The derivation of equation (7)

The demand curve for the ith class of consumers for a good (Q), when income is measured in real terms, may be written as

$$Q_i = \left(\frac{Y_i}{P^{\beta_i} P_m^{1-\beta_i}} \right)^{\psi_i} P_m^{\varepsilon_{mi}} P^{-\bar{\varepsilon}_i}, \tag{7a}$$

where

$\quad Q = $ the quantity of grain
$\quad P = $ the price of Q
$\quad P_m = $ the price of all other goods, Q_m
$\quad Y = $ nominal income
$\quad \beta = $ the share of Q in consumption expenditures
$1 - \beta = $ the share of all other goods in consumption expenditures
$\quad \psi = $ the income elasticity of the demand for Q
$\quad \varepsilon_m = $ the cross-elasticity of the demand for Q with respect to P_m
$\quad \bar{\varepsilon} = $ the own-price elasticity of the income-adjusted demand for Q
$\quad i = $ a subscript referring to the ith class of consumers

Differentiating (7a) totally and rearranging terms yields

$$\overset{*}{Q}_i = \psi_i \overset{*}{Y}_i + [\varepsilon_{mi} - \psi_i(1 - \beta_i)] \overset{*}{P}_m - (\psi_i \beta_i + \bar{\varepsilon}_i) \overset{*}{P}. \tag{7b}$$

Since by assumption Q_m is the numeraire, $\overset{*}{P}_m = 0$ and equation (7b) reduces to

$$\overset{*}{Q}_i = \psi_i \overset{*}{Y}_i - (\psi_i \beta_i + \bar{\varepsilon}_i) \overset{*}{P}. \tag{7c}$$

Now, by definition,

$$Y_i = PQ_i + P_m Q_{mi}. \tag{7d}$$

Differentiating (7d) totally yields

$$\overset{*}{Y}_i = \theta_i (\overset{*}{P} + \overset{*}{Q}_i) + (1 - \theta_i)(\overset{*}{P}_m + \overset{*}{Q}_{mi}), \tag{7e}$$

where θ_i is the share of PQ_i in Y_i. Since Q_m is the numeraire and $\overset{*}{Q}_m = 0$ by assumption, (7e) reduces to

$$\overset{*}{Y}_i = \theta_i(\overset{*}{P} + \overset{*}{Q}_i). \qquad (7f)$$

If it is also assumed that all classes that own farm land suffer or benefit from random fluctuations in yields proportionately,

$$\overset{*}{Q}_i = -\varepsilon_t \overset{*}{P}, \qquad (7g)$$

so that (7f) reduces to

$$\overset{*}{Y}_i = (1 - \varepsilon_t)\theta_i\overset{*}{P}, \qquad (7h)$$

where ε_t is the aggregate price elasticity of demand over all classes of consumers of grain (see equation (10)). Substituting (7h) into (7c) and rearranging terms yields

$$\overset{*}{Q}_i = \{ \psi_i[\theta_i(1 - \varepsilon_t) - \beta_i] - \bar{\varepsilon}_i \} \overset{*}{P}. \qquad (7i)$$

Hence the price elasticity of demand for the ith class of consumers (ε_i) is the coefficient of $\overset{*}{P}$ in (7i), or

$$\varepsilon_i = [\theta_i (1 - \varepsilon_t) - \beta_i] \psi_i - \bar{\varepsilon}_i, \qquad (7j)$$

which is the same as equation (7).

The derivation of equation (8) and (10)

The derivation of equation (8) follows directly from the identity

$$Q_c = Q_1 + Q_2 + Q_3 + Q_4 = \sum_{i=1}^{4} Q_i, \qquad (8a)$$

where

Q_c = the aggregate demand for foodgrains
Q_1, Q_2, Q_3, Q_4 = demand for foodgrains of each of the four
classes defined in Table 9.5.

Differentiating (8a) totally yields

$$\overset{*}{Q}_c = \sum_{i=1}^{4} \varphi_i \overset{*}{Q}_i, \qquad (8b)$$

where φ_i = the share of Q_i in Q_c. Substituting $-\varepsilon_i \overset{*}{P}$ for $\overset{*}{Q}_i$ in (8b) yields

$$\overset{*}{Q}_c = -\overset{*}{P} \sum_{i=1}^{4} \varphi_i \overset{*}{Q}_i. \qquad (8c)$$

Hence by definition, we have

$$\varepsilon_c = \sum_{i=1}^{4} \varphi_i\varepsilon_i = \varphi_1\varepsilon_1 + \varphi_2\varepsilon_2 + \varphi_3\varepsilon_3 + \varphi_4\varepsilon_4, \qquad (8d)$$

which is the same as equation (8).

The derivation of equation (10) is symmetrical to the derivation for (8), except that the initial identity is

$$Q_t = Q_c + Q_s \qquad (10a)$$

where

Q_t = the aggregate quantity demanded for grain for all uses

Q_s = the quantity demanded for grain used as seed, feed,
and carry-over inventories

The sources for the estimation of parameters in equations (4), (5), (6), and (11)

The estimate for σ_q was obtained by fitting a normal distribution to the ratio of the residuals to trend values of annual wheat yields obtained from a linear regression of yields on time. Per-acre yields, rather than annual wheat production or wheat production plus net imports, were used because of the assumption in the literature that the distribution of arable land across crops remained fixed from year to year by conventions that changed only very slowly over time (cf. p. 282 above). The estimated standard deviation of the residuals around yields is greater than those around the production or around the annual production plus net imports. The data on wheat yields for the period 1884–1913 are from Mitchell and Deane (1962:92–3). The root mean square errors around quadratic trends were lower than those around the linear trends.

The estimates of α were based on two time series of prices that were spliced at the overlap to provide a continuous series for the period 1540–1738. The series for 1540–1649 are from Bowden (1967:814–70), and the series for 1640–1749 are from Bowden (1985:827–902). 'Grains' was defined to include wheat, barley, oats, rye, and peas and beans. 'Food' was defined to include the preceding crops plus livestock and animal products. The grain price index and the food price index were constructed by giving equal weight to the prices of each of the commodities. The reasons for choosing equal weights are discussed by Bowden (1967: 870). Plausible alternative weighting schemes (such as those indicated in Phelps Brown and Hopkins 1956; Thirsk 1983; Shammas 1983, 1988; and Komlos 1988) tend to reduce both α and σ_{gp} because the prices of livestock and animal products are less variable than those of grains. The data on crop yields and total output are reported in Mitchell and Deane (1962:92–3) and in the sources cited there.

The standard deviations of prices from trend during 1540–1738 were computed around a 25-year moving average in which the trend value of the price was standardized at 1. A similar procedure was followed in computing the standard deviation around a moving average of the real wage series developed by Wrigley and Schofield (1981:638–44) from the series of Phelps Brown and Hopkins as well as around the original price series. The estimates of the standard deviation around trend from these series over 1541–1871 were quite close to those computed from the Bowden all-food series for 1540–1738. Use of an 11-year moving average instead of a 25-year moving average also had negligible effects on the estimates of the standard deviation around trend in the several series.

Sources for the parameter estimates in Table 9.5

Column (1) The population shares are based on King's table (Laslett 1984), except that out-servants were divided among the top three classes on the assumption that there were an average of 5 out-servants for each household of a landlord ('landlords' include the gentry down through 'Persons in the Law'), an average of 0.44 out-servants for each farm and lesser landlord household (a category that includes households of freeholders and ordinary clergy in addition to farmers), and an average of 0.24 out-servant for each household in the category of shopkeepers, minor professionals, and craftsmen (including military officers). The remainder of the households in King's table, which comprise the fourth class of Table 9.5, are presumed to hire no out-servants. The analysis stemming from the table is not particularly sensitive to reasonable alternative definitions of classes or of other distributions of out-servants, nor to re-estimates of King's table like the one proposed by Lindert and Williamson (1982), since such redistribution would have little effect on the inequality of the caloric distribution by income or social class.

Column (2)   The shares of the four classes are based on the assumption that the English distribution of calories was lognormal with $\bar{x} = 2.700$ kcal per equivalent adult and $s/\bar{x} = 0.3$ (see Table 9.8 above). The means of the four classes are obtained from

$$Z_{mi} = \frac{N_i}{(2\pi)^{0.5}} \int_{Z_i}^{Z_{i+j}} Z e^{-0.5 Z^2} \, dZ. \tag{A1}$$

and

$$\bar{X_i} = e^{S_{mi} \sigma + \mu} \tag{A2}$$

where
Z_{mi} = the Z scores of the mean of the ith class
Z_{j+i} and Z_i = the Z scores of the upper and lower bounds of the
             interval for the ith class
$\bar{X_i}$ = the mean of the ith interval in the lognormal distribution
N_i = the reciprocal of the area between Z_i and Z_{i+j}.
For a further discussion of this procedure see Fogel (1988).

Column (3)   The shares of grain in the expenditure of the four classes is based on the assumptions listed in Table 9.10. Values in column (3) were rounded to the nearest 5 per cent. These estimates are rough approximations based on data in Stigler (1974), Crafts (1980), Shammas (1983, 1984), and Phelps Brown and Hopkins (1956); cf. Thirsk (1983). The share of grain and of food in total expenditures for landlords may seem high, but it should be kept in mind that the majority of the persons in their households were from the lower classes and that bread and beer or ale were the main components of their ration (cf. Dyer 1983).

Column (4)   Estimates of King (1973:52–5) and Davenant (1699:71–4) indicate that foodgrains accounted for about 43 per cent of value added in agriculture *c*.1700 and animal products about 30 per cent (cf. Chartres 1985:443–8; O'Brien and Keyder 1978:44; Deane and Cole 1969:156). The remaining 27 per cent was accounted for by feed crops, other crops (e.g. flax, hemp), timber,

Table 9.10. Assumed shares of grain in class-specific expenditure

Class	(1) Share of food in total expenditure	(2) Share of grain in food expenditure	(3) (1) × (2)
1	0.30	0.50	0.15
2	0.40	0.40	0.15
3	0.60	0.60	0.35
4	0.80	0.90	0.70

and firewood. It is likely, however, that non-grain products, particularly animal products, represented a larger share of the agricultural income of wealthy land-holders (class 1) than of farmers and lesser landlords (class 2). I have assumed that $1 - \varepsilon_t = 0.82$, that class 1 had claims upon or produced about one-quarter of annual grain output, and that the remaining three-quarters belonged to class 2.

Column (5)   The income elasticity for grains for class 4 was estimated directly by Shammas (1984:259) from the Edens and Davies surveys of *c.*1790. Her figure (0.92) is quite close to the elasticity of grain (rice) derived from Timmer's equation for contemporary Indonesia (Timmer *et al.* 1983:59). For classes 2 and 3 I used Timmer's equation, and the income per household relatives for classes 2 and 3 computed from King's table (Laslett 1984), with the per-household income of class 4 standardized at 100. Since the relative average income of class 1 was far beyond the range of observations on which Timmer's equation was computed, I arbitrarily assumed that the value of ψ for class 1 was one-half of that for class 2.

Column (6)   Timmer's procedure (Timmer *et al.* 1983:59) was followed, employing the income relatives computed from King's table, as indicated in the paragraph above relating to column (5). For the reason indicated in the previous note, and Timmer's finding that the $\bar{\varepsilon}$ declines more rapidly than ψ with income, I arbitrarily assumed that $\bar{\varepsilon}$ for class 1 was 0.02.

10

Intra-Household Allocation of Nutrients and Gender Effects: A Survey of Structural and Reduced-Form Estimates

J. R. Behrman

10.1 INTRODUCTION

For most individuals in most developing countries intra-household food allocation is responsible for the provision of most nutrients. Since households generally include individuals of both sexes, there is the possibility of a systematic influence of gender on the nutrients that a specific individual receives; that is, the sex of the person who controls the allocation of critical resources and the sex of each individual recipient may affect the allocation of nutrients to a specific individual. A number of studies, particularly of southern and western Asian societies, conclude that females often receive fewer nutrients relative to their needs than do males.[1] Other studies suggest that gender may have an impact in that,

I thank the participants in the WIDER Conference in July 1987, particularly C. Gopalan, Siddiq Osmani, Philip Payne, Amartya Sen, and T. N. Srinivasan, and I also thank Susan Horton for useful comments on the version presented at the conference. The usual disclaimer applies.

[1] See Bardhan (1974), Das Gupta (1987), Behrman (1988*b*), Harriss (1987), Horton (1988), Kakwani (1986), Makinson (1986), Sen and Sengupta (1983), Valenzuela (1978), and Waldron (1986, 1987). Though most systematic studies focus on South Asia, Sen (1984) and Waldron (1987) give references to evidence for Africa, the Middle East, Latin America, Europe, and North America. Even within South Asia, Harriss (1987) reports a range of behaviour, with more gender distinction in the north than in the south and with males in some cases absorbing food shortfalls. Kakwani (1986), moreover, shows that conclusions about the direction of gender bias in some aggregate South Asian data are sensitive to the definitions of the index used. Das Gupta (1987) also suggests that, in the Punjab and Haryana in India, sex and birth order interact in that mortality rates are much higher for higher-birth-order girls than for low-birth-order girls. Studies of mortality in South Asia, further, suggest that gender differences persist, where they exist, across social classes (see Weinbergen and Heligman 1987). Langsten (1987), finally, suggests that a review of the evidence regarding the distribution of nutrients in South Asia in fact does not generally (though there are some exceptions, such as Chen *et al.* 1981*a*) indicate that females receive less relative to their requirements than do males (with the possible exception of some micro nutrients), though in much of South Asia age-specific female mortality is high relative to male mortality compared with some other parts of the world; she also indicates that cultural norms that seem to favour males in intra-household food distributions often are not followed.

the greater the share of resources controlled by women, the more of a given level of resources is devoted to nutrients for children.[2]

This chapter considers the intra-household allocation of nutrients and gender effects within the framework of household models of intra-household allocation, and surveys a number of studies of structural relations and reduced-form relations that can be interpreted within such frameworks.[3] Section 10.2 considers analytical frameworks for investigating these issues. Section 10.3 discusses some data problems. In Section 10.4 a number of existing empirical studies are reviewed. Section 10.5 presents concluding remarks.

10.2 ANALYTICAL FRAMEWORKS

An analytical framework helps as an organizing device for interpreting empirical evidence, particularly for a topic for which the available information is as imperfect as it is regarding the intra-household distribution of nutrients in poor societies.[4] I outline two standard static economic stories about intra-household distribution of nutrients and gender.

10.2.1 Constrained maximization of a unified preference function

Within this framework, the household is assumed to have a unified preference function defined over outcomes for each of the I household members. Such a preference function is consistent with there being a dictator in the household, benevolent or malevolent, as well as with the situation in which everyone in the household has the same preferences defined over the consumption of all household members.[5] The latter

[2] See Brown (1975), Caldwell (1979), Dey (1981), Dwyer (1983), P. Engle (1980, 1984), Guyer (1980), Kumar (1979), and Leslie et al. (1986). However, Harriss (1987) expresses doubts for some south Asian contexts. Also, Horton and Miller (1989) report that female-headed households in a Jamaican sample do not orient their expenditure more to children and basic needs than do male-headed households, though they claim that the former choose diets with higher nutrient quality (see Section 10.4.2).

[3] I do not attempt to resurvey the many studies that consider whether there are bivariate associations between sex and nutrient intakes or between sex and outcomes that are related to nutrient intakes. See the references in nn. 1 and 2 for evidence regarding such bivariate associations, particularly the surveys by Harriss (1987), Sen (1984), and Waldron (1987).

[4] I do not explore here the usefulness of the household as an analytic concept, though (as Cloud 1986; Guyer 1986; Peters 1986, and others emphasize) reservations have been expressed about this use in anthropology and in economic surveys at least since the 1940s, because of the ethnographic complexity of 'households', perhaps particularly in Africa. The work unit, consumption unit, residential unit, budgetary unit, etc., may be far from coterminous. Guyer seems to agree, however, that the 'as if' fiction of economic household analysis may be useful for some purposes.

[5] Economists often assume identical preferences over one's own consumption. But the requirement here is that there are identical preferences over every household member's consumption, so A weighs B's consumption just as does B, and vice versa.

might not be completely implausible if there is strong enough identification with the household or family line, whether for sociobiological, altruistic, or economic reasons (e.g. Ben-Porath 1980; Pollak 1985).[6] However, the requirement that each household member weigh the arguments of all other members of the household identically does seem quite strong. Nevertheless, if there is a household member close enough to a dictator or a situation does enough to identical preferences, a unified household preference function may be an adequate approximation for considering the intra-household allocation of nutrients.[7] Moreover, for most existing data-sets, the estimable relations that come out of the constrained maximization of a unified household preference function cannot be identified from those that come out of a bargaining framework, as is discussed in Section 10.2.3.

For the purposes of the present paper, it is useful to be explicit about some of the arguments in the preference function: individual consumption ($\mathbf{C}_i$), human resource quality ($\mathbf{Q}_i$), time use ($\mathbf{T}_i$), and assets ($\mathbf{A}_i$):

$$U = U(\mathbf{C}_i, \mathbf{Q}_i, \mathbf{T}_i, \mathbf{A}_i, I, \dots) \qquad \text{for all } i = i, \dots, I. \qquad (1)$$

Each of these variables has a subscript i to reflect that it is individual household members' consumption that enters into the preference function. Each variable is represented as a vector to reflect that there are multiple dimensions for each.

Consumption of goods and services ($\mathbf{C}_i$) is included because of the standard assumption that, *ceteris paribus*, increased consumption improves satisfaction. A subset of the elements in this vector refers to food consumption ($\mathbf{C}_i^f$), which is important in itself because of the direct satisfaction that food consumption provides in addition to its impact on the health component of quality and possibly on productivity. I include the whole consumption vector and not just the food component to emphasize that there generally are trade-offs between food consumption and other consumption for fixed total household resources, in addition to trade-offs among the food consumption of various household members. Further, the food consumption of some household members, through productivity effects, may alter the total resources available to the household, and thus probably both food and non-food consumption.

The human resource quality ($\mathbf{Q}_i$) of each individual includes health ($\mathbf{Q}_i^h$), schooling ($\mathbf{Q}_i^s$), and other human resource attributes. These affect the current welfare of individuals and the household. They also have an investment dimension with effects in the future, beyond the period of immediate relevance for this static one-period framework. For example,

---

[6] Maclachlan (1983) seems to argue, for example, that in rural south India the traditional gender roles amplify sexual differences and work towards creating a harmonious consistency of preferences held by different household members.

[7] Such a framework would not seem adequate for investigating certain phenomena, such as household formation and dissolution (or the entrance or exit of a particular individual).

in the absence of good capital markets and old-age pensions plans, parents may be interested in the human resource qualities of their children because they relate to the children's potentialities for providing income transfers to the parents, particularly support for them in their old age (e.g. Greenhalgh 1985; Willis 1980). As is discussed below, these human resource qualities may be 'produced' in part by nutrients.

The time use (T_i) of individuals affects preferences directly because different time uses provide different degrees of satisfaction (e.g. leisure versus work versus schooling). Different time uses also feed back indirectly on household welfare by altering indirectly the other arguments in the preference function, as is discussed further below.

The assets of individuals (A_i) are included for reasons parallel to the non-food consumption and the investment dimension of human resources. Asset accumulation represents an alternative use of current resources and an alternative to human resource investments regarding the future. Improvements in capital markets, for example, might make such assets relatively more attractive than human resource investments in children for parental old-age security, and could cause a shift away from human resource investments, *ceteris paribus*. While assets are indicated to be associated with individuals, if the household pools all its resources, pooled rather than individual assets enter into household preferences.

The last argument that is indicated explicitly is household size (I). This may have some immediate direct impact on household welfare if, for example, the household places positive value on pleasures of having more children (I^c). There also may be an indirect effect through changing the total resources to be allocated, the number of individuals among whom they are allocated, and the potential for exploiting economies of scale.[8] The number of children also has an investment dimension, and there may be a trade-off among human resource investments, other assets, and number of children regarding alternative strategies for providing for parental old-age security.[9]

One observation worth making explicit is that nutrients (N_i) do not appear directly in this preference function. That is, nutrients are not posited to affect preferences directly, but only indirectly, through their association with foods consumed (C_i^f) or their impact on human resource quality (Q_i), both of which reflect production relations that are considered below.

The preference function is maximized subject to two sets of constraints. The first is the production functions, broadly defined. For the present purpose, among the most important are those for the health

---

[8] Economies of scale appear to be important in nutrient determination in some studies (e.g., Behrman and Wolfe 1984a; Iyengar *et al.* 1968; Ward and Sanders 1980; Wolfe and Behrman 1983).

[9] The well-known quantity–quality fertility models of Becker (1981 and references therein) and Willis (1973) focus on such trade-offs.

$(\mathbf{Q}_i^h)$ and schooling $(\mathbf{Q}_i^s)$ components of human resource quality $(\mathbf{Q}_i)$, nutrition $(\mathbf{N}_i)$, births (B), mortality (M_i), and possibly wages $(\mathbf{W}_i)$ and farm/firm production (Y).

The health of the ith household member $(\mathbf{Q}_i^h)$ is posited to be produced by nutrients consumed by that individual $(\mathbf{N}_i)$, other health-related inputs $(\mathbf{C}_i^h)$,[10] the general environment $(\mathbf{R})$, endowments related to the inherent robustness and capabilities of the individual $(\mathbf{E}_i)$ and of the primary health care provider in the household (hereafter 'mother', $\mathbf{E}_m$), the time use of the individual $(\mathbf{T}_i)$ and of the mother $(\mathbf{T}_m)$, the schooling of the individual $(\mathbf{Q}_i^s)$ and of the mother $(\mathbf{Q}_m^s)$, and the health status of all other individuals in the household $(\mathbf{Q}_k^h, k \neq i)$:

$$\mathbf{Q}_i^h = Q^h(\mathbf{N}_i, \mathbf{C}_i, \mathbf{R}, \mathbf{E}_i, \mathbf{E}_m, \mathbf{T}_i, \mathbf{T}_m, \mathbf{Q}_i^s, \mathbf{Q}_m^s, \mathbf{Q}_k^h)$$
$$\text{(for all } k \neq i) \qquad \text{for each } i = 1, \ldots, I. \tag{2}$$

Nutrients are included in this production relation because nutrient intakes presumably are a major input into the production of health status. But five observations are useful regarding the role of nutrients in producing health.

1   Nutrients are not equivalent to health status. They may not be a good indicator of health status, moreover, unless one of two conditions are satisfied. First, the health production function in (2) must have fixed coefficients between nutrients and the other inputs so that there is not substitution between nutrients and the other inputs:[11]

$$\mathbf{Q}_i^{h*} = \min [\mathbf{Q}^{h*}(\mathbf{N}_i), \mathbf{Q}^{h**}(\mathbf{C}_i^h, \mathbf{R}, \ldots)]. \tag{2a}$$

Such a condition seems very strong, suggesting, for example, that nutrition inputs result in the same level of health for individuals who have much different inherent robustness (which is related to $\mathbf{E}_i$) or much different time use patterns $(\mathbf{T}_i)$. Second, all individuals in society (or at least in the sample) must face the same relative prices for all of the inputs in the health production function (2) and therefore, in their maximizing behaviour, must select the same non-nutrient and nutrient input combinations; thus, nutrients (or any other single input) are a perfect proxy for the composite input.[12] This too seems to be a very strong condition that is unlikely to be satisfied. Relative market prices are likely to differ for individuals across space because of transportation costs and even in a given location if prices of some items are subsidized for some members

---

[10] These may (e.g. medicines) or may not (e.g. automobile usage) be consumed consciously because of their relation to the individual's health.

[11] This includes the extreme case in which only nutrients count in producing health status, and not other health-related consumption or the environment $(\mathbf{R})$ or endowments $(\mathbf{E}_i)$.

[12] This statement is a little strong in that it would suffice for prices to be such that the composite non-nutritive input be the same for everyone and that the trade-off between nutrients and the composite non-nutritive input be the same for everyone.

of society (e.g. subsidized food,[13] or medical services for the poor). Effective prices for endowments, moreover, are likely to vary since no market exists for, say, genetic endowments, with the result that effective prices differ even for members of the same household (with the possible exception of identical twins). Therefore nutrients are not necessarily very good indicators of health status, nor vice versa. In fact, nutrients may not even be associated positively with health status.[14] If endowments are very important in the production of health, and if nutrients are allocated so as to compensate for endowment inadequacies, for example, nutrients may be inversely associated with health status.[15]

2   Basal metabolism also plays a role in the absorption of nutrients, apparently varying considerably across individuals, and possibly adapting to nutrient intakes (e.g. see Dasgupta and Ray 1990; Sukhatme 1982*d* and the references therein; Chapters 2, 3, and 4 in this volume; and the discussion of point 5 in Section 10.3 below). In the health production function, metabolism is reflected partially in the individual's endowments but also, if it is affected by nutrient intakes, in those intakes. The variance and possible endogeneity of basal metabolism may weaken further the association between nutrient intakes and health status.

3   Time use and associated energy expenditure also alter how a given level of nutrient intakes affects health status, at least as measured by the usual health indicators. Two persons with identical basal metabolism may absorb vastly differing amounts of current nutrient intakes through different physical activities, and thus have much different quantities of nutrients remaining to affect longer-run health status. While the importance of time use patterns is widely recognized (see e.g. Chapters 2 and 3 above), empirical estimates of health production functions generally do not control for time use differences.

4   Besides nutrients, there are a number of other inputs in this health production function. For example, human resources may affect significantly the knowledge of or efficiency of use of other inputs, so these are included for both the individual himself and the household's primary health care provider/mother. To the extent that these human resources result in individuals being better informed about options, one would expect a positive association between human resources such as schooling and the use of modern inputs or good nutrition practices, as, for

[13] Food subsidy programmes have been widespread in developing economies. Behrman (1990), Horton and Taylor (1986), and Pinstrup-Andersen (1985) provide recent surveys of some of these programmes.

[14] Langsten (1987) claims that a review of existing studies about differences in nutrients consumed by sex in south Asia does not suggest that such distributions (or those of medical care) account for the relatively high female mortality there.

[15] Analytically, this situation is exactly parallel to the possible lack of association or inverse association between child quality and schooling discussed in Behrman (1987). Also see Sect. 10.4.1 below.

example, Strauss (1990) reports for the Ivory Coast. On the other hand, more human resources may substitute for other inputs if, for example, better educated food preparers boil bad water but less educated ones do not. Rosenzweig and Schultz (1982a) present some evidence for Colombia consistent with this possibility. The other non-nutrient inputs include the health status of other household members. These are included primarily to capture the possibility of contagion,[16, 17] though that for the mother may also represent her energy and effectiveness in providing household health care services. Health-related inputs for a particular individual, including nutrients, might through contagion (as well as through other means such as labour productivity) have impact on the health of other household members.

5   There is a lot that we do not know about the biological technology of the health production function. The marginal product in terms of health status of increasing nutrients is likely to be positive for poorly nourished individuals. But at higher levels of nutrient intakes the marginal products may become negative, leading to obesity, arteriosclerosis, etc. Even at moderate nutrient intake levels, whether the marginal product is positive or negative may depend upon exactly what dimension of health is of interest. For example, increased calorie consumption may increase current energy levels at the same time that it contributes somewhat to longer-run obesity problems. Moreover, many nutrients may interact, and all may interact with other inputs, such as the environment, endowments and non-nutrient health-related inputs. Furthermore, some effects have considerable lags, which may make them hard to detect. A casual examination of the nutrition literature over the past several decades reinforces the observation that we do not know many details of these biological processes, as indicated by changing fads about the importance of proteins versus calories, etc.

Although the individual health status production function is critical in understanding the roles of intra-household distribution of nutrients, other production functions also are important. I discuss these more briefly now.

Mortality (M_i) can be considered to result when an individual's health status falls below a critical level ($\bar{\mathbf{Q}}_i^h$):

$$M_i = M\left(\mathbf{Q}_i^h - \bar{\mathbf{Q}}_i^h\right) \qquad \text{for each } i = 1, \ldots, I. \tag{3}$$

---

[16] There also may be contagion effects from non-household members, which for simplicity I assume are in **R**.

[17] They are not meant to represent genetic tendencies to be susceptible to diseases shared by relatives, since in principle those are incorporated in the endowments; however, in empirical estimates the health status of relatives may represent in part such endowments because of the lack of direct observations on endowments (e.g. Barrera 1990; Horton 1986 and Thomas et al., 1991).

The critical level, of course, may vary across individuals. Thus, in a sense, mortality is just another (albeit extreme and irreversible) health status indicator, so the comments above about the health production function and the associations between health status and nutrients carry over, except that the irreversibility of mortality limits sharply some substitutions over time.

Nutrient intakes of the ith individual in the household ($\mathbf{N}_i$) depend on food intakes of that individual ($\mathbf{C}_i^f$) and on time use and capacities of the mother ($\mathbf{T}_m$, $\mathbf{Q}_m^e$, $\mathbf{E}_m$):

$$\mathbf{N}_i = N(\mathbf{C}_i^f, \mathbf{T}_m, \mathbf{Q}_m^s, \mathbf{E}_m, \dots) \qquad \text{for each } i = 1, \dots, I. \qquad (4)$$

For given expenditures on food, the nutrient intakes can vary enormously because of different food composition (see Section 10.4.2) and different preparation.

Education of the ith individual ($\mathbf{Q}_i^s$) is posited to depend on the endowments ($\mathbf{E}_i$), the number of grades (S_i^g) and quality (S_i^q) of schooling, the health ($\mathbf{Q}_i^h$), and the nutrition ($\mathbf{N}_i$) of that individual:

$$\mathbf{Q}_i^s = Q^s(\mathbf{Q}_i^h, \mathbf{N}_i, S_i^g, S_i^q, \mathbf{E}_i, \dots) \qquad \text{for each child } i = 1, \dots, I_c. \qquad (5)$$

Health and nutrition are included because of evidence that at best the former is associated with schooling success through increasing students' productivity (e.g. Sirilaksana 1982, 1986; Moock and Leslie 1986; Jamison 1986; Section 10.4.2). The quality of schooling is included in addition to grades of schooling because of recent evidence in the developing country context that schooling quality is very important in understanding the impact of schooling on some important outcomes, and estimates that ignore it may be very misleading (e.g. Behrman and Birdsall 1983, 1985; Birdsall 1985; Fuller et al. 1986; Heyneman and Loxley 1983; Heyneman and White 1986). Endowments are included because of similar evidence that the failure to control for the attitudes and abilities relating to the adults' childhood family backgrounds may cause misunderstanding of both the determinants of schooling and its impact in developing countries (e.g. Barrera 1990; Behrman and Wolfe 1984b, 1987a; 1987b; 1989; Horton and Miller 1989; Thomas et al. 1991; Wolfe and Behrman 1986, 1987; 1991).

Births (B) are determined by a 'biological supply function' in the spirit of Easterlin et al. (1980) and Rosenzweig and Schultz (1983, 1987) as dependent on contraceptive use (C_m^c), the efficiency of the mother and father in using contraceptives as related to their education ($\mathbf{Q}_m^s$, $\mathbf{Q}_f^s$) and endowments ($\mathbf{E}_m$, $\mathbf{E}_f$), their fecundity as related to their health and nutritional status and their endowments ($\mathbf{Q}_m^h, \mathbf{Q}_f^h, \mathbf{N}_m, \mathbf{N}_f, \mathbf{E}_m, \mathbf{E}_f$), and the frequency of intercourse (F):

$$B = B(C_m^c, \mathbf{Q}_m^s, \mathbf{Q}_f^s, \mathbf{Q}_m^h, \mathbf{Q}_f^h, \mathbf{N}_m, \mathbf{N}_f, \mathbf{E}_m, \mathbf{E}_f, F). \tag{6}$$

There is some controversy about the role of nutrition in affecting births.[18] If there is a role, it might provide another channel through which intra-household nutrient allocations feed back upon intra-household allocations by changing the size and the composition of the household.

The number of household members (I) equals births (B) minus mortality (M) minus other net outflows (O_i):

$$I = B - \sum_i (M_i - O_i). \tag{7}$$

Other net outflows may occur because of migration, marriages, etc., that are not modelled easily within this simple framework.

To this point, I have been agnostic about whether income generation can be treated separately from consumption/demand. If it can, wages and income can be treated as predetermined variables from the point of view of the determination of individual nutrient intakes and health status. But if there are immediate impacts of health and nutrition on labour productivity, or impacts of labour time use on health (or if, for farm/firm production, there are sufficiently incomplete markets),[19] the separability assumption is not valid. Recently, moreover, a considerable literature has developed that emphasizes the integration of decisions regarding the gender allocation of a farm's production labour with those regarding the gender allocation of household consumption (see Dey 1981; Guyer 1980; Feldstein 1987; Okali and Sumberg 1986; Rogers 1985 and the references therein).[20] In such cases, production relations must be added for wages for the ith individual and for farm/firm production:

---

[18] Bongaarts (1980) and Menken et al. (1981) review the literature on the impact of nutrition on fecundity and conclude that there is not a biological effect except in cases of severe malnutrition. Nevertheless, there may be a positive association for behavioural reasons if, for example, frequency of intercourse depends on health status. Easterlin and Crimmins (1985) and Wolfe and Behrman (1987a) present indirect evidence consistent with such a possibility, with nutrition, contraceptive use, and fertility all increasing with income.

[19] Leibenstein (1957), Mazumdar (1959), Stiglitz (1976), and Bliss and Stern (1978), among others, have emphasized the productivity link possibility. Behrman and Deolalikar (1989), Deolalikar (1988), Sahn and Alderman (1988), and Strauss (1986) provide recent estimates that support this possibility, with health and nutrition treated as being simultaneously determined. If separability is not possible, the consumption/demand and income/production decisions must be explored simultaneously within the so-called household/farm model (see Barnum and Squire 1979; Lau et al. 1978; Singh et al. Strauss 1986 and the references therein), though this literature has intended to emphasize incomplete markets as a reason for the lack of separability.

[20] The link might be purely in terms of a nutrient and health productivity impact, but this literature seems to suggest that it goes beyond that link to include the nature of work and consumption norms, information flows (e.g. regarding own produced food quality, as in Ashby 1987), and perhaps power relations.

$$W_i = W(\mathbf{Q}_i^s, \mathbf{Q}_i^h, \mathbf{N}_i, E_i, \dots) \qquad \text{for each } i = 1, \dots, I, \qquad (8)$$

and

$$Y = Y(\mathbf{Q}_i^s, \mathbf{Q}_i^h, \mathbf{N}_i, E_i, \dots) \qquad \text{for all } i = 1, \dots, I. \qquad (9)$$

These relations allow for the possible impact of health and nutritional status on individual labour market productivity, as reported in recent studies by Behrman and Deolalikar (1989), Deolalikar (1988), Sahn and Alderman (1988), and Strauss (1986).[21] If there are such effects, the total resources available to the household may increase if more resources are used for nutrients so that productivity and income increase. If such effects differ by gender, then within the maximizing framework they feed back with optimal intra-household nutrient allocations favouring those individuals for whom at the margin the productivity effects are greater. Of course, in such an allocation any health and nutrient impact on household productivity, presumably primarily through the mother, given her dominance in time use for household production (e.g. Engle 1980, 1989; King 1978, 1980, 1983; Leslie et al. 1986), also should be incorporated into the analysis.

The second constraint is on time and monetary resources, as is summarized in a full-income budget constraint in which the $\mathbf{P}_c$ refer to prices that incorporate money and time costs:

$$\sum_i W_i T_i + Y = \sum_i \mathbf{P}_c \mathbf{C}_i + \sum_i W_i T_i^l + \sum_i W_i T_i^s + \sum_i \Delta \mathbf{A}_i, \qquad (10)$$

subject to the constraints that the total time use for each individual must equal the total time ($\overline{T}_i$) available for that individual. The left-hand side (LHS) of (10) gives the total value of full income: the total time of each household member $\overline{T}_i$ valued at the relevant wage (W_i) plus net income from all sources other than labour of members of the household (Y). The right-hand side (RHS) gives total resource expenditures: the sum of consumption ($\mathbf{P}_c \mathbf{C}_c$) plus the value of leisure time ($W_i T_i^l$) plus time spent in schooling ($W_i T_i^s$) plus asset changes ($\Delta \mathbf{A}_i$) for all individuals in the household.

Under the assumption that the underlying functions have the desirable characteristics, the first-order conditions for the constrained maximization lead to reduced-form demand relations:

$$\mathbf{V} = f(\mathbf{Z}) \qquad (11)$$

where

$$\mathbf{V} = (\mathbf{C}_i, T_i, \mathbf{Q}_i, S_i^g, S_i^q, \mathbf{N}_i, \mathbf{W}_i, Y, B, M_i, F, \Delta \mathbf{A}_i)$$
$$\text{for all } i = 1, \dots, I$$

---

[21] These studies control for the simultaneity or reverse causality in that higher wage or income may cause better health and nutrition rather than vice versa. A number of other studies have explored the association between health and nutrition and labour productivity, but without control for simultaneity. See Behrman and Deolalikar (1988a) for a survey of some of these studies and references to others.

except $i \neq m$ or f for S_i^g ans S_i^q, and

$$\mathbf{Z} = (\mathbf{P}_c, \mathbf{P}_f, \mathbf{E}_i, \mathbf{R}, \bar{\mathbf{A}}_i, S_m^g, S_f^g, S_m^q, S_f^q) \qquad \text{for all } i = 1, \ldots, I.$$

The dependent variables (**V**) include the food consumption, health, and nutrition of all household members, in addition to the grades and quality of schooling for all children, births, mortality, unearned income, and time use, wages, and asset accumulation for all individuals. The RHS variables (**Z**) include all of the consumption prices (**P**$_c$), farm/firm prices (**P**$_f$), the general environment (**R**), and all predetermined assets of the household—all individual endowments (**E**$_c$), grades and quality of schooling for the adults (S_m^g, S_m^q, S_f^g, S_f^q), and initial assets ($\bar{\mathbf{A}}_i$).

10.2.2 Bargaining model of intra-household allocation of nutrients

A number of people (e.g. Cain 1979; Dey 1981; P. Engle 1980, 1989; Folbre 1984*a*, 1984*b*, 1986; Guyer 1980, 1982; C. Jones 1983; S. Kumar 1979; Sen 1984) argue that the unified preference assumption of the framework outlined in Section 10.2.1 is misleading. Instead, they advocate a bargaining framework in which each individual has his or her own preferences and assets and bargaining occurs over the allocation of resources, including nutrients, among household members. Such a framework seems plausible on the basis of casual observation. While household members may be altruistic about one another and share important concerns about the perpetuation of the household, there generally also appears to be some differences in preferences and conflicts regarding intra-household allocation at each point in time and over the life-cycle of the household.

Manser and Brown (1980) and McElroy and Horney (1981) have developed theoretical bargaining models for intra-household allocations. A critical element of these models is the existence of threat points that relate to the possibility of an individual leaving the household if his/her utility is less than some fixed level determined by his/her options outside the household, and thus by his/her assets (both human resource and physical/financial).[22] Within this framework, the intra-household allocation can be interpreted in terms of a generalized (i.e. non-symmetric) Nash bargaining model. In work in progress, Behrman et al. (1988) develop this framework for the investigation of intra-household allocation of nutrients and leisure within Indian and Malaysian households.

The structural relations for the formal bargaining model are very similar to those described in Section 10.2.1. All production functions

---

[22] C. Jones (1983) emphasizes the possibility of shirking instead of exiting as part of a bargaining strategy in a repeated game regarding intra-household allocations.

for individual health, nutrition, wages, etc. remain. The major differences are that there are preference functions for each individual rather than the unified household preference function in relation (1), threat points (TP_i) regarding the possibility of exit from the household for all household members, and full-income budget constraints for each individual rather than the overall household budget constraint in (10). The resulting reduced forms are identical to those in relation (11) except that $\mathbf{Z}$ is augmented to include the threat points of all I household members. If certain household members systematically favour one gender, then increasing their threat points increases the nutrient (and other resource) allocation to individuals of that gender.

10.2.3   Empirically estimable relations pertaining to the intra-household allocation of nutrients and gender effects

Structural relations One interesting question is whether equal outcomes are weighted differently depending upon the gender of the individual in the unified preference function (1) or the in individual preference functions for the bargaining framework. Direct estimation of preference functions is not possible, of course, because utility is not observed. But preference parameters can be estimated in some cases from reduced-form relations, though simultaneity and the absence of exogenous gender-specific instruments may limit the possible inferences (see Section 10.4.1).

Direct estimation of the structural production function relations for health status, schooling, wages, firm/farm production, and possibly time use may be informative regarding gender effects of intra-household nutrient allocations. Such estimates may suggest, for example, whether the return to marginal nutrients is greater for one sex than for the other, given markets and customs that determine those returns. At least three major problems, however, need to be surmounted in such estimates. First, most of the RHS variables in the production functions are simultaneously determined with the outcomes of interest within the frameworks described in Sections 10.2.1 and 10.2.2. This means that there must be a sufficient number of exogenous variables (i.e. those in Z) to permit identification of the coefficients of the endogenous variables and appropriate estimation procedures must be used to avoid simultaneity bias. Second, some of the RHS variables are not easily observed, most notably endowments. If these unobserved variables are associated with observed variables, then the failure to control for the unobserved variables causes omitted variable bias, since the observed variable partially represents the effects of the omitted unobserved one. Third, lags may be critical, but theory provides little or no guidance regarding these lags.

Finally, the alternative unified preference function versus the bargaining frameworks has no differential implications for estimating these production relations.

Reduced-form relations The reduced-form relations may reveal whether there are gender differences in the intra-household allocation of nutrients in response to exogenous changes in prices, the environment, and the other variables in **Z** in relation (11). Are nutrients adjusted more (or less) for females than for males, for example, when food prices change? Such differences may exist because of preference weights that differ according to the sex of individuals, because of bargaining among household members of both sexes, and because of differences in production functions or individual endowments by sex. Generally, reduced-form relations cannot distinguish among these possibilities. Estimation problems include possible omitted variable biases and lag structures as for structural relations, but not simultaneity bias if the relations are truly reduced forms (since, in such a case, all of the RHS variables are exogenous). In principle, the two frameworks discussed in Sections 10.2.1 and 10.2.2 lead to different reduced forms in that the reduced-form relations for the bargaining model include the variables that determine individual threat points in addition to the variables that are explicit in **Z** in relation (11). But note that these variables have to be in addition to those in **Z** and therefore cannot include the human capital variables that might be representing shadow prices of time rather than threat points (see Rosenzweig and Schultz 1984). Since such variables are difficult (though not impossible) to obtain in most data-sets, most, if not all, existing empirical studies that claim to provide evidence in favour of the bargaining model (or vice versa) are not persuasive. A significant impact of women's schooling or women's wages (even if one ignores possible simultaneity problems) simply does not discriminate between the unified preference versus the bargaining model. Either further structure or predictions (e.g. differences in the restrictions on coefficients, as in Behrman and Taubman 1989, 1990) or else observations on variables that might affect threat points without affecting the shadow price of time (e.g. assets bought into the marriage by the husband and by the wife as in Behrman *et al.* 1988) are required.

Quasi-reduced form relations Sometimes estimates of quasi-reduced forms are made, in which some endogenous RHS variables are included in addition to some of the prices and other variables in **Z**. Such relations may be derived from the reduced-form relations by solving a particular reduced-form relation that determines one endogenous variable (say Y) for one exogenous variable (say P_f treated as a scalar) and then using that relation (say for N_i). The relation so obtained has all but one of the exogenous variables in $\mathbf{Z}$ plus one endogenous variable on the RHS.[23] In the example indicated in the parentheses immediately above, for instance, nutrients could be expressed as a function of consumer prices, (endogenous) farm/firm income, and the other exogenous variables in $\mathbf{Z}$ (other than $\mathbf{P}_f$). This basically is the standard demand relation.

Three observations about quasi-reduced forms are useful. First, to estimate them correctly requires the same information as to estimate the reduced-form relations, since the excluded exogenous variable must be used to identify statistically the influence of the included endogenous one. Second, a number of estimates that have a mixture of endogenous RHS variables and exogenous variables in $\mathbf{Z}$ are not truly quasi-reduced forms, in the sense that this term is used here, because they could not be derived by the above-described process of substituting endogenous variables for exogenous ones using reduced forms.[24] It is not clear how to interpret such relations. Third, the interpretation of even true quasi-reduced forms may be murky since a given change in any exogenous variable may work in part through the included endogenous variable(s). Therefore these estimates may reflect only the partial, not the total, effect of changes in exogenous variables.

10.3   MEASUREMENT PROBLEMS

Measurement problems may be severe for an empirical exploration of the intra-household allocation of nutrients and gender effects. For estimation of many of the possible structural, reduced-form, or quasi-reduced-form relations of interest, direct observations on individual nutrient intakes are required. Such observations are difficult to obtain and currently are available for only a few (though a growing) number of data-sets for developing countries that also include other socioeconomic data, which permits estimation of the relations of interest. There are at least six measurement problems, moreover, that are almost inherent in these data.

First, the necessary raw data are individual consumption data for different categories of food. These usually depend on direct observations by the surveyer or on recall data, sometimes from a key respondent such as the mother in the household. The basic problem is that both of these procedures well may lead to systematic biases in reported individual food consumption towards what the respondent(s) considers appropriate norms. That is, if local norms are that older males are favoured or that

[23] Of course, further substitutions from other reduced forms could replace other variables in $\mathbf{Z}$ with other endogenous variables.

[24] For example, there must be at least one excluded exogenous variable for each included endogenous one.

equality is desired, the allocations reported by key respondents or under-taken in the presence of outside observers are likely to be biased towards those norms as compared with usual allocations. The problem for the researcher is all the more severe because it is not clear *a priori* whether this bias is likely to lead towards an understatement or an overstatement of gender inequalities in nutrient allocations.

A second measurement problem is that food consumed outside of regular meals is likely to be undercounted either by key respondents or by outside observers. Such an undercount may have a systematic impact on measured allocations between the sexes. For example, food preparers (usually females) may consume relatively great quantities of food while preparing meals; on the other hand, males may eat more outside of the household. The problem for the researcher is all the more severe, once again, because the net direction of such systematic gender biases may not even be clear.

A third measurement problem is that there often is considerable vari-ation in food intakes for a given individual over time. In part this may result in random measurement error, which should not cause problems in the estimation of gender differences for the reduced-form nutrient intake relations, though it biases towards zero the estimated impact of nutrients on other outcomes, such as health in estimates of relation (2). But there may be systematic gender biases if, for example, nutrient intakes tend to vary seasonally more for one sex than the other but data collection tends to be concentrated in particular seasons. For example, suppose that food is allocated to ensure that males receive adequate quantities, with females receiving the residual quantities, so that gender inequalities are large when food is scarce but disappear when it is relatively abundant:[25] then, if data collection is concentrated in the seasons when food is relatively scarce (abundant), gender inequalities will be overstated (understated).[26]

A fourth measurement problem relates to the translation of foods into nutrients, typically by using fixed food-to-nutrient conversion factors, which effectively suppress all but the first argument in the nutrient production function of relation (4). This may result in systematic bias in measured nutrient allocations, but it is not clear that it results in a gender bias. For example, suppose that actual nutrient intakes from given foods (as categorized by the researcher) are greater for households with better educated food preparers (i.e. that $\mathbf{Q}_m^s$ is greater in (4)) and

[25] Abdullah and Wheeler (1985) report, incidently, that in their rural Bangladeshi sample, if anything, seasonal shortages are absorbed by men rather than by women—con-trary to the example in the text.

[26] Chambers (1982, 1983), Chambers *et al.* (1981), Sahn (1989), and S. Schofield (1974) and many of the references therein emphasize the possible importance of seasonal variations in food allocations and in data collection.

that better educated mothers allocate relatively more food to females than do less educated mothers. In such a case it is not obvious that the measured relative allocation between males and females within a household is distorted (though differences among households may be mispresented), although it might be if there are gender distinctions in the relative quantities of food consumed that happen to be associated with systematic errors in the conversion factors (e.g., males eat relatively more meat, and the conversion factors for meat involve more—or less— error than for non-meat).

A fifth measurement problem pertains to the need often to standardize for nutrient requirements in order to make comparisons among individuals of different ages and between males and females. As a number of nutritionists and economists have emphasized recently (e.g., Dasgupta and Ray 1990; Payne 1989; Payne and Cutler 1984; Seckler 1980, 1982; Srinivasan 1981, 1983a, 1985; Sukhatme 1982d, and the chapters in this volume), the use of such standards is tricky because of both inter- and intra-personal variations. With respect to representing relative nutrient intakes by gender, the effective question is whether the standardization adopted is free of gender bias. For example, often the nutrient intakes for some relatively healthy and well-off population are used to construct age- and gender-specific standards (e.g. middle- and upper-income urban residents for Indian Nutrient Institute standards described in Ryan et al. 1984); but if there is gender bias in the nutrient allocations in that reference population, then the use of the standards themselves will tend to misrepresent gender biases in the samples under study. Sen (1984), Chen et al. (1981a), and Epstein (1984) suggest that standards based on energy use for various activity levels systematically may understate the actual energy use of women because they assume too short work-days and too sedentary activities. If this is the case, and if nutrient intakes have a nonlinear impact on productivity with diminishing marginal returns after intakes above those necessary to maintain basal metabolism are consumed, then one might expect to find that measured nutrients relative to the (gender-biased) standards have larger estimated productivity effects for females than for males.

A sixth measurement problem pertains to sample selectivity. The only individuals observed at a particular point of time are those who have survived to that time. If previous nutrient and other health-care-related allocations have favoured males and the better endowed of both sexes, for example, then the currently existing pool of females may be relatively well endowed because of relatively high mortality rates among poorly endowed females as compared with those among poorly endowed males.

Such measurement problems may thus result in systematic biases in the extent of measured gender biases in nutrient allocations. Moreover, for many of these reasons, there are likely to be random measurement errors as well, which are likely to result in biases towards zero in the impact of measured nutrients on outcomes of interest.

For such reasons, reinforced by the relatively great cost of obtaining individual food data, many studies use health or morbidity indicators instead of nutrient intakes. For example, anthropometric and morbidity indicators are often used, and even referred to as indicators of nutritional status[27] (e.g. Barrera 1990; Bhuiya et al. 1986; Garcia and Pinstrup-Andersen 1987; Horton 1985, 1986, 1988; Jamison 1986; Moock and Leslie 1986; Sirilaksana 1982, 1986; Sen 1984; Thomas *et al.* 1991). Such indicators have some measurement problems parallel to those mentioned above for nutrients (e.g. the problem of defining standards) that I shall not go into here in the interest of brevity. But the more basic point, as is discussed above following the health production function in relation (2), is that these indicators need not be highly, or even positively, correlated with nutrient intakes. Therefore it may be very misleading to act as if they are representing nutrient intakes, even though they may be representing health outcomes of substantial interest in themselves.

Measurement problems also may affect other variables used in the analysis of the determinants, and the impact, of nutrient intakes. I shall not discuss these at length here except to note that there may be systematic gender bias in some relevant variables that are difficult to measure (e.g. schooling quality and individual endowments), which may result in a gender-specific omitted variable bias in estimates of the impact of nutrient intakes on outcomes of interest.[28]

---

[27] Some users seem merely to be defining nutritional status, for example, to be anthropometry. At a certain level one should not quibble with such a definition if it is clear to the audience as a whole. But since anthropometric indicators reflect not only nutrient intakes, but also genetic endowments, disease experience, the nature of water, etc., it is not clear why logically they should be associated with nutrient intakes by using the term 'nutritional status' for them rather than, e.g., 'genetic status', since they are also associated with genetic endowments. In fact, the use of 'nutritional status' for such indicators seems to lead to some confusion about the role of nutrients in what they represent. Perhaps it would be best to refer to such indicators simply as 'anthropometric indicators', though it seems to me that they refer to important dimensions of health status, so I use them that way in this paper.

[28] In simultaneous estimates such variables often should be used as instruments for endogenous nutrient intakes. If they are not observed, however, they cannot be used for such a purpose. As a result, the first-stage estimated nutrient intakes may be devoid of systematic gender factors that should be there, so the second-stage estimates may misrepresent gender effects.

10.4 EMPIRICAL STUDIES OF THE INTRA-HOUSEHOLD ALLOCATION OF NUTRIENTS AND GENDER EFFECTS

I shall now survey a number of recent studies that fit into the frameworks developed in Section 10.2.

10.4.1 Estimates of structural relations

Preference parameters Preference functions generally cannot be estimated directly, of course, because utility is not observed. They are estimable from first-order conditions, however, subject to assumptions about functional forms. In Behrman (1988*b*) I present estimates of preference function parameters relevant for intra-household nutrient distributions for rural south India, conditional on explicit assumptions about functional forms. I begin with the assumptions that there is a unified parental preference function as in (1), which has a separable CES component defined over the health outcomes of all I_c children:[29]

$$U_H = (\sum_i a_i (\mathbf{Q}_i)^c)^{1/c} \qquad \text{for all } i = 1, \ldots, I_c. \tag{1a}$$

Two characteristics of this utility function are of interest. The first is the curvature, which relates to inequality aversion of the equity–productivity trade-off. If the preference curve is L-shaped, as in Fig. 10.1 (*a*), parents obtain no additional satisfaction if, starting from a corner *A*, the health of one or the other child is improved (to *B* or *C*). To increase their satisfaction, the health of both children must be improved: equity is of paramount concern. If the preference curve is linear, as in part (*b*), parents do not care about the distribution of health improvements, but only about obtaining the largest sum of the health improvements for their children: they are indifferent among *A*, *B*, and *C* despite the very different distributional implications of these combinations of $\mathbf{Q}_1^h$ and $\mathbf{Q}_2^h$. Between these two extremes, there are many intermediate possibilities with different degrees of equity–productivity trade-offs (as in part (*c*)). In part (*a*), *C* refers to the curvature of the preferences, i.e. the degree of inequality aversion: $C \to \infty$ is the case of complete inequality aversion of Fig. 10.1(*a*), $C = 1$ is the pure productivity case of Fig. 10.1(*b*), and intermediate values of *C* are intermediate cases such as in Fig. 10.1(*c*). A particularly interesting intermediate case is the Cobb–Douglas case in which $C = 0$. With the health production function described below, if *C* is less than zero, nutrients are allocated to

---

[29] In relation (1*a*), health is represented as a scalar for each child for simplicity. In the actual study, health is represented by a weighted average of the available multiple indicators of health. For an alternative formulation in which health is treated as an unobserved latent variable for which there are multiple imperfect indicators, see Behrman (1988*a*).

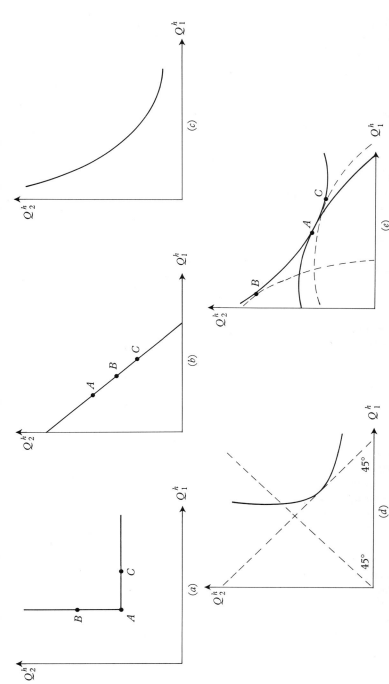

Fig. 10.1. Model of intra-household allocation of nutrients among children to produce a distribution of expected health among the children; (a) Square-cornered parental preferences (Rawlsian or infinite inequality; aversion case) with equal concern; (b) Linear parental preferences (pure investment or no-inequality aversion case) with equal concern; (c) Equity–productivity trade-off in parental preferences with equal concern; (d) Equity–productivity trade-off in parental preferences with unequal concern favouring child 1; (e) Constrained maximization of parental preferences at point A for solid health production possibility frontier (and at B and C for dashed frontiers)

compensate for inequality in endowments (i.e., the inherently weaker get more), and with C greater than zero, nutrients are allocated to reinforce inequality (i.e., the inherently stronger get more).

Second, preferences may be symmetrical over health outcomes of the children in the sense that equal health is weighted equally in the household preferences as in Fig. 10.1(a)–(c). Alternatively, parents may weigh equal health outcomes differently depending on the gender or birth order or other characteristics of the children, which is called 'unequal concern'. Unequal concern implies that the preference curves are asymmetrical around a 45° ray from the origin as in Fig. 10.1(d), in which case the health of child 1 is weighted more heavily than the health of child 2. The a_i refer to unequal concern; if they depend on sex, the preferences reflect unequal concern related to sex.

The next assumption concerns the technology of the health production function, which is assumed to be quasi-Cobb–Douglas. For simplicity, I write it with one nutrient and one health outcome for each child, though in the actual study both have multiple indicators:

$$Q_i^h = N_i^\alpha g(E_i, \ldots).\tag{2b}$$

Under the assumption that there is an interior solution and that the prices of nutrients are the same for all children, the critical parameters of the preference function are explicit in the ratio of the first-order conditions for two children:

$$\frac{N_1}{N_2} = \frac{a_1}{a_2}\left(\frac{Q_1^h}{Q_2^h}\right)^c.\tag{12}$$

With data on individual nutrient intakes and individual health outcomes, the utility function parameters relating to inequality aversion (c) and unequal concern by gender (a_1, a_2) can be estimated from (12). Effectively, these estimates exploit the fact that the preference-maximizing allocation of nutrients between two children is given by the tangency of the health production possibility frontier with a preference curve as at point A in Fig. 10.1(e); but for different pairs of children the health production possibility frontiers differ in shape because of different relative endowments (perhaps in part related to sex), so a series of such tangencies trace out the shape and location of a preference curve (B, C in part (e)). If ordinary least squares estimates are made, however, the estimate of C is upward-biased, since the nutrient and the health ratios are determined simultaneously. (See Behrman and Taubman (1986) for details.)

I obtained estimates for rural south Indian households using the ICRISAT VLS (International Crops Research Institute for the Semi-Arid

Tropics Village Level Studies) panel data.[30] Because of great emphasis by some on seasonality (e.g. Chambers *et al.* 1981; Chambers 1982, 1983; Sahn 1989; S. Schofield 1974), I distinguished in the estimates between the lean season (when food is in relatively short supply) and the (relatively) surplus season by effectively allowing for separability in preferences between the seasons. The estimates indicate significant inequality aversion; i.e., parents care about the distribution of health among their children and not just about the productivity of nutrients used to produce health. During the surplus season the inequality aversion is strong enough that parents adopt compensating behaviour, giving more nutrients to those children with less endowments. In other words, as is suggested as a possibility in the first point regarding the health production function in relation (2), nutrients are negatively associated with health indicators during this season because of parental efforts to compensate. During the lean season, however, the estimated inequality aversion is much less, indicating that parents may reinforce inequalities by giving more nutrients to children who are better endowed. During the lean season, moreover, the estimates indicate significant unequal

---

[30] These data are described in a little detail here since they are also used for several other studies that are summarized below. The data have been collected from 240 households in six carefully selected 'typical' villages in three different agroclimatic zones in two states in SAT India over the 1975–84 period. Within each village 10 households are randomly selected representatives of agricultural labour and non-landholding households and another 30 are a stratified (by size of landholding) random sample of cultivating households. For the 1976–7 and 1977–8 crop years special nutritional surveys were undertaken, from which individual food intakes during the previous 24 hours and anthropometric health indicators were recorded by nutritionists and medical doctors. The special nutritional surveys provide information on nine nutrient intake measures: calories, proteins, calcium, iron, carotene, thiamine, riboflavin, niacin, and ascorbic acid. These nutrients were calculated by applying Indian food-to-nutrient conversion factors from Gopalan *et al.* (1971) to 120 foods for which direct observations on individual consumption were made in the nutrient surveys. Examination of these data (see Behrman 1988*a*, 1988*b*; Behrman and Deolalikar 1987, 1988*b*; Harriss 1987; Ryan *et al.* 1984) suggests that this sample generally is malnourished in comparison with Indian standards, particularly for carotene and ascorbic acid—in which cases less than half of the Indian standards are met at the sample means. Also, less than three-quarters of the Indian standards are met at the sample means for calcium and riboflavin. Only for proteins, iron, and thiamine among these nine nutrients are the sample averages above Indian standards. The coefficients of variation for these nutrient intakes are relatively large for carotene and riboflavin, both with values greater than 0.90, indicating substantial fluctuations in consumption across households. At the other end of the spectrum, the variations across households are relatively small (below 0.40) for calories, proteins, niacin, and iron. Gender differences in nutrient intakes, however, are not large and usually are not significant.

Anthropometric data were collected on weight, arm circumference, triceps skinfold thickness, and height. These data were subsequently standardized for weight and height by age-specific standards for higher-income groups in Hyderabad as determined by the National Institute of Nutrition (and are at about the 50th percentile of the widely used Harvard standards), and for weight-for-height, arm circumference, and triceps skinfold thickness by international standards, in Jelliffe (1966). These data are used as indicators of health status. For further details concerning the ICRISAT VLS data, see Binswanger and Jodha (1978) and Ryan *et al.* (1984).

concern, weighing health outcomes by about 5 per cent more for boys than for girls (and more so for lower-caste than for higher-caste households).[31] Thus, there is substantial concern about equity and no unequal concern favouring boys when food is relatively available; but when food is relatively scarce, the less well endowed female and lower-caste children are placed at greater nutritional risk. That there is estimated gender preference in the lean season is all the more striking because for this south Indian sample the raw nutrient intake data do not indicate sharp gender differences.[32] Apparently, the gender differences entering through the endowments that favour girls in the health production function roughly offset the preference weights that favour boys in the lean season so that gender effects are not clear in simple bivariate associations between sex and nutrient intakes or between sex and health status, but they do appear in the structural estimates of preferences.

Health production functions A priori, there may be gender differences in the impact of nutrient intakes on health—as represented by anthropometric, mortality, and morbidity experience indicators—in relation (2). However, I am aware of very few efforts to explore such a possibility, and those estimates that are available do not indicate much in the way of gender differences. For example, Behrman and Deolalikar (1990) present 2SLS LISREL[33] estimates of health production functions for men, women, boys, and girls for the ICRISAT south rural Indian sample, also used in the study described immediately above. While they

[31] As noted above, these estimates are conditional on the specific functional forms used, which assume homotheticity within a season. In a personal communication, Siddiq Osmani has developed an example in which the lack of homotheticity might be misidentified as a gender bias. In this example the preference curves are sharper at higher preference levels and the observations are heavily concentrated on one side of the 45° ray at such preference levels (and vice versa at lower preference levels). This example is provocative, and suggests the possible gains to be made in future work with more flexible functional forms, though the peculiar concentration of the observations on opposite sides of the 45° ray for low versus high preferences does not make it persuasive to me as an explanation as to what is going on. (Why should the health production frontier be oblong to favour one sex at low preference levels and to favour the other at higher preference levels, since it depends only on the production functions, endowments, and budget constraints?)

[32] These estimates use anthropometric indicators as measures of the health outcome of interest. An alternative would be to posit that the nutrient intakes affect expected labour market outcomes, and those should be used as the relevant measure of the health status as in Rosenzweig and Schultz (1982b)—see Sect. 10.4.2 below. If the impact of nutrients on expected labour market outcomes is well represented by current effects for adults in the ICRISAT villages, the expected labour market outcomes can be added as an additional health indicator. When this is done multicollinearity is considerable, so it is difficult to sort out the effects with confidence. But the expected labour market variables do not dominate statistically the direct anthropometric health indicators for this sample. Of course there may be still other returns, such as the high dowry costs for girls emphasized by Carter (1984) and others.

[33] In these LISREL estimates health and nutrients are treated as unobserved variables for which there are imperfect indicators.

find some evidence of significant differences across types of individuals, they do not report any significantly positive estimates of coefficients for nutrient inputs in the health production process.

Lewis (1986) presents logistic estimates of quasi-reduced-form relations that include some elements of production functions for post-neonatal mortality for 5481 male and female Jordanian infants in the mid-1970s. Her results suggest some significant gender differences in health production, with the length of breast-feeding and mother's education being of significantly greater importance in reducing male than female mortality. These results are the most compelling of any that I know in suggesting gender-specific differences in the impact of nutrient intakes on health outcomes. They must be qualified, however, because it is not clear exactly what is being estimated, and there probably is simultaneity bias arising from the failure to treat variables such as the length of breast-feeding as endogenous.

Other studies that approximate individual health production functions have restricted themselves to additive gender effects, without interactions with nutrient intakes. For example, Magnani et al. (1985) present estimates of production functions for weight-for-age for Philippine infants and small children (aged 1–59 months) with a number of inputs. They report that male children are significantly (about 6 per cent) less likely to be 25 per cent or more below Filipino anthropometric standards than are female children independent of nutrient intakes. However, the lack of control for simultaneity makes interpretation difficult. Heller and Drake (1979) estimate health production functions with additive gender effects for three anthropometric measures (weight-for-height, height-for-age, and weight-for-age) and three morbidity indicators (mild diarrhoeal disease, severe diarrhoeal disease, and number of days with illness) for 1270 children under 6 years of age in the early 1970s in Candelaria, Colombia. They find significant positive effects for weight-for-height for girls age 0–11 months and 12–23 months, significant negative effects for weight-for-age for girls age 0–11 months, but no other significant additive effects. Their results do not appear very conclusive about possible gender discrimination, but their procedure of including the lagged endogenous variables may obscure actual gender effects. Wolfe and Behrman (1982) estimate quasi-reduced forms that are close to health production functions for child mortality and standardized child height, weight, and biceps circumference for a random area-stratified sample for 1281 households with children under 5 years of age in Nicaragua in 1977–8. For the nation and for three regions (by degree of urbanization), they find significant additive gender effects only for males for biceps circumference in the national and other urban (i.e. other than the capital city) samples, though the quasi-reduced-form nature of their specification and the lack of control for simultaneity means that their results must be qualified. Horton (1988) presents estimates of the determinants of height-for-age and weight-for-height for 1570 Filipino children aged 15 or less in the Bicol sample with a sibling control for unobserved fixed effects. She reports significant birth-order effects, but no significance for gender.[34] Pitt and Rosenzweig (1985) likewise report no significant additive gender effect in a production function for number of adult days ill in the previous week in rural Indonesia. Sirilaksana (1982, 1986), finally, estimates simultaneous health production functions for three anthropometric outcomes for 1006 preschool children in north-east Thailand. She finds one significantly negative additive impact (at the 5 per cent level) for a child being female in 24 regressions for different age–anthropometric combinations—about what one would expect to occur by chance if in fact there is no true effect.

Thus, there seems to be very little or no evidence that the impact of nutrient intakes on health indicators depends systematically on gender. However, this may just be part of the problem of our general ignorance of the nature of the health production technology and the failure in existing estimates to control well for metabolism, time use, and lags. For further discussion, see Behrman and Deolalikar (1988a) and Behrman (1990).

Wages Only recently, as noted above with regard to relation (8), have there been some estimates of the impact of nutrient intakes on productivity that control for the possible simultaneity of higher wages causing better nutrition. In only two of these studies, to my knowledge, is there an exploration of gender differences. Behrman and Deolalikar (1989) present such estimates for adults in the ICRISAT rural south Indian sample. Their results suggest that the wage impact of nutrients (actually, calories) does not differ significantly between males and females but that the impact of weight-for-height does, with significant effects in the slack season for males but not for females. Sahn and Alderman (1988) also estimate wage determination relations with household calories as a simultaneously determined RHS variable for 2125 men and 625 women in rural Sri Lanka with data from the 1980/1 Labour Force and Socioeconomic Survey. They report a statistically significant elasticity of real wage with respect to calories of about 0.2 for men that is robust to different estimation approaches, but an insignificant one for women. Behrman and Deolalikar speculate that the results in these studies may reflect the gender division of tasks, with males specializing in tasks involving more physical strength (e.g. those involving the use of bullocks). If so (and if weight-for-height reflects nutrient intakes in the Behrman–Deolalikar

---

[34] Her estimates control for possible systematic differences by gender in nutrients consumed not by including individual nutrients, but only through including an additive gender variable.

study), then with the current division of labour there may be gains to the household as a whole from allocating somewhat more nutrients at the margin to males than to females than would be optimal without labour productivity effects. Note that these results are not consistent with the conjecture in point 5 of Section 10.3 that estimated nutrient impacts may be greater for females than for males because of measurement problems.

Schooling Sirilaksana (1982, 1986), Jamison (1986), and Moock and Leslie (1986) present recent studies which claim to investigate the impact of child malnutrition on schooling performance, but in fact consider the association between anthropometric health indicators (and, in the last case, haemoglobin count) and schooling performance. Sirilaksana estimates the determinants of school grades for 582 children aged 7–13 in north-east Thailand. Jamison explores the determinants of grade retardation (or 'grades behind') for a Chinese sample. Moock and Leslie investigate the determinants of schooling enrolment and grade attainment in Nepal. All of these estimates generally indicate a positive association between the anthropometric indicators and school performance. However, that better health and better schooling performance both may be due to other factors such as endowments and family background, as is suggested in Section 10.2, is not recognized by using simultaneous estimators, so the authors' interpretation of causality must be heavily qualified. Additive gender effects are included in all of the estimates, but are significantly non-zero (negative for girls) only for schooling enrolment in Nepal. Therefore these estimates do not provide much clarification of whether nutrient and health effects on schooling performance differ by gender.

10.4.2 Reduced-form relations

The reduced-form relation for nutrients in equation (11) is of particular interest for this paper. But other reduced-form relations may also be of interest if, through differential responses to food prices for outcomes of individuals identified by gender, there is evidence of the intra-household allocation of nutrients having an impact through gender effects.

Nutrient intakes To estimate these reduced-form relations to test for most gender effects, data on *individual* nutrient intakes are required.[35,36]

[35] Data on nutrients at household, rather than individual, level are much easier to obtain since they often can be constructed from household expenditure surveys. If inferences about individual nutrient intakes could be made from such household data, it would be possible to use many existing data-sets to augment the few estimates on intra-household nutrient allocations and gender effects based on relatively rare data on individual nutrient consumption. Deaton (1987) presents a procedure for estimating gender discrimination in food

Some of the relatively few data-sets with such information do not have much information on prices or the other RHS variables in **Z** in relation (11). Therefore perhaps it is not surprising that I am aware of only two studies that contain estimates that include prices.

The first study is for the rural south Indian ICRISAT data-set, once again, by Behrman and Deolalikar (1988*b*). In this study the authors first observe that the impact of a food price change on nutrient intakes may be positive for at least one food price, depending upon the extent of induced substitution to foods with higher food-to-nutrient conversion factors. That is, an increase in the price of a high-cost nutrient source may improve nutrition (though not welfare) by inducing substitution by a lower-cost nutrient source. The authors then present estimates of the price elasticities of nutrient intakes for boys, girls, men, and women with a latent variable representation of nutrient intakes and with control for unobserved fixed effects through using differenced panel data. Their estimates suggest that the nutrient elasticities with respect to income are small and do not differ with the recipient of the nutrients.[37] The nutrient

consumption from household expenditure data (and finds, incidently, that there is no systematic gender differences in overall food consumption for data from the Ivory Coast). His procedure could be extended to link nutrient intakes to food consumption and, subject to the necessary assumptions on functional forms for this method, applied to other household data sets.

[36] Of course, nutrients are but one input in the production of health status, though other inputs are not the subject of this survey. See Behrman (1990) and Behrman and Deolalikar (1988*b*) for surveys of estimates of reduced-form demand relations for other health-related inputs. Generally, these studies do not explore gender differences although there are some exceptions, such as Horton and Claquin's (1983) estimates for diarrhoea treatment in Bangladesh, in which they report significant additive estimates that suggest that boys are taken for treatment more often than are girls.

[37] The small income impact may be surprising given the conventional wisdom that income is critical for the determination of nutrition. For example the World Bank (1981: 59) articulates this view forcefully: 'There is now a wide measure of agreement on several broad propositions . . . . Malnutrition is largely a reflection of poverty: people do not have income for food. Given the slow income growth that is likely for the poorest people in the foreseeable future, large numbers will remain malnourished for decades to come . . . . The most efficient long-term policies are those that raise the income of the poor . . . .' However, as Behrman and Deolalikar (1987, 1988*c*) demonstrate empirically, both for this Indian sample and for an international cross-country sample, the elasticity of nutrients with respect to income may be quite small even though the elasticity of food expenditure with respect to income is almost unity for poor people. The reason is that these people may value highly at the margin non-nutritive food attributes—tastes, appearance, status value, processing, variety—that are not highly correlated with nutrients (also see Shah 1983, and Behrman and Wolfe 1984*a*). Some recent systematic studies based on food expenditure systems with relatively few food groups report high nutrient elasticities with respect to income—e.g. Murty and Radhakrishna (1981), Pitt (1983), and Strauss (1984). But their procedure of applying food-to-nutrient conversion factors to fairly aggregate food groups misses the intra-group substitution that occurs when income increases, and guarantees by construction that the nutrient elasticities with respect to income are about the same order of magnitude as the food expenditure elasticities with respect to income. For direct evidence that nutrient unit prices increase systematically with income in various societies, see Horton (1985), Pitt (1983), Radhakrishna (1984), Williamson-Gray (1982), Behrman and Deolalikar (1988*c*),

elasticities with respect to price, in contrast, are large (generally greater than 1 in absolute value) and are negative for the basic staple (sorghum) but positive for the other foods.[38] Most important for this survey, the response of nutrients to price changes differs significantly among the types of individuals, with smaller adjustments in the nutrient intakes of girls in response to changes in the sorghum price (the basic staple) and larger adjustments in the nutrient intakes of girls in response to other price changes. Therefore nutrient intakes for girls are treated as relative 'necessities' with respect to sorghum price changes, with little significant adjustment in light of favourable or unfavourable sorghum price movements. In contrast, nutrient intakes for girls are treated as relative 'luxuries' with respect to *other* price changes, with considerable adjustments in response to favourable and unfavourable price movements.

The second such study is Garcia and Pinstrup-Andersen (1987) for a panel of 840 households in 14 villages (selected for their high incidence of malnutrition and poverty) in three provinces in the Philippines in 1983–4 to evaluate price discounts for rice and cooking oil and nutrient education programmes. Half of the households were covered by the programme; the other half were a control group. On the average, food distribution as compared with Filipino standards was biased in favour of adults, with limited evidence of pro-male biases for children; the calorie adequacy rate was 0.80 for adults, 0.60 for male preschoolers, and 0.55 for female preschoolers. Regression results are presented for reduced forms for calorie intakes for 509 individual children aged 13–83 months. With controls for a number of other variables (including income and some major prices and assets), boys still receive significantly more calories than girls, on the order of magnitude of 100 calories per day. Unfortunately, however, only additive gender effects are explored.

Besides there being different parameters in the reduced-form individual nutrient demand relations depending on the sex of the individual, gender may enter into the nutrient allocation decision in another way. As is discussed above in Section 10.2, the nature of predetermined control of or investment in human resources by gender may affect nutrient intakes. Existing studies focus on such effects for women's schooling, and in a few cases for women's wages. The rationale for including such variables is based on the fact that better schooled women are more

and Garcia and Pinstrup-Andersen (1987). For other recent studies besides Behrman and Deolalikar (1987, 1988c) that report much lower nutrient than food expenditure elasticities for developing countries, see Knudsen and Scandizzo (1979) for Sri Lanka and India; Greer and Thorbecke (1984) for Kenya; Garcia and Pinstrup-Andersen (1987) for the Philippines; G. Kumar (1987) for Kerala, India; and Alderman (1987) for Sri Lanka, Thailand, Egypt, Sudan, Indonesia, Nigeria, Malaysia, Brazil, Bangladesh, and Morocco.

[38] Pitt (1983), Pitt and Rosenzweig (1985), and Sahn and Alderman (1988) also report a number of positive estimates of food price impacts on household nutrition for Bangladesh, Indonesia, and Sri Lanka, respectively.

efficient in household production, that better schooled women bargain more effectively over household resources, and that women are more interested in nutrition than are their husbands. (As noted in Section 10.1.4, these possibilities are hard to test against one another with most existing data.) In any case, women's schooling is included in a number of estimated reduced-form nutrient relations. The results from these are mixed. Horton (1985) reports significantly negative effects for a sample of 366 rural households from Gujarat, India, primarily because of an inverse impact on the share of food expenditures in total expenditures. She also obtains a positive impact for the male household head's education, which in large part apparently is an income effect. Sirilaksana (1982, 1986) finds no significant impact of women's schooling (working through predicted women's wages), nor of men's schooling, on household nutrient intakes in her study of 582 north-east Thailand households, though there is a significant impact of women's schooling (through predicted wages) on food expenditure. Ward and Sanders (1980) report no significant effects for a north-eastern Brazilian sample, as do Behrman and Deolalikar (1990) for rural south India. Garcia and Pinstrup-Andersen (1987) report a significant positive effect of women's schooling on food expenditure, but not a significant effect on the acquisition of calories in their Filipino study cited above. On the other hand, Valenzuela (1978) reports significant positive effects on calories and, in interaction with food expenditures, on protein and vitamin C for the Laguna Philippine data. Behrman and Wolfe (1987a, 1989) and Wolfe and Behrman (1987, 1991) also report strong positive effects for their Nicaraguan data. The latter group of studies, moreover, find that the impact of mother's schooling remains strong even with random effects or with latent variable or sibling-differenced fixed-effects control for unobserved ability and attitudes related to the woman's childhood family background, in contrast to the strong effect of such controls on the estimated impact of schooling for a number of other outcomes.[39]

Horton and Miller (1989) explore whether women have preferences favouring children and basic needs, as suggested by S. E. Brown (1975), Dwyer (1983), P. Engle (1980, 1989), and others, by estimating household-level reduced-form relations for expenditure shares (including

[39] Bishop (1976) and Griliches (1979) have argued that sibling deviation estimates may result in coefficient estimates biased towards zero because of the greater relative role of measurement error in such differenced estimates than in standard estimates. In Behrman (1984), however, I demonstrate that this result does not hold if there is strong enough correlation in measurement error across the variable being differenced. For schooling, for example, the failure to control for schooling quality is likely to result in measurement error that is highly correlated across siblings. Similar arguments apply, of course, if differenced panel data are used to control for fixed effects, in which case serial correlation in measurement errors for income, prices etc., may mean that biases arising from measurement error are less for the estimates based on differenced data than for those based on non-differenced data.

some detail for food), calories per capita, and diet quality for a low-income non-random 1984/5 sample of 145 Jamaican households, 43 per cent of which were headed by females. For aggregate expenditure shares, no difference is found between male- and female-headed households. For major food groups, female-headed households spend a significantly larger share on starch from yams, plantain, etc., a significantly smaller share on dairy products, and have no significant differences for the other nine food groups. If foods are divided by the share of luxury, necessity, and intermediate food groups (where the economic definition concerning the relation between budget share and income is used to define these categories), female-headed households spend significantly less on necessity and intermediate foods. There is no difference in calories per capita, but female-headed households have higher diet quality (as defined in an index utilizing nine nutrients other than calories). Thus, the authors conclude that there is some limited support for the hypothesis that female-headed households exhibit greater concern for basic needs and children in the diet quality results. However, their diet quality index almost seems contrived in order to find some positive impact of female headship on food and nutrients after more direct explorations did not show significant effects. For this reason, and because of their peculiar sample, it would seem inappropriate to conclude that this study provides much evidence that women are more concerned with nutrients than are males.

Health status I am aware of nine studies that explore reduced forms for health status—once again, as measured by anthropometric and morbidity indicators—with some dimensions of gender differences that may be attributable to gender effects in intra-household nutrient allocations.

Pitt and Rosenzweig (1985) present ordered probits for the male household head being ill in the previous week and his wife being ill in the previous week and a fixed-effect logit for household head being ill relative to the wife being ill for a random sample 2347 farm households in the April–June 1978 sub-round of the National Socio-Economic Survey of Indonesia (SUSENAS). Their empirical representation of Z in relation (11) is extensive, including 13 consumption prices, 8 community or environmental variables, wages, education of the head and his wife, and owned land and farm profits. Their estimates prima facie suggest the possibility of some significant gender differences. At the 5 per cent level of significance, the probability of the household head being ill is affected positively by his education and the price of vegetables, and negatively by the price of sugar; the probability of the wife being ill is affected positively by the price of fish and the presence of public lavatories in the community. Such evidence is hardly overwhelming, however, given that only 5 of 56 coefficient estimates are statistically

significant at the 5 per cent level, not much more than would be expected to occur by chance if there were no true associations. In part
this may reflect the considerable measurement problems in using self-
reported illness for only one week as the health indicator.

Bhuiya *et al.* (1986) estimate separate (almost) reduced forms for
weight-for-age for about 700 (each) boys and girls aged 2–60 months in
Matlab in Bangladesh using data from the International Centre for
Diarrhoeal Disease Research Demographic Surveillance System. Their
estimates suggest some definite gender differences in these relations,
though the presentation of their results does not permit an easy untangling of all the effects. For example, they report a significant positive
impact of mother's education (larger for Hindus than for Muslims) on
boys' but not on girls' health. They also find a significantly positive
impact of possession of articles, reinforced by the male head's education,
on boys', but not girls', health. However, the interpretation of this last
result as a wealth effect is clouded by confusing gender effects associated
with their land-tax variables. Thus, their results suggest that young boys
benefit more in terms of weight-for-age from more educated mothers
than do young girls, presumably because of intra-household allocations,
including those for nutrients. It is interesting to note that, in this case,
having more educated mothers favours sons and more educated fathers
with low wealth favours the daughters (but vice versa if there is some
wealth, as represented by the ownership of items such as a quilt, hurricane lamps, bicycle, or radio).

Behrman and Deolalikar (1988*b*) present reduced-form estimates for
the determinants of individual health status (as represented by multiple
anthoropometric indicators within a LISREL latent variable framework)
for men, women, girls, and boys in the rural south Indian ICRISAT
sample, with control for unobserved fixed effects through differencing
panel data. Their estimates indicate a significant impact of half of the
food prices on health status, but no significant gender differences among
the price, income, or wage coefficients.

Khan (1984) estimates relations for height as a function of age and
simultaneously determined household nutrients (from basic grains) for
males and females in four age groups (2–5, 5–14, 14–19, and 19 years
and over) for a 1976–7 rural survey of about 6000 individuals conducted
by the Bangladesh Institute of Development Studies. Significant effects
are reported for males aged 19 and over and for females aged 14–19 and
5–14, but not for the other age–sex combinations considered. These
results might be interpreted to mean that at the margin household
nutrition allocations favour females aged 5–19 and males aged 19 and
over, or that the marginal productivity of nutrients in terms of height is
the greatest for such groups. The latter interpretation seems doubtful
since the marginal health impact probably is greatest for small children,

so probably these results reflect intra-household allocation patterns as much as differential nutrient productivities. If so, they constitute some evidence of intra-household allocation patterns in which sex and age interact. But the strength of the results is limited, since in the majority of cases there is no significant impact of nutrients on height, and since the instruments used for the first-stage estimates for household nutrients (i.e. land and socioeconomic status) are limited.

In addition, five other studies permit only additive gender effects. Strauss's (1990) extensive estimates for the rural Ivory Coast report no significant impact of gender. Akin *et al.* (1985) present logit estimates of infant feeding in the Bicol Philippines 1978 sample and also report no significant gender effects; but Horton (1986) reports a significant gender effect favouring girls for height-for-age for children under 15 in the same sample, which Barrera (1990) also finds for the older children in this sample using different techniques. Garcia and Pinstrup-Andersen (1987), for the same 509 Filipino children aged 13–83 months described above, report a significantly higher additive Z-score for weight-for-age for boys, but not for weight-for-height, nor for either weight or height as a percentage of age standards. They also find no significance of women's education for all of these outcomes.

Mortality Rosenzweig and Schultz (1982*b*) have estimated reduced-form differential male–female child survival rates with rural district data from the 1961 Indian census in a well-known study. They argue that such survival rates reflect intra-household resource allocations, presumably including nutrients. They find that the relative survival rate is significantly responsive to expected differential labour force options by gender, which they represent by current adult gender employment rates.[40] Therefore they conclude that intra-household allocations are responsive to and reinforce market-determined relative returns by gender, rather than being compensating. Such results are provocative regarding the role of longer-run expected returns in intra-household allocation, though one might question the exact representation of those expected returns in this study (i.e., why employment rates and not expected wages?).

10.5 CONCLUSIONS

There is some evidence of systematic gender differences in intra-household nutrient allocations, particularly in southern and western Asia.

---

[40] B. D. Miller (1981) comes to a similar conclusion after relating the juvenile sex ratio (used as an indicator of differential mortality by sex) to female labour force participation based on secondary analysis of anthropological studies.

Such patterns tend to favour males, though not always in the best documented cases, even in south Asia.

Household models provide frameworks with which to organize information pertaining to the determinants and impact of these phenomena, given the changing economic and social environment in which households operate. I have sketched out the frameworks for two such models: one based on maximization of a unified preference function, and the second based on bargaining among household members. These frameworks suggest structural and reduced-form relations about which it would be desirable to have more empirical information in order to understand better the determinants and impact of gender differentials in intra-household nutrient allocations and what is likely to ensue with changes in factors exogenous to the household, such as market prices. They also suggest some estimation problems related to simultaneity and unobserved variables, such as endowments, the exclusion of which may cause omitted variable biases. Finally, particularly for the reduced forms, there are questions of interpretation that make it difficult to know whether estimated effects are due to preference biases, differential health production functions, or the nature of intra-household allocation decisions.

For estimation of most of the relations of interest, critical data are individual nutrient intakes.[41] Such data may be subjected to a number of gender-specific biases, including distortions arising from the process of making observations, the construction of nutrient standards, and the diurnal and seasonal timing of observations. It is not clear in what direction nutrient gender differentials are likely to be biased for these reasons. In addition, there may be random measurement errors that lead to an underestimation of the impact of nutrient intakes. Because of the cost of obtaining information on individual nutrients, many have used anthropometric, morbidity, and mortality indicators to represent nutritional status. While such indicators may have less (though still possibly considerable) measurement problems, their use to represent nutrient intakes is dubious since they may not be highly correlated, or even necessarily positively correlated, with nutrient intakes.

In part because of the data difficulties and in part because of conceptual problems, the number of existing estimates of relevant structural and reduced-form relations is small.

Estimates of some of the structural parameters do suggest some interesting possibilities. Under the assumption of unified preferences, nutrients may be allocated to compensate for other factors (including endowments), so health status is poorly correlated with nutrient intakes;

---

[41] But see n. 35 about the possibility of using household data and imposing more *a priori* structure, as recently suggested by Deaton (1987).

when food is very scarce, however, there apparently is a reinforcement of endowment differentials and male preference even in a context in which the raw data do not obviously reflect gender differentials. Wages may be affected differently by health and nutrient indicators, given customary task divisions, for males versus females. Similarly, nutrient intakes may affect mortality differentially for boys versus girls.

Estimates of the reduced-form relations also suggest some additional interesting results. Individual nutrient intakes may be adjusted different-ly in response to price changes for individuals according to gender; in the specific example explored, adjustments are greater for girls' nutrient intakes for price changes in non-staple foods (and less for those in the basic staple) than for other household members. Thus, in this case girls bear the brunt and reap the rewards of price fluctuations in non-staple foods more than do other household members. Gender-specific expected labour market returns also appear to affect differential male–female child survival rates. In some studies, mother's school appears to have a strong and robust impact on nutrient intakes, thus suggesting another dimen-sion of gender effects.

Despite such suggestions, the available empirical evidence to date must be considered quite meagre. No completed systematic studies exist which discriminate satisfactorily between the unified preference function and the bargaining frameworks, though this is an important distinction in understanding how households operate. Almost all of the results sum-marized in the previous two paragraphs are based upon a single study or two, with little bases for knowing the extent of legitimate generalization. A critical link in the relation between nutrient intakes and many outcomes of interest is the health production function, about which we know very little because of data problems, lags, and possible misspecifications (e.g. excluding time use). Furthermore, most existing estimates of health pro-duction functions and of most other relevant relations ignore the possible interaction of gender with other observed variables, and thus are much less informative than they might be. Further empirical work on health production functions, therefore, may have significant payoffs in improv-ing our understanding of gender effects and intra-household nutrient allocation. Finally, the studies that I have reviewed have accepted (often implicitly) that the household is a useful unit of analysis, despite consid-erable longstanding reservations among some anthropologists (e.g. Guyer 1986) that the household is the appropriate unit for many important decisions, particularly in Africa, where there often appears to be a whole set of relevant overlapping units for micro decisions and activities. Rec-ognition of the more complicated nature of decision-making and alloca-tion may be necessary for such cases.

The expected improvements in our understanding may well be worth the costs of more such investigations. Learning more about how households or other relevant micro units function in regard to such critical allocations would be useful in itself, as well as giving a better basis for making judgements about individual welfare, as Sen (1984) argues. Some gender-specific welfare effects may become clearer, such as who bears adjustment burdens to food shortages or food price changes, which may alter our perceptions of individual welfare. Empirical work also may improve the basis for policy formulation if more is known about how individual physical and human resource assets ('entitlements') affect and are affected by the process. However, to the extent that there is substantial fungibility within the household, successful targeting of policies for specific types of individuals (e.g. females) may be quite difficult. It is not clear, therefore, that greater knowledge of the empirical structural and reduced-form relations pertaining to intra-household nutrient allocations and gender effects is likely substantially to improve policy formation.

Given the data and estimation problems, it also seems appropriate to ask, Why do we care about the intra-household allocation of nutrients instead of other outcomes? I have argued above that in part it is useful to understand better the process of nutrient allocations in itself. But the role of nutrients should be kept in perspective. As is suggested by my specification of the preference function, they are perhaps best viewed as a means, not an end. Of greater interest would seem to be direct anthropometric and morbidity indicators of individual health status—not as proxies for nutrients (for which they may not be very good proxies in any case), but because health is of great interest in itself. While information on these indicators, too, is difficult to obtain and is subject to some measurement problems, it does not have all of the measurement problems that plague the individual nutrient data. Perhaps, both for measurement reasons and because of their interest as ends in themselves, the returns would be greater from focusing in further research more on such health indicators than on nutrient intakes.

REFERENCES

Abdullah, M. and Wheeler, E. F. (1985) 'Seasonal Variations and the Intra-Household Distribution of Food in a Bangladeshi Village', *American Journal of Clinical Nutrition*, 41.

Abel, W. (1980) *Agricultural Fluctuations in Europe from the Thirteenth to the Twentieth Centuries*. New York: St Martin's Press.

Adbritton, E. C. (1954) *Standard Values in Nutrition and Metabolism*. Philadelphia: W. B. Saunders.

Agarwal, D. K., Upadhyay, S. K., Tripathi, A. M., and Agarwal, K. N. (1987) 'Nutritional Status, Physical Work Capacity and Mental Function in School Children', Scientific Report no. 6. New Delhi: Nutrition Foundation of India.

Akin, J. S., Griffin, C. C., Guilkey, D. K., and Popkin, B. M. (1985) 'Determinants of Infant Feeding: A Household Production Approach', *Economic Development and Cultural Change*, 34.

Alderman, H. (1987) *Cooperative Dairy Development in Karnataka, India: An Assessment*, Research Report no. 64. Washington, DC: International Food Policy Research Institute.

Anand, S. (1977) 'Aspects of Poverty in Malaysia', *Review of Income and Wealth*, 23.

—— (1983) *Inequality and Poverty in Malaysia: Measurement and Decomposition*. New York: Oxford University Press.

—— and Harris, C. J. (1985) 'Living Standards in Sri Lanka, 1973–1981/82: An Analysis of Consumer Finance Survey Data'. Mimeo, April, Oxford University.

—— —— (1987) 'Changes in Nutrition in Sri Lanka, 1978/79–1981/82'. Mimeo, September, WIDER, Helsinki.

—— —— (1990) 'Food and Standard of Living: An Analysis Based on Sri Lankan Data', in Drèze and Sen (1990).

—— —— (forthcoming) *Food, Nutrition and Standard of Living: Methodology and Applications to Sri Lanka*. Oxford: Clarendon Press.

Apfelbaum, M. (1978) 'Adaptation to Changes in Calorie Intake', *Progress in Food and Nutrition Science*, 2.

—— Bostsarron, J., and Lacatis, D. (1971) 'Effects of Calorie Restriction and Excessive Calorie Intake on Energy Expenditure', *American Journal of Clinical Nutrition*, 24.

Appleby, A. B. (1978) *Famine in Tudor and Stuart England*. Stanford, Cal.: Stanford University Press.

—— (1979a) 'Grain Prices and Subsistence Crises in England and France, 1590–1740', *Journal of Economic History*, 39.

Appleby, A. B. (1979*b*) 'Diet in Sixteenth-Century England: Sources, Problems, Possibilities', in C. Webster (ed.), *Health, Medicine and Mortality in the Sixteenth Century*. Cambridge University Press.

Ashby, J. A. (1987) 'Production and Consumption Aspects of Technology Testing in Pescador, Colombia: A Case Study'. Mimeo, Centro Internacional de Agricultura Tropical, Colombia.

Ashworth, A. (1968) 'An Investigation of Very Low Energy Intakes Reported in Jamaica', *British Journal of Nutrition*, 22.

Astrand, P-O. and Rodahl, K. (1977) *Textbook of Work Physiology*. New York: McGraw-Hill.

Atkinson, A. B. (1970) 'On the Measurement of Inequality', *Journal of Economic Theory*, 2.

Bairoch, Paul (1973) 'Agriculture and the Industrial Revolution 1700–1914', in Carlo M. Cipolla (ed.), *The Fontana Economic History of Europe: The Industrial Revolution*. London: Collins.

—— (1988) *Cities and Economic Development: From the Dawn of History to the Present*, trans. Christopher Braider. Chicago: University of Chicago Press.

Balazs, R., Lewis, P. D., and Patel, A. J. (1979) 'Nutritional Deficiencies and Brain Development', in Falkner and Tanner (1979), iii.

Barac-Nieto, M., Spurr, G. B., Maksud, M. G., and Lotero, H. (1978) 'Aerobic Capacity in Chronically Undernourished Adult Males', *Journal of Applied Physiology*, 44.

Bardhan, P. K. (1974) 'On Life and Death Questions', *Economic and Political Weekly*, Special Number, August.

Barnes, D. G. (1930) *A History of the English Corn Laws from 1660 to 1846*. London: George Routledge & Sons.

Barnicot, N. A., Bennett, F. J., Woodburn, J. C., Pilkington, T. R. E., and Antonis, A. (1972) 'Blood Pressure and Serum Cholesterol in the Hadza of Tanzania', *Human Biology*, 44.

Barnum, H. N. and Squire, L. (1979) 'An Econometric Application of the Theory of Farm-Household', *Journal of Development Economics*, 6.

Barrera, A. (1990) 'The Role of Maternal Schooling and its Interaction with Public Health Programs in Child Health Production', *Journal of Development Economics*, 32.

Barrett, D. E., Radke-Yarrow, M., and Klein, R. E. (1982) 'Chronic Malnutrition and Child Behaviour: Effects of Early Caloric Supplementation on Social and Emotional Functioning at School Age', *Development of Psychology*, 18.

Battaglia, F. C. and Simmons, M. A. (1979) 'The Low-Birth-Weight Infant', in Falkner and Tanner (1979), i.

Beaton, G. H. (1983) 'Energy in Human Nutrition', *Nutrition Today*, 18.

—— (1984) 'Adaptation to and Accommodation of Long-Term Low Energy Intake: A Commentary on the Conference on Energy Intake and Activity', in Pollitt and Amante (1984).

—— (1985) 'The Significance of Adaptation in the Definition of Nutrient Requirements and for Nutrition Policy', in Blaxter and Waterlow (1985).

—— and Ghassemi, H. (1982) 'Supplementary Feeding Programmes for Developing Countries', *American Journal of Clinical Nutrition*, suppl., 35.

Becker, G. S. (1981) *A Treatise on the Family*. Cambridge, Mass.: Harvard University Press.

Behrman, J. R. (1984) 'Sibling Deviation Estimates, Measurement Error and Biases in Estimated Returns to Schooling'. Mimeo, University of Pennsylvania.

—— (1987) 'Is Child Schooling a Poor Proxy for Child Quality?', *Demography*, 24.

—— (1988*a*) 'Nutrition, Health, Birth Order and Seasonality: Intrahousehold Allocation in Rural India', *Journal of Development Economics*, 28.

—— (1988*b*) 'Intrahousehold Allocation of Nutrients in Rural India: Are Boys Favored? Do Parents Exhibit Inequality Aversion?' *Oxford Economic Papers*, 40.

—— (1990) 'Nutrition and Health and Their Relations to Economic Growth, Poverty Alleviation, and General Development', in G. Psacharopoulos (ed.), *The Political Economy of Poverty, Equity and Growth: Cross-Country Perspectives*. Washington, DC: World Bank.

—— and Birdsall, N. (1983) 'The Quality of Schooling: Quantity Alone is Misleading', *American Economic Review*, 73.

—— —— (1985) 'The Quality of Schooling: Reply', *American Economic Review*, 75.

—— and Deolalikar, A. B. (1987) 'Will Developing Country Nutrition Improve with Income? A Case Study for Rural South India', *Journal of Political Economy*, 95.

—— —— (1988*a*) 'Health and Nutrition', in H. B. Chenery and T. N. Srinivasan (eds.), *Handbook on Development Economics*. Amsterdam: North-Holland.

—— —— (1988*b*) 'How Do Food Prices Affect Individual Nutritional and Health Status? A Latent Variable Fixed-Effects Analysis'. Mimeo, University of Pennsylvania.

—— —— (1988*c*) 'Do the Poor Really Elect to Consume so Few Calories at the Margin? Evidence from Cross-Country Estimates'. Mimeo, University of Pennsylvania.

—— —— (1989) 'Wages and Labor Supply in Rural India: The Role of Health, Nutrition and Seasonality', in Sahn (1989).

—— —— (1990) 'The Intrahousehold Demand for Nutrients in Rural South India: Individual Estimates, Fixed Effects and Permanent Income', *Journal of Human Resources*, 25.

Behrman, J. R., Deolalikar, A. B., King, E. M., Pollak, R. A., and Taubman, P. (1988) 'Intrahousehold Allocation of Nutrients in India and Malaysia: Is Bargaining Critical?' Mimeo, University of Pennsylvania.

—— and Taubman, P. (1986) 'Birth Order, Schooling and Earnings', *Journal of Labor Economics*, 4.

—— —— (1989) 'A Test of the Easterlin Fertility Model, *Demography*, 26.

—— —— (1990) 'A Comparison and Latent Variable Test of Two Fertile Ideas', *Journal of Population Economics*, 3.

—— and Wolfe, B. L. (1984a) 'More Evidence on Nutrition Demand: Income Seems Overrated and Women's Schooling Underemphasized', *Journal of Development Economics*, 14.

—— —— (1984b) 'The Socioeconomic Impact of Schooling in a Developing Country', *Review of Economics and Statistics*, 66.

—— —— (1987a) 'How Does Mother's Schooling ' Affect Family Health, Nutrition, Medical Care Usage, and Household Sanitation?' *Journal of Econometrics*, 36.

—— —— (1987b) 'Investments in Schooling in Two Generations in Pre-Revolutionary Nicaragua: The Roles of Family Background and School Supply', *Journal of Development Economics*, 27.

—— —— (1989) 'Does More Schooling Make Women Better Nourished and Healthier? Adult Sibling Random and Fixed Effects Estimates for Nicaragua', *Journal of Human Resources*, 24.

Beisel, W. R. (1977) 'Magnitude of the Host Nutritional Responses to Infection', *American Journal of Clinical Nutrition*, 30.

——, Sawyer, W. D., Ryll, E. D., and Crozier, D. (1967) 'Metabolic Effects of Intracellular Infections in Man', *Annals of Internal Medicine*, 67.

Benedict, F. G., Miles, W. R., Roth, P., and Smith, H. M. (1919) *Human Vitality and Efficiency Under Prolonged Restricted Diet*. Washington, DC: Carnegie Press.

Ben-Porath, Y. (1980) 'The F-Connection: Families, Friends, and Firms and the Organization of Exchange', *Population and Development Review*, 6.

Bernard, R.-J. (1975) 'Peasant Diet in Eighteenth-Century Gevaudan', in E. Forster and R. Forster (eds.), *European Diet from Pre-Industrial to Modern Times*. New York: Harper and Row.

Bhalla, S. (1980) 'Measurement of Poverty: Issues and Methods'. Mimeo, World Bank.

Bhaskaram, P., Satyanarayana, K., Prasad, J. S., Jagadeesan, V., Naidu, A. N., and Reddy, V. (1980) 'Effect of Growth Retardation in Early Life on Immunocompetence in Later Life,' *Indian Journal of Medical Research*, 72.

Bhuiya, A., Yojtyniak, B., D'Souza, S., and Zimicki, S. (1986) 'Socio-Economic Determinants of Child Nutritional Status: Boys versus Girls', *Food and Nutrition Bulletin*, 8.

Bielicki, T. W. *et al.* (1981) 'The Influence of Three Socioeconomic Factors on Body Height in Polish Military Conscripts', *Human Biology*, 53.

Billewicz, W. Z. and McGregor, I. A. (1982) 'A Birth-to-Maturity Longitudinal Study of Heights and Weights in Two West African [Gambian] Villages, 1951–1975', *Annals of Human Biology*, 9.

Binswanger, H. P. and Jodha, N. S. (1978) *Manual of Instructions for Economic Investigators in ICRISAT's Village Level Study*. Patancheru, Andhra Pradesh, India: ICRISAT.

Birdsall, N. (1985) 'Public Inputs and Child Schooling in Brazil', *Journal of Development Economics*, 18.

Bishop, J. (1976) 'Reporting Errors and the True Return to Schooling'. Mimeo, University of Wisconsin.

Black, R. E., Brown, K. H., and Becker, S. (1984) 'Malnutrition as a Determining Factor in Diarrhoeal Duration but not in Incidence among Young Children in a Longitudinal Study in Rural Bangladesh', *American Journal of Clinical Nutrition*, 37.

Blaxter, K. (1985) 'Energy Intake and Expenditure', in Blaxter and Waterlow (1985).

—— and Waterlow, J. C. (eds.) (1985) *Nutritional Adaptation in Man*. London: John Libbey.

Bliss, C. and Stern, N. (1978) 'Productivity, Wages and Nutrition', Parts I and II: 'The Theory', *Journal of Development Economics*, 5.

Blum, J. (1978) *The End of the Old Order in Rural Europe*. Princeton, NJ: Princeton University Press.

BMA (1933) 'British Medical Association Committee on Nutrition', *British Medical Journal*, 25 November.

Bongaarts, J. (1980) 'Does Malnutrition Affect Fecundity? A Summary of the Evidence', *Science*, no. 208.

Bourgeois-Pichat, J. (1965) 'The General Development of the Population of France since the Eighteenth Century', in D. V. Glass and D. E. C. Eversley (eds.), *Population in History: Essays in Historical Demography*. Chicago: Aldine.

Bowden, P. (1967) 'Statistical Appendix', in J. Thirsk (ed.), *The Agrarian History of England and Wales*, iv. Cambridge University Press.

—— (1985) 'Appendix III, Statistics', in J. Thirsk (ed.), *The Agrarian History of England and Wales*, v. ii. Cambridge University Press.

Bray, G. (ed.) (1978) *Recent Advances in Obesity Research, ii*. London: Newman.

Brown, K. H., Black, R. E., and Becker, S. (1982) 'Seasonal Changes in Nutritional Status and the Prevalence of Malnutrition in a Longitudical Study of Young Children in Rural Bangladesh', *American Journal of Clinical Nutrition*, 36.

Brown, S. E. (1975) 'Lower Economic Sector Female Mating Patterns in the Dominican Republic', in R. Rohrlich-Leavitt (ed.), *Women Cross-Culturally: Change and Challenge*. The Hague: Mouton.

Brozek, J. (1979) 'Behavioural Effects of Energy and Protein Deficits', NIH Publication no. 79–1906. Bethesda, Md: DHEW/National Institute of Health.

—— (1982) 'The Impact of Malnutrition on Behaviour', in Scrimshaw and Wallerstein (1982).

Burnett, J. (1979) *Plenty and Want*, 2nd ed. London: Scolar Press.

Cain, M. T. (1979) 'The Household Life Cycle and Economic Mobility in Rural Bangladesh'. Mimeo.

Caldwell, J. C. (1979) 'Education as a Factor in Mortality Decline: An Examination of Nigerian Data', *Population Studies*, 33.

Calloway, D. H. (1982) 'Functional Consequences of Malnutrition', *Reviews of Infectious Diseases*, 4.

Carrion, J. M. M. (1986) 'Estatura, Nutricion y Nivel de Vida en Murcia, 1860–1930', *Revista de Historia Economica*, 4.

Carter, A. T. (1984) 'Sex of Offspring and Fertility in South Asia: Demographic Variance and Decision Procedures in "Joint Family" Households', *Journal of Family History*, 9.

Casley, D. J. and Lury, D. A. (1981) *Data Collection in Developing Countries*. Oxford: Clarendon.

Cavalli-Sforza, L. L. and Bodmer, W. F. (1971) *The Genetics of Human Populations*. San Francisco: W. H. Freeman.

Chambers, R. (1982) 'Health, Agriculture, and Rural Poverty: Why Seasons Matter', *Journal of Development Studies*, 18.

—— (1983) 'Bad Times for Rural Children: Countering Seasonal Deprivation', *Journal of the Society for International Development*, 1.

——, Longhurst, R., and Pacey, A. (eds.) (1981) *Seasonal Dimensions to Rural Poverty*. London: Frances Pinter.

Chamla, M. C. (1964) 'L'Accroissement de la stature en France de 1880 à 1960: comparaison avec les pays d'Europe Occidentale', *Bulletin Société Anthropologie de Paris*, 11.

—— (1983) 'L'Evolution recente de la stature en Europe Occidentale (periode 1960–1980)', *Bulletin et memoire de la Société d'Anthropologie de Paris*, 13.

Chandra, R. K. (1980) *Immunology of Nutritional Disorders*. London: Edward Arnold.

—— (1982) 'Malnutrition and Infection', in Scrimshaw and Wallerstein (1982).

Chartres, J. A. (1985) 'The Marketing of Agricultural Produce', in

J. Thirsk (ed.), *The Agrarian History of England and Wales*, v. ii. Cambridge University Press.

Chase, H. C. (1969) 'Infant Mortality and Weight at Birth: 1960 United States Birth Cohort', *American Journal of Public Health*, 59.

Chase, H. P. (1976) 'Undernutrition and Growth and Development of the Human Brain', in Lloyd-Still (1976*b*).

Chavez, A. and Martinez, C. (1982) 'Growing up in a Developing Community'. Mimeo, Institute of National Nutrition, Mexico.

Chen, L. C. (1986) 'Primary Health Care in Developing Countries: Overcoming Operational, Technical and Social Barriers', *Lancet*, 29 November.

—— and Scrimshaw, N. S. (eds.) (1983) *Diarrhea and Malnutrition*. New York: Plenum Press.

——, Chowdhury, A. K. M., and Huffman, S. L. (1980) 'Anthropometric Assessment of Energy–Protein Malnutrition and Subsequent Risk of Mortality among Pre-school-aged Children', *American Journal of Clinical Nutrition*, 33.

——, Huq, E., and D'Souza, S. (1981*a*) 'Sex Bias in the Family Allocation of Food and Health Care in Rural Bangladesh', *Population and Development Review*, 7.

——, Huq, E., and Huffman, S. L. (1981*b*) 'A Prospective Study of the Risk of Diarrheal Diseases according to Nutritional Status of Children', *American Journal of Epidemiology*, 114.

—— et al. (1982) 'Malnutrition and Mortality', *Nutrition Foundation of India Bulletin*, 3.

Chittenden, R. H. (1905) *Physiological Economy in Nutrition*. London: Heinemann.

Cloud, K. (1986) 'Sex Roles in Food Production and Distribution Systems in the Sahel', in L. E. Creevey (ed.), *Women Farmers in Africa: Rural Development in Mali and the Sahel*. Syracuse, NY: Syracuse University Press.

Cole, G. D. H. and Postgate, R. (1938) *The Common People, 1746–1946*. London: Methuen, 1976.

Cole, T. J., Gilson, J. C., and Olsen, H. C. (1974) 'Bronchitis, Smoking and Obesity in an English and a Danish Town: Male Deaths after a 10-year Follow-up', *Bulletin de Physiopathologie Respiratoire*, 10.

Coleman, D. C. (1977) *The Economy of England 1450–1750*. Oxford University Press.

Crafts, N. F. R. (1980) 'Income Elasticities of Demand and the Release of Labor by Agriculture During the British Industrial Revolution'. *Journal of European Economic History*, 9.

Crafts, N. F. R. (1985) *British Economic Growth During the Industrial Revolution*. Oxford: Clarendon Press.

Cravioto, J. and Delicardie, E. R. (1979) 'Nutrition, Mental Development and Learning', in Falkner and Tanner (1979), iii.

Damon, A. (1984) 'Stature Increase among Italian-Americans: Environmental, Genetic, or Both?' *American Journal of Physical Anthropology*, 23.

Dandekar, V. (1981) 'On Measurement of Poverty', *Economic and Political Weekly*, 25 July.

—— (1982) 'On Measurement of Undernutrition', *Economic and Political Weekly*, 6 February.

—— and Rath, N. (1971) 'Poverty in India', *Economic and Political Weekly*, 2 January.

Danforth, E., Burger, A. G., Goldman, R. F., and Sims, E. A. H. (1978) 'Thermogenesis during Weight Gain', in Bray (1978).

Dasgupta, P. and Ray, D. (1990) 'Adapting to Undernourishment: The Biological Evidence and Its Implications', in Drèze and Sen (1990).

Das Gupta, M. (1987) 'Selective Discrimination against Female Children in India', *Population and Development Review*, 13.

Davenant, C. (1699) *An Essay Upon the Probable Methods of Making a People Gainers in the Ballance of Trade.* London: James Knapton.

Davidson, J. (1986) 'Cointegration in Linear Economic Systems', Discussion Paper in Econometrics, London School of Economics and Political Science.

Davies, C. T. M. (1973a) 'Physiological Responses to Exercise in East African Children', *Journal of Tropical Pediatric and Environmental Child Health*, 19.

—— (1973b) 'Relationship of Maximum Aerobic Power Output to Productivity and Absenteeism of East African Sugarcane Workers', *British Journal of Industrial Medicine*, 30.

Dawkins, R. (1982) *The Extended Phenotype.* Oxford University Press.

DDH/INCAP (1975) 'Nutrition, Growth and Development', *Boletin Oficina Sanitaria Panamericana*, 78.

De Maeyer, E. M. (1976) 'Protein–Energy Malnutrition', in G. H. Beaton and J. M. Bengoa (eds.), *Nutrition in Preventive Medicine.* Geneva: World Health Organization.

Deane, P. and Cole, W. A. (1969) *British Economic Growth*, 2nd edn. Cambridge University Press.

Deaton, A. (1981) 'Three Essays on a Sri Lanka Household Survey', LSMS Working Paper no. 11. Washington, DC: World Bank.

—— (1987) 'The Allocation of Goods within the Household: Adults, Children and Gender'. Mimeo, Princeton University.

Deolalikar, A. B. (1988) 'Do Health and Nutrition Influence Labor Productivity in Agriculture? Econometric Estimates for Rural South India', *Review of Economics and Statistics*, 70.

Desai, I. D. *et al.* (1984) 'Marginal Malnutrition and Reduced Physical Work Capacity of Migrant Adolescent Boys in Southern Brazil', *American Journal of Clinical Nutrition*, 40.

Dey, J. (1981) 'Gambian Women: Unequal Partners in Rice Development Projects?' *Journal of Development Studies*, 17.

Dowler, E. A., Payne, P. R., Seo, Y. O., Thomson, A. M., and Wheeler, E. F. (1982) 'Nutritional Status Indicators: Interpretation and Policy Making Role', *Food Policy*, 7.

—— and Seo, Y. O. (1985) 'Assessment of Energy Intake: Estimates of Food Supply vs Measurement of Consumption', *Food Policy*, 10.

Drèze, J. and Sen, A. K. (1990) *The Political Economy of Hunger: Vol. I.* Oxford: Clarendon Press.

Drummond, J. C. and Wilbraham, A. (1958) *The Englishman's Food: A History of Five Centuries of English Diet*, 2nd edn. London: Jonathan Cape.

Dugdale, A. E. (1985) 'Family Anthropometry: A New Strategy for Determining Community Nutrition', *Lancet*, 21 September.

—— and Eaton-Evans, J. (1985) 'The Seasonality of Infant Growth in Brisbane, Queensland, Australia', Human Nutrition Research Group Working Paper, Department of Child Health, University of Queensland.

—— and Payne, P. R. (1987) 'A Model of Seasonal Changes in Energy Balance', *Ecology of Food and Nutrition*, 19.

Durnin, J. V. G. A. (1979) 'Energy Balance in Man with Particular Reference to Low Intakes', *Bibliotheca Nutritio et Dieta*, 27.

Dwyer, D. H. (1983) 'Women and Income in the Third World: Implications for Policy', International Programs Working Papers no. 18, Population Council, New York.

Dyer, C. (1983) 'English Diet in the Later Middle Ages', in T. H. Aston *et al.* (eds.), *Social Relations and Ideas: Essays in Honour of R. H. Hilton.* Cambridge University Press.

Easterlin, R. A. and Crimmins, E. M. (1985) *The Fertility Revolution: A Supply–Demand Analysis.* Chicago and London: University of Chicago Press.

Easterlin, R. A., Pollak, R. A., and Wachter, M. L. (1980) 'Towards a More General Model of Fertility Determination', in R. A. Easterlin (ed.), *Population and Economic Change in Developing Countries.* Chicago: University of Chicago Press.

Edholm, O. G., Adam, J. M., Healy, M. J. R., Wolff, H. S., Goldsmith, R., and Best, T. W. (1970) 'Food Intake and Energy Expenditure of Army Recruits', *British Journal of Nutrition*, 24.

Edmundson, W. (1977) 'Individual Variations in Work Output per Unit Energy Intake in East Java', *Ecology of Food and Nutrition*, 6.

Edmundson, W. (1979) 'Individual Variations in Basal Metabolic Rate and Mechanical Work Efficiency in East Java', *Ecology of Food and Nutrition*, 8.

—— (1980) 'Adaptation to Undernutrition: How Much Food Does Man Need?' *Social Science and Medicine*, 14D.

Engle, P. (1980) 'The Intersecting Needs of Working Women and their Young Children', Report to the Ford Foundation, New York City.

—— (1989) 'Intrahousehold Resource Allocations: Issues and Methods for Development Policy and Planning, *United Nations Nutrition Bulletin*, suppl.

Engle, R. and Granger, C. W. J. (1987) 'Co-integration and Error Correction: Representation, Estimation and Testing', *Econometrica*, 55.

Epstein, T. S. (1984) 'Even Women Have to Eat: Analysis and Policy Issues'. Mimeo, University of Sussex.

Essemer, M. (1983) 'Food Consumption and Standard of Living: Studies on Food Consumption Among Different Strata of the Swedish Population 1686–1933', Uppsala Papers in Economic History, Research Report no. 2.

—— and Morell, M. (1986) 'Changes in Swedish Nutrition since the Seventeenth Century', in Fogel (1986).

Eveleth, P. B. and Tanner, J. M. (1976) *Worldwide Variation in Human Growth*. Cambridge University Press.

Everitt, A. (1967) 'The Marketing of Agricultural Produce', in J. Thirsk (ed.), *The Agrarian History of England and Wales 1500–1640*, iv. Cambridge University Press.

Falkner, F. and Tanner, J. M. (1979) *Human Growth*, 3 vols. New York and London: Plenum Press.

FAO (1950) 'Calorie Requirements', *FAO Nutrition Studies*, no. 5.

—— (1957) 'Calorie Requirements', *FAO Nutrition Studies*, no. 15.

—— (1977) *The Fourth World Food Survey*. Rome: FAO.

—— (1978) 'Requirements for Protein and Energy: An Examination of Current Recommendations', report by a group of consultants. Rome: FAO.

—— (1985) *The Fifth World Food Survey*. Rome: FAO.

FAO/WHO (1973) *Energy and Protein Requirements*, WHO Technical Report Series no. 522 (and FAO Nutrition Meetings Report Series no. 52). Geneva: World Health Organization.

FAO/WHO/UNU (1985) *Energy and Protein Requirements*, WHO Technical Report Series no. 724. Geneva: World Health Organization.

Feldstin, H. S. (1987) 'Intra-household Dynamics and Farming Systems Research and Extension: Conceptual Framework and Worksheets'. Mimeo, Centro International de Agricultura Tropical, Colombia.

Ferro-Luzzi, A. (1985) 'Work Capacity and Productivity in Long Term Adaptation to Low Energy Intakes', in Blaxter and Waterlow (1985).

——, D'Amicis, A., Ferrini, A. M., and Mariale, G. (1979) 'Nutrition, Environment, and Physical Performance of Preschool Children in Italy', *Bibliotheca Nutrito et Dieta*, 27.

Fitt, A. B. (1924) 'The Human Energy-Rhythm through the Year', in W. A. G. Skinner (ed.), *Report of the Sixteenth Meeting of the Australian Association for the Advancement of Science*, xvi.704–42. Wellington, NZ: Government Printer.

Flatt, J. P. (1978) 'The Biochemistry of Energy Expenditure', in Bray (1978).

Flinn, M. W. (ed.) (1965) *Report on the Sanitary Condition of the Labouring Population of Britain*, by Edwin Chadwick. Edinburgh University Press.

—— (1970) *British Population Growth, 1700–1850*. London: Macmillan.

—— (1974) 'The Stabilization of Mortality in Pre-industrial Western Europe', *Journal of European Economic History*, 3.

—— (1981) *The European Demographic System, 1500–1820*. Baltimore: Johns Hopkins University Press.

—— (1982) 'The Population History of England, 1541–1871', *Economic History Review*, 35.

Floud, R. (1983) 'Inference from the Heights of Volunteer Soldiers and Sailors'. Mimeo, Birkbeck College.

—— (1984) 'The Heights of Europeans since 1750: A New Source for European Economic History', Working Paper Series no. 1318, National Bureau of Economic Research, Cambridge, Mass.

—— (1986) 'Science, Medicine and the Community: A Case of Slow Diffusion', in A. Briggs and J. Shelley (eds.), *Science, Medicine and the Community: The Last One Hundred Years*. Amsterdam: Elsevier.

—— (1989) 'Measuring European Inequality: The Use of Height Data', in J. Fox (ed.), *Health Inequalities in European Countries*. Aldershot: Gower.

—— and Wachter, K. W. (1982) 'Poverty and Physical Stature: Evidence on the Standard of Living of London Boys, 1770–1870', *Social Science History*, 6.

——, Gregory, A., and Wachter, K. W. (1990) *Height, Health and History: Nutritional Status in the United Kingdom, 1750–1980*. Cambridge University Press.

Fogel, R. W. (1986*a*) 'Nutrition and the Decline in Mortality Since 1700: Some Preliminary Findings', in S. L. Engerman and R. E. Gallman (eds.), *Long-Term Factors in American Economic Growth*. Chicago: University of Chicago Press for NBER.

Fogel, R. W. (ed.) (1986*b*) *Long-Term Changes in Nutrition and the Standard of Living*. Berne: 9th Congress of the International Economic History Association.

Fogel, R. W. (1986c) 'Nutrition and the Decline in Mortality Since 1700: Some Additional Preliminary Findings', Working Paper no. 1802, National Bureau of Economic Research, Cambridge, Mass.

—— (1987) 'Biomedical Approaches to the Estimation and Interpretation of Secular Trends in Labor Productivity, Equity, Morbidity, and Mortality in Western Europe and America, 1780-1980'. Unpublished paper, University of Chicago.

—— (1989) *Without Consent and Contract: The Rise and Fall of American Slavery*. New York: W. W. Norton.

—— (1991a) 'New Sources and New Techniques for the Study of Secular Trends in Nutritional Status, Health, Mortality, and the Process of Aging', Historical Working Paper Series no. 26. Cambridge, Mass.: National Bureau of Economic Research.

—— (1991b) 'The Conquest of High Mortality and Hunger in Europe and America: Timing and Mechanisms', in D. Landes, P. Higgonet and H. Rosovsky (eds.), *Technological Constraints and Entrepreneurial Responses: Essays in Modern and Contemporary History*. Cambridge, Mass.: Harvard University Press.

—— and Engerman, S. L. (1974) *Time on the Cross*, 2 vols. Boston: Little Brown.

——et al. (1983) 'Secular Changes in American and British Stature and Nutrition', *Journal of Interdisciplinary History*, 14.

—— and Floud, R. (1991)'Nutrition and Mortality in France, Britain, and the United States, 1700–1938' (typescript). Chicago: University of Chicago.

——, Galantine, R. A., and Manning, R. L. (1992) *Without Consent or Contract: The Rise and Fall of American Slavery—Evidence and Methods*. New York: W. W. Norton.

——, Pope, C. L., Preston, S. H., Scrimshaw, N., Temin, P., and Wimmer, L. T. (1986) 'The Aging of Union Army Men: A Longitudinal Study, 1830–1940'. Unpublished paper, NBER.

Folbre, N. (1984a) 'Household Production in the Philippines: A Non-neoclassical Approach', *Economic Development and Cultural Change*, 32.

—— (1984b) 'Market Opportunities, Genetic Endowments, and Intra-family Resource Distribution: Comment', *American Economic Review*, 74.

—— (1986) 'Cleaning House: New Perspectives on Households and Economic Development', *Journal of Development Economics*, 22.

Foreign Office Commission (1985) *Famine in Africa*. London: HMSO.

Foster, J., Greer, J., and Thorbecke, E. (1984) 'A Class of Decomposable Poverty Measures', *Econometrica*, 52.

Freudenberger, H. and Cummings, G. (1976) 'Health, Work and Leisure Before the Industrial Revolution', *Explorations in Economic History*, 13.

Friedman, G. C. (1980) 'The Heights of Slaves in Trinidad', *Social Science History*, 6.

Frijhoff, W. and Julia, D. (1979) 'The Diet in Boarding Schools at the End of the Ancien Regime', in R. Foster and O. Ranum (eds.), *Food and Drink in History: Selections from the Annales, Economies, Societies, Civilisations*. Baltimore and London: Johns Hopkins University Press.

Frisancho, A. R., Sanchez, J., Pallerdel, D., and Yanez, L. (1973) 'Adaptive Significance of Small Body Size Under Poor Socio-economic Conditions in Southern Peru', *American Journal of Physical Anthropology*, 39.

Fuller, B., Gorman, K., and Edwards, J. (1986) 'School Quality and Economic Growth in Mexico', in S. P. Heyneman and D. S. White (eds.), *The Quality of Education and Economic Development*. Washington, DC: World Bank.

Garby, L. (1987) 'Metabolic Adaptation to Decrease in Energy Intake Due to Changes in the Energy Cost of Low Energy Expenditure Regimen'. Mimeo, FAO.

—— and Lammert, O. (1984) 'Within-subjects Between-days-and-weeks Variation in Energy Expenditure at Rest', *Human Nutrition: Clinical Nutrition*, 38C.

—— —— and Nielsen, E. (1984) 'Within-subjects Between-weeks Variation in 24-hours Energy Expenditure for Fixed Physical Activity', *Human Nutrition: Clinical Nutrition*, 38C.

Garcia, M. and Pinstrup-Andersen, P. (1987) 'The Pilot Food Price Subsidy Scheme in the Philippines: Impact on Incomes, Food Consumption, and Nutritional Status'. Mimeo, International Food Policy Research Institute, Washington, DC.

Garrow, J. S. (1978a) *Energy Balance and Obesity in Man*, 2nd edn. Amsterdam/New York: Elsevier.

—— (1978b) 'The Regulation of Energy Expenditure in Man', in Bray (1978).

Ghesquiere, J. L. A. (1972) 'Physical Development and Working Capacity of Congolese', in D. J. M. Vorster (ed.), *Human Biology of Environmental Change*. London: International Biological Programme.

Girardier, L. and Stock, M. J. (1983) *Mammalian Thermogenesis*. London: Chapman and Hall.

Gittinger, J. P., Leslie, J., and Hoisington, D. (1985) *Food Policy: Integrating Supply, Distribution and Consumption*. Washington, DC: World Bank.

Goldstein, W. (1971) 'Factors Influencing the Height of Seven-Year-Old Children: Results from the National Child Development Study', *Human Biology*, 43.

Goldstein, W. and Tanner, J. M. (1980) 'Ecological Considerations in the Creation and the Use of Child Growth Standards', *Lancet*, 15 March.

Gomez, F. *et al.* (1956) 'Mortality in Second and Third Degree Malnutrition', *Journal of Tropical Paediatrics*, 2.

Gopalan, C. (1955) 'Clinical Aspects and Treatment', in J. C. Waterlow (ed.), *Protein Malnutrition*. Rome: FAO.

—— (1978) 'Adaptation to Low Calorie and Low Protein Intake: Does it Exist?' in Margen and Ogar (1978).

—— (1983*a*) 'Measurement of Undernutrition: Biological Considerations', *Nutrition Foundation of India Bulletin*, 4.

—— (1983*b*) ' "Small is Healthy?" for the Poor, Not for the Rich', *Nutrition Foundation of India Bulletin*, 4; also reprinted in *Future*, Autumn 1983 (page references relate to the reprint).

—— (1984) 'Classification of Undernutrition: Their Limitations and Fallacies', *Nutrition Foundation of India Bulletin*, 5.

—— (1989) 'Growth Standards for Indian Children', *Nutrition Foundation of India Bulletin*, 10.

——, Sastry, B. V. R., and Balasubramanian, S. C. (1971) *Nutritive Value of Indian Foods*. Hyderabad, India: National Institute of Nutrition.

——, Swaminathan, M. C., Kumar, K. K., Hanumantha Rao, D., and Vijayaraghavan, K. (1973) 'Effect of Calorie Supplementation on Growth of Undernourished Children', *American Journal of Clinical Nutrition*, 26.

Goubert, P. (1960) *Beauvais et le Beauvaisis de 1600 à 1730*. Paris: SEVPEN.

—— (1973) *The Ancien Régime*. New York: Harper and Row.

Gould, B. A. (1869) *Investigations in the Military and Anthropological Statistics of American Soldiers*. Cambridge, Mass.: Riverside Press.

Grande, F. (1964) 'Man Under Calorie Deficiency', in D. Dill *et al.* (eds.), *Handbook of Physiology*, Sect. 4: *Adaptation to the Environment*. Washington, DC: American Physiological Society.

——, Anderson, J. T. and Keys, A. (1958) 'Changes of Basal Metabolic Rate in Man in Starvation and Refeeding', *Journal of Applied Physiology*, 12.

Grantham-McGregor, A. (1984) 'The Social Background of Childhood Malnutrition', in J. Brozek and B. Schurch (eds.), *Malnutrition and Behaviour: Critical Assessment of Key Issues*. Lausanne: Nestle Foundation.

Gras, N. S. B. (1915) *The Evolution of the English Corn Market from the Twelfth to the Eighteenth Century (Harvard Economic Studies, xiii)*. Cambridge, Mass.: Harvard University Press.

Greene, L. S. and Johnston, F. E. (eds.) (1980) *Social and Biological Predictors of Nutritional Status, Physical Growth, and Neurological Development*. New York: Academic Press.

Greenhalgh, S. (1985) 'Sexual Stratification: The Other Side of "Growth with Equity" in East Asia', *Population and Development Review*, 11.

Greer, J. and Thorbecke, E. (1984) 'Pattern of Food Consumption and Poverty in Kenya and Effects of Food Prices'. Mimeo, Cornell University.

Grigg, D. (1982) *The Dynamics of Agricultural Change: The Historical Experience*. New York: St Martin's Press.

Griliches, Z. (1979) 'Sibling Models and Data in Economics: Beginnings of a Survey', *Journal of Political Economy*, 87.

Guyer, J. I. (1980) 'Household Budgets and Women's Income', African Studies Center Working Paper no. 28, Boston University.

—— (1982) 'Dynamic Approaches to Domestic Budgeting: Cases and Methods from Africa', in D. Dwyer and J. Bruce (eds.), *A Home Divided: Women and Income in the Third World*. Stanford, Cal.: Stanford University Press.

—— (1986) 'Intra-Household Processes and Farming Systems Research: Perspectives from Anthropology', in J. L. Moock (ed.), *Understanding Africa's Rural Households and Farming Systems*. Boulder, Colo., and London: Westview Press.

Habicht, J. P., Martorell, R., Yarbrough, C., Malina, R. M., and Klein, R. E. (1974) 'Height and Weight Standards for Pre-school Children: How Relevant are Ethnic Differences in Growth Potential?' *Lancet*, 7 April.

Hadar, J. and Russell, W. R. (1969) 'Rules for Ordering Uncertain Prospects', *American Economic Review*, 59.

Hansson, J. E. (1965) 'The Relationship between Individual Characteristics of the Worker and Output of Logging Operations', Studia Forestalia Suecia no. 29, Skogshogskolan, Stockholm.

Hanumantha Rao, D. and Sastry, G. (1977) 'Growth Pattern of Well-to-do Indian Adolescents and Young Adults', *Indian Journal of Medical Research*, 66.

Harper, A. E. (1985) 'Origin of Recommended Dietary Allowances: An Historic Overview', *American Journal of Clinical Nutrition*, 41.

Harriss, B. (1990) 'The Intrafamily Distribution of Hunger in South Asia', in Drèze and Sen (1990).

Heckscher, E. F. (1954) *An Economic History of Sweden*, trans. G. Ohlin. Cambridge, Mass.: Harvard University Press.

Hegsted, D. M. (1974) 'Energy Needs and Energy Utilisation', *Nutrition Reviews*, 32.

Helleiner, K. F. (1967) 'The Population of Europe from the Black Death to the Eve of the Vital Revolution', in E. E. Rich and C. H. Wilson (eds.), *The Cambridge Economic History of Europe*, iv. *The Econ-*

omy of Expanding Europe in the Sixteenth and Seventeenth Centuries. Cambridge University Press.

Heller, P. S. and Drake, W. D. (1979) 'Malnutrition, Child Morbidity and the Family Decision Process', *Journal of Development Economics*, 6.

Heyneman, S. P. and Loxley, W. (1983) 'The Effects of Primary School Quality on Academic Achievement Across 29 High and Low Income Countries', *American Journal of Sociology*, 88.

—— and White, D. S. (1986) *The Quality of Education and Economic Development*. Washington, DC: World Bank.

Heywood, P. F. (1983) 'Growth and Nutrition in Papua New Guinea', *Journal of Human Evolution*, 12.

—— (1986) 'Nutritional Status as a Risk Factor for Mortality in Children in the Highlands of Papua New Guinea', *Proceedings of the XIII International Congress of Nutrition*. London and Paris: John Libbey.

Hiernaux, J. (1965) 'Hérédité, milieu et morphologie', *Biotypologie*, 26.

Himmelfarb, G. (1983) *The Idea of Poverty: England in the Early Industrial Age*. New York: Random House.

Holderness, B. A. (1976) *Pre-Industrial England: Economy and Society, 1500–1750*. London: J. M. Dent.

Horton, S. (1984) 'Nutritional Status and Living Standards Measurement'. Mimeo, Washington, DC: The World Bank.

—— (1985) 'The Determinants of Nutrient Intake: Results from Western India', *Journal of Development Economics*, 19.

—— (1986) 'Child Nutrition and Family Size in the Philippines', *Journal of Development Economics*, 23.

—— (1988) 'Birth Order and Child Nutritional Status: Evidence on the Intrahousehold Allocation of Resources in the Philippines', *Economic Development and Cultural Change*, 36.

—— and Claquin, P. (1983) 'Cost-Effectiveness and User Characteristics of Clinic-Based Services for the Treatment of Diarrhea: A Case Study in Bangladesh', *Social Science and Medicine*, 17.

—— and Miller, B. D. (1989) 'The Effect of Gender of Household Head on Expenditure: Evidence from Low Income Households in Jamaica'. Mimeo.

—— and Taylor, L. (1986) 'Food Subsidies in Developing Countries: Theory, Practice and Policy Lessons'. Mimeo, Massachusetts Institute of Technology.

Hoskins, W. G. (1964) 'Harvest Fluctuations and English Economic History, 1480–1619', *Agricultural History Review*, 12.

—— (1968) 'Harvest Fluctuations and English Economic History, 1620–1759', *Agricultural History Review*, 16.

Hufton, O. H. (1974) *The Poor of Eighteenth-Century France*. Oxford: Clarendon Press.

—— (1983) 'Social Conflict and the Grain Supply in Eighteenth-Century France', *Journal of Interdisciplinary History*, 14.

ICMR (1981) *Recommended Dietary Intakes for Indians*. New Delhi: Indian Council of Medical Research.

Illsley, R. (1955) 'Social Class Selection and Class Differences in Relation to Still Births and Infant Deaths', *British Medical Journal*, 2.

Italy (1978) *Historical Statistics of Italy, 1861–1965*. Rome: Office of the Census.

Iyengar, N. S., Jain, L. R., and Srinivasan, T. N. (1968) 'Economies of Scale in Household Consumption: A Case Study', *Indian Economic Journal*, 15.

James, W. P. T. (1985) 'Appetite Control and Other Mechanisms of Weight Homeostasis', in Blaxter and Waterlow (1985).

—— and Shetty, P. S. (1982) 'Metabolic Adaptation and Energy Requirements in Developing Countries', *Human Nutrition: Clinical Nutrition*, 32C.

Jamison, D. T. (1986) 'Child Malnutrition and School Performance in China', *Journal of Development Economics*, 20.

Jaya Rao, K. S. (1986) 'Perpetuating Undernutrition', *Economic and Political Weekly*, 14 June.

Jelliffe, D. B. (1966) *The Assessment of the Nutritional Status of the Community*. Geneva: World Health Organization.

Jones, C. (1983) 'The Mobilization of Women's Labor for Cash Crop Production: A Game-Theoretic Approach', *American Journal of Agricultural Economics*, 65.

—— (1986) 'Intra-Household Bargaining in Response to the Introduction of New Crops: A Case Study from North Cameroon', in J. L. Moock (ed.), *Understanding Africa's Rural Households and Farming Systems*. Boulder, Colo., and London: Westview Press.

Jones, E. L. (ed.) (1967) *Agriculture and Economic Growth in England 1650–1815*. London: Methuen.

Jordan, W. K. (1959) *Philanthropy in England 1480–1660*. London: George Allen & Unwin.

Kakwani, N. (1984) 'Welfare Ranking of Income Distributions', in R. L. Basmann and G. F. Rhodes Jr. (eds.), *Advances in Econometrics*, iii. Greenwich, Conn.: JAI Press.

—— (1986) 'Is Sex Bias Significant?' Working Paper no. 8, World Institute for Development Economics Research, Helsinki.

—— (1988) 'On Measuring Undernutrition', *Oxford Economic Papers*, 40.

Kaplan, S. L. (1976) *Bread, Politics and Political Economy in the Reign of Louis XV*. The Hague: Martinus Nijhoff.

Kerridge, E. (1968) *The Agricultural Revolution.* New York: Augustus M. Kelley.

Keys, A. (1980) 'Overweight, Obesity, Coronary Heart Disease and Mortality', *Nutrition Reviews,* 38.

——, Brozek, J., Henschel, A., Mickelson, O., and Taylor, H. L. (1950) *The Biology of Human Starvation.* Minneapolis: University of Minnesota Press.

Khan, Q. M. (1984) 'The Impact of Household Endowment Constraints on Nutrition and Health: A Simultaneous Equation Test of Human Capital Divestment', *Journal of Development Economics,* 15.

Kielmann, A. A. and McCord, C. (1978) 'Weight-for-Age as an Index of Risk of Death in Children', *Lancet,* 10 June.

Kiil, V. (1939) 'Stature and Growth of Norwegian Men during the Past 220 Years', *Skrifter av det Norske Videnskaps-Akademie,* 6.

King, E. M. (1978) 'Time Allocation and Home Production in Rural Philippine Households', *Philippine Economic Journal,* 17.

—— (1980) 'Nutrition, Work and Demographic Behaviour in Rural Philippine Households: A Synopsis of Several Laguna Household Studies', in H. Binswanger et al. (eds.), *Rural Household Studies in Asia.* Singapore: Agricultural Development Council/Singapore University Press.

—— (1983) 'Time Allocation and Home Production in Philippine Rural Households', in M. Buvinic *et al.* (eds.), *Women and Poverty in the Third World.* Baltimore: Johns Hopkins University Press.

King, G. (1973) 'Natural and Political Observations and Conclusions upon the State and Condition of England in 1696', in Laslett (1973).

Klein, R. E. (1979) 'Malnutrition and Human Behaviour: A Backward Glance at an Ongoing Longitudinal Study', in D. A. Levitsky (ed.), *Malnutrition, Environment and Behaviour.* Ithaca: Cornell University Press.

——, Habicht, J. P. and Yarbrough, C. (1971) 'Effects of Protein–Calorie Malnutrition on Mental Development', *Advances in Paediatrics,* 18.

Knight, I. and Eldridge, J. (1984) *The Heights and Weights of Adults in Great Britain.* London: HMSO, for the Office of Population Censuses and Surveys and the Department of Health and Social Security.

Knudsen, O. K. and Scandizzo, P. L. (1979) 'Nutrition and Food Needs in Developing Countries', Staff Working Paper no. 328, World Bank.

Koenker, R. (1977) 'Was Bread Giffen? The Demand for Food in England circa 1790', *Review of Economics and Statistics,* 49.

Komlos, J. (1985) 'Stature and Nutrition in the Habsburg Monarchy: The Standard of Living and Economic Development', *American Historical Review,* 90.

—— (1988) 'The Food Budget of English Workers: A Comment on Shammas', *Journal of Economic History,* 48.

—— (1990) 'Stature, Nutrition and the Economy in the Eighteenth-Century Habsburg Monarchy'. Unpublished Ph.D. thesis, University of Chicago.

Krishnaji, N. (1981) 'On Measuring the Incidence of Undernutrition: A Note on Sukhatme's Procedure', *Economic and Political Weekly*, 30 May.

Kumar, B. G. (1987) 'Poverty and Public Policy: Government Interventions and Levels of Living in Kerala, India'. Unpublished doctoral dissertation, Oxford University.

Kumar, S. (1979) *Impact of Subsidized Rice on Food Consumption and Nutrition in Kerala*. Washington, DC: International Food Policy Research Institute.

—— (1987) 'The Nutrition Situation and its Food Policy Links', in J. Mellor, C. Delgado and M. Blackie (eds.), *Accelerating Food Production in Sub-Saharan Africa*. Baltimore: Johns Hopkins University Press.

Lancet (1984) 'A Measure of Agreement on Growth Standard', (editorial), *Lancet*, 21 January.

Langsten, R. (1987) 'Determinants of High Female Mortality in South Asia: Are the Data Consistent with Theory?' Mimeo, American University, Cairo.

Laslett, P. (ed.) (1973) *The Earliest Classics: John Graunt and Gregory King*. Farnborough, Hants: Gregg International.

—— (1984) *The World We Have Lost: England before the Industrial Age*, 3rd ed. New York: Scribner.

Lau, L. J., Lin, W.-L., and Yotopoulos, P. A. (1978) 'The Linear Logarithmic Expenditure System: An Application to Consumption–Leisure Choice', *Econometrica*, 46.

Laurence, M., Lamb, M. H., Lawrence, F., and Whitehead, R. G. (1984) 'Maintenance Energy Cost of Pregnancy in Rural Gambian Women and Influence of Dietary Status', *Lancet*, 18 August.

Le Brun, F. (1971) *Les Hommes et la mort en Anjou aux 17e et 18e siècles*. Paris: Mouton.

Lee, R. (1981) 'Short-Term Variation: Vital Rates, Prices and Weather', in E. A. Wrigley and R. S. Schofield (eds.), *The Population History of England, 1541–1871: A Reconstruction*. Cambridge, Mass.: Harvard University Press.

Leibenstein, H. A. (1957) *Economic Backwardness and Economic Growth*. New York: John Wiley.

Leonard, E. M. (1965) *The Early History of English Poor Relief*. New York: Barnes & Noble.

Leslie, J., Lycelle, M., and Buvinic, M. (1986) 'Weathering Economic Crisis: The Crucial Role of Women in Health'. Mimeo, International Center for Research on Women, Washington, DC.

Lewis, M. A. (1986) 'Postneonatal Mortality: The Importance of Intra-household Resource Allocations and Gender in Jordan'. Mimeo, The Urban Institute, Washington, DC.

Lindert, P. H. (1980) 'English Occupations, 1670–1811', *Journal of Economics History*, 40.

—— (1983) 'English Living Standards, Population Growth, and Wrigley–Schofield', *Explorations in Economic History*, 20.

—— (1985) 'English Population, Wages, and Prices, 1541–1913', *Journal of Interdisciplinary History*, 15.

—— and Williamson, J. G. (1982) 'Revising Britain's Social Tables, 1688–1812', *Explorations in Economic History*, 20.

Lindgren, G. (1976) 'Height, Weight and Menarche in Swedish Urban School Children in Relation to Socio-Economic and Regional Factors', *Annals of Human Biology*, 3.

Lipson, E. (1971) *The Economic History of England*, ii and iii. *The Age of Mercantilism*. London: Adam and Charles Black.

Lipton, M. (1983) 'Poverty, Undernutrition and Hunger', Staff Working Paper no. 597. Washington, DC: World Bank.

—— (1988) 'The Poor and the Poorest: Some Interim Findings', Discussion Papers no. 25. Washington, DC: World Bank.

Lloyd-Still, J. D. (1976a) 'Clinical Studies on the Effects of Malnutrition during Infancy on Subsequent Physical and Intellectual Development', in Lloyd-Still (1976b).

—— (ed.) (1976b) *Malnutrition and Intellectual Development*. Lancaster (UK): MTP Press.

Longhurst, R. and Payne, P. (1981) 'Seasonal Aspects of Nutrition', in Chambers *et al.* (1981).

Lusk, G. (1906) *The Science of Nutrition*. Philadelphia and London: W. B. Saunders.

Maclachlan, M. D. (1983) *Why They Did Not Starve: Biocultural Adaptation in a South Indian Village*. Philadelphia: Institute for the Study of Human Issues.

Magnani, R. J., Clay, D. C., Adlakha, A. L., and Tourkin, S. C. (1985) 'Breastfeeding, Water/Sanitation, and Childhood Nutrition in the Philippines'. Mimeo, US Bureau of Census.

Makinson, C. (1986) 'Sex Differentials in Infant and Child Mortality in Egypt'. Mimeo, Princeton University.

Mann, G. V., Roels, O. A., Price, D. L., and Merril, J. M. (1962) 'Cardiovascular Disease in African Pygmies', *Journal of Chronic Diseases*, 15.

Manser, M. and Brown, M. (1980) 'Marriage and Household Decision-Making: A Bargaining Analysis', *International Economic Review*, 21.

Margen, S. and Ogar, R. A. (eds.) (1978) *Progress in Human Nutrition*, ii. Westport, Conn.: AVI Publishing.

Marmot, M. G., Shipley, M. J., and Rose, R. (1984) 'Inequalities of Death: Specific Explanations of a General Pattern', *Lancet*, 5 May.

Marshall, J. D. (1968) *The Old Poor Law, 1795–1834*. London: Macmillan.

Martorell, R. (1979) 'Responses to Chronic Protein–Energy Malnutrition: Adaptation or Malady?' Paper presented to the 48th Annual Meeting of the American Association of Physical Anthropologists, San Francisco.

—— (1980) 'Interrelationships between Diet, Infectious Disease, and Nutritional Status', in Greene and Johnston (1980).

—— (1984) 'Genetics, Environment and Growth: Issues in the Assessment of Nutritional Status', in A. Velazaques and H. Bourges (eds.), *Genetic Factors in Nutrition*. New York: Academic Press.

—— (1985) 'Child Growth Retardation: A Discussion of its Causes and its Relationship to Health', in Blaxter and Waterlow (1985).

—— and Ho, T. J. (1984) 'Malnutrition, Morbidity and Mortality', *Population and Development Review*, 10, Suppl.

——, Lechtig, A., Yarbrough, C., Delgado, H., and Klein, R. E. (1978) 'Small Stature in Developing Countries: Its Causes and Consequences', in Margen and Ogar (1978).

——, Klein, R. E., and Delgado, H. (1980) 'Improved Nutrition and its Effects on Anthropometric Indicators of Nutritional Status', *Nutrition Reports International*, 21.

——, Delgado, H. L., Valverde, V., and Klein, R. E. (1981) 'Maternal Stature, Fertility and Infant Mortality', *Human Biology*, 53.

Mazumdar, D. (1959) 'The Marginal Productivity Theory of Wages and Disguised Unemployment', *Review of Economic Studies*, 26.

McCance, R. A. and Widdowson, E. M. (1967) *The Composition of Foods*, Medical Research Council Special Report Series no. 297. London: HMSO.

McElroy, M. B. and Horney, M. J. (1981) 'Nash-Bargained Household Decisions: Toward a Generalization of the Theory of Demand', *International Economic Review*, 22.

McLaren, D. S. (1974) 'The Great Protein Fiasco', *Lancet*, 2 November.

McNeill, G. (1986) 'Patterns of Adult Energy Nutrition in a South Indian Village'. Unpublished Ph.D. thesis, University of London.

—— and Payne, P. R. (1985) 'Energy Expenditure of Pregnant and Lactating Women', *Lancet*, 30 November.

——, Rivers, J. P. W., Payne, P. R., de Britto, J. J., and Abel, R. (1987) 'Basal Metabolic Rate of Indian Men: No Evidence of Metabolic Adaptation to a Low Plane of Nutrition', *Nutrition Research*, 41C.

Medical Research Institute (MRI) (1972) 'Food Value Tables'. Mimeo, MRI, Colombo, Sri Lanka.

Mehta, J. (1982) 'Nutritional Norms and Measurement of Malnourishment and Poverty', *Economic and Political Weekly*, 14 August.

Mellor, J. W. and Gavian, S. (1987) 'Famine: Causes, Preventation, and Relief ', *Science*, no. 235.

Menken, J., Trussell, J., and Watkins, S. (1981) 'The Nutrition Fertility Link: An Evaluation of the Evidence', *Journal of Interdisciplinary History*, 11.

Merimee, T. J., Zarf, J., Hewlett, B., and Cavalli-Sforza, L. L. (1987) 'Insulin-like Growth Factors in Pygmies: the Role of Puberty in Determining Final Stature', *New England Journal of Medicine*, no. 316.

Meuvret, J. (1965) 'Demographic Crisis in France from the Sixteenth to the Eighteenth Century', in D. V. Glass and D. E. C. Eversly (eds.), *Population in History: Essays in Historical Demography*. London: Edward Arnold.

Meerton, N. A. von (1989) 'Croissance economic en France et accroissement des français: une analyse "Villermetrique" ', (typescript). Leuven: Center voor Economische Studiën.

Miller, B. D. (1981) *The Endangered Sex: Neglect of Female Children in Rural North India*. Ithaca, NY: Cornell University Press.

Miller, D. S. (1975) 'Thermogenesis in Everyday Life', in E. Jequier (ed.), *Regulation of Energy Balance in Man*. Geneva: Medicine & Hygiene.

—— , Mumford, P., and Stock, M. J. (1967) 'Gluttony, 2: Thermogenesis in Overeating Man', *American Journal of Clinical Nutrition*, 20.

Milligan, L. P. and Summers, M. (1986) 'The Biological Basis of Maintenance and its Relevance to Assessing Responses to Nutrients', *Proceedings of the Nutrition Society*, 45.

Mitchell, B. R. and Deane, P. (1962) *Abstract of British Historical Statistics*. Cambridge University Press.

Mokyr, J. (1985) *Why Ireland Starved: A Quantitative and Analytical History of the Irish Economy, 1800–1850*. London: George Allen & Unwin.

Moock, P. R. and Leslie, J. (1986) 'Childhood Malnutrition and Schooling in the Terai Region of Nepal', *Journal of Development Economics*, 19.

Morowitz, H. J. (1978) *Foundations of Bioenergetics*. New York: Academic Press.

Morris, M. D. (1979) *Measuring the Condition of the World's Poor: The Physical Quality of Life Index*. New York: Pergamon Press for the Overseas Development Council.

Mueller, W. H. (1986) 'The Genetics of Size and Shape in Children and Adults', in F. Falkner and J. M. Tanner (eds.), *Human Growth*, iii. *Methodology*, 2nd ed. New York: Plenum.

Munro, H. N. (1985) 'Historical Perspective on Protein Requirements: Objectives for the Future', in Blaxter and Waterlow (1985).

Murty, K. N. and Radhakrishna, R. (1981) 'Agricultural Prices, Income Distribution and Demand Patterns in a Low-Income Country', in R. E. Kalman and J. Martinez (eds.), *Computer Applications in Food Production and Agricultural Engineering*. Amsterdam: North-Holland.

Narayana, N. S., Parikh, K. S., and Srinivasan, T. N. (1988) 'Indian Agricultural Policy: An Applied General Equilibrium Model', *Journal of Policy Modeling*, 10. 527–58.

National Nutrition Monitoring Bureau (1980) *Report on Urban Populations, 1975–1979*. Hyderabad: National Institute of Nutrition.

National Sample Survey (1976) *Calorie and Protein Values of Food Items Consumed per Diem per Consumer Unit in Rural Areas*, i. New Delhi: National Sample Survey Organization.

Netherlands (annual) *Statistical Yearbook of the Netherlands*. The Hague.

Neumann, R. O. (1902) 'Experimentalle Beigrage zur Lehre von dem täglichen Nahrungsbedarf des Menschen unter besonder Berucksichtigung der notwendigen Eiweissmenge', *Archives of Hygiene*, 36.

Norgan, N. G. (1983) 'Adaptation of Energy Metabolism to Level of Energy Intake', in J. Parizkova (ed.), *Energy Expenditure under Field Conditions*. Prague: Charles University.

—— and Durnin, J. V. G. A. (1980) 'The Effect of 6 Weeks of Overfeeding on the Bodyweight, Body Composition and Energy Metabolism of Young Men', *American Journal of Clinical Nutrition*, 33.

Norway (annual) *Statistical Arbok*. Oslo.

Nylin, G. (1929) 'Periodical Variations in Growth, Standard Metabolism and Oxygen Capacity of the Blood in Children', *Acta Medica Scandinavia Supplementum*, 31.

O'Brien, P. and Keyder, C. (1978) *Economic Growth in Britain and France 1780–1914: Two Paths to the Twentieth Century*. London: George Allen & Unwin.

Ojha, P. D. (1970) 'A Configuration of Indian Poverty', *Reserve Bank of India Bulletin*, 24.

Okali, C. and Sumberg, J. E. (1986) 'Examining Divergent Strategies in Farming Systems Research', *Agricultural Administration*, 22.

Orr, J. B. and Clark, M. L. (1930) 'A Report on Seasonal Variation in the Growth of School Children', *Lancet*, 16 August.

Osmani, S. R. (1987) 'Controversies in Nutrition and their Implications for the Economics of Food', Working Paper no. 16, WIDER, Helsinki.

—— (1990) 'Nutrition and the Economics of Food: Implications of Some Recent Controversies', in Drèze and Sen (1990).

Pacey, A. and Payne, P. (eds.) (1985) *Agricultural Development and Nutrition*. London: Hutchinson Press.

Palmer, C. E. (1933) 'Seasonal Variation of Average Growth in Weight of Elementary School Children', *Public Health Reports*, 48.

Pariza, M. W. (1987) 'Dietary Fat, Calorie Restriction, *ad libitum* Feeding and Cancer Risk', *Nutrition Reviews*, 45.

Parizkova, J. (1977) *Body Fat and Physical Fitness*. The Hague: Martinus Nijhoff.

Parliamentary Papers (1833) *British Parliamentary Papers 1833* xxi. *Report on the Sanitary Condition of the Labouring Population of Great Britain*, by Edwin Chadwick; reprinted in Flinn (1965).

Payne, P. R. (1985) 'Nutritional Adaptation in Man: Social Adjustments and their Nutritional Implications', in Blaxter and Waterlow (1985).

—— (1989) 'Public Health and Functional Consequences of Seasonal Hunger and Malnutrition', in Sahn (1989).

—— and Cutler, P. (1984) 'Measuring Malnutrition: Technical Problems and Ideological Perspectives', *Economic and Political Weekly*, 25 August.

—— and Dugdale, A. E. (1977) 'A Model for the Prediction of Energy Balance and Body Weight', *Annals of Human Biology*, 4.

—— and Waterlow, J. C. (1971) 'Relative Energy Requirements for Maintenance Growth and Activity', *Lancet*.

Peters, P. E. (1986) 'Household Management in Botswana: Cattle, Crops, and Wage Labor', in J. L. Moock (ed.), *Understanding Africa's Rural Households and Farming Systems*. Boulder, Colo. and London: Westview Press.

Phelps Brown, E. H. and Hopkins, S. V. (1956) 'Seven Centuries of the Price of Consumables, Compared with Builders' Wage-Rates', *Economica*, 23.

Pinstrup-Andersen, P. (1985) 'Food Prices and the Poor in Developing Countries', *European Review of Agricultural Economics*, 12.

Pitt, M. M. (1983) 'Food Preference and Nutrition in Rural Bangladesh', *Review of Economics and Statistics*, 65.

—— and Rosenzweig, M. R. (1985) 'Health and Nutrient Consumption Across and within Farm Households', *Review of Economics and Statistics*, 67.

Poleman, T. T. (1981a) 'Reappraisal of the Extent of World Hunger', *Food Policy*, 6.

—— (1981b) 'Quantifying the Nutrition Situation in Developing Countries', *Food Research Institute Studies*, 18.

Pollak, R. A. (1985) 'A Transaction Cost Approach to Families and Households', *Journal of Economic Literature*, 23.

Pollitt, E. and Amante, P. (eds.) (1984) *Energy Intake and Activity*. New York: Alan R. Liss.

—— and Thomson, C. (1977) 'Protein–Calorie Malnutrition and Behaviour: A View from Psychology', in R. J. Wurtman and J. J. Wurtman (eds.), *Nutrition and the Brain*. New York: Raven Press.

Post, J. D. (1976) 'Famine, Mortality and Epidemic Disease in the Process of Modernization', *Economic History Review*, 29.

—— (1977) *The Last Great Subsistence Crisis in the Western World*. Baltimore: Johns Hopkins University Press.

Power, C., Fogelman, K., and Fox, A. J. (1986) 'Health and Social Mobility during the Early Years of Life', *Quarterly Journal of Social Affairs*, 2.

Prakasa Rao, B. L. S. (1983) *Nonparametric Functional Estimation*. London: Academic Press.

Prentice, A. M. (1984) 'Adaptations to Long-term Energy Intake', in Pollitt and Amante (1984).

Pullar, P. (1970) *Consuming Passions: Being an Historic Inquiry into Certain English Appetites*. Boston: Little Brown.

Quenouille, M. H., Boyne, A. W., Fisher, W. B., and Leitch, I. (1951) 'Statistical Studies of Recorded Energy Expenditure in Man', Technical Communication no. 17, Commonwealth Bureau of Animal Nutrition.

Quetelet, L. A. J. (1871) *Anthropometrie ou Mesure des differentes facultes de l'Homme*. Brussels: Muquardt, C.

Quisumbing, Ma. A. R. (1985) 'Food Demand Parameters and their Application to Nutrition Policy Simulation'. Mimeo, University of the Philippines.

Radhakrishna, R. (1984) 'Distributional Aspects of Caloric Consumption: Implications for Food Policy', in K. T. Achaya (ed.), *Interfaces between Agriculture, Nutrition and Food Science*. Tokyo: United Nations University.

Rand, W. M. and Scrimshaw, N. S. (1984) 'Protein and Energy Requirements: Insights from Long-term Studies', *Nutrition Foundation of India Bulletin*, 5.

—— —— and Young, V. R. (1985) 'Retrospective Analysis of Data from Five Long-term Metabolic Balance Studies: Implications for Understanding Dietary Nitrogen and Energy Utilisation', *American Journal of Clinical Nutrition*, 42.

Rea, J. N. (1971) 'Social and Economic Influences on the Growth of Pre-school Children in Lagos', *Human Biology*, 43.

Reddy, V., Jagadeesan, V., Ragharamulu, N., Bhaskaram, C., and Srikantia, S. G. (1976) 'Functional Significance of Growth Retardation in Malnutrition', *American Journal of Clinical Nutrition*, 29.

Reutlinger, S. and Alderman, H. (1980) 'The Prevalence of Calorie-Deficient Diets in Developing Countries', *World Development*, 8.

Reutlinger, S. and Selowsky, M. (1976) *Malnutrition and Poverty: Magnitude and Policy Options*, World Bank Staff Occasional Paper, no. 23. Baltimore: Johns Hopkins University Press.

Richardson, T. L. (1976) 'The Agricultural Labourer's Standard of Living in Kent, 1790–1860', in D. Oddy and D. Miller (eds.), *The Making of the Modern British Diet*. London: Croom Helm.

Rimoin, D. L., Merimee, T. J., Rabinowitz, D., McKusick, V. A., and Cavalli-Sforza, L. L. (1967) 'Growth Hormone in African Pygmies', *Lancet*, 9 September.

Roberts, D. F. (1985) 'Genetics and Nutritional Adaptation', in Blaxter and Waterlow (1985).

Roberts, S. B. *et al.* (1982) 'Changes in Activity, Birth Weight and Lactational Performance in Rural Gambian Women', in *Transactions of the Royal Society of Tropical Medicine and Hygiene*, 76.

Rodriguez, M. G. (n.d.) 'La Estadisitica de Reemplazo y Reclutamiento de los Ejercitos'. Mimeo, Madrid.

Rogers, B. L. (1985) 'Incorporating the Intrahousehold Dimension into Development Projects: A Guide for Planners', paper prepared for USAID/PPC/Human Resources Division. Mimeo, Tufts University School of Nutrition, Medford, Mass.

Rona, R. J., Swan, A. V., and Altman, D. G. (1978) 'Social Factors and Height of Primary Schoolchildren in England and Scotland', *Journal of Epidemiology and Community Health*, 32.

Rose, G. A. and Williams, R. T. (1961) 'Metabolic Studies on Large and Small Eaters', *British Journal of Nutrition*, 15.

Rose, M. E. (1971) *The Relief of Poverty, 1834–1914*, Studies in Economic History. London: Macmillan.

Rose, R. B. (1961) 'Eighteenth Century Price Riots and Public Policy in England', *International Review of Social History*, 6.

Rosenzweig, M. R. and Schultz, T. P. (1982a) 'Child Mortality and Fertility in Colombia: Individual and Community Effects', in *Health Policy and Education*, ii. Amsterdam: Elsevier.

—— —— (1982b) 'Market Opportunities, Genetic Endowments, and Intrafamily Resource Distribution: Child Survival in Rural India', *American Economic Review*, 72.

—— —— (1983) 'Estimating a Household Production Function: Heterogeneity, the Demand for Health Inputs, and Their Effects on Birth Weight', *Journal of Political Economy*, 91.

—— —— (1984) 'Market Opportunities and Intrafamily Resource Distribution: Reply', *American Economic Review*, 74.

—— —— (1987) 'Fertility and Investments in Human Capital: Estimates of the Consequences of Imperfect Fertility Control in Malaysia', *Journal of Econometrics*, 36.

Rotberg, R. I. and Rabb, T. K. (1983) *Hunger and History: The Impact of Changing Food Production and Consumption Patterns on Society.* Cambridge University Press.

Rothschild, M. and Stiglitz, J. E. (1970) 'Increasing Risk: A Definition', *Journal of Economic Theory*, 2.

Rowntree, B. S. (1901) *Poverty: A Study of Town Life.* London: Macmillan.

Rutishauser, I. H. E. and Whitehead, R. G. (1972) 'Energy Intake and Expenditure in 1–3-Year-Old Ugandan Children Living in a Rural Environment', *British Journal of Nutrition*, 28.

Ryan, J. G., Bidinger, P. D., Rao, N. P., and Pushpamma, P. (1984) 'The Determinants of Nutritional Status in Six Villages of Southern India', *Research Bulletin* no. 7. Hyderabad: International Crops Research Institute for the Semi-Arid Tropics.

Sah, R. K. and Srinivasan, T. N. (1988) 'Distributional Consequences of Rural Food Levy and Subsidized Urban Rations', *European Economic Review*, 32.

Sahn, D. E. (ed.) (1989) *Causes and Implications of Seasonal Variability in Household Food Security.* Baltimore: The Johns Hopkins University Press.

—— and Alderman, H. (1988) 'The Effect of Human Capital on Wages, and the Determinants of Labor Supply in a Developing Country', *Journal of Development Economics*, 29.

Salmon, M. (1982) 'Error Correction Mechanisms', *Economic Journal*, 92.

Satyanarayana, K., Naidu, A. N., Chatterjee, B., and Rao, B. S. N. (1977) 'Body Size and Work Output', *American Journal of Clinical Nutrition*, 30.

—— —— and Rao, B. S. N. (1979) 'Nutritional Deprivation in Childhood and the Body Size, Activity and Physical Work Capacity of Young Boys', *American Journal of Clinical Nutrition*, 32.

—— —— —— (1980) 'Adolescent Growth Spurt among Rural Indian Boys in Relation to Their Nutritional Status in Early Childhood', *Annals of Human Biology*, 7.

——, Prasanna, K., and Rao, B. S. N. (1986) 'Effect of Early Childhood Undernutrition and Child Labour on Growth and Adult-Nutritional Status of Rural Indian Boys around Hyderabad', *Human Nutrition: Clinical Nutrition*, 40C.

Schofield, R. (1983) 'The Impact of Scarcity and Plenty on Population Change in England, 1541–1871', *Journal of Interdisciplinary History*, 14.

Schofield, S. (1974) 'Seasonal Factors Affecting Nutrition in Different Age Groups and Especially Preschool Children', *Journal of Development Studies*, 11.

Schultz, T. W. (1980) 'Nobel Lecture: The Economics of Being Poor', *Journal of Political Economy*, 88.

Scrimshaw, N. S. (1987) 'The Phenomenon of Famine'. Mimeo, Massachusetts Institute of Technology.

—— and Young, V. R. (1978) 'Biological Variability and Nutrient Needs', in Margen and Ogar (1978).

—— and Wallerstein, M. B. (eds.) (1982) *Nutrition Policy Implementation: Issues and Experience*. New York and London: Plenum Press.

Seckler, D. (1980) 'Malnutrition: An Intellectual Odyssey', *Western Journal of Agricultural Economics*, 5 reprinted in Sukhatme (1982*d*).

—— (1982) 'Small but Healthy: A Basic Hypothesis in the Theory, Measurement and Policy of Malnutrition', in Sukhatme (1982*d*).

—— (1984*a*) 'The "Small but Healthy?" Hypothesis: A Reply to Critics', *Economic and Political Weekly*, 3 November.

—— (1984*b*) 'The "Small but Healthy" Hypothesis: An Invitation to a Refutation', in P. Narain (ed.), Impact of P. V. Sukhatme on *Agricultural Statistics and Nutrition*. New Delhi: Indian Society of Agricultural Statistics.

Sen, A. K. (1976) 'Poverty: An Ordinal Approach to Measurement', *Econometrica*, 44.

—— (1981) *Poverty and Famines: An Essay on Entitlement and Deprivation*. Oxford: Clarendon.

—— (1984) 'Family and Food: Sex Bias in Poverty', *Resources, Values and Development*. Oxford: Basil Blackwell.

—— and Sengupta, S. (1983) 'Malnutrition of Rural Children and the Sex Bias', *Economic and Political Weekly*, Annual Number, May.

Shah, C. H. (1983) 'Food Preference, Poverty, and the Nutrition Gap', *Economic Development and Cultural Change*, 32.

Shammas, C. (1983) 'Food Expenditures and Economic Well-Being in Early Modern England', *Journal of Economic History*, 43.

—— (1984) 'The Eighteenth-Century English Diet and Economic Change', *Explorations in Economic History*, 21.

—— (1988) 'The Food Budget of English Workers: A Reply to Komlos', *Journal of Economic History*, 48.

Shetty, P. S. (1984) 'Adaptive Changes in Basal Metabolic Rate and Lean Body Mass in Chronic Undernutrition', *Human Nutrition: Clinical Nutrition*, 38.

Silverman, B. W. (1986) *Density Estimation*. London: Chapman and Hall.

Sims, E. A. H. (1976) 'Experimental Obesity, Dietary-Induced Thermogenesis, and their Clinical Implications', *Clinics in Endocrinology and Metabolism*, 5.

Singh, I., Squire, L., and Strauss, J. (eds.) (1986) *Agricultural Household Models: Extensions, Applications and Policy*. Washington, DC: World Bank.

Sirilaksana, C. (1982) 'An Economic Analysis of Malnutrition among Young Children in Rural Thailand'. Mimeo, University of Hawaii.

—— (1986) 'Malnourished Children: An Economic Approach to the Causes and Consequences in Rural Thailand'. Mimeo, East–West Population Institute, Honolulu.

Slicher von Bath, B. H. (1963) *The Agrarian History of Western Europe, AD 500–1850*. London: Edward Arnold.

Smith, A. M., Chinn, S., and Rona, R. J. (1980) 'Social Factors and Height Gain of Primary Schoolchildren in England and Scotland', *Annals of Human Biology*, 7.

Smout, T. C. (1977) 'Famine and Famine-Relief in Scotland', in L. M. Cullen and T. C. Smout (eds.), *Comparative Aspects of Scottish and Irish Economic and Social History 1600–1900*. Edinburgh: John Donald.

Sokoloff, K. L. and Villaflor, G. C. (1982) 'The Early Achievement of Modern Stature in America', *Social Science History*, 6.

Sommer, A. and Loewenstein, M. S. (1975) 'Nutritional Status and Mortality: A Prospective Validation of the QUAC Stick', *American Journal of Clinical Nutrition*, 28.

Spurr, G. B. (1983) 'Nutritional Status and Physical Work Capacity', *Yearbook of Physical Anthropology*, 26.

—— (1984) 'Physical Activity, Nutritional Status and Physical Work Capacity in Relation to Agricultural Productivity', in Pollitt and Amante (1984).

——, Barac-Nieto, M., and Maksud, M. G. (1977) 'Productivity and Maximal Oxygen Consumption in Sugarcane Cutters', *American Journal of Clinical Nutrition*, 30.

——, Reina, J. C. and Ramirez, R. (1984) 'Marginal Malnutrition in School-Aged Colombian Boys: Efficiency of Treadmill Walking in Submaximal Exercise 1–3, *American Journal of Clinical Nutrition*, 39.

—— *et al.* (1982) 'Maximum Oxygen Consumption of Nutritionally Normal White, Mestizo and Black Colombian Boys 6–16 Years of Age', *Human Biology*, 54.

——, Reina, J. C., Dahners, H. W., and Barac-Nieto, M. (1983) 'Marginal Malnutrition in School-Aged Colombian Boys: Functional Consequences in Maximum Exercise 1–3, *American Journal of Clinical Nutrition*, 37.

Srinivasan, T. N. (1981) 'Malnutrition: Some Measurement and Policy Issues', *Journal of Development Economics*, 8.

—— (1983a) 'Hunger: Defining It, Estimating its Global Incidence, and Alleviating It', in D. Gale Johnson and G. Edward Schuh (eds.), *The Role of Markets in the World Food Economy*. Boulder, Colo.: Westview Press.

—— (1983b) 'Malnutrition in Developing Countries: the State of Knowledge of the Extent of its Prevalence, its Causes and its Consequences', background paper prepared for FAO's Fifth World Food Survey. Mimeo, Economic Growth Center, Yale University.

Srinivasan, T. N. (1983c) 'Measuring Undernutrition', *Ceres*, 16.

—— (1985) 'Population, Food and Rural Development', background paper prepared for the Working Group on Population Growth and Economic Development, Committee on Population. Mimeo, National Research Council, Washington, DC.

—— (1986) 'Undernutrition: Extent and Distribution of Its Incidence', in A. H. Maunder and U. Renborg (eds.), *Agriculture in a Turbulent World Economy*. Aldershot: Gower.

Statistics Department, Central Bank of Ceylon (1984) *Report on Consumer Finances and Socio-Economic Survey 1981/82, Sri Lanka*, Part I (October 1984) and Part II (May 1985), Colombo.

Steckel, R. H. (1983) 'Height and Per Capita Income', *Historical Methods*, 16.

—— (1986) 'A Peculiar Population: The Nutrition, Health and Mortality of American Slaves', *Journal of Economic History*, 46.

—— (1987) 'Growth, Depression and Recovery: The Remarkable Case of American Slaves', *Annals of Human Biology*, 14.

Stephenson, L. S. *et al.* (1983) 'A Comparison on Growth Standards: Similarities between NCHS, Harvard, Denver and Privileged African Children and Differences with Kenyan Rural Children', International Nutrition Monograph Series no. 12.

Stigler, G. J. (1974) 'The Early History of Empirical Studies of Consumer Behavior', *Journal of Political Economy*, 62.

Stiglitz, J. (1976) 'The Efficiency Wage Hypothesis, Surplus Labour, and the Distribution of Income in LDCs', *Oxford Economic Papers*, NS 28.

Stoudt, H. W. (1961) *The Physical Anthropology of Ceylon*, Ethnographic Series Publication no. 2. Colombo: Colombo National Museum.

Strauss, J. (1984) 'Joint Determination of Food Consumption and Product in Rural Sierra Leone: Estimates of a Household-Firm Model', *Journal of Development Economics*, 14.

—— (1986) 'Does Better Nutrition Raise Farm Productivity?', *Journal of Political Economy*, 94.

—— (1990) 'Households, Communities and Preschool Children's Nutrition Outcomes: Evidence from Rural Côte D'Ivoire', *Economic Development and Cultural Change*, 38.

Sukhatme, P. V. (1961) 'The World's Hunger and Future Needs in Food Supplies', *Journal of the Royal Statistical Society* A, 124.

—— (1977a) 'Incidence of Undernutrition', *Indian Journal of Agricultural Economics*, 32.

—— (1977b) 'Economics of Nutrition', *Indian Journal of Agricultural Economics*, 32.

—— (1977c) *Malnutrition and Poverty*, Ninth Lal Bahadur Shastri Memorial Lecture. New Delhi: Indian Agricultural Research Institute.

—— (1978) 'Assessment of Adequacy of Diets at Different Income Levels', *Economic and Political Weekly*, Special Number, August.

—— (1981*a*) 'On Measurement of Poverty', *Economic and Political Weekly*, 8 August.

—— (1981*b*) 'On the Measurement of Undernutrition: A Comment', *Economic and Political Weekly*, 6 June.

—— (1982*a*) 'Measurement of Undernutrition', *Economic and Political Weekly*, 11 December.

—— (1982*b*) 'Poverty and Malnutrition', in Sukhatme (1982*d*).

—— (1982*c*) 'Improving Living Conditions in Villages: Interview with the Press', in Sukhatme (1982*d*).

—— (ed.) (1982*d*) *Newer Concepts in Nutrition and Their Implications for Policy*. Pune: Maharashtra Association for the Cultivation of Science.

—— (1987) 'Adaptation and Variability'. Mimeo, Maharashtra Association for the Cultivation of Science, Pune.

—— and Margen, S. (1978) 'Models of Protein Deficiency', *American Journal of Clinical Nutrition*, 31 also reprinted in Sukhatme (1982*d*).

—— —— (1982) 'Autoregulatory Homeostatic Nature of Energy Balance', *American Journal of Clinical Nutrition*, 35: 355–65; reprinted in Sukhatme (1982*d*) (page references are to the reprint).

—— and Narain, P. (1982) 'The Genetic Significance of Intra-Individual Variation in Requirement', in P. S. R. S. Rao and J. Sedransk (eds.), *Research Work of William J. Cochrane*, Memorial Volume. New York: John Wiley.

Supple, B. E. (1964) *Commercial Crisis and Change in England, 1600–1642*. Cambridge University Press.

Suskind, R. M. (ed.) (1977) *Malnutrition and the Immune Response*. New York: Raven Press.

Tanner, J. M. (1978) *Foetus into Man: Physical Growth from Conception to Maturity*. London: Open Books.

—— (1981) *A History of the Study of Human Growth*. Cambridge University Press.

—— (1982) 'The Potential of Auxological Data for Measuring Economic and Social Well-being', *Social Science History*, 6.

Taylor, H. L. *et al.* (1945) 'The Effect of Successive Fasts on the Ability of Men to Withstand During Hard Work', *American Journal of Physiology*, 143.

Taylor, L., Horton, S., and Raff, D. (1983) 'Food Subsidy Programs: Practice and Policy Lessons'. Mimeo, Department of Economics, Massachusetts Institute of Technology.

Thirsk, J. (1983) 'The Horticultural Revolution: A Cautionary Note on Prices', *Journal of Interdisciplinary History*, 14.

Thirsk, J. (1985) 'Agricultural Policy: Public Debate and Legislation', in J. Thirsk (ed.), *The Agrarian History of England and Wales*, v.ii. Cambridge University Press.

Thomas, D., Strauss, J., and Henriques, M.-H. (1991) 'How does Mother's Education Affect Child Height?', *Journal of Human Resources*, 26.

Thomson, A. M. (1966) 'Adult Stature', in J. V. Van der Werff, T. Bosch, and A. Hask (eds.), *Somatic Growth of the Child*. Springfield, Ill.: Charles C. Thomas.

—— (1980) 'The Importance of Being Tall', *Human Ecology Forum*, 10.

Tilly, C. (1975) 'Food Supply and Public Order in Modern Europe', in C. Tilly (ed.), *The Formation of National States in Western Europe*. Princeton, NJ: Princeton University Press.

Tilly, L. A. (1971) 'The Food Riot as a Form of Political Conflict in France', *Journal of Interdisciplinary History*, 2.

—— (1983) 'Food Entitlement, Famine, and Conflict', *Journal of Interdisciplinary History*, 14.

Timmer, C. P., Falcon, W. P., and Pearson, S. R. (1983) *Food Policy Analysis*. Baltimore: Johns Hopkins University Press.

Tobias, P. V. (1962) 'On the Increasing Stature of the Bushmen', *Anthropos*, 57.

Tomkins, A. M. (1981) 'Nutritional Status and Severity of Diarrhoea among Pre-school Children in Rural Nigeria', *Lancet*, 18 April.

—— (1986) 'Protein–Energy Malnutrition and the Risk of Infection', *Proceedings of the Nutrition Society*, 45.

—— and Watson, F. (1989) 'Malnutrition and Infection', Nutrition Policy Discussion Paper no. 5, UN ACC/SCN.

Torun, B., Schutz, Y., Bradfield, R., and Viteri, F. E. (1975) 'Effect of Physical Activity upon Growth of Children Recovering from Protein Calorie Malnutrition (PCM)', *Proceedings of Tenth International Congress of Nutrition*. Kyoto:

Toutain, J. (1971) 'La Consommation alimentaire en France de 1789 à 1964', *Economies et sociétés*, Cahiers de L'ISEA, v.

US Bureau of the Census (1975) *Historical Statistics of the United States: Colonial Times to 1970*, Bicentennial Edition, pts. I and II. Washington, DC: Government Printing Office.

Valenzuela, R. E. (1978) 'Nutrient Distribution within the Family', *Philippine Economic Journal*, 17.

van Wieringen, J. C. (1978) 'Secular Growth Changes', in F. Falkner and J. M. Tanner (eds.) *Human Growth*, iii. *Methodology*. New York: Plenum.

—— (1986) 'Secular Growth Changes', in F. Falkner and J. M. Tanner (eds.), *Human Growth*, iii. *Methodology*, 2nd edn. New York: Plenum.

Vijayaraghavan, K., Singh, D., and Swaminathan, M. C. (1971) 'Heights and Weights of Wellnourished Indian School Children', *Indian Journal of Medical Research*, 59.

Villermé, L. R. (1829) 'Memoire sur la taille de l'homme en France', *Annales d'Hygiene Publique*, 1.

Viteri, F. (1971) 'Considerations on the Effect of Nutrition on the Body Composition and Physical Capacity of Young Gautemalan Adults', in N. Scrimshaw and A. M. Altshull (eds.), *Amino-acid Fortification of Protein Foods*, pp. 350–75. Cambridge, Mass: MIT Press.

Waaler, H. T. (1984) 'Height, Weight and Mortality: The Norwegian Experience', *Acta Medica Scandinavia*, Suppl. no. 679.

Wachter, K. W. (1981) 'Graphical Estimation of Military Heights', *Historical Methods*, 14.

—— and Trussel, J. (1982) 'Estimating Historical Heights', *Journal of the American Statistical Association*, 77.

Waldron, I. (1986) 'What Do We Know about Causes of Sex Differences in Mortality? A Review of the Literature', *Population Bulletin of the United Nations, 1985*, 18.

—— (1987) 'Patterns and Causes of Excess Female Mortality among Children in Contemporary Developing Countries', *World Health Statistics Quarterly*, 44.

Ward, J. O. and Sanders, J. H. (1980) 'Nutritional Determinants and Migration in the Brazilian Northeast: A Case Study of Rural and Urban Areas', *Economic Development and Cultural Change*, 29.

Waterlow, J. C. (1972) 'Classification and Definition of Protein-calorie Malnutrition', *British Medical Journal*, 3.

—— (1984) 'The Meaning of Adaptation in Nutritional Adaptation in Man', in Blaxter and Waterlow (1985).

—— (1985a) 'What Do We Mean by Adaptation?', in Blaxter and Waterlow (1985).

—— (1985b) 'Postscript', in Blaxter and Waterlow (1985).

—— (1986) 'Mechanisms of Adaptation to Low Protein and Energy Intakes', *Annual Review of Nutrition*, 6.

—— et al. (1977) 'The Presentation and Use of Height and Weight Data for Comparing the Nutritional Status of Groups of Children under the Age of 10 Years', *World Health Organization Bulletin*, 55.

Weinberger, M. B. and Heligman, L. (1987) 'Do Social and Economic Variables Differentially Affect Male and Female Child Mortality?' Mimeo, United Nations.

Weir, D. R. (1984) 'Life Under Pressure: France and England, 1670–1870', *Journal of Economic History*, 44.

Widdowson, E. M. (1962) 'Nutritional Individuality', *Proceedings of Nutrition Society*, (London), 21.

Williams, M. W. (1985) 'Improvements in Western European Diets and Economic Growth'. Mimeo.

Williamson-Gray, C. (1982) 'Food Consumption Parameters for Brazil and their Application to Food Policy'. Mimeo, International Food Policy Research Institute, Washington, DC.

Willis, R. J. (1973) 'A New Approach to the Economic Theory of Fertility Behavior', *Journal of Political Economy*, 81.

—— (1980) 'The Old Age Security Hypothesis and Population Growth', in T. Burch (ed.), *Demographic Behavior: Interdisciplinary Perspectives on Decision-Making*. Boulder, Colo.: Westview.

Wilson, C. A. (1973) *Food and Drink in Britain: From the Stone Age to Recent Times*. London: Constable.

Wolanski, N. (1970) 'Genetic and Ecological Factors in Human Growth', *Human Biology*, 42.

Wolfe, B. L. and Behrman, J. R. (1982) 'Determinants of Child Mortality, Health and Nutrition in a Developing Country', *Journal of Development Economics*, 11.

—— —— (1983) 'Is Income Overrated in Determining Adequate Nutrition?' *Economic Development and Cultural Change*, 31.

—— —— (1986) 'Child Quantity and Quality in a Developing Country: Family Background, Endogenous Tastes and Biological Supply Factors', *Economic Development and Cultural Change*, 34.

—— —— (1987) 'Women's Schooling and Children's Health: Are the Effects Robust with Adult Sibling Control for the Women's Childhood Background?' *Journal of Health Economics*, 6.

—— —— (1991) 'The Synthesis Economic Fertility Model: A Latent Variable Investigation of Some Critical Attributes', *Journal of Population Economics*, 4.

Woodham-Smith, C. (1962) *The Great Hunger: Ireland 1845–1849*. London: Hamilton.

Woolf, B. (1946) 'Poverty Lines and Standards of Living', *Proceedings of the Nutrition Society*, 5.

World Bank (1981) *World Development Report 1981*. Washington, DC: World Bank.

—— (1984) *World Development Report 1984*. Washington, DC: World Bank.

—— (1986) *Poverty and Hunger: Issues and Options for Food Security in Developing Countries*. Washington, DC: World Bank.

—— (1987) *World Development Report 1987*. Washington, DC: World Bank.

World Health Foundation of Sri Lanka (1979) *Tables of Food Composition for Use in Sri Lanka*, compiled by W. D. A. Perera, Padma M. Jayasekera, and Sithy Z. Thaha. Colombo: Medical Research Institute.

World Health Organization (1974) *Handbook on Human Nutritional Requirements*, WHO Monograph Series no. 61. Geneva: World Health Organization.

—— (1978) *Habitual Physical Activity and Health*, WHO Regional Publications European Series no. 6. Copenhagen: World Health Organization Regional Office for Europe.

Wrigley, E. A. (1969) *Population and History*. London: Weidenfeld & Nicolson.

—— (1987) 'Some Reflections on Corn Yields and Prices in Pre-Industrial Economies', in *People, Cities and Wealth: The Transformation of Traditional Society*. Oxford: Basil Blackwell.

—— and Schofield, R. S. (1981) *The Population History of England, 1541–1871: A Reconstruction*. Cambridge, Mass.: Harvard University Press.

Wyndham, C. H. (1970) 'Man's Adaptation to the Physical Environment in South Africa', *Materiaty i Prace Antropogiczne*, 78.

Zurbrigg, S. (1983) 'Ideology and the Poverty Line Debate', *Economic and Political Weekly*, 3 December.

INDEX OF NAMES

SUBJECT INDEX